The Financial Development of India, 1

The Financial Development of India, 1860–1977

RAYMOND W. GOLDSMITH

Yale University Press
NEW HAVEN AND LONDON

Published with the assistance of
the Samuel W. Meek Publication Fund.

Designed by James J. Johnson
and set in Times Roman type.
Printed in the United States of America by
Murray Printing Co., Westford, Mass.

Library of Congress Cataloging in Publication Data

Goldsmith, Raymond William, 1904–
 The financial development of India, 1860–1977.

 Bibliography: p.
 Includes index.
 1. Finance—India—History. I. Title.
HG187.I4G64   332.1'0954   82–7094
ISBN 0–300–02030–9   AACR2

10 9 8 7 6 5 4 3 2 1

TO J., D., AND P.

Contents

Tables

Preface

Habent sua fata libelli, if it is permitted to apply the diminutive to a project that comprises three volumes totaling about 600 pages—consisting of parallel volumes on Japan and India and a short volume comparing them with the United States*—and they do so not only after their publication but also during their gestation.

This study of the financial structure and development of India since 1860 was started about a decade ago as the second of a planned set of a good half-dozen comparative case studies intended to supplement and illustrate the approach developed in my *Financial Structure and Development* (1969). I soon realized that this plan was beyond the powers of an author then in his mid-sixties, and that studies of the two largest Asian countries, which now have modern financial systems, would have to stand on their own feet. The book presented here is essentially the result of work done during the years 1970 to 1973, updated and not insubstantially shortened and revised in 1976 and again in 1979. This will explain why statistics, description, and analysis generally end with 1977; why developments before the early 1970s are covered more fully than those of the last few years, and why, with a few exceptions, nothing published after early 1979 has been taken into account.

I have tried in these volumes to come as close as possible, without becoming tedious and exceeding the publisher's indulgence, to the principle of reproducibility of the statistics used, that is, to permit the reader to derive the figures in the tables from the sources specified in the notes to them. This has not always been possible in the case of figures in the text not taken from the tables, though an attempt has been made to identify the sources of these in the notes where it seemed important.

The source notes to the tables, the footnotes, and the bibliography will indicate the multifarious nature of the materials from which text and tables had to be pieced together. It is only fair to add that the book could not have been written except for the existence of the Reserve Bank of India's *Banking and Monetary Statistics of India* (1954) and many of its more recent publications.

The tables present the information mostly for benchmark years or as averages for groups of years and, in the interest of comparability, in the form of percentage distributions or other relatives, particularly as relations to national product. However, in almost all cases enough absolute figures have been preserved to enable the reader to recover, or approximate, the underlying absolute values. This procedure has been followed in order to emphasize longer-term developments and structural changes and has in any case been unavoidable in order to keep the book to manageable proportions. Absolute annual figures are shown for only a limited number of

---

The Financial Development of Japan, 1868–1977 and *The Financial Development of India, Japan, and the United States: A Trilateral Institutional, Statistical, and Analytic Comparison* (New Haven and London: Yale University Press, 1983).

basic series; many others, as well as numerous supplementary tables, were eliminated in shortening the manuscript. It hardly needs to be added that, because of rounding, some totals, products, or ratios do not agree exactly with the sums, products, and ratios of components or factors.

It will be evident to anyone familiar with the literature of a subject as broad as the economic and financial development of India over the last century, that I can have used only part of the relevant publications, even in the narrower field of financial institutions and instruments. All I can hope is that not too many major statistical sources, institutional descriptions, or analytical explanations have escaped me. The List of Publications Cited is just what it says, not a systematic or even selective bibliography of the subject, nor even an enumeration of sources consulted or used.

There are about 25,000 figures in the tables and text of this book. It is obvious that I cannot have avoided mistakes. Again, I can only hope that the percentage is small and that they do not affect any of the main findings or conclusions. While most of the figures come from accepted statistical sources, which does not mean that all of them are accurate, I have not hesitated to make even rough estimates where I felt they were preferable to silence or circumlocution and were likely to shed light on the subject. I shall be only too glad if critics produce better ones; that challenge is indeed a main reason for making these estimates.

There is, in summary, not much that I can say *pro illi opere suo* except that I am convinced that the subject is important for understanding financial and hence economic development; that it should have been shorter; that it could have been done better; and that to the best of my knowledge nothing similar to it exists.

The writing of this book has essentially been a solitary job; it has been made possible through the assistance, mainly in the form of travel grants, of the National Science Foundation, which of course is in no way responsible for its contents. I am also grateful for the hospitality and help I received on the occasion of my two visits to Bombay in 1971 and 1976 from the staff of the research and statistics divisions of the Reserve Bank of India, in particular to K. S. Krishnaswamy, now a deputy governor of the Reserve Bank. I have not felt justified in asking friends and colleagues to go over hundreds of pages of complex tables and text, so the book may suffer from my (I still feel commendable) considerateness. I am also indebted to Marian Ash of Yale University Press and James Blackman of the National Science Foundation for their patience and understanding during the book's long gestation process. Finally, the manuscript would never have reached the publisher without the efficient help, over many years, of my former secretary, Mrs. Anne Tassi.

R.W.G.

New Haven, Conn.
1983

Abbreviations

BMS	Reserve Bank of India, *Banking and Monetary Statistics of India*, 1954
BMSS	Reserve Bank of India, *Banking and Monetary Statistics of India*, Supplements 1 and 2, 1964
BR	Bina Roy, ''Estimation of Capital Formation in India,'' Ph.D. dissertation, University of Calcutta, 1975
D-V	V. V. Divatia and T. R. Venkatachalam, ''Household Demand for Money in India: Some Evidence from Time Series,'' *Reserve Bank of India Bulletin 26*, no. 6 (June 1972)
NAS	Government of India, Central Statistical Organization, *National Accounts Statistics 1960/61–1973/74*, 1976
NII	M. Mukherjee, *National Income of India: Trends and Structure*. Calcutta: Statistical Publishing Society, 1969
PEI	Government of India, Ministry of Finance, *Pocket Book of Economic Information*, New Delhi, annual
RBC	Government of India, *Report of the Banking Commission*, 1972
RBIB	Reserve Bank of India, *Reserve Bank of India Bulletin*, monthly
RBSOP	Reserve Bank of India, *Reserve Bank Staff Occasional Papers*
RCF	Reserve Bank of India, *Report on Currency and Finance*, annual
SOI	Tata Services Ltd., *Statistical Outline of India*. Bombay, annual
V-S	T. R. Venkatachalam and Y. S. R. Sarma, ''Structure and Trends in the National Balance Sheet of India,'' *Indian Journal of Income and Wealth*, vol. 2. (1977)

1   Victorian India, 1860–1913[1]

Selecting a date at which to start an analysis of the financial structure and development of modern India presents little difficulty. The year 1860, or one of its close neighbors, marks a watershed not only in the political field but also in the economic and financial fields. Here the watershed is marked by the introduction of railways and factory industry in the mid-1850s, by James Wilson's reform of the central government's finances in the early 1860s, and by the extension of the principle of limited liability to banking.[2]

The selection of 1913 as the closing year of the period is more arbitrary. In the financial field, however, the imported inflation connected with World War I and the marked progress in the Indianization of the economy since the 1910s lead to 1913 rather than to a year around 1900, which would be almost equally defensible. Although a number of indicators mark some acceleration of economic growth after the turn of the century, such growth has not been regarded as sufficiently large or widespread to call for the division of the 1860–1913 span into two or more subperiods.[3]

1. THE INFRASTRUCTURE

At the beginning of the period, that is, around 1860, the Indian economy did not differ basically, except in a few port cities, from that of one or two centuries earlier, say, at the death of Akbar (1605).[4] The country had neither railways nor surfaced roads nor factories. The bulk of the population was engaged in subsistence agriculture. Although income had probably nearly doubled since 1600,[5] real income per head had probably not increased at all. Politically, more than half the peninsula was inefficiently administered by a private foreign organization—the East India Company of London—for the purpose of maximizing its profits, whereas the remainder of

1. For readers who follow the literature on Indian economic history, it should be pointed out that this study was completed before publication of A. Heston's contribution to *Cambridge Economic History of India*. The only use of material contained in that volume is of Professor Heston's estimates of national product (cf. table 1-2), which the author kindly made available before publication.

2. *Report of the Indian Central Banking Enquiry Commission*, 1931, p. 18; Spear, p. 677.

3. The years between 1860 and 1913, treated here as one period, have been subdivided by Gadgil (p. 194) into three subperiods, which, however, he did not regard as structurally different. The first, from 1860 to 1875, is characterized as a period of prosperity arrested by famine. The second subperiod of prosperity, from 1880 to 1895, was arrested by two famines. And finally, the years from 1900 to 1914 are regarded as a subperiod of mild prosperity. A somewhat differing periodization is used by P. Ray (p. 47), who distinguishes three periods of "commercial development" between 1870 and 1913. The first period, from 1870 to 1893, is characterized as "checkered development"; the brief second period, 1894 to 1900, as "stagnation"; and the third, from 1901 to 1913, as "unimpeded" progress.

4. Cf. Moorehead, *India at the Death of Akbar*, 1962.

5. Starting from either Moorehead's estimate of "at least somewhere about 100 million" people (ibid., p. 21) or Davis's estimate of 125 million in 1600 (p. 26), the increase in population in the two and a half centuries before 1860 averaged 0.33 or 0.21 percent per year.

1

the country was equally or even more inefficiently and autocratically administered—with varying degrees of independence from the East India Company—by several hundred native princes,
who ruled over territories ranging in size from a few square miles to an area equal to the size of a
small European country.

a. Population

Population growth was slow and irregular. Between 1871, when the first census was
taken, and 1911, population in the territory of undivided India grew (after adjustments to
improve comparability) by 48 million, or 19 percent, that is, at an average annual rate of slightly
less than one-half of 1 percent (table 1-1). Because of the varying incidence of famines and
epidemics, and possibly also differences in the accuracy of the enumerations, growth was
concentrated in the 1880s and in the first decade of this century and was close to zero in the
1870s and the 1890s. Birth and death rates apparently failed to show a definite trend in the
period, both staying at high levels.

The predominantly rural character of the Indian economy is reflected in the fact that
agriculture (including livestock, forestry, and fishing) absorbed nearly three-fourths of the labor
force in 1901 and 1911, the first dates for which this information is available. If rural artisans,
traders, and service workers are also included, the ratio would be well in excess of four-fifths. It
is unlikely that the ratio was substantially different during the second half of the nineteenth
century.

The degree of urbanization remained low. In 1911 the thirty cities with 100,000 or more
inhabitants accounted for not much more than 2 percent of the total population—the same
proportion as forty years earlier—whereas more than half the population lived in the more than
600,000 villages of less than 1,000 inhabitants each and another one-third in the more than
60,000 towns having between 1,000 and 5,000 inhabitants.[6]

b. National Product

The trend of real national product of India during the half century prior to World War I is
still in dispute.[7] Practically all estimators agree, however, that if any increase in real income per
head occurred during this period it was very small. The latest estimates yield an annual aggregate
growth rate of real product per head of approximately 0.4 percent between 1857 and 1913.[8] This
implies an average growth rate of slightly less than 1 percent in aggregate real product.

Whether to describe such a situation as stagnation or as very slow growth is a matter of
taste. It is important, however, not to overlook the fact that, despite the very slow increase in
conventionally measured national product, there developed in this half century a "modern"
sector consisting mainly of railroads, light industries—primarily cotton and jute—and banks.
This sector, except for the railroads, was essentially limited to a few port cities, mainly Calcutta,
Madras, and Bombay, and developed relatively few backward or forward linkages with the rest
of the economy, which retained its traditional technology and organization. Consequently, India
displayed throughout most of this period many of the features of a dual economy, as the country
still does today.

Estimates of national product in current prices for the forty years prior to 1900 are still
more hazardous. Because neither of the two most recent estimates provides these figures, which

6. *Statistical Abstract for British India 1911–21; Census of India, 1911.* vol. 1, pt. 2, pp. 6, 16.
7. Some students have gone so far as to doubt or to deny that any estimate can be made. Thus Thorner and Thorner
(1962, p. 102) declared more than fifteen years ago: "As of 1953 we remain without reliable and comparable national
income estimates for any phase of India's economic development." Saini (p. 258) was even more skeptical, asserting more
recently that "it is not possible to construct estimates of the national income of India for the period 1860–1913."
8. This figure is a result of a combination of Mukherjee's estimate for 1859 to 1900 (*NII*, p. 98) and the estimates
for 1901 to 1913 in table 1-2. A more recent estimate (Heston) puts the average rate of growth in per head real national
product at 0.6 percent per year for the 1869–1913 period.

TABLE 1-1. Demographic Background, 1871–1971

	Population Undivided India (mill.) (1)	Population Indian Union (mill.) (2)	Population growth rate (percent per year)[a] (3)	Birth rate (per thou.)[a] (4)	Death rate (per thou.)[a] (5)	Literacy rate (percent) (6)	Urbanization; all towns (percent) (7)	Urbanization; towns over 100 thou. (percent) (8)
1871	255.2	218.8	0.08	·	·	·	·	·
1881	257.4	212.4	0.09	·	·	·	·	·
1891	282.1	233.1	0.92	49	41	6.1	·	·
1901	285.3	236.2	0.10	46	44	6.2	10.9	2.5
1911	303.0	252.1	0.60	49	43	7.0	10.3	2.5
1921	305.7	251.4	0.09	49	49	8.3	11.2	2.8
1931	338.2	279.0	1.02	46	36	9.2	12.0	3.3
1941	389.0	318.7	1.41	45	31	15.1	13.9	4.9
1951	437.0	360.2	1.23	40	27	·	17.3	7.2
1961	533.7	439.0	2.00	42	23	24.0	18.0	8.7
1971	667.4	561.0[b]	2.30	40	16	29.4	19.9	10.1

[a]Decade ending with year indicated; average for 1856–1971 for line 1; rates refer to col. 2 from 1941 on.   [b]1977, 625.8; growth rate 1972–77: 2.14 percent.

SOURCES: **Col. 1:** 1871–1941, Davis, pp. 27, 151; 1951–71, col. 2 plus figure for Pakistan (*IFS, 1972 Supplement*).   **Col. 2:** 1871–91, Mukherjee, *NII,* p. 99; 1901–41, Davis, loc. cit.; 1951–71, *IFS, 1972 Supplement.*   **Col. 3:** 1881–1971, derived from col. 1 for 1881–1941 and from col. 2 for 1951–77.   **Cols. 4 and 5:** 1891–1901, Sinha, p. 106; 1911–61, Delhi School of Economics, *Selected Tables Relating to Indian Economic History,* n.d., table 2, decadal averages; 1961–70, *India, 1971–72,* p. 104.   **Col. 6:** 1891–1961, *Selected Tables,* table 1; percentage of population over 10 years; 1971, *Records and Statistics (Eastern Economist)* 1971–72, p. 181.   **Cols. 7 and 8:** 1901–71, op. cit. 22: 249.

are needed as scalars for the many financial statistics that are always expressed in current prices, it has been necessary to reflate the only continuous set of estimates for the second half of the nineteenth century with the help of a far from satisfactory price index and to link the resulting figure in 1900 to the only annual estimate of current prices that is available for the 1900–13 period. The results of these calculations are shown in table 1-2 for a few benchmark years and in table 1-3 on an annual basis. Although subject to a substantial margin of error, in level as well as in movement, the estimates are compatible with the more elaborate contemporary estimates available for a few years of this period.[9] The resulting estimates of gross national product in current prices—slightly more than R. 6 bill. in 1860 and nearly R. 21 bill. in 1913—imply an average annual growth rate of 2.3 percent a year, resulting from average annual increases of about 1.4 percent in the price level, of about 0.5 percent in population, and of about 0.4 percent in real product per head.

The small advance in real income per head resulted from irregular shorter movements. Almost the entire increase for the period seems to have occurred between the late 1860s and the middle 1880s and in the decade prior to World War I, whereas the trend was downward between the mid-1880s and the end of the century.

Although the growth rate of national product may be in dispute, there is no doubt that the level of average real product per head remained very low throughout the period. The estimates accepted here imply values for national product per head in current prices of about R. 25 in 1860 and nearly R. 70 in 1913, values equal, at current rates of exchange, to about $12 in 1860 and $22 in 1913. (United States averages were about $125 in 1860 and about $400 in 1913.)[10] These

9. For a discussion of these estimates, cf. S. J. Patel, *The Indian Economic Journal* 5 (1958): 234, and Mukherjee, *NII,* pp. 31–52, 81 ff.

10. For 1913, U.S. Bureau of the Census, *Historical Statistics of the United States,* 1960, p. 139. The estimate for 1860 was obtained by linking with Gallman's series for commodity output (*Studies in Income and Wealth,* 1960, 24:16).

TABLE 1-2. National Product, 1900–1946

	Current prices	Constant prices aggregate				Constant prices per head		
	Sivasubramonian[a] (1)	Sivasubramonian[a] (2)	Maddison[b] (3)	Heston[c] (4)	Mukherjee[a] (5)	Sivasubramonian[a] (6)	Maddison[b] (7)	Heston[c] (8)
	I. Indices (1913 = 100)							
1900	63	83	89	85	90	89	95	91
1913	100	100	100	100	100	100	100	100
1920	167	100	94	96	115	100	94	95
1929	164	127	110	126	118	116	100	115
1939	132	138	119	134	120	110	95	107
1946	349	149	127	142	116	109	93	104
	II. Rate of growth (percent)							
1901–13	3.61	1.44	0.90	1.26	0.81	0.93	0.42	0.74
1914–20	7.62	0.03	−0.86	−0.58	2.02	−0.05	−0.88	−0.70
1921–29	−0.20	2.69	1.76	3.06	0.03	1.67	0.69	2.14
1930–39	−2.15	0.82	0.79	0.59	0.02	−0.54	−0.51	−0.72
1940–46	14.95	1.10	0.93	0.63	−0.48	−0.13	−0.30	−0.41
1914–46	3.86	1.22	0.73	1.08	0.04	0.26	−0.22	0.13

[a]National income. [b]Net domestic product at factor cost. [c]Net domestic product.

SOURCES: **Cols. 1, 2, and 6:** Sivasubramonian, pp. 337–38; 1938–39 prices for cols. 2 and 6. **Cols. 3 and 7:** Maddison, pp. 167–68; 1938–39 prices. **Cols. 4 and 8:** Heston, chap. 4. **Col. 5:** Mukherjee, *NII*, p. 61; 1948–49 prices. Figures are nine-year averages centered on 1900, 1910, 1920, 1930, 1940, 1945, and refer to Indian Union.

TABLE 1-3. Production, Prices, Interest Rate, and Exchange Rate, 1860–1913

	Gross national product (R. bill.) (1)	Real income per head[a] (2)	Agricultural production[a] (3)	Industrial production[a] (4)	Wholesale prices[a] (5)	Cost of living[a] (6)	Bank rate (percent) (7)	Exchange rate (pence per R.) (8)
1860	6.14	80[b]			48.5	50.4	4.23	26.0
1861	6.56	·			52.7	54.8	4.17	23.9
1862	6.95	·			52.7	54.8	5.14	23.9
1863	7.47	·			55.8	58.1	5.51	23.9
1864	7.85	·			59.6	61.8	8.69	23.9
1865	8.06	·			61.9	64.2	6.95	23.8
1866	8.37	·			71.2	74.0	9.15	23.2
1867	8.53	78			66.9	69.6	5.05	23.3
1868	8.58	·			60.8	63.2	5.85	23.1
1869	8.62	·			66.9	69.6	6.00	23.3
1870	8.51	·			60.0	63.2	5.73	22.6
1871	8.60	·			52.7	54.8	4.72	23.1
1872	8.58	·			55.8	57.8	4.96	22.8
1873	8.47	84			56.5	58.8	3.93	22.4
1874	8.45	82			61.9	64.2	6.22	22.2
1875	10.20	92			54.6	56.7	5.66	21.7
1876	9.88	81			56.5	58.8	6.76	20.5
1877	9.06	78			73.1	75.9	8.40	20.8
1878	10.55	92			78.5	81.5	5.28	19.9
1879	9.69	84			72.3	76.3	6.34	19.9
1880	10.21	89			61.9	64.2	4.65	20.0
1881	10.22	92			56.5	58.8	5.29	19.9
1882	10.04	92			55.8	58.1	6.60	19.6
1883	10.11	95			56.5	63.2	6.78	19.5
1884	10.22	96			60.8	63.2	6.38	19.4
1885	10.58	97		22	60.8	61.1	5.38	18.3
1886	10.58	94			58.8	61.1	6.04	17.5
1887	10.62	91			58.8	61.1	5.64	16.9
1888	10.78	90			63.1	65.6	5.46	16.4
1889	11.52	92			66.9	69.6	6.99	16.6
1890	11.79	91		40	66.9	69.6	5.79	18.0
1891	11.72	88			68.1	70.5	3.06	16.8
1892	12.11	90			75.4	78.2	3.50	15.0
1893	11.94	87	104		73.1	75.9	4.88	14.6

(continued)

are extremely low values even if the internal purchasing power of the rupee is certain to have been considerably in excess of its foreign exchange value. In 1913 it may have been as high as five to seven times its exchange value of 32 cents.[11]

Throughout the period, India continued to be a predominantly agricultural, and more specifically a grain-growing, country. It is impossible to determine whether and to what extent

11. These figures are obtained by applying to the purchasing-power/exchange-rate ratio of 3.35 in 1970 (Kravis, et al., p. 10) changes in the price levels of the United States and India and changes in the rupee/dollar exchange rate between 1913 and 1970. Using gross national product deflators to measure changes in the price level, the ratio is about 7, but using cost-of-living indices, it is below 5. The reason for the higher ratio of the purchasing power/exchange rate in 1913 is the fact that the rupee/dollar exchange rate fell much more, from about 32 cents to 13 cents, than the increase in the Indian price level exceeded that of the United States (by only about 15 percent for GNP deflators, though by more than 70 percent for the cost-of-living indices). The limitations of most comparisons over long periods of time are obvious, and nothing more than an indication of the orders of magnitude involved is intended.

TABLE 1-3. (*continued*)

	Gross national product (R. bill.) (1)	Real income per head[a] (2)	Agricultural production[a] (3)	Industrial production[a] (4)	Wholesale prices[a] (5)	Cost of living[a] (6)	Bank rate (percent) (7)	Exchange rate (pence per R.) (8)
1894	12.38	86	108	·	69.2	71.9	5.39	13.1
1895	12.19	84	98	51	68.1	70.5	4.33	13.4
1896	13.08	91	80	·	74.2	77.0	5.69	14.4
1897	13.04	90	106	·	87.7	91.1	7.92	15.4
1898	13.89	94	111	·	71.2	74.0	8.06	16.0
1899	12.86	86	94	·	69.0	71.9	5.91	16.0
1900	13.17	89	101	47	81.5	79.2	5.34	15.9
1901	13.05	89	97	72	77.3	78.2	5.48	15.9
1902	13.38	96	110	76	74.2	79.6	4.86	16.0
1903	13.08	97	108	79	69.2	73.5	4.88	16.0
1904	14.27	97	103	82	71.2	77.3	4.87	16.0
1905	15.99	95	100	97	77.3	80.6	5.09	16.0
1906	17.61	97	106	100	90.8	87.6	6.42	16.0
1907	18.23	91	90	87	95.8	91.6	6.10	16.0
1908	17.08	91	97	88	100.0	106.3	5.83	16.0
1909	17.86	102	117	95	103.1	97.4	5.24	16.0
1910	18.13	103	117	90	85.8	92.3	5.33	16.0
1911	19.03	103	113	90	90.8	88.5	5.51	16.0
1912	20.52	103	110	107	95.8	97.1	5.42	16.0
1913	20.76	100	100	100	100.0	100.0	5.95	16.0

[a]1913 = 100.   [b]1857.

SOURCES: **Col. 1:** 1860–99, Mukherjee's estimate of real income per head (*NII*, p. 98) multiplied by population (Maddison, pp. 164–65), using straight-line interpolation between census dates before 1900, multiplied by seven-year moving average of Mukherjee's price index (*NII*, p. 94), multiplied by 1.143 to link to Sivasubramonian's estimate for 1900 (*NII*, p. 337), raised by 10 percent to shift from national income to gross national product; 1900–13, Sivasubramonian, raised by 10 percent.   **Col. 2:** 1860–1900, Mukherjee, loc. cit., 1901–13, Sivasubramonian (p. 338), linked in 1900 to Mukherjee's figure.   **Col. 3:** 1893–1913, Blyn, p. 251.   **Col. 4:** 1885–95, Sahni, p. 106, linked in 1905 to Sivasubramonian's estimate; 1900–13, Sivasubramonian, p. 226 (net output of manufacturing industries).   **Col. 5:** 1860–1913, Mukherjee, *NII*, p. 94.   **Col. 6:** 1860–1913, Mukherji, p. 657 ff. ("working class cost of living index," shifted from 1944 to 1913 basis).   **Col. 7:** 1860–1913, *BMS*, p. 690.   **Col. 8:** 1860–97, *Statistical Abstract for British India*, various issues; 1898–1913, *BMS*, pp. 855 ff. Average of monthly averages of Calcutta rate on council bills.

this predominance declined in the half century preceding World War I because sufficiently accurate figures are not available for the share of agriculture in the labor force or in national product before 1900. In 1911 the share of agriculture in the labor force is estimated at nearly 70 percent.[12] Of the two available estimates of the sectoral distribution of national product in constant prices, one (Maddison) puts the share of agriculture (including forestry and fishing) at slightly below 60 percent throughout the period 1900–13 and the other (Sivasubramonian) shows a substantial decline from two-thirds to slightly less than three-fifths. Because part of the labor force in, and part of the product of, the secondary and tertiary sectors are connected with the trading in, and the transportation or processing of, agricultural products, nonagricultural activities cannot have employed more than about one-fifth of the total labor force or accounted for more than approximately one-fourth of national product in the decade before World War I, and it is unlikely that the nonagricultural share was substantially smaller and the share of agriculture substantially larger in the preceding half century.

　　The information now available does not permit an examination of the output trend of the

12. J. N. Sinha, pp. 112–13.

main economic sectors in quantitative terms throughout the period. Blyn's index of agricultural production, generally regarded as the best available estimate, begins in the 1890s and indicates an average rate of expansion from 1891/93 to 1912/14 of 1.1 percent, with sharp annual fluctuations reflecting mainly the vagaries of the monsoon. The increase in food-grain output of 0.8 percent a year was only slightly in excess of population growth. Part of this modest growth was due to increased inputs of land and labor, as yields per acre rose by less than 15 percent between 1891/93 and 1912/14 and did so mostly in cash crops rather than in food grains.[13]

The most rapidly growing sector was manufacturing—particularly cotton and jute, as might be expected, as these industries were practically nonexistent at the beginning of the period. The average rate of increase in manufacturing output between 1880 and 1913 has been put at somewhat more than 7 percent per year,[14] which is not much in excess of the increase in the industrial labor force.[15] This increase, however, cannot be regarded as a net addition to national product, because part of the manufacturing output displaced handicraft products. The increase was most rapid in the 1880s, with nearly 15 percent a year; growth declined thereafter, averaging slightly less than 5 percent from 1890 to 1913.

Within the agricultural sector the main change was the substantial increase in cash crops (particularly cotton, jute, and sugar) and the stagnation in the production of food crops. Thus from 1893/95 to 1912/14 the output of food grains fell by about 5 percent, whereas that of other crops increased by more than 50 percent, or from 23 to 28 percent of total crop output. This meant a substantial increase in the monetization of the agricultural sector and in the volume of production that required financing by indigenous or organized lenders.

The main change within the secondary and tertiary sectors, of course, was the rise of factory industry and the railroads, both of which hardly existed at the beginning of the period. By 1913 factories and railroads employed 1.0 million and 0.6 million workers, respectively, or together about 4 percent of the total nonagricultural labor force, and accounted for about one-seventh of the nonagricultural product and for nearly two-fifths of the product of the secondary sector.

At least three contemporary attempts were made to obtain regional income estimates for this period. Naoroji put the per head income of Bombay province at 180 percent of the average for British India for 1867–68 and that of the Punjab at 135 percent. On the other hand, the per head income of the Central Provinces was estimated at 90 percent of the average, that of Bihar and Orissa at 75 percent, and those for the United Provinces and for Madras at 70 percent of the country average. Although Naoroji's methods of estimation were rough, the ranking of the different provinces is nevertheless similar to that obtaining in the 1930s and in the post-independence period, with the exception of Bombay province, which appears to be exaggerated.[16]

As the methods of calculation and coverage varied among the estimates, it seems best to

13. Blyn, p. 349.
14. Saini, p. 260.
15. Myers, p. 17.
16. Digby's estimate for 1901 (p. 613) provides figures for only four of the six provinces, putting the per head income of Bombay at 206 percent of the country average, that of the Central Provinces at 123 percent of the average, that of Bengal at 107 percent, and that of Madras at 98 percent. An estimate by Barbour for 1882 is limited to agricultural income. Because at that time agriculture accounted for more than two-thirds of total national product, his estimates regarding the relative position of the various provinces are of some interest. Barbour ranked the Central Provinces and Bombay first and second, followed by Madras and Punjab in the third and the fourth positions with a per head income of about one-sixth below that of the two leaders, whereas Madras and the United Provinces occupied the fifth and the sixth positions with per head incomes of nearly three-fourths that of the leaders. Although the ranking is similar in Naoroji's, Barbour's, and Digby's estimates, the range between leading and lagging provinces is much larger in Naoroji's and particularly in Digby's estimates than it is in Barbour's. Part of this difference is probably due to the fact that Barbour's estimates omit the large cities with their presumed considerably higher average incomes, a fact that lowers the relative position of Bengal and Bombay provinces. This effect, however, can be of only limited importance, because at that time Calcutta accounted for less than 2 percent of the population of Bengal and even Bombay city sheltered only 5 percent of the inhabitants of Bombay province.

emphasize the ranks of the different areas rather than the numerical relationships among the provinces. It then appears that the ranks of the individual provinces are fairly similar in the three estimates referring to the years 1867–68, 1882, and 1901. Bombay always holds first or second position and the United Provinces are always close to the bottom, as would also be Bihar and Orissa if the combined estimate for Bengal and Bihar could be split up. The only definite trends in rank are shown by Madras, which moved up from near the bottom in 1867–68 to the middle of the ranking in 1882 and 1901, and by the Punjab, which moved down from second place in 1867–68 to fifth in 1901. The Central Provinces also moved upward, though erratically.

c. National Wealth

Information on the growth of national wealth is even less accessible. The only available estimate shows a 45 percent increase in the stock of reproducible tangible assets between 1860 and 1900, or 0.9 percent per year.[17] This estimate, however, is based on the assumption of an average capital-output ratio of 2 in both years and thus is nothing more than an estimate of the increase in aggregate real product. From scattered indications, however, there is little doubt that the growth rate of real national wealth per head was very low. A new estimate of national wealth and its components is attempted in section 7.

d. Economic Policy

The role of the government under the British Raj in the economic development of India has been acrimoniously debated for more than a century. Although the government and most of its British officials were emphatic in claiming to have initiated or aided and accelerated much of the modernization of the Indian economy,[18] many Indian as well as some British observers qualified such claims. Some pointed out that the modernization that had occurred had been achieved at too high a price for the Indian taxpayer and in addition had been warped so as to benefit primarily British investors and exporters, and others denied that any progress at all had been made when the living standard of the entire Indian population was considered.[19]

The question of whether the monetary and financial policies followed by the government were the best that could have been adopted in the existing situation, the welfare of India being the test, is unanswerable if put in absolute terms; rather, one must ask whether other countries, similar to India in economic development and in natural and human resources, did better or worse than India. Although an attempt at a considered answer would far transcend the scope of this study, it would seem that a negative answer—that is, that India did worse—is difficult to defend if the development of some politically independent countries in the region—Siam, Persia, Turkey, China, Afghanistan, and Tibet—is used as the criterion. The British introduced, or at least improved, law and order; financed India's railroad system on better terms than any independent non-European country could then have obtained in the international capital market; and provided the country with the nucleus of a modern banking structure and with a currency system that, by chance rather than by design, was more modern than that then used by most countries, rich or poor. These three contributions may have been in the Victorian world the main preconditions for the economic development of backward countries. Karl Marx recognized this,[20] though many Marxists did not then and still do not.

17. Mukherjee, *NII*, p. 78.

18. The government typically issued its annual reports under the title *The Moral and Material Progress of India*.

19. Although most authors blame the British Indian government's do-nothing attitude—except for its vigorous public works activities ("The government's gospel in the post-mutiny years was public works," as Spear formulates it, p. 282)—for the slowness of the country's modernization and industrialization, even the government's limited role was of importance. Sen (p. 150) starts his "Concluding Remarks" with the statement: "In the period 1858–1914 government spending was a factor of crucial importance in India's industrialization, particularly the liberalization of store purchase rules in 1909." Stimulation is regarded as "undeniable . . . for coal, paper, woolen and leather industries," mainly, however, after the turn of the century (ibid.). For a more negative conclusion, cf. Lamb, p. 471 ff.

20. K. Marx, *Articles on India* (1943), a reprint of his articles that appeared in the *New York Daily Tribune* of 1853.

2. MONEY, PRICES, AND INTEREST RATES[21]

a. Money

A uniform rupee coinage was introduced for the territory then controlled by the East India Company in 1835, and from then on India was on a silver bullion standard. Although gold coins continued in use to a limited extent, money in circulation consisted mainly of silver rupees, supplemented by fractional coins and by notes issued by the three Presidency banks until 1862 and thereafter by the government. Until the early 1870s the value of the rupee kept fairly close to 2 shillings (24d) as the ratio of the market price of silver to gold remained in the neighborhood of 1 : 15. From then on, however, the international decline of the silver price, in part reflecting the transition of Germany and an increasing number of other countries to a monometallic gold standard, led to a depreciation of the rupee in terms of gold and sterling. The value of the rupee reached a low of only 13d in 1894, a depreciation of 45 percent compared to the earlier level of 2 shillings and of more than one-third from the level of the early 1880s when the rupee had a value of 20d. The difficulties created by a fluctuating and depreciating exchange, in particular the increase in the rupee amounts necessary to pay interest, pensions, and other foreign liabilities, led in 1893 to the suspension of the free coinage of silver and thus to the abandonment of the monometallic silver standard. It was replaced in the late 1890s, after a few years of floating exchange rates, by a gold (or more correctly sterling) exchange standard at the practically fixed rate of 16d per rupee. This ratio was maintained until World War I essentially by the willingness, never expressed in statutory form, of the government of India to buy or sell London (sterling) funds and, with some limitations, gold sovereigns or bullion at or very close to the ratio of 15 rupees per pound sterling. From the late 1890s to World War I India thus was an integral part of the international gold standard system, though without the use of gold coins in internal circulation. Because it lacked a central bank and because the volume of notes in circulation depended on the inflow and outflow of sterling funds, which were governed primarily by the seasonally fluctuating balance of trade, the system was much less elastic than that of most other countries that adhered to the gold standard.

In the absence of trustworthy, comprehensive, and continuous estimates of money in circulation before the mid-1930s as well as because of the shortcomings of the available price indices, it is difficult to measure changes in the money supply or to assess their effect on price movements or on other aspects of the economy before World War I. There is no doubt, however, that the trend in both money supply and prices was substantially upward and that the money supply increased more rapidly than total national product and probably also more rapidly than the part of national product that was sold in the market, that is, exchanged against money.

Given a rate of increase of total real national product from 1860 to 1913 of slightly less than 1 percent a year, monetized real product can hardly have increased at a rate of more than, say, 1¼ percent. The price level approximately doubled according to the available indices of wholesale and retail prices, a movement that implies an average annual rate of increase of nearly 1½ percent. Assuming other factors, particularly the velocity of circulation, to have been constant, one would expect an increase in the money supply at an average annual rate of 2½ to 3 percent, that is, a rise by 250 to 350 percent between 1860 and 1913.

The only component of the money supply for which fairly reliable information is available throughout the period are the notes issued by the Treasury since 1862. The amount in circulation rose fairly rapidly during the 1860s to about R. 100 mill., which was then equal to slightly more

---

21. No adequate modern history of the development of the monetary system of India before World War I exists. Keynes's *Indian Currency and Finance* remains in some respects the most informative source even though published in 1913. The main sources used for this section are, in alphabetical order: J. E. Coyajee, *The Indian Currency System 1835–1926*, 1930; S. V. Doraiswami, *Indian Finance, Currency and Banking*, 1915; H. S. Jevons, *Money, Banking and Exchange in India*, 1922; D. K. Malhotra, *History and Problems of Indian Currency 1835–1959*, 1960; G. F. Shirras, *Indian Finance and Banking*, 1920; C. N. Vakil, *Financial Developments in Modern India 1860–1924*, 1925; C. N. Vakil and S. K. Muranjan, *Currency and Prices in India*, 1927.

TABLE 1-4. Money Supply, 1860–1913

	Level (R bill.) (1)	Change (R bill.) (2)	Rate of growth (percent) (3)	Ratio (percent of GNP)[a] (4)	New issue ratio (percent of GNP) (5)
1860	0.61	.	.	9.6	.
1870	1.23	0.63	7.3	14.4	0.80
1880	1.48	0.24	1.9	14.5	0.25
1890	1.74	0.26	1.6	14.8	0.24
1900	1.90	0.17	0.9	14.5	0.13
1913	3.54	1.63	4.9	16.5	0.74
1861–1913	—	2.93	3.4	—	0.47

NOTE: Denominator is, as throughout the volume, the year-end rate of national product defined as the average of value of GNP of the year and the year following. The exception is 1946, because no estimate for 1947 exists.

SOURCES: **Col. 1:** Table 1-6, col. 5.   **Cols. 4 and 5:** Cols. 1 and 2 divided by gross national product of benchmark year or period between benchmark dates from table 1-3.

than 1 percent of national product. Note circulation increased only slowly up to the turn of the century, the ratio to national product remaining in the neighborhood of 1 percent. From then on, note circulation grew considerably more rapidly than national product, the rate of expansion exceeding 6 percent in the 1901–13 period, to reach a level of 2½ percent of national product on the eve of World War I.

Estimates of the volume of silver rupee coins in circulation, the largest single component of the money supply, are subject to a wide margin of error, particularly for the first two decades of the period. They indicate, as in the case of notes, a rapid increase in the early 1860s, possibly exaggerated in the only available estimate, which was made nearly eighty years ago; slow growth from then to the turn of the century; and finally rapid expansion from then to 1913. The ratio of rupee coin circulation to national product, however, remained in the neighborhood of 10 percent from 1865 to 1913.

The ratio of notes to coin showed an upward trend during the period, rising from about one-tenth between the mid-sixties and the mid-eighties to about one-fifth at the turn of the century and to more than one-fourth in 1913. This movement, together with the increase in check deposits, indicates a slow but steady modernization of India's monetary system.

No reliable information is available on the three other components of the money supply: small coin (which may be omitted because of negligible size—an increase of about R. 7 mill. per year between 1901 and 1913),[22] gold coins (British sovereigns, because no gold rupee coins were minted), and check deposits. Gold coins present a particular problem because most of them were hoarded and only a fraction, difficult to measure, of the net import of gold coins actually served as means of payment.[23]

There are no statistics of the volume of commercial bank checking deposits, which may be regarded as having functioned as a means of payment. In 1915 nearly three-fifths of the deposits of the Calcutta and Madras Presidency banks were classified as "current accounts," which probably were subject to check. If one is willing to assume, first, that this proportion applied to all commercial banks in 1913 and, second, that the proportion had been increasing slowly over the preceding thirty years, then approximately R. 40 mill. in 1870, R. 180 mill. in 1900, and nearly R. 600 mill. in 1913 would have to be regarded as part of the effective circulation.

The structure of the assets of the paper currency reserve reflects some of these changes. Thus the reserve consisted entirely of silver coins and bullion until 1863. By the turn of the

22. *BMS*, p. 665.
23. Cf. discussion of gold circulation in Keynes, pp. 53 ff.

century the reserve was more diversified, holding nearly two-fifths in the form of silver coins and bullion and about 30 percent each in that of gold and securities. By 1913 the share of gold coin and bullion had risen to one-half of the total, whereas that of rupee and sterling securities had declined to 15 and 6 percent, respectively, leaving nearly one-third to be covered by silver and thus exposed to changes in value.

In this situation any estimate of the volume of money in circulation must accept a substantial margin of error, particularly because of the uncertainty about the proportion of gold sovereigns imported into India that formed part of the active circulation. For the purposes of this study, money circulation has been defined as the sum of silver rupees and Treasury notes in circulation, of the roughly estimated amounts of current deposits of commercial banks, and of one-fifth of the net import of gold coins. Slightly narrower or broader definitions of money in circulation are equally defensible, but their adoption would not give a substantially different picture of the level, and particularly of the trend, of the money supply in India in the half century preceding World War I. Table 1-6 shows the estimates of money in circulation at six decadal

TABLE 1-5. Money, Bank Deposits, Government Debt, and Capital of Joint Stock
Companies, 1860–1913 (R. Mill.)

	Money in circulation				Funded rupee debt		
	Rupee coins (1)	Notes (2)	Coins and notes (3)	Bank deposits (4)	Total (5)	Held by Indians (6)	Corporate stock (7)
1860	440				635		
1861	451				634		
1862	508	40	548		634		
1863	611	45	656		634		
1864	717	67	784		634		
1865	851	67	918		624		
1866	891	90	981		630		
1867	909	93	1002		638		
1868	943	93	1036		634	147	
1869	979	102	1081		656	·	
1870	930	94	1024	125	668	·	
1871	892	98	990	145	686	155	
1872	898	116	1014	155	665	171	
1873	872	98	970	134	664	·	
1874	903	98	1001	108	699	193	
1875	870	101	971	116	728	·	
1876	874	109	983	103	719	·	
1877	1008	138	1146	127	750	226	
1878	1031	109	1140	127	788	230	
1879	1073	128	1201	137	829	210	
1880	1080	134	1214	161	860	187	
1881	1067	108	1175	141	887	216	157
1882	1073	111	1184	145	907	244	171
1883	1077	111	1188	149	932	243	188
1884	1090	132	1222	160	932	253	208
1885	1130	142	1272	183	927	249	210
1886	1110	129	1239	194	927	294	214
1887	1110	159	1269	216	981	300	223
1888	1120	137	1257	231	1009	305	230
1889	1170	127	1297	236	1028	298	237
1890	1200	156	1356	349	1028	291	245
1891	1260	180	1440	363	1027	203	266

(continued)

TABLE 1-5. (*continued*)

	Money in circulation				Funded rupee debt		
	Rupee coins (1)	Notes (2)	Coins and notes (3)	Bank deposits (4)	Total (5)	Held by Indians (6)	Corporate stock (7)
1892	1380	209	1589	361	1029	310	267
1893	1360	183	1543	357	1056	345	269
1894	1300	202	1502	395	1044	297	273
1895	1280	212	1492	414	1038	296	291
1896	1200	199	1399	401	1091	325	306
1897	1200	192	1392	381	1117	478	323
1898	1150	200	1350	396	1127	464	348
1899	1120	222	1342	420	1125	485	347
1900	1200	230	1430	443	1153	473	363
1901	1370	225	1595	494	1162	443	374
1902	1270	257	1527	565	1176	484	382
1903	1290	278	1568	598	1194	507	387
1904	1320	298	1618	664	1223	509	403
1905	1420	316	1736	684	1261	548	417
1906	1600	365	1965	749	1305	586	443
1907	1860	341	2201	798	1328	597	508
1908	1920	342	2262	828	1346	619	570
1909	1900	384	2284	930	1368	612	614
1910	1860	395	2255	1041	1381	652	641
1911	1800	446	2246	1108	1400	696	694
1912	1850	474	2324	1175	1428	694	721
1913	1903	507	2410	1192	1457	766	766

SOURCES: **Col. 1:** 1860–83, Atkinson's estimate (*Journal of the Royal Statistical Society*, 1897, p. 144), linked in 1884 to Datta's estimate; 1884–1912, Datta, 1:270; 1913, extrapolated on basis of absorption of rupee coin (*BMS*, p. 666).   **Col. 2:** 1862–1913, *BMS*, pp. 650 ff. Figures before 1874 reduced by 10 percent, approximately the difference between notes issued and notes in circulation in the decade 1874–83.   **Col. 4:** 1870–1913, *BMS*, p. 7. Covers Presidency banks, exchange banks, and class A Indian joint stock banks and Post Office Saving System.   **Col. 5:** 1870–1913, *BMS*, pp. 880–81. Until 1885, figures refer to April 30 of the year following; thereafter, to March 31 of the year following.   **Col. 6:** 1868–1913, Vakil, pp. 576–77. The sharp increase in 1897 is due to rectification of previous errors in allocation.   **Col. 7:** 1881–1913, *BMS*, p. 781; paid-up capital of all joint stock companies at work as of March 31 of the year following.

benchmarks and of the relation of the stock of money and of changes in it to national product. Table 1-5, finally, shows annual data for the two components for which more or less reliable information is available on an annual basis, that is, for Treasury notes, for which the margin of error should be small, and for rupee silver coins, for which the estimates are much more uncertain, particularly until the mid-1880s. All estimates of the total money supply and changes in it should be regarded as indicating orders of magnitude rather than as close estimates, which could support sophisticated statistical analysis. Notwithstanding the substantial margin of error in the estimates, particularly that in the active gold coin circulation, a few conclusions from the figures brought together in tables 1-5 and 1-6 seem nevertheless justified.

First, the total money supply increased somewhat more rapidly than national product. For the period 1861–1913 the expansion of the money supply by 3.4 percent a year compares with a growth rate of national product in current prices of 2.3 percent. If the 1860s are excluded because the estimates are even less certain than those for the following decades, the difference is less—2.5 percent for money supply compared to 2.1 percent for national product for the 1871–1913 period. The difference is considerably less for the 1870s, 1880s, and 1890s, indeed so minute that it may not be statistically significant. It is large enough, however, for the 1901–13 period—4.9 percent for money supply against 3.6 percent for national product—to make it

TABLE 1-6. Main Components of the Money Supply, 1860–1913[a]

	Rupee coins (1)	Gold coins (2)	Notes (3)	Current bank deposits (4)	Total[b] (5)
			I. Level (R. mill.)		
1860	440	530	40	20	606
1870	930	901	94	40	1244
1880	1080	1004	134	60	1475
1890	1200	1266	156	135	1744
1900	1200	1548	230	175	1915
1913	1903	2768	507	575	3539
		II. Average annual rate of growth (percent)			
1861–1870	7.8	5.5	8.9	7.2	7.5
1871–1880	1.5	1.1	3.6	4.1	1.7
1881–1890	1.1	2.3	1.5	8.5	1.7
1891–1900	0	2.0	4.0	2.6	0.9
1901–1913	3.6	4.6	6.3	9.6	4.8
1861–1913	2.8	3.2	4.9	6.5	3.4
		III. Distribution (percent)			
1860	73	17	7	3	100
1870	75	14	8	3	100
1880	73	14	9	4	100
1890	69	15	9	8	100
1900	63	16	12	9	100
1913	54	16	14	16	100
		IV. Ratio to gross national product (percent)			
1860	6.9	8.3	0.6	0.3	9.5
1870	10.9	10.5	1.1	0.5	14.6
1880	10.6	9.8	1.3	0.6	14.5
1890	10.2	10.7	1.3	1.1	14.7
1900	9.1	11.8	1.7	1.3	14.5
1913	8.9	12.9	2.4	2.7	16.5
		V. Ratio of change to period's gross national product (percent)			
1861–1870	0.62	0.47	0.07	0.03	0.81
1871–1880	0.16	0.11	0.04	0.02	0.24
1881–1890	0.11	0.25	0.02	0.07	0.25
1891–1900	0.00	0.22	0.06	0.03	0.13
1901–1913	0.32	0.56	0.13	0.18	0.73
1861–1913	0.23	0.36	0.07	0.09	0.47

[a]March 31 of following year for I and III; period ending March 31 of following year for II and IV.   [b]Sum of cols. 1, 3, and 4, and one-fifth of col. 2.

SOURCES: **Cols. 1 and 3:** 1860–1913, table 1-5.   **Col. 2:** 1860–1893, nearly two-thirds of net gold imports (*BMS*, pp. 940, 961), the relationship between total net imports of gold and imports of British gold coins in 1894–1913; 1894–1913, net imports of British gold coins (*BMS*, p. 961). The figures given by Keynes (1971, p. 54) for 1901–12 are about one-fifth lower.   **Col. 4:** 1860, rough estimate; 1870–1913, assumed to rise from about 40 to nearly 60 percent of total deposits of all commercial banks (*BMS*, p. 7).

unlikely that the difference is a statistical artifact rather than the reflection of a decline in the velocity of circulation of money.

Second, the ratio of money supply to gross national product, that is, the income velocity of money, declined substantially in the 1860s—if the figures can be trusted—but showed no trend from 1870 to 1913, keeping between 6 and 7.[24] A decrease over the period as a whole is what

24. *BMS*, pp. 647–48.

one would expect as the degree of monetization of the Indian economy is almost certain to have increased during this period and the degree of layering, that is, the average number of economic units in the money circuit, is likely to have become larger. Rather, what requires explanation is the apparent stability of income velocity after 1870.

Third, and a corollary of the movements discussed in the two preceding paragraphs, the money issue ratio (i.e., the increase in the money supply divided by the period's national product), as shown in table 1-6, was much higher in the 1860s (again, provided the rough estimates are accepted) and in the 1901–13 period than in the last thirty years of the nineteenth century. The average ratio for the period as a whole of slightly below 0.5 percent of national product is very low in international comparison but is in line with the limited financial development of Victorian India.

Fourth, though this remains to some extent a matter of judgment, the increase in the money supply, which in turn was largely determined by India's balance of payments, seems to have been a major, if not the determining, force in the increase of the current price level. At an average annual rate of nearly 1½ percent—somewhat lower than the difference between the rate of increase in the money supply of 3½ percent and that of real national product of slightly less than 1 percent—the increase of the current price level contrasts with the practical equality of the measured wholesale price levels of 1860 and 1913 in Great Britain and the United States.

The method by which notes and coins were issued and redeemed by the Treasury makes it possible to observe regional differences in the case of notes throughout the period and in that of coins from 1894 on.[25] The one characteristic regional difference in India's financial structure that stands out in the figures is the dominating role of Calcutta and Bombay, which together provided in the 1894–1913 period the country's entire money supply, the other regions together showing a small net reduction in their holdings of rupee coins and notes. There is no obvious explanation for the relatively high share of Bombay in the supply of coins and its low share in that of notes in comparison to the approximate equality of the two shares of Calcutta. Although no information is available on the regional distribution of check deposits, one may regard the total deposits of the three Presidency banks as reflecting the regional distribution of check deposits in all commercial banks. The share of Calcutta, then, is about the same as it is in the supply of notes and rupee coins, namely, close to one-half, whereas that of Bombay is considerably higher in deposits (about one-half) than in the supply of notes and coins (about one-fifth). This may reflect the relatively larger importance of financial activities in Bombay and its position as the chief import point of precious metals.

b. Prices

The Indian price level in the half century before World War I moved substantially though irregularly upward (table 1-7).[26] Both the wholesale and the retail price indices doubled between 1860 and 1913. They rose by about one-fourth during the 1860s (using moving three-year averages) and moved sideways during the 1870s and 1880s when prices declined substantially in many countries,[27] the difference reflecting in part the fall in the price of silver, which was the basis of India's currency at that time. The price level then advanced slowly during the 1890s and more rapidly in the last decade before World War I, as it also did in the rest of the world. As would be expected from the increase in the difference between the rates of expansion of the money supply and of real national product, the rise in the price level was considerably more pronounced after the turn of the century than in the preceding four decades. In the period from

25. The calculation should use as the denominator only the monetized part of national product. Because no estimates are available for this magnitude, total national product has been used, resulting in values for the income velocity of money that are too high by something like one-third to one-fourth, the difference presumably declining over time.

26. *BMS*, pp. 661–62.

27. If the devaluation of the rupee is considered, it appears that the Indian price level rose only at an average annual

TABLE 1-7. Price and Wage Movements, 1860–1913

	National income (1)	Cost of living (2)	Wholesale prices (3)	Export prices (4)	Import prices (5)	Agricultural wages (6)	Skilled wages (7)	Exchange rate (pence per R.) (8)
			I. Change during period (percent)					
1860–1913	·	+98.4	+106.3	+75.0[a]	+23.2[a]	+250.5[b]	+143.4[b]	−35.1
1860–1880	·	+27.4	+ 27.8	+25.0[a]	− 7.4[a]	+100.0[b]	+ 81.0[b]	−19.4
1880–1900	·	+23.4	+ 31.7	+12.7	+ 9.1	+ 14.3	+ 29.3	−19.5
1900–1913	+30.8	+26.3	+ 22.6	+24.2	+21.9	+ 53.3	+ 4.0	− 0.6
			II. Average rate of change (percent per year)					
1861–1913	·	+1.30	+1.38	+1.08[a]	+0.40[a]	+2.39[b]	+1.69[b]	−0.81
1861–1880	·	+1.22	+1.23	+1.18[a]	−0.37[a]	+3.06[b]	+2.61[b]	−1.07
1881–1900	·	+1.06	+1.39	+0.60	+0.44	+0.67	+1.29	−1.08
1901–1913	+2.09	+1.81	+1.58	+1.68	+1.53	+3.34	+0.03	−0.05

[a]1861 instead of 1860.   [b]1857 instead of 1860.

SOURCES: **Cols. 1 and 2:** Sivasubramonian, pp. 337–39. Implicit deflator for col. 1.   **Cols. 2 and 3:** Table 1-3.   **Cols. 4 and 5:** Shirras, p. 447; figures refer to March 31 of the year following.   **Cols. 6 and 7:** 1860–1900, Mukherjee, *NII,* p. 91; 1900–13, Sivasubramonian, p. 240; refers to rural, field, and skilled urban wages in up-country areas in Bombay province.   **Col. 8:** Shirras, pp. 456–58.

1900 to 1913 wholesale prices, the cost of living, and the general price level (national product deflator) all showed substantial increases.

Although information about wages is fragmentary and in part contradictory, and wage earners represented only a minority of the working population, wages for the period as a whole seem to have at least kept up with the rise in the price level.[28] The financial development of India during the period thus took place against the background of a moderate secular inflation, although the rise in the price level may not have been, and probably was not, recognized and treated as such by contemporaries.

c. Interest Rates

At least three sets of interest rates with hardly any interconnection existed throughout the period. The first set was represented by the discount rate of the Presidency banks. This rate was the weathervane for rates charged by banks for short-term business credit and was subject to sharp seasonal fluctuations—high in the busy season of fall and winter and low in the slack

---

rate of 0.8 percent for the entire period from 1860 to 1913 and by 1 percent for the period following the stabilization of the rupee, that is, the late 1890s.

	India	Great Britain[a]	United States[b]
1860–1880	+1.2	−0.6	+0.4
1880–1900	+1.4	−0.8	−1.0
1900–1913	+1.6	+0.8	+1.7
1860–1913	+1.4	−0.3	+0.2

[a]Sauerbeck; cf. B. R. Mitchell and Ph. Deane, *Abstract of British Historical Statistics,* 1962, p. 474.
[b]Warren and Pearson, 1860–1890; *BLS,* 1890–1913; U.S. Bureau of the Census, *Historical Statistics of the United States,* 1960, pp. 115 ff.

28. Cf., in addition to table 1-7, Mukherjee's "final wage series" (*NII,* p. 91), according to which wage rates of both agricultural workers and skilled workers rose by 130 percent from 1857 to 1900, that is, somewhat more rapidly than retail prices.

season—because of the inelasticity of note circulation or rather its dependence on the state of the trade balance and of the very limited development of check deposits. The second set of interest rates prevailed in the bazaars of large urban centers and was charged by unincorporated indigenous bankers to the small- and medium-sized traders and manufacturers who borrowed from them through bills of exchange (*hundis*). The third set of interest rates, which applied to the largest volume of funds throughout most of the period, were the much higher rates charged by rural and urban moneylenders to their clients. The first set of rates was considerably influenced by movements in interest rates in London, as were the yields on Indian government bonds; the second and third sets were determined almost exclusively by domestic conditions.

Statistics, for all or most of the period, are available only for the first set of interest rates. They show (table 1-7) considerable year-to-year and cyclical changes but no long-term trend, the averages for the beginning (1860–64), the middle (1885–89), and the end (1909–13) of the period all lying between 5½ and 6 percent. They were thus substantially above the rates prevailing in London, generally by about 2 percent. The bazaar rates were considerably higher, but they showed much less short-time fluctuations, reflecting their partly conventional character. They appear to have been in the neighborhood of 9 percent from 1867–79; somewhat lower— around 7½ percent—in the 1880s; again at about 9 percent in the 1890s; and considerably lower, in the neighborhood of 6 percent, in the first decade of the twentieth century. Effective rates were somewhat higher because of commission charges and other extras. Moneylenders' rates varied over a broad range. Effective rates apparently were hardly ever below 12 percent a year and often reached 18 and 24 percent and even higher levels.

3. THE BALANCE OF PAYMENTS AND FOREIGN INVESTMENTS

India's balance of payments throughout the period was characterized by a large export surplus of commodities, which was used in part to acquire gold and silver, primarily for hoarding by the population, and in part to pay the so-called home charges to the United Kingdom, mainly interest on sterling loans raised by the government or the railroads and pensions and similar charges, payment being effected by Indian Council bills. Home charges—regarded as "tribute" not only by Indian nationalists but also by some British observers[29]—stayed close to 1½ percent of national product throughout the period.[30] The only estimate of the balance of payments that covers most of the period is reproduced in table 1-8. Balance of payments statistics prepared in line with the more detailed economic breakdowns now in use or statistics covering the first two decades of the period do not seem to be available.

For the half century from 1865 through 1913 the surplus on merchandise account was nearly R. 20 bill., or 3.3 percent of gross national product.[31] Annual fluctuations, largely reflecting weather conditions and food production, were large, but five-year averages began to rise fairly sharply in absolute amount from the 1890s on. Compared to national product, however, the surplus, which measures the extent to which India's disposable income lagged behind its domestic output, fell from more than 3 percent in the 1860s to not much more than 2 percent in the 1880s but then rose to nearly 4 percent in 1909–13. Well over half the surplus was needed for home charges and about one-third was taken in precious metals, with neither form contributing directly to the growth of the Indian economy.

Between 1879 and 1915 net gold and silver imports were equal to three-fifths of the commodity export surplus. The estimated stock of gold and silver more than doubled, from fully R. 5 bill. to more than R. 11 bill., between 1860 and 1913, with gold accounting for three-

29. The term was explicitly used as early as 1859 by Wingate (p. 8), a high official of the government.
30. Absolute figures from Vakil, pp. 580–81.
31. For trade figures for 1864 to 1878, cf. Shirras, p. 441.

TABLE 1-8. Components of Balance of Payments, 1879–1913ᵃ (£ Mill.)

Annual average of	Net merchandise exports (1)	Net gold and silver imports (2)	Net commodity exports (1−2) (3)	Transactions in R. paper (4)	Council drafts (net) (5)	Balance (6)
1879–1883	20.7	6.9	13.8	0.1	13.2	0.7
1884–1888	20.0	8.0	12.0	−0.5	12.0	−0.5
1889–1893	24.8	9.5	15.3	−0.3	14.5	0.4
1894–1898	25.1	5.7	19.4	−0.9	17.4	1.2
1899–1903	30.7	9.8	20.9	−1.1	18.5	1.4
1904–1908	35.6	14.0	21.6	−0.7	22.1	−.1.2
1909–1913	52.2	24.0	28.2	−0.9	27.5	−0.2
1879 to 1913						
£ mill.	30.8	11.4	19.4	−0.6	18.4	0.3
R. mill.	462	171	291	9	276	24
Percent of GNP	3.33	1.23	2.10	−0.07	1.99	0.04

ᵃFiscal year starting April 1.   ᵇInterest on enfaced rupee paper and export and imports of enfaced rupee paper.   ᶜAt 4.15 per £ (Shirras, p. 442, footnote 2).

SOURCE OF BASIC DATA: Shirras, p. 442.

fourths of the increase. By 1913 the stock of the two metals was equal at near R. 6 bill. each, or somewhat more than one-fourth of the national product.[32]

Because the few available estimates of foreign investment in India refer to different dates and differ in scope and method of estimation, stringing such estimates together can only provide an idea of the orders of magnitude involved.[33] Foreign, that is, essentially British, investment in India before the Mutiny appear to have been small, consisting essentially of the holdings of British investors in East India Company stock.[34] The first estimates available refer to 1860 and put total foreign investment in India at about £70 mill., that is, R. 700 mill., two-fifths each of government sterling loans and railway securities and one-fifth of rupee government securities.[35,36] Ten years later foreign investments were estimated at about £150 mill. (about R. 1,600 mill.). In the late 1890s foreign investments seem to have been close to R. 3,500 mill.,[37]

32. The estimates are derived from the quantity figures of Prakash (p. 286), using the metal prices in Shirras.
33. For a careful review of the estimates of foreign investments in India, cf. Saini (pp. 127 ff.), who finally accepted the following estimates: 1860, £153 mill.; 1884, £294 mill.; 1910, £430 mill. (p. 141). Using the current rates of exchange, these four estimates correspond to about R. 700 mill. in 1860; R. 1,600 mill. in 1870; R. 3,500 mill. in 1884; and R. 6,500 mill. in 1910. For the early history and an interpretation, cf. Jenks, p. 207.
34. Bose (p. 487) states that there were hardly any British investments in India before the Mutiny, whereas G. Rosen (cited by Saini, p. 133) estimates British investments in India before 1854 at only £3.4 mill. (R. 34 mill.), then on the order of less than 1 percent of a year's national product. This contrasts with the considerably higher estimate of Wingate (footnote 36).
35. Saini, p. 132.
36. A contemporary estimate, made by a member of the finance wing of the British administration, put total British investments in India in 1859 at about £120 mill. (R. 1.2 bill.) (Wingate, p. 13), quite out of line with Saini's estimate for 1860 as well as with later estimates. About R. 0.35 bill. of this total was supposed to be invested in Indian government securities; R. 0.12 bill. in East India Company stock; R. 0.21 bill. in other loans and deposits; and—the most doubtful item—R. 0.40 bill. in "Indian public works capital." If the last item is omitted, because it is not usually regarded as a foreign investment in India, the estimate is reduced to about R. 0.8 bill., which is somewhat, but not radically, higher than other estimates.
37. E. Crammond, cited in Bose, p. 494. Crammond's estimates were R. 3.5 bill. in 1897, R. 4.6 bill. in 1906 (of which R. 3.9 bill. was in government and railroad securities), and R. 6.5 bill. for 1910.

and near the end of the period the estimates are on the order of R. 6 bill. to R. 7 bill.[38,39] This would mean an increase between 1860 and 1913 by about R. 6 bill., or about 1 percent of the period's national product. The absolute and relative size of the flow appears to have been definitely larger in the period since 1898, at about 1.5 percent of national product, than it was in the preceding forty years when the ratio was only on the order of 0.7 percent.[40] In comparison to India's annual national product, foreign investments increased from about one-tenth in 1860 to about one-fourth in 1900 and to about one-third in 1913.

More significant is the comparison of capital imports with total capital formation. Capital imports appear to have been equal to nearly one-fifth of gross domestic capital formation for the period as a whole, rising from about one-seventh in the first four decades to one-fifth for the last fifteen years of the period. The ratios are, of course, higher in relation to net capital formation, namely, nearly one-fourth for the earlier and about one-third for the latter part of the period and fully one-fourth for the period as a whole.[41] None of the figures should be taken too literally, given the large margins of error in the underlying magnitudes involved. They should, however, be able to sustain and to concretize two conclusions. First, capital imports provided a very important complement to domestic capital formation, particularly in the modern sector, and second, the importance of capital imports was substantially larger in the later rather than in the earlier part of the period.

These conclusions are supported by a comparison of the stock, rather than the flow, dimensions. The stock of foreign investments, equal in 1860 to about 4 percent of all reproducible tangible assets (including gold and silver), had increased to close to 15 percent in 1913.[42] The ratio would, of course, be considerably higher, but probably also rising, if the comparison could be limited to the modern sector of the Indian economy.

Railroad and government securities, part of which went to finance the railways, accounted for the bulk of capital imports. One estimate[43] puts the share of government securities in British investments in India around 1910 at about one-half, followed closely by railway (including other transport) securities with nearly two-fifths. Because most of the proceeds of government securities were used to finance the railways,[44] the share of this industry in total foreign investment would be in excess of three-fourths. Plantations, mainly tea, accounted for only 7 percent of the total and the remaining private investments for about 10 percent.

Although their size may have been relatively small compared to that of foreign investments in Indian government and railway securities, direct foreign, that is, mainly British, investments in industry, commerce, and banking (made partly through managing agencies, for which satisfactory estimates are not available) were of crucial importance in developing the modern sector of the Indian economy and were the means by which a large part of the modern sector came under foreign control and remained under it throughout the period, although to a diminishing extent after the turn of the century. This will become evident in the discussion of managing agencies in section 6d. Notwithstanding the rapid and substantial increase of foreign,

38. Paish's estimate for about 1910 of £365 mill. (R. 5.5 bill.) includes Ceylon but excludes direct investments by British companies or individuals in India.

39. Other estimates for this period are those of Keynes, £350 mill. (R. 5.4 bill.) for 1910, and of Howard (p. 95), also for about 1910, of £424 mill. (R. 6.3 bill.), of which one-half was in government securities. Inclusion of direct investments would bring this to at least £450 mill. (R. 6.8 bill.).

40. Another later estimate puts net capital imports for the period 1898–1913 at about R. 2.2 bill., or 1.0 percent of national product (Pandit, p. 103).

41. These ratios are based on the estimates of capital formation in table 1-9. The ratio for 1901–13 would be much lower if B. Roy's estimates (table 1-10) were used.

42. Based on the estimate of tangible assets in table 1-28.

43. Paish, p. 180.

44. Cf. table 1-23.

that is, mainly British, investment in India and in spite of its financial attractiveness,[45] India lost in importance as an outlet for British capital, its share in total British foreign investments declining from about one-fifth in 1860–85 to about one-eighth after the turn of the century.[46]

4. CAPITAL FORMATION AND SAVING

a. Capital Formation

For most of the period, conjectures and guesses are our only sources. For the years 1901 to 1913, however, an estimate has recently become available that puts aggregate gross capital formation at about R. 14 bill. and net capital formation at nearly R. 9 bill. This estimate is shown in table 1-10 together with the distribution and the rate of increase of its components and their relation to the flow of gross national product.

TABLE 1-9. Rough Estimates of Fixed Capital Formation, 1861–1913[a]

	Capital formation			
	Gross (R. bill.) (1)	Net (R. bill.) (2)	Gross (percent of GNP) (3)	Net (percent of GNP) (4)
1861–1900	20	8	5	2
1901–1913	14	9	6	4
1861–1913	34	17	5½	2½

[a]Figures rounded to emphasize rough nature of estimates.

SOURCES: **Cols. 1 and 2:** 1861–1900, cf. discussion in text. Figures exclude consumer durables and precious metals, which may have added about 1-1/2 percent in 1861–1913 to cols. 3 and 4. **Cols. 1 and 2:** 1901–13, *BR*. **Cols. 3 and 4:** Cols. 1 and 2 divided by gross national product estimates of table 1-3.

On the basis of these estimates, gross capital formation averaged 6 percent of gross national product for the 1901–13 period with only small year-to-year variations, the annual ratios fluctuating without trend within a range of 6 and 8 percent. Net capital formation is estimated at 4 percent of national product. These estimates include neither consumer durables, which may well be ignored, nor the increase in gold and silver hoards, which may have been equal to nearly 1 percent of national product, bringing the gross capital formation ratio more broadly defined to close to 7 percent and the net ratio to 5 percent.[47] Such low capital formation ratios are not unexpected in an economy with as low a standard of living and as low a rate of growth of national product as Victorian India, particularly when non-monetized investment, which should have been substantial in agriculture, is not included.

More than 90 percent of the entire gross capital formation was in the form of fixed assets, as inventory accumulation is estimated at less than one-tenth of the period's total capital formation, or fully one-half percent of its national product. Construction accounted for fully 60 percent of total gross capital formation and machinery and equipment for 30 percent. For a country in which more than two-thirds of the labor force and more than one-half of its output were agricultural, the one-fourth share of agriculture in total gross capital formation was lamentably

45. An anonymous author, writing under the pseudonym "A Manchester Man," advocated British investments in India by pointing out that "Indian investments are particularly eligible because they unite the profits of an Asian operation with the security of an English one," p. 10.

46. Saini (p. 145), using Imlah's estimates of total British foreign investments.

47. Figures arrived at by relating estimated increase in gold and silver hoards of R 2 bill. between 1895 and 1913 (table 1-28) to the sum of the period's gross national product (table 1-3).

TABLE 1-10. Capital Formation and Saving, 1901–1913

	Amounts (R. bill.)[a] (1)	Distribution (percent)[a] (2)	Ratio to GNP[a] (3)	Rate of growth (percent)[a,b] (4)	Rate of growth (per year)[b,c] (5)
Gross fixed capital formation	13.80	91.0	6.30	4.01	2.62
Construction	9.28	61.2	4.24	3.15	1.50
Urban	5.64	37.2	2.58	3.30	1.86
Rural	3.64	24.0	1.66	2.46	1.00
Machinery	4.52	29.8	2.06	5.87	4.02
Agricultural	0.31	2.0	0.14	6.12	3.99
Other	4.21	27.8	1.92	5.85	4.02
Inventories	1.36	9.0	0.62	−3.26	.
Gross total capital formation	15.16	100.0	6.92	3.00	2.44
Depreciation	6.40	42.2	2.92	7.43	5.90
Net total capital formation	8.76	57.8	4.00	0.07	−1.72
Net capital inflow	0.45	3.0	0.21	.	.
Net saving	8.31	54.8	3.79	0.78	−1.10
Gross public capital formation	4.98	32.7	2.21	5.71	4.00

[a]Current prices.   [b]Between averages of 1900–02 and 1912–14.   [c]1951–52 prices.

SOURCE OF COL. 1: *BR*, p. 205, increased by 20 percent to shift from Indian Union territory to undivided India.

low. An average total gross investment of about R. 6 per year per agricultural household (i.e., about $2.00) indicates the almost complete absence of mechanization, even if allowance is made for non-monetized capital formation in the form of structures and equipment produced in the household or by villagers. As public gross capital formation appears to have accounted for nearly one-third of the total, about two-fifths of the total must have taken place in the private non-agricultural sector. In view of the relatively small size of the corporate sector, about two-fifths of the national total must thus be attributed to the urban noncorporate business and household sectors. These relations are important indicators of the demand for finance.

For the preceding four decades the void is complete.[48] It is fairly certain that the average domestic capital formation ratio was lower for the last four decades of the nineteenth century than for the 1901–13 period. On the evidence of the creation of the railway system and of a few modern industries, none of which existed in 1860, as well as of the extension and improvement of the country's road and canal system and of a substantial number of public and private structures, which are visible in most of India's larger cities even today, net capital formation must have been positive and of not altogether negligible size. Such a conclusion is further substantiated by the housing investment required for a rural population increase of about 20 percent and an increase of about 5 million in the urban population, where a considerably larger average housing investment per head is required.[49] A rather flimsy basis for an estimate, it is nevertheless all that is available. Putting gross fixed capital formation at 5½ percent and net fixed capital formation at 2½ percent and adding about one-half percent for inventories and about 1½ percent for consumer durables and precious metals yields a broad gross capital

48. Mukherjee's estimates (*NII*, p. 78) of the stock of reproducible tangible wealth, presumably in 1948 prices, excluding inventories and referring to undivided India, of R. 65 bill. for 1860 and of R. 94 bill. for 1900 imply a net capital formation for the intervening forty years of R. 29 bill. in 1948 prices and one about R. 5 bill. in current prices, which would be equal to only about 1¼ percent of national product. Unfortunately, however, the estimates are based on the assumption of a capital-output ratio of 2 for both dates. The growth rate, in real terms, of the stock of reproducible tangible assets of 0.9 percent per year for the 1861–1900 period, therefore, is nothing but the growth rate of real national product.

49. Assuming a share of town population of 10 percent throughout the period (table 1-1, col. 7).

formation ratio of about 7½ percent of national product for the 1860–1913 period and a net ratio of about 4½ percent, little more than a guess but basically of the right order of magnitude.

Hardly anything is known quantitatively about the structure of capital expenditures in the nineteenth century, either by type of asset or by ownership or by location. Only a few series on capital expenditures for specific purposes are available, the most important of which refer to the railroads and to irrigation.

Capital expenditures on railroads through 1913 are reported at nearly R. 5 bill.,[50] which is equivalent to slightly less than 1 percent of this period's total gross national product and to about one-seventh of estimated total gross fixed capital expenditures. Although the reported figures may cover expenditures on land and other items not included in total capital expenditures, for example, costs of purchasing existing private railroads, there is little doubt that in this period the railways were one of the most important objects of capital expenditures and certainly the most important one in the modern sector. The relative importance of the railroads as objects of capital expenditures was highest in the 1860s and again in the closing two decades of the century. And for some shorter periods railroad capital expenditures were even more important. In 1895–99, for example, expenditures averaged about R. 170 mill. a year, equal to a little more than 1 percent of gross national product. Although reported expenditures on irrigation, which probably were limited to the major projects undertaken by the government, were considerably smaller (only about one-tenth of 1 percent of the period's national product), they still accounted for nearly 5 percent of total gross capital formation.

b. Saving

Saving suffers from an almost total lack of data or estimates before 1900. Hence the only way to estimate total national saving is to determine the difference between capital formation and net capital imports, the resulting residual estimate necessarily subject to the shortcomings of the estimates of minuend and subtrahend. This approach leads to estimates of saving for the 1901–13 period of close to 4 percent of national product excluding, and fully 4½ percent including, consumer durables and precious metals. The ratios should have been somewhat lower for the entire period from 1860 to 1913.

Similarly low figures are obtained when the problem is approached from the financial side, that is, by estimating as well as possible the various forms of financial saving. The national balance sheets (table 1-28) suggest that the net increase in deposits of financial institutions, in government securities held by private Indian investors, and in the paid-up stock of corporations during the period from 1860 to 1913 are equal to only about 1 percent of the period's national product. Most of these amounts are probably attributable to individuals. Saving in other forms— primarily retained earnings of business enterprises, housing financed by owners, self-financed capital expenditures in agriculture, and government saving—taken together, were probably larger than financial saving. Gross government saving alone is estimated at 1.7 percent of national product (table 1-11). The substantial increase in agricultural debt does not affect the volume of net saving as the saving of the creditor is offset by the dissaving of the debtors in the household and unincorporated business sector.

A confirmation, finally, of a low level of saving is provided by the use of Harrod's famous formula, according to which a country's net saving rate is equal to the product of its real rate of

---

50. "Railway capital at charge" in 1900 alone amounted to R. 3.3 bill. Although the accounting methods by which this figure was derived, particularly the treatment of depreciation and replacement, are in doubt, the R. 3.3 bill. would appear to fall between a gross and a net figure as it should be calculated for national accounting purposes. Even if the net capital stock of the railways in 1900—practically all created since 1860—is put as low as R. 2 bill., the net investment in railways alone would be equal to one-half of 1 percent of the period's national product and might have been as high as three-fourths of 1 percent. It is difficult to put total net fixed capital formation at less than about four times the figure for this single sector.

TABLE 1-11. Public Investment and Saving, 1898–1938[a]

	A. Amounts (R. bill.)				B. Distribution (percent)				C. Relation to GNP (percent)			
	1898 to 1913	1919 to 1929	1930 to 1938	1919 to 1938	1898 to 1913	1919 to 1929	1930 to 1938	1919 to 1938	1898 to 1913	1919 to 1929	1930 to 1938	1919 to 1938
I. Total public investment												
Gross	4.69[b]	7.49	3.33	10.82	100	100	100	100	1.82	1.94	1.55	1.80
Depreciation	1.55	2.48	2.10	4.58	33	33	63	42	0.60	0.64	0.97	0.76
Net	3.14	5.01	1.23	6.24	67	67	37	58	1.22	1.30	0.57	1.04
II. Gross investment by government												
Central	4.20	4.74	1.55	6.29	80	62	47	57	1.63	1.23	0.72	1.05
Provincial	0.50[c]	2.10[d]	1.28	3.38	10	28	48	31	0.19	0.54	0.59	0.55
Municipal	0.20	0.38	0.23	0.61	4	5	7	6	0.08	0.10	0.11	0.10
District and local	0.29	0.39	0.27	0.66	6	5	8	6	0.11	0.10	0.13	0.11
III. Gross investment by type												
Railways	2.38	3.64	0.89	4.53	51	48	27	42	0.92	0.94	0.41	0.75
Irrigation	0.55	0.84	0.55	1.39	12	11	16	13	0.21	0.22	0.26	0.23
Roads and buildings	1.49	2.59	1.54	4.13	31	35	46	38	0.58	0.67	0.71	0.69
Other	0.28	0.43	0.35	0.78	6	6	11	7	0.11	0.11	0.16	0.13
IV. Gross public saving	4.45	4.30	2.78	7.08	95	57	83	65	1.72	1.11	1.29	1.18

[a]Fiscal year starting April 1. [b]This compares with R. 4.96 bill. for 1901–13 in table 1-10, gross public capital formation. [c]Roughly estimated; not included in I and III.
[d]Roughly estimated for 1919; not included in I and III.

SOURCE OF A: Thavaraj, 1: 220–24.

growth and its capital-output ratio.[51] Using a growth rate of aggregate real gross national product of about 1 percent for the period 1861–1913, an average capital-output ratio of about 2½ percent, i.e., the intermediate ratio of table 1-32 (p. 64), one obtains an aggregate net saving ratio for the period of about 2½ percent. Although both the real rate of growth and the capital-output ratio are subject to a substantial margin of error, it is difficult to find a reasonable combination of the two components of the net saving ratio that could bring it below 2 percent or above about 3 percent. These rates, thus, are of the same order of magnitude, or smaller, than the ratios obtained from either the investment side or the saving side of the national accounts as here estimated.

Both approaches—from the investment side and from the saving side—must consider the accumulation of gold and silver stocks by the population, which may be estimated at about R. 8 bill. for the period as a whole (the figure differs from the estimated change in the value of the stock of R. 6 bill. shown in table 1-28 as a result of upward changes in the price of gold and downward changes in that of silver) and thus equaled about 1¼ percent of national product. The hoarding of precious metals thus constituted, if it is included in both investment and saving, as it should be, a substantial proportion of total gross investment and saving and an even larger share of net investment and saving because of the negligible amount of depreciation. Accepting the very rough estimates for saving and investment discussed above, the hoarding of gold and silver would have been equal for the period as a whole to at least one-fourth of total net capital formation, including inventories and precious metals. The ratio apparently was somewhat higher in the 1896–1913 period, with nearly 1½ percent of national product, than in the 1861–95 period, with about 1 percent of national product. The economic and financial development of India in the half century before World War I thus does not seem to have decreased the population's propensity to hoard gold and silver. Even if these calculations overstate the ratio of precious-metal hoarding to capital formation in the form of structures, equipment, livestock, and inventories, either by overestimating hoarding or by underestimating capital formation and saving, the relation between the hoarding of precious metals and total capital formation as high as that observed in India from 1860 to 1913 must nevertheless be unique for a large country and a protracted period, except possibly for India before 1860.

For the end of the period the net reproducible capital stock has been estimated at nearly R. 20 bill., fixed assets accounting for more than two-thirds; livestock about one-fifth, a relatively high ratio; and inventories about one-tenth (table 1-12). If gold and silver are included, the value of the stock of reproducible assets rises to R. 31 bill., with precious metals then accounting for more than one-third of the more broadly defined stock, again a very high ratio in international comparison.

Between 1900 and 1913 the stock of narrowly defined reproducible assets has been estimated to have increased by 75 percent in current, but only by 45 percent in constant, prices, or at an annual rate of 4.4 percent in current and of 2.9 percent in constant prices for the aggregate and 2.3 percent for the per head stock, astonishingly high rates given the character of the Indian economy at that time. Differences in the structure of the capital stock between 1900 and 1913 were minor.

5. THE DEVELOPMENT OF FINANCIAL INSTITUTIONS

In 1860 the Western-type financial superstructure of India was limited to about a half-dozen commercial banks with assets on the order of one-fourth of 1 percent of the country's national product, which coexisted, with hardly any direct contacts, with hundreds of indigenous bankers and many thousands of rural moneylenders. By 1913 the assets of Western-type financial institutions, which then numbered well over a hundred and included, in addition to commercial

51. Harrod, pp. 7ff. The calculation is based on reproducible tangible assets, including precious metals.

TABLE 1-12. Reproducible Net Capital Stock, 1900 and 1913

	Current prices		1951–52 prices		Rate of growth		Ratio to GNP[a]	
					Current prices	1951–52 prices		
	1900	1913	1900	1913			1900	1913
	(1)	(2)	(3)	(4)	(5)	(6)	(7)	(8)
Fixed assets	71.4	70.5	67.7	67.4	4.28	2.89	1.07	1.13
Livestock	16.6	19.7	18.8	21.8	5.78	4.14	0.25	0.32
Inventories	12.0	9.8	13.5	10.8	2.75	1.17	0.18	0.16
Total, percent	100.0	100.0	100.0	100.0	4.39	2.93	1.50	1.61
Total, R. bill.	19.7	34.4	94.8	137.8	—	—	—	—

[a]Current prices.

SOURCE: *BR*, increased in cols. 1–4 by 20 percent to shift from Indian Union to Undivided India.

banks (though not yet a central bank), savings banks, credit cooperatives, and insurance companies, had risen to nearly 10 percent of national product, still an extremely low ratio in international comparison. Much of the growth had taken place after the turn of the century, as was the case in the money supply, indicating the advent of a new phase in the country's financial development. This section will highlight the development of the different groups of financial institutions during the half century preceding World War I and in the final subsection will look at the development of financial institutions from the perspective of the growth of the country's real infrastructure.

Table 1-13 shows the number and assets of the banks that were the dominant financial institutions for five benchmark years between 1870 and 1913. In 1913 the two types of non-bank financial institutions, life insurance companies and state pension funds, for which data are available, had only R. 130 mill. of assets compared with R. 1,375 mill. for banks. Only rough estimates are available for indigenous bankers and moneylenders, but their combined assets were undoubtedly still much larger than those of Western-type financial institutions.

a. Indigenous Bankers[52]

It is fitting to start the description of the development of financial institutions in India in the period between the Mutiny and World War I with the indigenous bankers, not because they were during this period the most important group of financial institutions, but because they, like the rural moneylenders, who will be discussed in section 6b, antedate by many hundreds of years the Western-type financial institutions, which were introduced into India beginning with the second half of the eighteenth century.

Although indigenous bankers and moneylenders have been operating for many centuries, usually combining the business of banking with some other commercial activities, they seem to have become much more important during the Mughal dynasty when the monetization of the Indian economy made substantial progress.[53] As in medieval and Renaissance Europe, the main clients of the larger firms, as well as the cause of the ultimate ruin of many of them, were the princes and their courts. Another important part of their business, which was especially important to the smaller firms, was the exchange of the numerous types of coins then circulating in India and the transfer of money within the country. It is likely that, again as in Europe, most of

52. There is no satisfactory history of indigenous Indian bankers that goes back beyond the Mughal period and covers all of India. Jain complained in 1929 that "literature on the subject is almost non-existent" (p. *vii*). This is still the situation except for a number of articles on banking in the Mughal empire, for example, Habib and more recently Timberg. Bhargava is an enthusiastic amateur, whose book, a defense of indigenous bankers, is short on documentation.

53. Habib, pp. 1, 20.

TABLE 1-13. Number and Assets of Banks, 1870–1913

Year	All banks (1)	Presidency (2)	Commercial (3)	Exchange (4)	Savings[a] (5)	Cooperative (6)
I. Number						
1870	8	3	2	3	—	—
1880	4248	3	3	4	4238	—
1890	6467	3	4	5	6455	—
1900	6652	3	5	8	6636	—
1913	22204	3	41	12	9824	12324
II. Assets (R. mill.)[b]						
1870	173	155	3	5	10	—
1880	226	155	8	34	29	—
1890	410	229	32	75	74	—
1900	512	213	94	105	100	—
1913	1375	498	282	310	232	53
III. Growth of assets (percent per year)						
1871–1880	2.7	0.0	10.3	21.1	11.2	—
1881–1890	6.1	4.0	14.9	8.2	9.8	—
1891–1900	2.3	−0.7	11.4	3.4	3.1	—
1901–1913	7.9	6.8	8.8	8.7	6.7	.
1871–1913	4.9	2.8	11.1	10.1	7.6	.
IV. Relation of assets to GNP (percent)						
1870	2.04	1.82	0.04	0.06	0.12	—
1880	2.21	1.52	0.08	0.33	0.28	—
1890	3.47	1.94	0.27	0.64	0.62	—
1900	3.89	1.62	0.71	0.80	0.76	—
1913	6.42	2.32	1.32	1.45	1.08	0.25
V. Distribution of assets (percent)						
1870	100.0	89.6	1.7	2.9	5.8	—
1880	100.0	68.6	3.5	15.0	12.8	—
1890	100.0	55.9	7.8	18.3	18.0	—
1900	100.0	41.6	18.4	20.5	19.5	—
1913	100.0	36.2	20.5	22.5	16.9	3.9

[a]Offices for I.   [b]Approximated by capital, reserves, and deposits for cols. 2 and 3, deposits for cols. 4 and 5, and working capital for col. 6.

SOURCE OF BASIC DATA: *BMS,* pp. 10 ff., 237 ff., and 368 ff.

their funds represented their own capital and that deposits from outside the circle of the family and close business associates played only a secondary role. The bankers had, however, created at least one important type of financial instrument, the hundi, which is similar to a bill of exchange and was used as a means of short-term financing as well as for the interlocal transfer of funds.

With the advent of the British, or more correctly the assumption of the direct administration of large parts of the peninsula, particularly of Bengal and the Carnatic, by the East India Company in the second half of the eighteenth century, the business of the indigenous bankers, or at least of the more important firms among them, began a rapid decline.[54] By eliminating many of the indigenous princes and their courts, the company drastically reduced the number and importance of the large bankers' chief clients and further curtailed their business by organizing, not so much directly as through some of its officials, banks of the Western type, which came to handle much of the company's financial transactions. Finally, the unification of the currency of British India in 1835, which introduced the standard silver rupee, put an end to much of the

54. Cf. Savkar, pp. 12 ff.

money-exchange business on which many of the indigenous bankers, particularly the smaller ones, had depended.

Indigenous bankers nevertheless continued to operate throughout the period from the middle of the nineteenth century to 1913 in most cities of importance, apparently without substantial change in their methods of operation, and continued to be characterized by "fine traditions concerning [their] respectability, resourcefulness and integrity . . . their hereditary relations and close personal contact with their clientele and simple, inexpensive and popular methods of work."[55] Although all observers agree that the relative importance of the indigenous bankers within the Indian credit system continued to decline throughout the nineteenth century and beyond it, quantitative evidence appears to be entirely lacking.[56] It is difficult to believe, however, that at the end of this period, that is, around 1913, the resources of the indigenous bankers, as distinguished from those of the much more numerous rural and urban small-scale moneylenders, amounted to a substantial fraction of the nearly R. 1.5 bill. of the resources of Western-type banks.[57,58,59]

b. The Presidency Banks[60]

The three Presidency banks were not the first Western-type banks to operate in India, having had a number of predecessors in Bengal with often short and tumultuous careers, beginning in 1770 with the Bank of Hindostan.[61] The Presidency banks proved to be, however, the most durable and successful institutions of this type, lasting in their original form until 1921 and continuing to operate as before after their merger as the Imperial Bank of India until 1935, when several of their functions were taken over by the new Reserve Bank of India. Nationalized soon after independence, the Presidency banks carry on today as the State Bank of India, the largest commercial bank. The Bank of Bengal was the oldest of the three banks, which were limited to operating within the territory of their Presidency. It was chartered in 1809 by the East India Company as the successor to the Bank of Calcutta, which had been organized three years earlier. More than thirty years later similar banks were chartered in the other two Presidencies, the Bank of Bombay in 1840 and the Bank of Madras in 1843. All three banks were, first, banks

55. Savkar, p. 14.
56. Comprehensive, but still limited, statistics of the indigenous bankers' business—though for one benchmark only—had to wait until the Bank Commission's Report of 1972 (cf. chap. 3, sec. 4). For estimates of assets of rural moneylenders, cf. sec. 6b.
57. One piece of statistical information that turns up several times in the literature (e.g., Savkar, p. 14; Gubbay, p. 11; and even as late as 1952 in Wilson, p. 177), ascribed to Sir George Schuster, sometime finance member of the government of India, is the statement that 90 percent of the country's banking business was done—at an unspecified date but apparently well into the twentieth century—by the indigenous bankers. This estimate must be treated with great skepticism, unless it is intended to include rural and urban moneylenders, as it is in complete contradiction to the firsthand evidence produced by the Central Banking Enquiry Commission of 1931 and to all fragmentary and quasi-quantitative information on the subject.
58. Even the number of indigenous bankers is unknown and the figures depend entirely on the definition of banker used. Thus Atkinson's estimate (p. 234), which put the number of "bankers" at 64,000 in 1875 and 85,000 in 1895, must refer to what essentially were moneylenders, although separate figures are given for "moneylenders," numbering 114,000 in 1875 and 141,000 in 1895. Around 1930 the number of "indigenous bankers" was given as 250, or 5.5 per million inhabitants, for the United Provinces and as 66, or 3.2 per million inhabitants, for the Punjab (Central Banking Enquiry, 1-94). On that basis, the total number for the country would have been between 1,000 and 2,000.
59. The Indian Chamber of Commerce in Calcutta went so far as to say that "the position today is that the indigenous bankers in India are like Lilliputians who in spite of their numbers are helpless in tackling the financial problems of the country" (Central Banking Enquiry, 2:529). Although this statement was formulated around 1930, it would also seem applicable to the situation prevailing two decades earlier.
60. The history of the Presidency banks is discussed in almost all books dealing with India's monetary, banking, and credit system. The basic studies dealing with their early history are still Cooke and Brunyate, whose book served as one of Keynes's sources of information. Although it is difficult to believe that the balance sheets of all three Presidency banks have now disappeared, none of these three authors nor any later student of the financial history of India seems to have collected them for dates before 1870 or to have made more than casual use of them when available.
61. For the history of Western-type banks in Bengal before 1860, cf., apart from Cooke, H. Sinha and Tripathi.

of issue, authorized by their charters to issue bank notes, originally up to the amount of their capital (R. 500,000 for the Calcutta and Bombay banks and R. 300,000 for the Madras bank) so long as their cash reserve exceeded one-third of their liabilities; second, banks of the East India Company and after 1857 of the British government of India, keeping the cash reserves and handling most of the financial business of the company or the government; and, third, British-type deposit banks which concentrated on the solicitation of deposits from the public and on granting short-term credit.

When the Bank of Bengal was organized, the East India Company itself bought one-fifth of the stock. Although the owners of the other four-fifths apparently have not been identified, it is likely that most of them belonged to the British colony of company officials and businessmen in Calcutta. The East India Company originally held slightly more than half of the shares of the Bank of Bombay, the remainder being fairly widely distributed among about 330 shareholders, with an average holding of about R. 750. Although the number of European and Indian share-holders was about the same, the average holding of European subscribers (nearly R. 1,000) was considerably above that of the Indian shareholders (not much above R. 500), with Parsees accounting for about two-thirds of the Indian subscriptions.[62]

Early in 1856, the first date for which a balance sheet of one of the three banks appears in the literature,[63] at a time when none of the three banks had any branches, the total assets of the Bank of Bengal amounted to R. 34 mill., consisting of nearly one-fifth cash and 7 percent each of government securities and of mercantile bills and loans slightly above one-half of the total. Nearly one-third of total funds was provided by capital and reserves, almost one-fourth by current accounts, and more than two-fifths by bank notes, including post bills. In 1868, the first year for which figures for all three banks are available, the resources of all three Presidency banks were almost twice as large as those of the Bank of Bengal. If the same relation obtained in 1856, their combined resources would have been on the order of R. 65 mill. and their notes nearly R. 30 mill., that is, R. 0.27 and R. 0.13 (about 13 cents and 6 cents in U.S. money) per head, or approximately 1.3 and 0.6 percent, respectively, of the very roughly estimated gross national product of that year. Thus, the Western-type financial institutions in the company's India were still minuscule size, and at that time no other Western-type banks nor any sizable insurance organizations existed.

In 1870, shortly after continuous statistics become available, the resources of the three Presidency banks amounted to R. 155 mill., indicating an increase of 140 percent, or 6.4 percent per year, since 1856, only part of which can be attributed to the approximately 50 percent increase in the price level.[64] This is the more remarkable because the banks had lost the privilege of issuing notes in 1862. The growth of the banks stopped during the 1870s when the banks lost their status of government depositories; resumed at the relatively slow pace of 4 percent per year during the 1880s; stopped again in the 1890s as a result of the depression, which lasted through a good part of that decade; but resumed growth at the faster pace of more than 130 percent, or 6.7 percent per year, during the 1901–13 period. As a result, the ratio of the three banks' resources to gross national product fell from 1.8 percent in 1870 to 1.6 percent in 1900 but then advanced, still at a slow pace, to 2.4 percent in 1913.

Although detailed balance sheets for the three banks apparently are unavailable, table 1-14 shows that in the more than forty years between 1870 and 1913 the share of capital and reserves declined from 23 to 15 percent, the entire reduction occurring after 1900, and that of government deposits, which fell from 35 to 19 percent between 1870 and 1880, declined even further, to 12 percent, in 1913. On the assets side, cash balances declined sharply but irregularly from 65

62. Cooke, p. 165.
63. R. B. Rao, p. 648. Condensed balance sheets of the Bank of Bengal as of July 21, 1857, and October 2, 1857, are given in Brunyate, p. 12.
64. Mukherjee, NII, p. 94.

TABLE 1-14. Main Assets and Liabilities of Presidency Banks, 1870–1920

End of	Capital and reserves	Deposits			Cash	Investments
		Total	Government	Other		
		I. Absolute figures (R. mill.)				
1870	36.2	118.3	54.3	64.0	99.7	13.0
1880	40.5	114.0	29.1	84.9	74.1	25.5
1890	44.8	183.6	35.9	147.6	129.7	33.4
1900	56.0	156.9	28.1	128.8	50.4	30.3
1913	74.8	423.6	58.9	364.7	153.8	68.2
1920	75.3	862.9	90.3	772.6	260.3	142.4
		II. Distribution (liabilities[a] = 100)				
1870	23.4	76.6	35.1	41.4	64.5	8.4
1880	26.2	73.8	18.8	55.0	48.0	16.5
1890	19.6	80.4	15.7	64.6	56.8	14.6
1900	26.3	73.7	13.2	60.5	23.7	14.2
1913	15.0	85.0	11.8	73.2	30.9	13.7
1920	8.0	92.0	9.6	82.3	27.7	15.2

[a]Capital, reserves, and deposits.

SOURCE: *BMS*, pp. 10–11.

percent in 1870 to 31 percent in 1913, although investments, probably mainly in government securities, rose only from 8 percent in 1870 to 17 percent a decade later and thereafter declined slowly to 14 percent in 1900 and 1913. By inference, the share of advances must have increased substantially.[65]

Because each of the Presidency banks was by far the largest financial institution in its territory, each bank's resources should be an indicator of the relative financial progress of its territory. The distribution of resources among the three banks was very similar in 1870 and 1913: the Bank of Bengal accounted for about one-half of the total and the other two banks for about one-fourth each. In 1880, however, the share of the Bank of Bengal was considerably above this level, and the Bank of Bombay experienced a similar situation in 1890 and 1900, whereas the share of the Bank of Madras was much smaller in 1880 and 1890.

c. The Exchange Banks

As the brightest jewel in the British crown, India was not likely to be overlooked when joint stock banks began to expand beyond the confines of the British Isles in the second quarter of the nineteenth century. However, notwithstanding earlier attempts, which constituted a long and dismal record of failure,[66] it was only in the 1850s that British banking actually reached India. In that decade four banks started to function as chartered institutions, then common for British banks operating abroad: the Chartered Bank of India, Australia and China and the Chartered Bank of Asia in 1853, the Chartered Mercantile Bank of India, London and China and the Agra and United Services Bank in 1857. Because the Chartered Bank of Asia was dissolved after four years, only three exchange banks were in operation in 1860. These banks, which

65. Because complete balance sheets are unavailable, it is not possible to trace the absolute and relative development of loans. If loans accounted for most of the difference between capital, reserves, and deposits, on the one hand, and cash and investments, on the other, they would have increased sharply from about R. 50 mill. in 1870–90 to R. 130 mill. in 1900 and to nearly R. 400 mill. in 1913, or from about 30 percent of total resources in 1870, 1880, and 1890 to about 60 and 55 percent in 1900 and 1913, respectively.

66. Baster, p. 88.

concentrated on the financing of the country's imports and exports and which limited their operations to the three Presidency towns and a few other large cities, were joined by another bank in the late 1870s, another in the late 1880s, three in the 1890s, and four between 1904 and 1911, bringing their number at the beginning of World War I to twelve. Although local deposits were solicited wherever they operated, most of the exchange banks were British, in the sense that they were incorporated in Great Britain, had their main office in London, and most of their shares were owned by British investors. Four of the exchange banks, however, were branches of non-British institutions, specifically of French, German, Japanese, and Russian banks. By that time the exchange banks constituted an important part of the modern enclave in the Indian economy.

In 1870, the first date for which statistics are available,[67] the deposits of the three exchange banks in India, which had then been operating for more than a decade, amounted to only R. 5 mill., a mere 4 percent of the deposits of the three Presidency banks. From the 1870s on, however, the growth of the exchange banks was very rapid, with deposits increasing by 580 percent in the 1870s, 120 percent in the 1880s, 40 percent in the 1890s, and nearly 200 percent between 1900 and 1913, or at an average annual rate of 10 percent for the period 1870 to 1913. As a result, in 1913 the deposits of the twelve exchange banks had grown to be equal to fully 70 percent of those of the three Presidency banks and to more than 25 percent of those of the whole banking system, including Indian joint stock banks, savings banks, and cooperatives.[68] Because the forty-odd offices of the exchange banks were concentrated in a few large cities,[69] their share in the banking resources of these centers must have been considerably in excess of one-fourth, which may be taken as an indication of the importance of the exchange banks in the modern sector of the Indian credit system at the outbreak of World War I.

Unfortunately, no breakdown is available for either the assets or the liabilities of the exchange banks, except for their cash, which amounted to more than two-fifths of their Indian deposits in the 1870s but by 1913 had declined to one-fifth.

d. Indian Joint Stock Banks[70]

Although not facing any legal obstacles after 1860, joint stock banks incorporated in India were rather slow in developing, as can be seen in tables 1-13 and 1-15. In 1870 only two such banks were in operation (or, more correctly, were reporting to the authorities), and their capital, reserves, and deposits amounted to only R. 2.6 mill. compared with the R. 155 mill. of the three Presidency banks. Even twenty years later the number of Indian joint stock banks had risen to only four, with capital, reserves, and deposits of R. 32 mill., still a mere 14 percent of that of the Presidency banks and a bit more than 40 percent of the exchange banks. Growth accelerated in the following quarter century, particularly after 1900, under the influence of the Swadeshi movement, which tried to induce Indians to do business primarily with Indian financial institutions. By 1913 the number of reporting Indian joint stock banks had risen to forty-one, including twenty-three so-called class B banks for which no earlier statistics are available. Because the class B banks in 1913 accounted for only 8 percent of the deposits of the class A banks, their omission from the earlier statistics cannot affect the picture substantially (e.g., the average annual growth rate of resources of fully 11 percent in the 1890s and of more than 8 percent between 1900 and 1913). However, even in 1913 the resources of the forty-odd Indian joint

---

67. *BMS*, p. 14.

68. Because the statistics of exchange banks are limited to Indian deposits, their total resources can only be roughly estimated on the assumption that resources bore the same relationship to deposits as in the Presidency and Indian joint stock banks. In that case, the resources of the twelve exchange banks in 1913 would have amounted to about R. 370 mill.

69. For the location of branches of Presidency, exchange, and Indian joint stock banks around 1916, see map following p. 497 in Shirras.

70. Most of the statistics in this section are taken from *BMS*, pp. 6 ff.

TABLE 1-15. Growth of Large Indian Joint Stock Banks, 1880–1946
(Liabilities: R. Mill.)

	1880	1900	1913	1929	1939	1946
Allahabad Bank	2	26	74	122	118	278
Punjab National Bank	—	1	15	59	73[b]	635
Bank of India	—	—	28	130	208	679
Central Bank	—	—	6	152	324	1193
Bank of Baroda	—	—	10	63	77[b]	347
Indian Bank	—	—	4	21	41	186
Bank of Mysore	—	—	1	22	28[b]	142
Bank of Bihar	—	—	1	4	13	54
Union Bank of India	—	—	—	7	14	58
Total, R. mill.	2	27	139	580	896	3572
Total all banks, percent[a]	1.0	6.6	13.0	24.5	27.1	246
Total class A banks, percent	25.0	28.7	57.4	78.1	73.3	42.1
Rate of growth, percent per year		13.9	13.4	9.3	4.4	21.8

[a]Presidency banks, exchange banks, and Indian joint stock banks.   [b]1938.

Source: Muranjan, pp. 188 ff.

stock banks were equal to less than three-fifths of the resources of the three Presidency banks and to about nine-tenths of those of the twelve exchange banks.[71]

Although the average resources of the forty-one banks operating in 1913 amounted to only about R. 7 mill., compared with averages of more than R. 160 mill. for the three Presidency banks and with R. 26 mill. for the twelve exchange banks, a few of the older Indian joint stock banks had by that time attained a substantial size, as can be seen in table 1-15. The largest, the Allahabad Bank, was founded in 1865 and located away from the port cities, which were dominated by the Presidency and exchange banks. In 1913 the Allahabad Bank alone accounted for about one-fourth of the resources of all reporting Indian joint stock banks, and although still considerably smaller than any of the three Presidency banks, it was nearly three times as large as the average exchange bank. The next four banks together held a little more than one-fifth of the resources of all forty-one Indian joint stock banks. Hence, the top five banks accounted for one-half of the resources of the group, a substantial degree of concentration.

e. Thrift Institutions

The first Western-type thrift institutions introduced in India were the savings departments of the three Presidency banks, which opened in the mid-1840s. They were followed in 1870 by district savings banks operated by the Treasury and in 1882 by the Post Office Saving System, which utilized the facilities of that department and took over the district savings banks in 1886 and the savings business of the three Presidency banks in 1896. Some commercial banks also opened savings departments around the turn of the century, but no separate statistics are available for them.

71. A large number of generally small institutions registered as banks under the Indian Companies Act are not included in the banking statistics because banking was not their only or even their main activity (Keynes, p. 162). There were nearly 400 such institutions at the end of 1899 and nearly 480 ten years later. The volume of their deposits is not known. Their paid-in capital of R. 30 mill. in 1899 and of about R. 50 mill. in 1909 was equal to nearly 40 percent of that of the Presidency and the class A banks in 1899 and 1909. Although it is very likely that their ratio of deposits to paid-in capital was much lower than that of the Presidency and the class A banks, these small institutions constituted a considerable part of the Indian banking system. The absence of relevant statistics on the volume of their banking activities, and in particular on their assets and deposits, is therefore a serious hindrance in obtaining a comprehensive picture of the Indian banking system prior to World War I.

In 1860 deposits of the Presidency savings banks amounted to less than R. 4 mill., most of which was probably deposited by the inhabitants of the three Presidency towns. Ten years later deposits had risen to nearly R. 10 mill., the smallness of the average balance of about R. 300 giving a clue as to the economic status of the depositors. In 1880 deposits reached R. 22 mill., with 61,000 depositors having an average balance of R. 360. At the same time the district savings banks held another R. 7 mill. of deposits, with the average deposit of R. 370 indicating a similarity of clientele with the savings depositors of the Presidency banks.

In 1900 when the Post Office Saving System was the only such institution left in the field, deposits amounted to R. 100 mill., or 817,000 depositors with an average deposit of only R. 122. Both the number of depositors and the volume of deposits more than doubled between 1900 and 1913, the average deposit balance rising moderately to R. 142. These figures indicate that in 1913 the Post Office Saving System with its 9,800 urban and semi-urban offices drew on groups of depositors with apparently considerably lower incomes and savings than the Presidency and district savings banks, which had been essentially limited to large cities.

The deposits collected by the savings banks were throughout the period put at the disposal of the Treasury. These funds, however, constituted only secondary sources of central government financing, as they were equal in 1913 to only 5 percent of the total debt and to one-eighth of the rupee debt of the central government.[72]

In addition to these Western-type thrift institutions, which operated uniformly throughout the country and whose liabilities were implicitly guaranteed by the central government, there always existed indigenous private institutions, varying regionally and locally in character and importance. Very little is known about these institutions, the *chit* funds and *nidhis*,[73] and no quantitative information exists that would permit an evaluation of their size in comparison to other financial institutions, of changes in that relationship over time, and of differences in various parts of the country. Nor can the character of their assets and liabilities be specified or their intertemporal changes or interregional differences be identified. It is known, however, from the descriptive literature, which is sparse for the period before World War I and even up to independence, that such institutions were more common in western and southern India, where they provided home financing, and in Bengal, where they provided loans, than in the rest of the country. Whatever fragmentary material exists points to the small size of these institutions, which seem to have originated in the mid-nineteenth century, and indicates fairly clearly a rapid decline in their size and importance relative to that of financial institutions of the Western type, which developed in India during the nineteenth century.

Because information on regional differences in financial structure within the subcontinent is rare for this period, table 1-17 shows the distribution of postal-savings offices and accounts and deposit balances as well as average deposits per office and per account for eight large subdivisions of British India as of 1910. A full exploitation of the data shown in tables 1-16 and 1-17, as well as of similar material available for some geographic subdivisions since 1900—in particular an attempt to explain the regional differences, which are evident in the table, by differences in urbanization, income, and other possibly relevant factors—would greatly exceed the scope and resources of this study. A few conclusions, however, appear justified without econometric analysis of the data.

A comparison of the share of each of the six territorial divisions in population (instead of the unavailable data for income) with the number of offices and of deposits in savings accounts shows large regional differences. The fact that Bombay's share in savings deposits as well as its average deposit per account and per office was higher with respect to the national average than

---

72. The assets of savings banks made available to the Treasury were equal to less than 2 percent of the total debt and to about 3 percent of the rupee debt of the central government in 1880, and to 3 and nearly 8 percent, respectively, in 1900.

73. The most detailed information on two types of these institutions operating mainly in western and southern India will be found in Nicholson, pt. 2, chap. 3.

TABLE 1-16. Savings Banks, 1860–1946

March 31 of following year	Number of offices (1)	Number per million inhabitants (2)	Accounts		Deposits			
			Number (thou.) (3)	Per thousand inhabitants (4)	Total (R. mill.) (5)	Per account		Percent of GNP (8)
						Current rupees (6)	R. of 1913 (7)	
I. Presidency and Government District Savings Banks								
1860	·	·	·	·	3.7	·	·	0.1
1870	·	·	32	0.1	9.8	306	510	0.1
1880	·	·	80	0.3	29.3	366	591	0.3
1890	·	·	39	0.1	10.2	262	392	0.1
II. Post Office Saving System								
1882	4238	16	39	0.2	3	77	138	0.0
1890	6455	23	409	1.5	64	156	233	0.5
1900	6636	23	817	2.9	100	122	150	0.8
1913	9824	33	1639	5.4	232	142	142	1.1
1920	10713	35	1878	6.1	229	122	59	0.7
1929	12768	38	2305	6.9	371	161	111	1.2
1939[a]	11870	31	4583	11.9	783	171	153	2.8
1946[a]	11189	27	3973	9.5	1424	358	128	2.0

[a]Excluding Aden and Burma.

SOURCES: **Cols. 1, 3, and 5:** *BMS,* pp. 368–69.   **Cols. 2, 4, and 8:** Cols. 1 and 3 divided by population of undivided India or gross national product (table 1-3), hence slightly too high for dates from 1882 to 1929 because figures include Burma and Aden.   **Col. 6:** Col. 5 divided by col. 3.   **Col. 7:** Col. 6 divided by index of wholesale prices (Mukherjee, *NII,* p. 94).   **Col. 8:** Col. 5 divided by gross national product (table 1-3).

that in any other region reflects the above average degree of urbanization and industrialization, the presumably higher per head income, and Bombay's position as one of the country's two financial centers. Although Bengal was also above the country average in the density of offices and accounts and in deposits, the distance from the national average is much smaller than in the case of Bombay, a difference not easy to explain, except possibly by the fact that Bombay city accounted for about 6 percent of the total population of the region, whereas Calcutta's share in the population of Bengal and Assam was only 2½ percent. The regions farthest from the national averages—Bihar and Orissa and the United Provinces—are known in the post-independence period to have had a relatively high share of agriculture, little urbanization and industrialization, and relatively low incomes per head, characteristics that most likely were already in evidence before World War I. Madras presents a special case. Its density of offices and accounts did not depart sharply from the national average, but its share of deposit balances was only 7 percent and the average deposits per office and per account were only at two-fifths of the national average, although the region accounted for 18 percent of the population of British India. Whether this is due to the fact that the Madras region was one of the areas in which nidhis and chit funds were of much greater importance than in the rest of India and thus provided an alternative outlet to small savers not available in most of the country, it is difficult to say.

f. Cooperative Credit Institutions

Credit cooperatives modeled after European institutions, have been regarded by Indian reformers and foreign advisors as an important, if not the most important, instrument for breaking, together with debt relief legislation, the stranglehold that local moneylenders were supposed to have had over cultivator-owners and tenants. The words that conclude the preface of Sir F. A. Nicholson's famous *Report* of 1895, "Find Raiffeisen," are typical of an entire

TABLE 1-17. Regional Distribution of Post Office Saving System Business, March 31, 1910[a]

Province	Number of offices (1)	Number of accounts (2)	Deposit balance (3)	Average deposits per office (4)	Average deposits per account (5)	Accounts per inhabitant[b] (6)	Deposits per inhabitant[b] (7)
Bengal and Assam	27.6	30.7	28.5	103	139	134	124
Bihar and Orissa[c]	8.4	7.3	6.0	72	82	49	40
Bombay	13.9	19.7	26.3	189	289	283	378
Central Provinces	6.8	4.8	5.2	77	117	79	87
Madras	19.0	13.9	7.2	38	42	78	40
Punjab[d]	8.8	10.6	12.3	140	116	113	131
United Provinces	13.5	11.2	12.0	89	135	55	59
Sinde[e]	1.9	1.8	2.6	133	142	106	149
Total, percent	100.0	100.0	100.0	100	100	100	100
Total, amounts	9,482 (number)	1449 (000)	168.2 (R. mill.)	17.7 (R.000)	116 (R.)	0.0063 (number)	0.73 (R.)

[a]Data refer to British India only. [b]Population from Statistical Abstract for British India, 1911–1921, p. 6. [c]March 31, 1915. [d]Includes Northwest Province. [e]Includes Baluchistan; data refer to March 31, 1905.

SOURCE: Cols. 1-3: BMS, pp. 370 ff.

literature.[74] In reality, however, the creation and operation of a system of rural and urban cooperatives throughout India, and in particular of credit cooperatives, proved to be a protracted and difficult process, even after the long-delayed enactment of the requisite legislation—the Cooperative Credit Societies Act of 1904, which dealt with primary (local) societies, and the Cooperative Societies Act of 1912, which provided the basis for central (district or provincial) institutions.

At the beginning of World War I, nearly 16,000 societies, more than 95 percent of them credit societies, had been formed with nearly 750,000 members and a working capital of R. 77 mill.[75] Although these are respectable absolute figures, they must be compared with the more than 620,000 villages then existing,[76] with the 70 million rural households,[77] and with a total rural indebtedness of more than R. 5,000 mill., all three figures given only to indicate orders of magnitude and to suggest that, again a very rough approximation, only one in forty villages had a credit cooperative, only one in more than one hundred rural households belonged to a credit cooperative, and loans made by credit cooperatives were equal to not much more than 1 percent of total rural credit.

Thus credit cooperatives in 1914 obviously were still in a very early stage in their development. This is also suggested by the fact that only about three-fifths of their working capital had been supplied by members—about one-fifth in the form of subscription to shares, two-fifths in that of deposits—and about two-fifths by central cooperative organizations, which in turn were mainly financed by public bodies and by banks. On the other hand, less than three-fifths of the societies' resources were lent to individual members. Most of the absolute and relative growth of credit cooperatives thus lay in the future.

g. Insurance[78]

Insurance, particularly life insurance, was still in an early stage of development at the beginning of World War I, and a substantial part of the relatively small volume of business was done by British rather than by Indian companies. In 1913, the first year for which comprehensive statistics are available, the total assets of the forty-odd Indian life insurance companies then active amounted to only R. 65 mill. and the business on their books came to slightly more than R. 200 mill.[79] Their assets at that time, with only R. 0.2 per head (i.e., less than 10 cents), were equal to 4 percent of the resources of all financial institutions and to only 0.3 percent of national product. Four-fifths of total assets consisted of Indian government securities (including about one-seventh in municipal and port trust bonds), partly because the largest company, the Oriental Government Securities Life Association, kept, as its name indicates, virtually all its resources in this type of investment. Real estate and policy loans accounted for 5 percent each of total assets and corporate securities for less than 2 percent (table 2-19).

The slow development of life insurance in India was due, apart from extremely low level of income of most of the population, to the absence of a satisfactory actuarial table for Indian lives; to the disinclination until 1866 of the few British companies that operated in India to insure any but European lives; and to the unsatisfactory performance of most of the early small Indian

74. Cf. Nicholson's conclusion, p. xv, "The future of rural credit lies with those who, being of the people, live among the people, and yet by their intelligence, prescience and energy, are above the people"—obviously not easy to find such paragons in sufficient numbers.

75. *BMS*, p. 384/7; these figures cover all cooperatives.

76. The number of towns of less than 1,000 inhabitants as given in the 1921 Census (*Statistical Abstract for British India from 1911–12 to 1920–21*, p. 9).

77. Based on the number of males (72 million) engaged in agriculture according to the 1921 Census (ibid. p. 36).

78. This section is based primarily on R. M. Ray, *Life Insurance in India*, 1941, and on two pamphlets by D. M. Slater, founder, actuary, and manager of Oriental Life, then the largest Indian life insurance company (*Rise and Progress of Native Life Insurance in India* and *Life Insurance in India: Its Origin and Development*, both published in 1897).

79. R. M. Ray, pp. 105 ff. and 154. No statistics are available on the Indian business of the foreign, that is, mainly British, companies. It is, however, unlikely that they invested any substantial amount of assets in India.

companies, the oldest one starting operation in 1818 in Calcutta, the center of the British expatriates, as well as of the two British companies (European and Albert) that had been most active in India.[80]

In 1870, four years after passage of the first Insurance Company Act, only about a half dozen each of domestic and foreign (British) life insurance companies were operating in the country.[81] The activities of most of them were on a very small scale,[82] and those of a few were ephemeral. The first successful and enduring company was the Oriental Government Securities Life Association, which was organized in 1874 under Indian laws by a British resident and concentrated on insuring Indian lives on participating policies. The company's assets, practically all Indian government securities, increased relatively rapidly to R. 2.2 mill. in 1886 and to R. 10.8 mill. ten years later.[83] However, even as late as 1896 the company had less than 25,000 policies with an average face value of R. 2,500 outstanding. It is, therefore, unlikely that the total number of Indians having life insurance was in excess of 100,000, or about 1 in 2,800 inhabitants, another indication of the shallowness of the penetration of life insurance.[84]

The first spurt in the life insurance business occurred near the end of the nineteenth century when several of the companies, which held leading positions until the nationalization of 1956, were organized, for example, the Indian Life, the first Indian stock life insurance company; the Punjab Mutual; the Bharat; and the Empire of India. This expansion, along with the failure of some weak companies, led to tighter regulation under the Insurance Act of 1912 and the Provident Insurance Act of 1912. By 1914 more than forty companies, including a dozen British companies, were in operation.

In addition to private companies, the Post Office began an insurance fund for its own employees in 1884 and extended it to all permanent government employees in 1898.[85] The volume of business must have been very small before World War I because even in 1920 there were only about 30,000 policies with a total face value of R. 47 mill. and hence a fund of probably not more than R. 10 mill.[86]

h. All Financial Institutions

The development of Indian financial institutions in the half century between 1860 and 1913 may be characterized by three figures: First, the average annual rate of increase in the total resources in current prices of a little more than 5 percent (4 percent in real terms) between 1870 (when most of the statistics begin) and 1913; second, the net new issue ratio (i.e., the ratio of the increase in the assets of financial institutions to total gross national product) of less than one-fourth of 1 percent (table 1-18); and, third, the ratio of the assets of financial institutions at the beginning and the end of the period to the national product of these two years, namely, about 2 percent in 1870 and fully 7 percent in 1913.

All the figures just cited refer to only those financial institutions for which statistics are available from 1870 on or for which rough estimates can be made, that is, the banking system,

80. The years from 1818 to 1870 have been called the "period of trial," during which "many pioneer companies, Indian and English, underwriting business in India, were either absorbed by other companies or went into liquidation" (ibid., p. 14).

81. Ibid., p. 17. Some of the Indian units were very small denominational associations.

82. Of these dozen companies, the Bombay Mutual had assets of not more than R. 47,000 in 1871.

83. Because information on Oriental Life's assets in 1914 is not available, it is not possible to calculate the company's share in the assets of all Indian life insurance companies; it may well have been, however, on the order of one-third to one-half of the total.

84. Assuming that the 1913 average assets per policy were the same size as they had been in 1896 in Oriental Life, that is R. 440, policyholders of Indian companies would have numbered about 135,000 or 1 in 2,250 inhabitants. The inclusion of holders of policies written by foreign companies might have increased the number to as much as 200,000, or 1 in about 1,500 inhabitants.

85. Clarke, p. 232.

86. Ray, *Life Insurance in India*, p. 40.

TABLE 1-18. Net Issue Ratio of Credit Institutions, 1871–1913
(Percent of Gross National Product)

	All banks[a]	Presidency banks	Exchange banks	Indian joint stock banks	Post Office savings banks	Other savings banks	Cooperative banks
1871–1880	0.06	0.00	0.03	0.01	—	0.02	—
1881–1890	0.18	0.07	0.04	0.02	0.07[b]	−0.02	—
1891–1900	0.09	−0.01	0.02	0.05	0.03	—	—
1901–1913	0.40	0.13	0.09	0.08	0.06	—	0.04[c]
1871–1913	0.20	0.06	0.05	0.04	0.04	0.00	0.01

[a]Does not include net issues of banks notes emitted by the Treasury, which represented 0.01 percent of gross national product in 1871–80; 0.04 percent in 1881–90; 0.05 percent in 1891–1900; 0.13 percent in 1901–13 and 0.07 percent for the whole period from 1871 to 1913, nor issues of life insurance companies and state pension funds, which amounted to about 0.02 percent for the 1871–1913 period.   [b]1882–90.   [c]1907–13.

SOURCES: Difference in assets between benchmark dates (tables 1-13 and *BMS*, p. 384) divided by period's gross national product.

consisting of the Presidency, exchange, and reporting Indian joint stock banks; the thrift institutions, that is, the postal saving system, other savings banks, and credit cooperatives; and insurance organizations. The figures, however, omit what during this period corresponded to a central bank, that is, the Treasury in its capacity to issue paper money, an omission that can be easily remedied. Although data are also missing for the small Indian joint stock banks, it is evident from the figures available for 1913 and later dates that their assets were so low that the omission cannot substantially affect the picture. The same applies to a few other institutions, the nidhis and chit funds in southern India and the loan offices in Bengal. Much more serious is the lack of data, except for very rough estimates at a few benchmark dates, for indigenous bankers and for urban and rural moneylenders because these very numerous units had throughout the period much larger assets than the Western-type financial institutions for which statistics are available. Thus the funds of rural moneylenders, by far the largest of the three groups in numbers as well as in resources, have been estimated very roughly as being on the order of R. 1¼ bill. in 1860, R. 2½ bill. in 1895, and R. 5 bill. in 1913.[87] Their inclusion, as well as that of Treasury notes, indigenous bankers, and rural moneylenders, would have reduced the estimated average growth rate of all financial institutions, indigenous as well as Western-type, for the period 1871–1913 to something on the order of 3¼ percent against a rate of nearly 5 percent for the statistically covered Western-type institutions. On the other hand, inclusion of these indigenous institutions would substantially increase the new issue ratio from one-fourth of 1 percent to about 1 percent and the ratio of the resources of financial institutions to gross national product from 2 to more than 20 percent in 1870 and from 8 to more than 35 percent in 1913. Even then, the Indian ratios are extremely low in international comparison. The new issue ratio of less than 1 percent of national product, for example, compares with ratios, for about the same period, on the order of fully 5 percent for developed countries.[88]

The movement of the three basic ratios for the Western-type financial institutions can be followed decade by decade in table 1-19. It is obvious that the modern financial system expanded much more rapidly in the 1880s and particularly from 1901 to 1913 than it did in the 1870s and

87. For estimates of assets of rural moneylenders, cf. sec. 6b.
88. Goldsmith (1969), p. 190.

TABLE 1-19. Growth of Financial Institutions, 1871–1913

	1871 to 1880	1881 to 1890	1891 to 1900	1901 to 1913	1871 to 1913
	I. Rate of growth of assets (percent a year)				
All financial institutions[a]	2.7	5.3	2.9	7.2	4.7
Banking system[b]	2.6	4.0	2.7	7.1	4.3
	II. New issue ratio (percent of GNP)				
All financial institutions[a]	0.09	0.21	0.15	0.54	0.31
Banking system[b]	0.08	0.17	0.11	0.47	0.25

[a]Banking system including government paper money, postal saving system, cooperatives, and insurance companies, the latter very roughly estimated.   [b]Presidency, exchange, and Indian joint stock banks plus government paper money.   [c]Ratios at end of period indicated. Values for 1870 are 0.20 for all financial institutions and 0.19 for the banking system alone.

SOURCES OF BASIC DATA: *BMS*, passim, and table 1-3.

1890s. These differences may in part be attributed to cyclical movements in business. Thus six years of the 1890s were classified as recession or depression phases of the cycle, whereas only three of the thirteen years starting in 1901 were so characterized.[89] The particularly rapid increase in the latter period may also reflect, however, the beginning of a structural change in the direction of a modernization of the country's financial structure.

In the present state of the statistics, any attempt to break down the issue ratios of financial institutions into their components—particularly the personal saving ratio, the share of financial saving in total personal saving, and the share of non-monetary household claims against financial institutions in total personal financial saving—is doomed to failure. All that can be said is that all three components must have been quite low, compared with the situation in financially developed countries before World War I or in India in the post-independence period, to produce a new issue ratio of about one-third of 1 percent.

The Presidency banks had no offices outside their headquarters in Calcutta, Bombay, and Madras throughout the early part of the period, and only three exchange banks and two reporting Indian joint stock banks were in operation in 1870. At that time, therefore, all Western-type financial institutions probably did not have more than a dozen offices in the entire subcontinent. On the other hand, the places of business, often hardly to be called offices, of indigenous bankers and urban moneylenders must have been countable by the hundreds, and those of rural moneylenders by the myriads.

In the following half century all three groups of Western-type banks began to build up small systems of offices. However, even in 1916, the first year for which the information is available, there were only 34 banks operating branches out of a total of 61 Presidency, exchange, and reporting Indian joint stock banks, and the total number of their branches was slightly below 300, or on the average of 9 branches per system.[90] The total of about 350 main and branch offices meant an average density of nearly 900,000 people per office; or if the fact is considered that practically all bank branches were located in cities (defining cities as places with more than 10,000 population), one office for about 70,000 urban inhabitants, still an exceedingly low density.

The three Presidency banks had the densest network, 65 branches, or 22 per bank. The

89. Thorp, pp. 333 ff.
90. *BMS*, p. 282.

exchange banks were not far behind with 45 branches, or 4½ per bank. The 48 reporting Indian class A and B joint stock banks had 180-odd branches, an average of 9 for each of the 20 banks having branches. The offices of the Post Office Saving System and of credit cooperatives were, of course, much more numerous—fully 10,000 for the postal saving system and possibly an approximately equal number for the 19,000 credit cooperatives, given the fact that some of the cooperatives were not large enough to afford a permanent office.

The branch network of the Western-type banks was heavily concentrated in a few large cities—about 30 percent of all branches were located in ten cities (table 1-20). This concentration also meant that only 140 out of 2,300 cities with a population of more than 5,000 had even one bank office[91] and that main or branch offices in smaller places were practically nonexistent. The three Presidency cities alone, which accounted for not more than 1 percent of the population, had about 50 offices, or one-seventh of the total (Bombay 26, Calcutta 19, and Madras about 10), around 1916.[92]

6. FINANCING THE NONFINANCIAL SECTORS OF THE ECONOMY

a. Financing the Government

Until World War I, and even beyond it, the British government of India tried as far as possible to minimize its direct economic activities, the main exception being substantial expenditures on public works, mainly railways, roads, and irrigation. This attitude was due, on the one hand, to the principle of laissez-faire to which the British government adhered as much as possible, both at home and in its overseas possessions. On the other hand, such an attitude also reflected the difficulty of the government's appropriating a large proportion of the national product of a country as poor as India. As a result, the central government's current revenue averaged only 5½ percent of gross national product for the period 1871–1913, with only small variations from decade to decade. The revenues of provinces, municipalities, and other public bodies were small compared with those of the central government. The land tax constituted the backbone of the central government's income, as it had done in the Mughal empire, accounting on the average for about one-third of total current receipts. Excise taxes, mainly that on salt, were the second largest revenue producers, contributing about one-fifth of the total. Income tax receipts were negligible until the late 1880s, and even in 1913 they produced less than 3 percent of total revenue.[93]

Using the figures in the government's published accounts, gross capital outlays for the period 1871–1913 at nearly R. 5 bill. amounted to about one-seventh of current expenditures, to 0.8 percent of the period's national product, and to about one-fourth of gross capital formation.[94] Better figures, resulting from a detailed analysis of the basic data, are available for the years 1898–1913 for all levels of government (table 1-11).[95] They put public gross investment at more than R. 4½ bill., or nearly 2 percent of national product. They also indicate that gross investment of other governmental units amounted to less than one-fourth of that of the central government and that the railways accounted for nearly one-half of gross public investment, followed by roads and buildings with nearly one-third and irrigation with one-eighth. For these fifteen years before World War I, public investment accounted for about one-third of total gross capital formation.

From the point of view of the financial development of India, the most important aspect of

91. Muranjan, p. 18.

92. Derived from the map following p. 497 in Shirras.

93. *BMS*, pp. 872 ff.

94. Assumes a government share of 20 percent in total gross capital formation for 1861 to 1900 compared with 32 percent for 1901 to 1913 (table 1-10).

95. Thavaraj's figure of R. 4.7 bill. for government gross capital formation for 1898 to 1913 (table 1-11) is close to B. Roy's estimate for 1901 to 1913 of R. 5.0 bill. Because the central government accounted for almost all government expenditures, both estimates are obviously far above the budget figures of R. 2.3 bill. for 1901 to 1913.

TABLE 1-20. Distribution of Main and Branch Commercial Bank Offices around 1916

Number of branches in town	Number of towns	Number of offices	Percent of towns	Percent of offices
One	93	93	58.5	25.5
Two	27	54	17.0	14.8
Three	16	48	10.1	13.2
Four	6	24	3.8	6.6
Five	5	25	3.1	6.8
Six	3[a]	18	1.9	4.9
Seven	3[b]	21	1.9	5.7
Eight	2[c]	16	1.3	4.4
Nine	1[d]	9	0.6	2.5
Twelve	1[e]	12	0.6	3.3
Nineteen	1[f]	19	0.6	5.2
Twenty-six	1[g]	26	0.6	7.1
Total[h]	159	365	100.0	100.0

[a]Bangalore, Delhi, and Rawalpindi.   [b]Allahabad, Amritsar, and Cawnpore.   [c]Lucknow and Madras.   [d]Karachi.
[e]Lahore.   [f]Calcutta.   [g]Bombay.   [h]Another source (Wadia and Joshi, p. 383) puts the number of offices at 402 in 165 places as of 1917.

SOURCE: Map following p. 497 in Shirras. (I have been unable to reconcile the figure for main and branch offices of 389, subtracting offices in Burma and Afghanistan, with the 365 offices shown on the map.)

public finance is the size of the government's requirements for funds and the ways by which they were met. Table 1-22 shows, therefore, the essential statistics of the central government's debt. Comparable information on the debt of other governmental units is lacking, but it is known that it was small compared with the debt of the central government.

The East India Company had borrowed in India on a fairly substantial scale, its total debt before the Mutiny standing at R. 558 mill., then about one-tenth of the country's annual national product, an increase of R. 225 mill. since 1820. Most of the debt had been raised to pay for the company's wars. After the British government took over, borrowing increased considerably, first in connection with the Mutiny—the debt rose by 45 percent in 1858 and 1859—and then

TABLE 1-21. Finances of Central Government, 1871–1913

Fiscal years beginning April 1	Current account		Capital account	
	Revenue	Surplus	Debt receipts	Capital outlay
	I. Amounts (R. mill.)			
1871–1880	5106	−15	137	300
1881–1890	5999	75	520	1086
1891–1900	7040	39	667	880
1901–1913	11804	430	1483	2308
1871–1913	29949	529	2807	4574
	II. Relation to gross national product (percent)			
1871–1880	5.45	−0.02	0.15	0.32
1881–1890	5.63	0.07	0.49	1.02
1891–1900	5.57	0.03	0.53	0.70
1901–1913	5.39	0.20	0.68	1.05
1871–1913	5.50	0.10	0.52	0.84

SOURCE OF I: *BMS*, pp. 872–73.

TABLE 1-22. Central Government Debt, 1860–1913

		Rupee debt					Sterling debt
					Other		
					Post Office saving system	State Provident funds	
Year[a]	Total	Total	Funded	Total			Total
I. Absolute amounts (R. mill.)							
1860	1014	729	635	94	.	.	285
1870	1131	755	668	87	.	.	376
1880	1673	958	860	98	.	.	715
1890	2184	1140	1028	112	75	6	1044
1900	3313	1311	1153	158	102	15	2002
1913	4454	1798	1457	341	232	62	2656
II. New issue ratio (percent of gross national product)							
1861–1870	0.16	0.03	0.04	−0.01	.	.	0.12
1871–1880	0.58	0.22	0.21	0.01	.	.	0.36
1881–1890	0.48	0.17	0.16	0.01	0.06	.	0.31
1891–1900	0.37[b]	0.14	0.10	0.04	0.02	0.01	0.23[b]
1901–1913	0.52	0.22	0.14	0.08	0.06	0.02	0.30
1861–1913	0.44[b]	0.17	0.13	0.04	0.04	.	0.27[b]
III. Distribution of net issues (percent)							
1861–1870	100.0	22.2	28.2	−6.0	.	.	77.8
1871–1880	100.0	37.5	35.4	2.0	.	.	62.5
1881–1890	100.0	35.6	32.9	2.7	14.7	.	64.4
1891–1900	100.0[b]	36.8	26.9	9.9	5.8	1.9	63.2[b]
1901–1913	100.0	42.7	26.6	16.0	11.4	4.1	57.3
1861–1913	100.0[b]	38.5	29.6	8.9	8.1	.	61.5[b]
IV. Distribution of outstanding debt (percent)							
1860	100.0	71.9	62.6	9.3	.	.	28.1
1870	100.0	66.8	59.1	7.7	.	.	33.2
1880	100.0	57.3	51.4	5.9	.	.	42.7
1890	100.0	52.2	47.1	5.1	3.4	0.3	47.8
1900	100.0	39.6	34.8	4.8	3.1	0.5	60.4
1913	100.0	40.4	32.7	7.7	5.2	1.4	59.6

[a]March 31 or April 30 of following year.   [b]After deduction of an increase of R. 664 mill. in 1900 representing write-up because of devaluation of rupee from 24 to 16 pence.

SOURCE OF I: *BMS*, pp. 880–81.

because of a sharp increase in expenditures on public works, primarily the new railroads. From 1861 through 1913 the central government's total debt increased by nearly R. 2,800 mill., or 0.44 percent of gross national product. The call on Indian resources was, however, much smaller as more than two-thirds of the additional debt was issued in London, most of it being bought by British private and institutional investors. Net rupee debt issues thus amounted to only slightly more than R. 1 bill., or less than one-fifth of 1 percent of national product. About one-fifth of the increase in domestic debt was supplied by the Post Office Saving System and more than 5 percent by state provident funds, so that net market offerings of long-term rupee securities in the half century before World War I were only slightly in excess of R. 750 mill., or about one-tenth of 1 percent of national product, without a definite trend during the period.

Gross issues of central government long-term rupee debt securities totaled almost R. 1.3 bill. between 1871 and 1913. They did not exceed the modest amounts of R. 61 mill. in 1896, then 0.5 percent of national product; and R. 55 mill. in 1887, or 0.6 percent of national product;

and were below R. 25 mill. in 19 years of the 42-year period. Because nearly R. 0.3 bill. of securities of the same type were redeemed, the increase in net funded rupee debt was held to not much more than R. 1 bill.

It is rather astonishing that both the absolute amount of gross and net new rupee issues and the ratio of net rupee issues to national product were considerably higher in the 1870s and 1880s than in the later part of the period. Indeed, for the quarter century from 1891 through 1913 net new rupee issues averaged only R. 10 mill. per year, or 0.07 percent of gross national product, against nearly R. 40 mill., or 0.37 percent of national product, in 1871–90. This pattern may be explained by heavier reliance on the London market and by surpluses in the current account of the government in the second half of the period.

Part of the rupee debt was held throughout the period by British investors living in Great Britain or temporarily domiciled in India.[96] The amount of rupee debt registered in London increased from about R. 150 mill., or nearly one-fourth of the total rupee debt in 1868, the first date for which this information is available, to about R. 225 mill., also one-fourth of the total, in the early 1880s, thus reducing the call on Indian resources by about R. 75 mill., or 0.06 percent of the period's national product. From then to the turn of the century the amount of rupee debt registered in London showed only small fluctuations. In the following dozen years the process of repatriation began, reducing the London registered rupee debt in 1913 to R. 100 mill., or 7 percent of the total. This means an additional call on Indian resources of about R. 125 mill., or 0.06 percent of the period's national product.

It is a moot question whether or not the purchase of rupee securities by foreigners living in India should be regarded as involving a call on Indian funds. In 1867 R. 475 mill., or more than 70 percent of the total funded rupee debt outstanding, was reported as held by "Europeans," a term that may have included foreigners who had returned to their home countries as well as those residing in India. From 1897 to 1913 their holdings were reported with only small changes at about R. 700 mill., their share declining from 58 percent to 47 percent of total rupee debt outstanding. For the period as a whole, holdings by Europeans thus seem to have increased by a little more than R. 200 mill. Because this is equal to only 0.03 percent of the period's national product, although to a considerably higher fraction of total saving, it may not matter too much how these holdings are treated. All these figures make it evident that the central government's security issues absorbed only a small fraction of the country's net saving, probably not much more than one-tenth.

There is little information about the distribution of the domestic funded debt held by Indian investors, which increased between 1860 and 1913 by R. 0.83 bill., or 0.13 percent of national product.[97] It may, however, be assumed that most of the "investments" reported by the Presidency banks[98] represented domestic funded debt of the government. On this assumption, the Presidency banks would have held about 2 percent of the government's domestic funded debt in 1870, 3 percent in 1890, and 4 percent in 1913. Because the Presidency banks accounted during this period for most of the assets of the entire banking system, it is evident that the bulk of the government's domestically owned funded debt must have been held outside Indian financial institutions, presumably by individual Indian investors for whom they must have constituted a substantial fraction of their portfolio of financial assets.[99]

The government's calls on the London market were chiefly determined, on the one hand, by the government's capital expenditures that exceeded its surplus and the absorptive capacity of the Indian market for government securities and, on the other hand, by the situation of the British

96. For annual data on rupee debt registered in London or held by Europeans, cf. Vakil, pp. 576–77.
97. *BMS*, pp. 880–81, and Vakil, pp. 576–77.
98. *BMS*, p. 11.
99. The ratio would be in the neighborhood of one-third if only marketable financial assets (money, bank deposits, and corporate shares) are considered, that is, if interhousehold claims, the most important of which are loans to agriculturalists, are excluded.

TABLE 1-23. Uses of Funds Raised through Public Debt Issues, 1875–1913

	Total	Railways	Irrigation	Other
		I. Amounts (R. mill.)		
1875	1224	117	87	1020
1880	1572	381	172	1019
1890	2070	1022	274	774
1900	3076	1677	351	1048
1913	4110	3328	591	191
		II. Distribution (percent)		
1875	100.0	9.6	7.1	83.3
1880	100.0	24.2	10.9	64.8
1890	100.0	49.4	13.2	37.4
1900	100.0	54.5	11.4	34.1
1913	100.0	81.0	14.4	4.6
		III. Rate of growth (percent per year)		
1876–1880	5.13	26.63	14.60	−0.02
1881–1890	2.79	10.36	4.77	−2.71
1891–1900	4.04	5.07	2.50	3.08
1901–1913	2.25	5.41	4.09	−12.27
1876–1913	3.24	9.21	5.17	−4.31
		IV. Relation of change in debt to period's gross national product (percent)		
1876–1880	0.71	0.54	0.17	0.00
1881–1890	0.47	0.60	0.10	−0.23
1891–1900	0.80	0.52	0.06	0.22
1901–1913	0.47	0.75	0.11	−0.39
1876–1913	0.57	0.64	0.10	−0.17

SOURCE OF I: Vakil, pp. 573–74.

capital market, the Indian government profiting from the 1880s on from the status of its obligations as trustee securities. Because bond yields in London were generally lower than in India, the government would, other conditions being equal, prefer to issue its bonds in the British market.

From 1861 through 1913 the net funded sterling debt (unfunded debt being minimal) increased by nearly R. 2.4 bill. More than one-fourth of this increase, however, reflects the depreciation of the rupee during this period from 24 to 16 pence, so that the net amount of sterling funds raised by bond issues came to only R. 1.7 bill.[100] The actual receipts from the net issues of government sterling securities, disregarding discounts and other costs of offering, therefore, amounted to only 0.3 percent of the period's national product.

Net issues of rupee securities were quite small in the 1860s after the sharp increase in 1857–59 due to expenses following the Mutiny, when the Indian market was in no position to absorb substantial amounts of government obligations. They rose to an annual average of about R. 25 mill. in the period from 1871 through 1885 and to one of about R. 45 mill. from 1886 through 1913. Sterling debt increased by, on the average, R. 32 mill. per year if the exceptional reported increase of R. 664 mill. in 1889, which represents a write-up of existing sterling debt rather than a flow of funds, is omitted from the average.[101] As a result of the predominance of the London market in the sale of central government securities as well as of the devaluation of the rupee by one-third, the share of the sterling debt increased from less than 30 percent in 1860

100. Such a revaluation is indicated by the fact that the rupee value of the government's sterling debt jumped between March 31, 1899, and March 31, 1900, from R. 1,198 mill. to R. 1,862 mill. (*BMS*, p. 881), whereas the face value of the sterling debt remained unchanged at £124 mill. (Vakil, p. 557). This means a write-up during the fiscal year 1899 of R. 664 mill. and implies £:R. ratios of 9.7 for March 31, 1899, but of 15.0 for March 31, 1900, the deviation from the ratio of 10 in 1899 possibly being due to a small difference in the types of debt covered by the two sets of statistics.

101. Years in which the sterling debt increased by more than R. 100 mill. are 1879, 1886, 1889, 1900, 1905, and 1907–10.

to 60 percent since the turn of the century. Interest charges payable in sterling (including guaranteed interest of railway and irrigation accounts) rose from £3.2 mill. (R. 32 mill.) in 1861 to more than £11 mill. (R. 165 mill.) in 1913, an increase from about 0.5 to 0.8 percent of national product, but in both years equal to about 7 percent of Indian merchandise exports.

The bulk of the proceeds of the central government's borrowing was used to finance capital expenditures, primarily for railways and secondarily for irrigation works. As a result, almost all the proceeds of the borrowings outstanding in 1913 had been used for productive purposes, whereas most of the debt incurred for other purposes, including the military, had been retired by that time, a striking contrast to the situation existing in 1875, when only one-sixth of the debt then outstanding had been raised for productive purposes.

b. Financing Agriculture[102]

Because agriculture constituted the largest sector of the Indian economy during the 1860–1913 period, as well as before and after, employing about three-fourths of the population and contributing about two-thirds of the national product, it is unfortunate that the data are inadequate to present a reasonably trustworthy picture in quantitative terms of the investment or saving or of the assets and liabilities of Indian agriculture, and hence of the uses and sources of funds of agriculture before independence. It is possible, however, to extract from the mainly descriptive literature enough information about two important aspects of the finances of Indian agriculture for the period of British government rule, namely, the size of agricultural indebtedness and the trend of prices of agricultural land.

In the period from 1860 to 1913 agricultural indebtedness was almost exclusively non-institutional. The smallness of the commercial banking system, the concentration of its offices in urban areas, and the character of its operations held its direct financing of agriculture to a minimum, although indirect credits in the form of loans to wholesalers and exporters were substantial. This was true not only of short-term credit but even more so of long-term mortgage credit. The two other potential sources of agricultural credit, rural credit cooperatives and insurance companies, were too small to make any significant contribution, even if they had invested a larger proportion of their assets in credits to agriculture than they did.[103]

The credit demands of agriculture, therefore, had to be met essentially by rural moneylenders. Although moneylending was the main permanent occupation for some, it was often secondary and occasional for a much larger number of local lenders such as landlords, merchants, officials, relatives, and fellow caste members. The agricultural debt would, therefore, disappear in a consolidated balance sheet of the household sector.

A great deal of the literature on rural indebtedness in India from the mid-nineteenth century to the present reiterates the theme that the mass of Indian peasants "are born in debt, live

---

102. The literature on the finances of Indian agriculture prior to World War I is voluminous but unfortunately weak in quantitative data. It concentrates on the problem of rural indebtedness and generally deals only with the situation in a limited area—hardly ever larger than one of the provinces of British India, particularly the Punjab—and during a limited period of time. The text is based primarily on the following publications, apart from the relevant sections of some of the general studies of Indian economic history: N. Benjamin, "Some aspects of agricultural indebtedness in British India (1850–1900)," *Indian Journal of Economics* 51 (1971); H. Calvert, *The Wealth and Welfare of the Punjab*, 1922; B. B. Chaudhuri, "Rural Credit Relations in Bengal, 1859–1885," *Indian Economic and Social History Review* 6 (1969); B. S. Cohn, "Structural Changes in Indian Rural Society," in R. E. Frykenberg, ed., *Land Control and Social Structure in Indian History*, 1969; N. Darling, *The Punjab Peasant in Prosperity and Debt*, 1925; T. B. Desai, *Economic History of India under the British*, 1968; D. Kumar, *Western India in the 19th Century*, 1965; M. B. Nanavati and J. J. Anjaria, *The Indian Rural Problem*, 1965; F. A. Nicholson, *Report Regarding the Possibility of Introducing Land and Agricultural Banks into the Madras Presidency*, 1895; S. C. Roy, *Agricultural Indebtedness in India and Its Remedies*, 1915; S. B. Singh and H. Calvert, *An Inquiry into Mortgages of Agricultural Land . . . in the Punjab*, 1925; P. J. Thomas, "Rural Indebtedness," in R. Mukherjee, ed., *Economic Problems of Modern India*, 1930, and *The Problem of Rural Indebtedness*, 1934; S. S. Thorburn, *Musalmans and Moneylenders in the Punjab*, 1886; R. D. Tiwari, *Indian Agriculture*, 1943.

103. This paragraph is based on the discussion in sec. 5 and therefore omits specific references to quantities and to sources.

in debt and die in debt."[104] There can be no doubt that a substantial proportion, although not the majority, of all rural households, cultivators as well as tenants and farm laborers, was in debt, often for a protracted period; that the agreed interest rates were very high, rarely below 1½ percent per month; and that a considerable proportion of the debtors ultimately lost their land to foreclosing creditors. This is true not only for the period of British rule but also for the long period preceding and following it.[105] However, if the official and unofficial jeremiads were taken literally, the creditors, and particularly the professional rural moneylenders, would have become immensely rich by 1913, or by now, and would have taken possession of much of the land. Because neither of these eventualities actually occurred, offsetting forces must have been at work, namely, among others, rather extensive defaults of debtors without loss of land, particularly tenants and landless farm laborers.[106] It is therefore necessary to obtain a quantitative picture of the volume and character of rural indebtedness, even if this is possible only in rough outline and with a substantial margin of error.

Most of the rough estimates of the total volume of agricultural indebtedness in India before World War I that have been published are based on an estimate made for Madras Presidency, an estimate that in turn was derived from data from only part of that area.[107] According to this estimate, total rural indebtedness in Madras Presidency in 1895 amounted to R. 450 mill., of which about R. 200 mill. were on mortgages and R. 250 mill. on personal security. This figure leads to an estimate for all of India of approximately R. 2½ bill., using in the absence of regional income or wealth data, either population or crop area as the basis for the blowup. In view of the nature of the derivation of the estimate, in particular of doubts about whether Madras Presidency can be regarded as representative of the whole country, it may be preferable to assert only that total agricultural indebtedness in the mid-1890s was probably between R. 2 and 3 bill. This would be equivalent to between two and three months of total gross national product and, more significantly, to between three and four months' agricultural income.[108,109] Assuming an average effective interest rate, that is, after defaults on interest and capital, of 1½ percent a month, the annual effective interest charge would have been between about R. 500 and 700 mill., or between 4 and 6 percent of the total income of Indian agriculture. The incidence of debt service and repayment was undoubtedly much heavier in many individual cases, although a substantial proportion of all agriculturalists always managed to keep free of debt.[110] Given the poverty of most Indian cultivators and farm workers,[111] even such apparently moderate ratios of debt

104. Tiwari, 1943, in preface and repeated on p. 250.

105. See statement by Kumar (p. 155) that in western India "rural indebtedness [was] widespread even before 1818" when British rule started.

106. Of 4.2 million acres of agricultural land changing hands in 1905–09 in Madras Presidency, 82 percent was purchased by agriculturalists and 9 percent each by traders and by other purchasers (Datta, 1:161).

107. Nicholson, p. 240.

108. This calculation is based on the national product estimate of table 1-3 and a share of agriculture in national product of two-thirds, which is close to Sivasubramonian's estimate for 1900–05 (p. 352).

109. Benjamin (p. 226) estimated that in the beginning of this century agricultural indebtedness was equal to from one-third to one-half of the total annual income of the peasants, figures only slightly higher than those derived independently in the text.

110. The proportion of agriculturalists free from debt varies enormously from sample to sample and practically any ratio between one-fifth and four-fifths can be found in the literature. (Cf., e.g., the proportions cited by B. B. Chaudhuri, pp. 213–18.) In 1880 the Famine Commission estimated that about one-third of all landowners in India were "deeply and inextricably in debt," whereas another third was less heavily indebted (cited by Tiwari, 1943, p. 253). These relations probably reflect the situation at the trough of an agricultural cycle. Roughly weighing the evidence, the proportion of debt-free agriculturalists seems to have been on the order of one-third to one-half. The burden of debt of the actual borrowers thus would be, of course, one and a half to two times as heavy as the figures in the text, which refer to all agriculturalists, in debt as well as debt-free.

111. In the absence of overall figures or even estimates, the result of two inquiries may be of some use. In the Bombay Deccan, a region with about 6 million inhabitants, the number of cattle decreased between 1886 and 1909 by 7 percent, whereas the population grew by 20 percent (Choksey, p. 70). In a small district of Bombay Presidency the number

TABLE 1-24. Estimate of Value of Agricultural Land, 1870–1915

	Crop area (acre mill.) (1)	Land tax revenue (R. mill.) (2)	Land price			Value of land (R. bill.)		
			R. per acre		Value tax ratio	A^a	B^b	C^c
			A (3)	B (4)	(5)	(6)	(7)	(8)
1870	200	206	19e	25	·	4.9e	6.5	·
1875	205	215	38	·	31	10.1	·	8.7
1880	210	211	34	36	32	9.3	9.8	8.8
1885	215	226	30	·	36	8.4	·	10.6
1890	220d	241	61	60	50	17.4	17.2	15.7
1895	230	254	59	·	56	17.6	·	18.5
1900	235	263	77	83	89	23.5	25.4	30.4
1905	240	284	85	·	105	26.5	·	38.8
1910	255	313	124	129	127	41.1	42.8	51.7
1915	250	331	216	·	·	70.2	·	·

[a]1.3 × col. 1 × col. 3 (step-up from British India to Undivided India).   [b]1.3 × col. 1 × col. 4.   [c]1.3 × col. 2 × col. 5.   [d]1891.   [e]1869.

SOURCES: **Col. 1:** 1890–1914, Blyn, p. 316; 1869–85, extrapolated on assumption of annual increase by 0.5 percent.   **Col. 2:** *BMS*, p. 872.   **Cols. 3 and 5:** Price and ratio for cultivated land in the Punjab as given in Calvert, p. 299. Estimate for 1869 to 1880 linked in 1885 to main series.   **Col. 4:** Mukerji, pp. 534 ff. Price of all land for 1870–90 linked to price of cultivated land in 1900. Figures refer to one year after the year indicated.

service to income constituted a heavy burden. The numerous debt riots, of which the Deccan riots of 1875 are probably the best-known example because they became the subject of a detailed official investigation, testify to the seriousness of the problem in certain areas and at certain times, particularly after repeated crop failures.

Possibly the most appropriate comparison is that between the value of debt and that of the land and other tangible assets of agriculturalists. In 1895 the crop acreage was on the order of 230 million acres.[112] If the average price of land sales in the Punjab in 1895, R. 59 per acre,[113] can be applied to all of India, a mighty "if," then the value of agricultural land would have been on the order of R. 18 bill. Another approach—multiplying the land tax revenue of 1895, R. 254 mill. for all of British India, with the value-to-tax ratio in the Punjab, 56—yields an estimated total value of land of R. 14 bill. for British India and one of about R. 18 bill. for all of India. On the basis of these figures, the derivation of which is shown in table 1-24 together with that of similar estimates for nine other benchmark years between 1869 and 1915, the ratio of agricultural debt to the value of agricultural land would be on the order of one-eighth to one-sixth.[114] Even if the average per acre value (or the value-to-land tax ratio) in the Punjab should be considerably above that for the entire country, it is difficult to arrive at a debt burden of more than about one-fifth of the value of agricultural land for all of India. The ratio of debt to all

of cattle increased by 8 percent from 1865 to 1895, after having fallen by 9 percent in the preceding thirty years, whereas the population increased in the earlier period by 31 percent and in the later period by 25 percent. Carts and wells increased more rapidly than population between 1865 and 1895, namely, by 55 percent and 86 percent, respectively.

112. Blyn's figure for British India of 176 million acres (p. 316) increased by 30 percent for princely states on the basis of population in 1891 and 1901.

113. Calvert, p. 219.

114. In one Deccan village near Poona the ratio of debt to the value of land around 1916 was close to 17 percent (Mann et al., p. 149). From the description of the settlement it would appear to have been even worse off than the average Indian village. The village's debt/land ratio may therefore be assumed to be higher than it was for India as a whole.

tangible agricultural assets would, of course, be lower.[115] These ratios imply a considerably higher debt-to-land (or debt-to-all-tangible-assets) ratio for that proportion of the land that is mortgaged; and still higher, and then indeed critical, values for peasants with an indebtedness well above the average. However, neither the flow (income) nor the stock (land value) approach seems to justify the pitch-black picture painted in most discussions of the problem of agricultural indebtedness, at least not for the country as a whole or for the average or "representative" agriculturalist.[116]

No reliable data exist that would permit an estimate of agricultural indebtedness at other dates between 1860 and 1913.[117] Three facts, however, make it likely that agricultural indebtedness showed an increasing trend over the period, so that its volume, though not necessarily its relation to agricultural income or to land value, was in 1860 substantially lower and in 1913 substantially higher than it had been in 1895. First, crop acreage increased from 1891 to 1913 at the rate of 0.5 percent a year.[118] Second, land prices advanced sharply, to judge by the information for the Punjab, by nearly 200 percent from 1869 to 1895 and by another 100 percent between 1895 and 1910.[119] Third, the value of national product doubled between 1860 and 1895 and rose by another 70 percent from 1895 to 1913, and it is doubtful that the share of agriculture in national product declined substantially during this period.[120] It is, therefore, not unlikely that total agricultural indebtedness in 1860 was as low as R. 1 bill. and might have risen to about R. 4

115. One of the very few estimates of the real assets of agriculture other than land for the period prior to World War I puts the possessions, other than land and inventories, of the "ordinary kumbi ryot" (i.e., peasant) at R. 125 for his livestock, R. 50 for his home, R. 20 for agricultural implements, and another R. 20 for all other real assets for a total of R. 215. It is not the minuscule total—about $70 at the then rate of exchange—that is of primary interest but the relative size of the components: 53 percent for livestock, 21 percent for house, and 9 percent each for agricultural implements and other utensils (Deccan Riots Commission of 1875, cited in Roy, p. 3). Multiplying these figures with the approximate number of rural households (about 40 million), one obtains the following figures for all of India:

Livestock	R. 5.0 bill.
Houses	R. 2.0 bill.
Agricultural implements	R. 0.8 bill.
Other implements	R. 0.8 bill.
Total	R. 8.6 bill.

This compares with an estimated value of agricultural land in 1875 of about R. 10 bill. (table 1-28). Such a ratio—approximate equality between land and reproducible assets including livestock—is not entirely unreasonable. In 1960 the value of reproducible tangible assets of agriculture was estimated at R. 120 bill. (excluding public land improvement and irrigation works), of which R. 23 bill. was for livestock on farms, R. 68 bill. for structures, and R. 4 bill. for agricultural implements (Gothoskar and Shanker). If one allocates about three-fourths of the total value of land (R. 213 bill.) to agriculture, the ratio of reproducible tangible assets to land is 160 : 120 = 1.33, which is not too far from the estimate for the situation seventy-five years earlier when the ratio was 1.16, particularly if account is taken of the fact that land prices rose more than the general price level. The distribution within reproducible assets, however, has changed radically. Moreover, the figure for livestock of R. 5.0 bill. is difficult to reconcile with Atkinson's estimate (p. 271) for the same year of R. 1.8 bill.

116. The situation reported by the Deccan Riots Commission for twelve villages in the Ahmednegar district probably was not typical for all of India, namely, mortgages of about 70 percent of land value topped by loans on personal security of 110 percent of land value for nearly 30 percent of the cultivators classified as "embarrassed" by their debts (cited in Roy, p. 13).

117. Thomas estimated, using documents from the Inspector General of Registration, that in Madras Presidency the volume of agricultural mortgages increased by nearly 60 percent, or by an average of 4.2 percent per year, between 1899 and 1910. On this basis one might estimate the agricultural debt to have doubled between 1895 and 1913. In one circumscription (taksil) of the Peshawar district, the volume of secured debt went up between 1896 and 1926 by slightly less than the rise in land prices, namely, by 365 percent and 400 percent, respectively (cited in Jain, p. 129). An estimate by McLaglen for 1911, based on Nicholson's estimate for 1895, is R. 3 bill. (cited in Jathar and Beri, p. 280). This seems too low.

118. Blyn, p. 316, for British India.

119. Calvert, p. 219, for land prices in the Punjab.

120. From 1900/04 to 1910/14 the decline, according to Sivasubramonian's estimates (p. 337) was only from 63.6 to 60.1 percent.

bill. by 1913.[121] If it is assumed that the relation between agricultural debt and land value remained the same as in 1895, one obtains somewhat higher estimates for agricultural debt, namely, R. 1½ bill. for 1875, the earliest date for which the calculation can be made, and R. 5 to 7 bill. for 1910.[122]

Apart from our knowledge, or guesswork, about the total volume of agricultural debt, information on other aspects, important for the evaluation of the significance and the consequences of agricultural indebtedness, may be more reliable, though fragmentary, than the aggregative estimates.

This material sheds some light on the character of lenders and borrowers, the purposes of the loans, the typical amounts and terms of the loans, and the rates of interest agreed upon. The material, usually based on small locally concentrated and not systematically selected samples of rural households, is too extensive and disparate to be presented here in detail. These data nevertheless seem to permit a few conclusions on points on which most of the sample inquiries agree. Because of the diversity of the samples and the impossibility of evaluating them, some dating from nearly a century ago, these conclusions must necessarily be stated in very general terms.

1. Most of the loans, particularly those made to proprietors, were secured by a mortgage on land.

2. Most of the borrowers, but also a substantial proportion of the lenders, were agriculturalists; the lenders were probably wealthier peasants for whom moneylending was a regular though secondary occupation.[123]

3. The loans were usually made for a short period, although often renewable and renewed to include accrued interest. In a study based on a large number of registered documents the mean term of payment was less than four years for mortgage loans and well under one year for other loans.[124]

4. The small size of the individual loan, often for less than R. 100—about $30—reflects the poverty of the Indian peasant.[125]

5. The interest rate was often relatively low—1 percent per month—in registered deeds but almost certainly was effectively much higher.

6. Possibly the most important characteristic of the loans is the fact that only a small amount was used in the borrowers' agricultural activities. Most loans were for debt repayment; for the fulfillment of social obligations, such as marriage and burial ceremonies; and for feeding the family after harvest failures or other calamities.[126]

Meaningful statements about the volume and composition of agricultural saving in India before World War I, and even up to independence, are difficult to make, partly because of the lack of data and partly because most lenders as well as borrowers belonged to the agricultural

121. This estimate is compatible with one of R. 5.2 bill. obtained by multiplying the average debt per household (R. 130), as determined around 1916 by an intensive study of one village near Poona of 103 families (Mann et al., p. 130), with the number of agricultural households in all of India (about 40 million), as total debt would be expected to be slightly higher in 1916 than in 1913.

122. To give the Devil his due, attention should be drawn to the fact that all figures on rural indebtedness so far discussed refer to monetary claims and obligations. Besides these, however, many cultivators incurred seasonal debts in seed grain, repayable after the harvest and usually carrying extremely high implicit interest rates. Some authors believe that seed loans were as important as money loans, at least in the earlier part of the period, but this is in contrast to the much better documented situation in the Indian Union.

123. In an inquiry covering R. 340 mill. worth of mortgages made in Madras Presidency in 1905–09 (Datta, 1:162), fully 70 percent of loans were made by agriculturalists, 17 percent by traders, and 11 percent by other lenders, so that the share of moneylenders could not have exceeded one-fourth of the total unless the category of "agriculturalists" includes many rural moneylenders.

124. Nicholson, 1:397.

125. Of about 1.1 million mortgages made in 1890–91 in Madras Presidency, the average amount was less than R. 190 (at that time about $60), and half of them were for amounts below R. 100 (Nicholson, 1:400).

126. E.g., Nicholson, 1:xii.

sector and, consequently, the bulk of agricultural indebtedness disappears from the calculations when the usual social accounting convention of netting intrasectoral claims and liabilities is followed.

There is little doubt, however, that during this period most of agricultural saving took the form of additions to farm buildings and implements and possibly to livestock; and it is quite unlikely that the increase did much more than to keep up with the growth of the agricultural population,[127] given the backward state of Indian agriculture on the eve of World War I when mechanization was still unheard of. Between 1860 and 1913 the only significant additions to the stock were in the form of irrigation, mainly new or improved canals and new wells. A large part of these expenditures were, however, undertaken by the government rather than by the agricultural sector.

Given the unlikelihood of any substantial increases in bank deposits or even in the postal saving banks[128] and in securities, the only financial assets embodying substantial amounts of agricultural saving are the increase in currency held and, still more important, the addition to gold and silver hoards, mainly in the form of jewelry. Because rupee coins in circulation in the country increased by nearly R. 1,500 mill. between 1860 and 1913 and notes in circulation rose by less than R. 500 mill. (table 1-6), agricultural saving in these two forms could hardly have exceeded R. 1,500 mill., or well under 1 percent of agricultural income, if agriculture's share in national product is used as the allocator, and it probably was considerably lower. The most important form of saving by the rural population may have been the hoarding of gold and silver, mainly in the form of ornaments. Because the country's stock of gold and silver is estimated to have increased from 1861 to 1913 by R. 6 bill. (table 1-28), the share of the rural population may well have been on the order of R. 3 to 4 bill. Total rural saving in these three forms of saving, which do not yield interest, may thus have amounted to between R. 4 and 6 bill., which would be equal to about 1 percent of gross national product originating in agriculture in the 1860–1913 period. Given the slow growth of the stock of reproducible capital in Indian agriculture, it is difficult to see how the rate of net saving in agriculture could have exceeded 2 percent of income.

The absence of estimates of capital formation in Indian agriculture before 1900 is fortunately not fatal for an investigation of the country's financial structure because, as argued above, most of capital formation in agriculture apparently was financed by agricultural saving, whereas the financing of agricultural investment by other sectors seems to have been limited to public works, particularly irrigation, undertaken and paid for by the government. Moreover, part of these government funds may be regarded as coming from agriculture, namely, to the extent that public works in agriculture were financed by government taxes and other levies originating in the agricultural sector. Although Indian agriculture was not entirely financially self-sufficient in the 1860–1913 period, most of its capital expenditures were financed by its own saving, and most of its saving was kept within the sector, so it was not very far from such a position.

For the years 1900 to 1913, the only years for which even rough estimates are available, gross rural construction (including public works financed by the government) and gross investment in agricultural implements have been estimated at about one-third of the country's total gross fixed investment, the share declining from somewhat more than one-third in 1900–02 to

127. One of the few relevant sets of data indicates for one district (*taluka*) in Bombay Presidency an average annual rate of increase in the period 1865 to 1895 of 0.7 percent for population; 1.9 percent for wells; 1.5 percent for carts; and 0.3 percent for cattle (Kumar, p. 302). In view of the dominating position of cattle among the reproducible tangible assets of Indian agriculture, this points to a low rate of growth of the agricultural total capital stock, indeed, one hardly in excess of the growth of the population.

128. The share of agricultural depositors in the total number of deposit accounts of the Post Office Saving System was only 1.3 percent in 1890 and even by 1911 had risen to only 2.3 percent (Datta, I: 164). Assuming the average balance in the accounts of agricultural depositors to equal the overall average—probably an overstatement—would yield an estimate of agriculturalists' total postal savings deposits of only R. 0.8 mill. in 1890 and R. 4.4 mill. in 1911. The increase of R. 3.6 mill. is equal to about 0.002 percent of the period's agricultural income.

fully one-fourth in 1911–12.[129] This is equal to about 2½ percent of the period's gross national income and to less than 4 percent of agricultural income. Because of the apparently rising trend in the proportion and of the slow growth of total, as well as agricultural, capital formation, the ratio of net agricultural saving to agricultural income can hardly have been in excess of 2 percent.

The financial situation of agriculture is strongly influenced by the movements of land prices, both absolutely and in relation to changes in the general price level, and specifically to the prices of commodities agriculturalists buy. Although we lack a continuous index, or even comparable benchmark estimates, of the movements in agricultural land prices in all of India for the period from 1860 to World War I and beyond, the fragmentary available data are sufficient to establish the direction of the trend of land prices and even to obtain a picture of the size of the movement, at least for one important region, the Punjab.

The preponderant view is that before British rule the land market was very restricted and that the prices in such transactions as occurred were very low.[130] One estimate, by a knowledgeable contemporary Indian author who is not an economist, put the increase in Bengal between 1793 and 1831 at 1,000 percent and in some instances even 2,000 percent.[131] For the Punjab the trend of agricultural land prices can be followed for almost the entire period from 1860 to 1913.[132] Here the price doubled between 1869 and 1890 and advanced by another 25 percent and 60 percent in the next two decades. The price thus was six times as high in 1910 as it had been a half century earlier. By way of comparison, the average mortgage per acre in one small district of the Punjab rose by 235 percent[133,134] between 1889 and 1910, a period during which land prices doubled. As the two series do not refer to the same area and undoubtedly are subject to considerable margins of error, one must be careful in drawing the conclusion that mortgage debt increased slightly more rapidly than land prices in the Punjab, let alone in all of India.

c. Financing Nonfarm Households

Although nonfarm households during this period accounted for a substantial proportion of the income of all households, even excluding their business activities, there is very little information on either their financial assets or their liabilities and hardly any comprehensive statistics. Assuming that these households held most of the private deposits in financial institutions, most of the claims against insurance organizations, most of the rupee securities of the government owned by Indians, and most of the stock of corporations as well as a proportion of money (coin and notes) corresponding to at least their share in national income, their total financial assets would have been on the order of R. 0.8 bill. in 1860, R. 1.3 bill. in 1890, and R. 3.0 bill. in 1913. Although it is possible to make a rough estimate of the relation of these figures to total national product—they are in the neighborhood of 15 percent at all three dates—the more relevant comparison with the total or disposable income of all nonfarm households is hampered by the absence of estimates of that income. Assuming a share of nonfarm households in personal income of one-third, the relation of the two very rough estimates of the numerator (financial

129. Roy.

130. Cf., e.g., Anstey, p. 97; S. C. Gupta, *Indian Economic Review* 4 (1956): 57; and Mukherji, p. 533. Chandra, "Some Aspects of the Growth of a Money Economy in India during the Seventeenth Century," *Indian Economic and Social History Review* 3 (1966): 325, however, asserts that "land was beginning to be a subject of sale and purchase" as early as the seventeenth century.

131. Estimate by Rammohun Roy in his *Questions and Answers on the Revenue System of India* (1831) as cited by Ganguli, p. 285. In a similar vein, Cohn (p. 112) asserts that "from the fragmentary evidence available the price paid for land [in central India] appears to have risen sharply after 1795."

132. Calvert, p. 219.

133. Singh and Calvert, p. 13.

134. Similar price rises, also for the Punjab—an increase by 250 percent between 1862/63 and 1889/90—are indicated by the figures given by Mukherji, p. 533. In the Ghazepur district (near Banaras) the price per acre increased in the thirty years between 1843/52 and 1872/82 by slightly more than 100 percent (Cohn, p. 112).

assets of nonfarm households) and of the denominator (annual disposable income of these households) is approximately one-half at the three benchmark dates.

Information is entirely lacking on either the business or the nonbusiness debt of nonfarm households. Because installment credit and policy loans were of negligible size during the period, only two categories of nonfarm household debts need to be considered, the housing debt and the debts of nonfarm households incurred in connection with marriages, funerals, sickness, and similar occasions. Given the attitudes of most of the urban, as well as the agricultural, population to sumptuary expenditures, it is difficult to believe that the total debt of nonfarm households was not at least equal to the ratio of their numbers to those of farm households. This would put them most roughly at R. 250 mill. in 1860, R. 500 mill. in 1896, and R. 1 bill. in 1913. These guesses are equal to about one-fourth of nonfarm households' annual income.

d. Financing Nonagricultural Business[135]

(i) GENERAL CHARACTERISTICS. As in the case of financial institutions, a modern sector also evolved in the nonagricultural business sector in the period from the middle of the nineteenth century to World War I. The modern sector, primarily in factory industry, operated in addition to, and often almost independently of, the traditional handicraft, trade, and service sectors, which continued to employ most of the nonagricultural labor force and which changed their methods of operation and financing only marginally, if at all. Although the modern sector was of great importance in initiating the modernization of the Indian economy, its absolute and relative size was still small at the end of the period. Thus, in 1913 modern (factory) industry employed fewer than 800,000 persons or about 2 percent of the total nonagricultural labor force,[136] and it accounted for only about 10 percent of nonagricultural product and 4 percent of total national product.[137]

Most Indian industry was concentrated in a few cities, primarily Calcutta, Bombay, Ahmadabad, and Madras. An idea of the geographic distribution of the modern nonagricultural business sector is given by the share of each province in the paid-up capital of all corporations. Thus, in 1900 Bengal (mostly Calcutta) and Bombay each accounted for more than 40 percent of the total, followed at great distance by Madras with 7 percent. None of the other eight provinces had a share of more than 1 percent of the total capital of corporations.[138]

Little is known about the financing methods of the traditional nonagricultural business sector, and quantitative information is completely lacking. It may be assumed that the new Western-type financial institutions employed only a small part of their resources in loans to nonagricultural businesses of the traditional type (which, of course, had no access to financing through the issuance of securities). Such enterprises must have been financed, therefore, in the same way they had been for hundreds of years, that is, partly, and probably to a large extent, by retained earnings and by loans from family members and close business and caste connections and partly by indigenous bankers and moneylenders.

Information, particularly of a comprehensive statistical nature, is, however, also scarce regarding the financing of the modern sector, even in the case of the more conspicuous factory industries. In particular, no statistics are available on the assets, liabilities, and the sources and

---

135. In addition to the sources on managing agencies, which are listed in footnote 147, the main sources for this section are: D. H. Buchanan, *The Development of Capitalistic Enterprise in India*, 1934; D. R. Gadgil, *The Industrial Evolution of India in Recent Times, 1860 to 1939*, 5th ed., 1971; P. S. Lokanathan, *Industrial Organization in India*, 1935; M. M. Mehta, *Structure of Indian Industries*, 1955; R. S. Rungta, *The Rise of Business Corporations in India—1851–1900*, 1970; N. S. R. Sastry, *A Statistical Study of India's Industrial Development*, 1947; S. K. Sen, *Studies in Industrial Policy and Development of India (1858–1914)*, 1966; H. R. Soni, *Indian Industry and Its Problems*, 1932.

136. Based on an estimate of employment in factories in 1911 of 786,000 persons (Myers, p. 17) and an estimate of total nonagricultural labor force in 1911 (J. N. Sinha, p. 112).

137. Sivasubramonian, p. 37.

138. Rungta, p. 301.

uses of funds of even a large part of the modern business sector, which operated predominantly as corporations.

The only comprehensive set of statistics of the modern nonfinancial business sector, which may be regarded as identical with the total of nonfinancial corporations, provides information on the number and the capital of nonfinancial corporations incorporated in India (table 1-25). Because a number of enterprises incorporated in Great Britain operated in India, the figures seriously understate the size of the corporate nonfinancial business sector, but this ommission should be crucial only in a few industries, for example, railways and tea gardens.[139]

Although a few business corporations, mostly in the financial field,[140] began operating in India in the late eighteenth century, nonfinancial corporations did not begin to be of any importance until the middle of the nineteenth century. In 1850 fewer than 30 nonfinancial corporations, including a dozen in maritime trade or transportation and five cotton mills,[141] are reported to have been in operation. From 1851 to 1865 only about 180 nonfinancial corporations, for which data on capitalization are available, were registered in India and raised a paid-up capital of nearly R. 85 mill.[142] Assuming that all paid-up capital represented a flow of new money into the sector and ignoring retirements and dissolutions, the stock issues of nonfinancial corporations would represent only approximately 0.10 percent of the period's national product. The movement accelerated in the following fifteen years as the main modern industries grew rapidly and the modern financial system expanded. From 1866 through 1881 the number of registered corporations, for which information on capitalization is available, almost doubled to 325 and their paid-up capital increased by 110 percent to R. 175 mill.[143] This was equal to about 0.13 percent of national product, only a modest increase over the ratio 0.10 percent for the preceding fifteen-year period. The average size per mill of about R. 1 mill. indicates the small size of many of the mills. About 80 cotton mills accounted for R. 75 mill. paid-up capital, or for nearly 30 percent of the total. Jute mills, with R. 13 mill., or 5 percent of the total, followed at a large interval. The two branches of the textile industry, together with their auxiliaries, accounted for more than one-third of the paid-in capital raised by nonfinancial corporations in the three decades from 1851 to 1881, their share being considerably higher in the second half of the period. There were, it appears, only a very few issues of corporations in the capital-goods industries. Coal mines, which are a borderline category, issued only R. 6 mill. worth of stock, or a little more than 2 percent of the total.

In 1881, the year with which a continuous set of statistics starts, the 360 reporting nonfinancial corporations had a paid-in capital of R. 135 mill., or not more than 1.3 percent of a year's national product.[144] By 1913 their number had increased to nearly 2,000 with a capital of R. 682 mill., or about 3½ percent of national product, indicating that, as might be expected, the nonfinancial corporate sector, if measured by the size of its paid-in capital, had been growing more than twice as rapidly as the economy as a whole, namely, at an average annual rate of 5.2 percent compared with a growth rate of national product of 2.2 percent.

In the absence of combined balance sheets and statements regarding the sources and uses

139. Macpherson (p. 186) concluded that "private" [British] capital showed no aversion to overseas [i.e., Indian] public utility construction provided that the principal and interest were duly guaranteed."

140. Rungta, pp. 11–13.

141. Rungta, pp. 274–75.

142. Rungta, p. 289. It may be assumed that the capital of the corporations for which data on capital were unavailable represented only a small fraction of that of the reporting corporations.

143. Of the 828 nonfinancial corporations registered from 1851 through 1881, 464 were wound up before 1881 and only 350-odd survived (Rungta, p. 284).

144. BMS, pp. 780 ff. It should be noted that the figures for the group of railways, including tramways, in col. 6 of table 1-25 seriously understate the size of that industry because they do not include railway companies incorporated outside India nor the lines owned by the government. Thus in 1913 the capital-at-charge of all railways in India (which is represented not only by paid-in capital but also by reserves and debentures) totaled more than R. 4,700 mill. (BMS, p. 876) compared to the paid-up capital of railway and tramway companies incorporated in India of only R. 71 mill. (BMS, p. 781).

TABLE 1-25. Number and Capital of Joint Stock Companies, 1881–1913[a]

March 31 of following year	All companies (1)	Financial[b] (2)	Nonfinancial (3)	Trading (4)	Mills and presses[c] (5)	Other nonfinancial (6)
			I. Number			
1881	505	144	361	86	104	171
1890	928	288	640	159	223	258
1900	1366	463	903	280	368	255
1913	2744	766	1978	902	518	558
			II. Paid-up capital (R. mill.)			
1881	157	22	135	20	67	48
1890	246	33	213	38	116	59
1900	363	39	324	70	184	70
1913	766	84	682	192	295	195
			III. Paid-up capital (percent)			
1881	100.0	14.0	86.0	12.7	42.7	30.6
1890	100.0	13.4	86.6	15.4	47.2	24.0
1900	100.0	10.7	89.3	19.3	50.7	19.3
1913	100.0	11.0	89.0	25.1	38.5	25.4
			IV. Paid-up capital per company (R. in thousands)			
1881	311	153	374	233	644	281
1890	265	115	333	239	520	229
1900	266	84	359	250	500	275
1913	279	110	345	213	569	349

[a]Excluding companies incorporated abroad operating in India, particularly railroads, whose capital was much larger than that of companies incorporated in India. [b]Banking, loan, and insurance. [c]Mainly cotton and jute.

SOURCE OF I AND II: *BMS*, pp. 780 ff.

of funds for all nonfinancial corporations, or for a representative sample, one is reduced to inferring financing needs and methods from fragmentary information,[145] particularly the relative importance of internal and external financing, and within the latter that of issuance of debentures, borrowing from managing agents, bank borrowing, trade credit, and deposits from the public.[146] Debentures provided only a small fraction of financing needs and were particularly small in the earlier part of the period. For bank borrowing, only an upper limit, a very rough approximation, can be obtained. Assuming that business loans of commercial and exchange banks at the beginning of this period bore approximately the same ratio to the banks' total assets as they did in the Bank of Bengal in 1856, namely, nearly 60 percent, and that at the end of the period the ratio applicable is that of the then dominating Imperial Bank of India in 1921, or that of the scheduled banks in 1935 when statistics of this type became available, namely, a ratio of slightly below one-half, then these loans would have amounted to somewhat more than R. 100 mill. in 1870 and to about R. 500 mill. in 1913. These figures undoubtedly overstate the bank borrowings of nonfinancial corporations from Western-type financial institutions because part of the bank advances went to unincorporated business and to individual borrowers. On the other hand, the figures make no allowance for the undoubtedly smaller borrowings of corporations from indigenous bankers. Accepting provisionally these estimates, bank loans would have constituted 30 percent of the paid-in capital of nonfinancial corporations in 1881 and 75 percent in 1913. Such ratios are not unreasonable, although the increase between 1881 and 1913 seems to be too large.

(ii) THE ROLE OF MANAGING AGENCIES.[147] The financing, as well as the operation, of a large proportion of nonfinancial corporations has been characterized by a specific Indian institution, the managing agency. These firms, partnerships or corporations, organized an industrial or mercantile corporation; assembled the board of directors, including a number of representatives of the agency; hired the top operating officers in India or Great Britain; arranged for the placement of the original and the later security issues of the corporation; assisted in securing the corporation's working capital, either by providing it themselves or by making the necessary arrangement with a bank; acted as purchasing and selling agents of the corporation; and, last but not least, were remunerated by the managed corporation for their services, generally on the basis of profits or of sales. In many cases, therefore, the agency constituted the effective, although not the legal, management of the corporation. At the least, the agency was an important factor in the managed corporation's operations.

The agency system originated in Bengal in the late eighteenth century.[148] It reached its maturity, covering all industrially or commercially important parts of the country, during the second half of the nineteenth century as modern industry developed in India. The early managing agencies, which often also acted as wholesalers and importers or exporters of commodities, were almost exclusively British. Later, however, a number of Indian managing agencies were formed, primarily by Parsees, and became dominant on the west coast, whereas the British agencies

145. One of the few statistics providing information on the methods of financing industry concerns 39 cotton mills in Jombay in 1894 with a paid-up capital of R. 41 mill., equal to 15 percent of the capital of all nonfinancial corporations (Rungta, p. 291). These mills had reserves of R. 17 mill., bringing their own capital to R. 58 mill., and they had borrowed R. 34 mill., indicating total funds of more than R. 90 mill. of which only about one-fifth were internally generated. Information on the sources of the loans is unfortunately lacking, but four groups of lenders are likely to have been involved, commercial banks, managing agents, suppliers (trade credit), and the general public (deposits).

146. "Unfortunately, no statistical information is available for estimating the nature and extent of intercompany investments in India in 1911" (M. M. Mehta, p. 294) or for any year of the period.

147. Although no study dealing specifically with managing agencies in the period before World War I appears to be available, most books covering the economic history of that period, particularly those dealing with India's industrial development, discuss the managing agencies in more or less detail. The discussion in the text is based primarily on Bagchi, chap. 6; Buchanan, chap. 8; Gadgil; Kidron, chap. 2; Lokanathan, chaps. 1, 6, 8, and 9; Samant and Mulky, chap. 3; Rungta, passim; Rutnagur, pp. 49 ff.; Soni, passim.

148. Lokanathan, p. 36.

retained the leading position in Bengal.[149] The characterization often applied to the German mixed banks that they accompanied a company from the cradle to the grave is even more apposite in the case of the Indian managing agencies.[150]

Although the statistics for this period are scarce, there is little doubt that a substantial, and probably even the major, part of nonfinancial corporations operating in India from the middle of the nineteenth century to World War I, particularly corporations in the textile industry, were associated with, or probably more correctly were controlled by, a managing agency. This control was exercised either by a management contract or by a share ownership, which seems to have averaged 40 percent of the capital in western India but to have been lower in Bengal,[151] or frequently by a combination of both devices.

Two types of managing agencies need to be distinguished. The first type managed only a single operating corporation or possibly a very few corporations in the same industry. In these cases the managing agency did little more than provide an additional layer beyond the board of directors and the officers, although it might have enabled the group controlling the corporation to cream off through the management contract a larger share of the corporation's profits than might otherwise have been possible. The rate of remuneration of the management in the early period was on the order of one sixty-fourth of sales, irrespective of whether the operating corporation was profitable or not; but from the 1880s on, the rate of remuneration was usually fixed at a given percentage—often 10 percent—of the operating corporation's profits.[152]

The other type of managing agency in essence anticipated the conglomerates that have recently become fashionable in developed countries. Such agencies had management contracts with a substantial number of operating corporations, often in various and technologically unconnected industries. This arrangement permitted the agency to control a group of corporations with no or little investment of its own funds, a feature that had great attraction compared with a Western-type holding company in a country in which capital was scarce. For the same reasons—the narrowness of the capital market, particularly for equity securities, and the scarcity of entrepreneurs familiar with Western production and financing techniques—the interposition of a managing agency, particularly of a well-known one, played the role, effectively though not legally, of debtor substitution and thus made financing possible or facilitated it. Such a function was particularly important when part of the funds had to be raised abroad, in the Indian case in Great Britain, a task that in many cases would have been very difficult and costly, if not impossible, for Indian operating corporations. The larger managing agencies thus, in addition to their other functions, to some extent substituted for investment bankers, who were nonexistent in Victorian India.

The extent of the control of these multi-firm management agencies is indicated by the fact that, limiting attention to only three important industries (tea, jute, and coal) concentrated in the eastern part of India, eight agencies managed at least 10 corporations each and in 1911 together controlled 120 corporations, the largest agency alone managing 27 corporations. Because most of these agencies also managed operating companies in other industries and in other parts of the country as well, their influence was even greater than these figures indicate.

Statistics of the activities and scope of control of managing agencies during the second half of the nineteenth century are apparently lacking, although it is known that the two then most

149. In Marxist terminology, "The managing agency system was a leading weapon in their [the Indian bourgeoisie's] hands to extend their grip over a number of industries" (Sen, p. 156).

150. The summary by a knowledgeable Indian economist merits quotation: "The managing agent became the very centre and life of every important industrial concern because he, and not the industry as such, established contact with the banking system"; and "the lack of an efficient banking system threw the whole burden of industrial finance on a limited class of entrepreneurs [managing agents] who were unwilling to pioneer new enterprises unless the chances of high profits were bright" (Lokanathan, pp. 140–41).

151. Lokanathan, p. 148.

152. Rutnagur, pp. 62–63.

TABLE 1-26. Distribution of Ownership and Management of 4,676 Industrial Concerns, 1911

	Agency managed		Directly managed		Total			
								Percent
	Europeans[a]	Indians	Europeans[a]	Indians	Europeans[a]	Indians	Together	Indians
Tea plantations	729	120	101	66	830	186	1016	18.3
Cotton mills and presses	60	556	—	303	60	859	919	93.5
Jute mills and presses	114	45	8	36	122	81	203	39.9
Collieries	153	175	13	142	166	317	483	65.6
Flour and rice mills	9	129	—	96	9	225	234	96.2
Oil mills	4	115	—	118	4	233	237	98.3
Brick and tile factories	18	183	12	159	30	342	372	91.9
Coffee plantations	86	18	56	11	142	29	171	17.0
Indigo plantations	117	2	93	14	210	16	226	7.1
Other industries	177	331	38	269	215	600	815	73.6
All industries	1467	1674	321	1214	1788	2888	4676	61.8

[a]Includes Anglo-Indians.

SOURCE OF BASIC DATA: Bagchi, p. 183, on basis of *Census of India*, vol. 1 (1913).

important industries, cotton and jute, were completely dominated by agencies, the cotton industry mostly by Indian agencies and the jute industry predominantly by British ones. In 1895 70 cotton mills in Bombay were under the control of 50 agencies. Of the agencies, in turn, 27 Hindu agencies controlled 30 mills; 15 Parsee agencies, 22 mills; 4 Muslim, 4 mills; 3 British, 6 mills; and 8 mills were controlled by the Jewish Sassoon family, originally from Baghdad but operating throughout the Near and Far East in the second half of the nineteenth century.[153]

In 1911 the *Census of India* listed about 2,850 industrial "concerns," many of which were not in corporate form, as agency-managed compared with 1,538 concerns directly managed by their officers and indirectly by their owners.[154] Table 1-26 shows the number of the agencies and the number of directly managed concerns for a dozen main industries with a further breakdown indicating the number of concerns managed by Europeans (and Anglo-Indians) and by Indians. Although the distribution by number of concerns is, of course, not identical with the more relevant distribution by size of capital or assets or by sales or by number of employees, it should nevertheless provide a picture that also reflects the broad characteristics of the other distributions.

It then appears that the agency-managed concerns were nearly twice as numerous as those directly managed if all industries are considered together. In some industries—tea gardens, jute mills, and collieries—agency-managed concerns predominated; in others—flour, rice, and vegetable-oil mills, brick and tile factories, and coffee and indigo plantations—the two categories are about equal. In general, agency-managed concerns tended to dominate export-oriented industries, whereas directly managed concerns worked mainly for the domestic market. A similar difference appears when concerns are classified into British- and Indian-controlled enterprises. Foreigners accounted for more than two-fifths of all concerns and dominated tea, coffee, and indigo plantations, all industries characterized by their export orientation. Indians, on the other hand, controlled the great majority of cotton mills, flour, rice, and oil mills, and brick and tile

153. Rutnagur, p. 55.
154. This is evident from the fact that in 1911 only about 2,300 corporations were reported in operation (*BMS*, p. 780) compared with the nearly 4,400 industrial concerns reported in the census, which was not quite complete (cf. Bagchi, p. 182).

factories, industries either working mainly for the home market or concentrated in the western part of the country as in the case of the cotton mills.

Although statistics providing quantitative evidence are not available, it is likely that the industries managed or owned by the British were financed partly in Great Britain and that to the extent that they were financed in India, they borrowed primarily from the Presidency or exchange banks. Indian-owned or -managed concerns, on the other hand, are most unlikely to have had direct access to the British credit market and probably borrowed mainly from Indian joint stock banks and native bankers, although they also had access to the Presidency banks, particularly in rediscounting bills of exchange.

(iii) THE BOMBAY SHARE MANIA OF 1861–1865. Early in the period, when corporate securities were still a novelty, Indian promotors and stock speculators showed, in what became known as the Bombay-share mania, that they had nothing to learn from the West.[155] As a result of the stoppage of American cotton exports to Great Britain and other countries during the American Civil War, cotton prices rose explosively, with the price of Indian raw cotton in Bombay increasing more than fourfold between 1861 and 1864. As the combined result of the price rise and the increase in the volume of exports of Indian cotton, (from about 500,000 bales a year to nearly 1.2 million bales in 1865), mostly shipped from Bombay, an extraordinary amount of funds became available in Bombay. More than R. 500 mill. worth of silver was imported into Bombay in 1861–64, equal to something like one-fifth of the total income of the Bombay Presidency at that time,[156] an inflow that led not only to feverish speculation in cotton, by the general public as well as by members of the cotton trade, but also to a boom in the organization of new corporate enterprises and to the issuance of shares on a scale not seen before or after in India. In the three years 1863 to 1865 the stocks of more than one hundred new corporations with a paid-up capital of nearly R. 300 mill. are reported to have been offered in the Bombay market—the city was as yet without an organized stock exchange—at a premium amounting on the average to 125 percent of par. The aggregate value of these offerings of R. 675 mill. was far in excess of the capital of all corporations then operating in India, or of the assets of all financial institutions, and was on the order of 10 percent of a year's national product of the entire country. Banks and other financial corporations contributed the lion's share of this avalanche of offerings, accounting for two-thirds of the number of issues and for slightly more than one-half of their aggregate offering price. Land reclamation companies, on which the mania centered, though numbering only a half dozen, absorbed nearly two-fifths of the total funds raised.

The house of cards collapsed in July 1865 as it became evident that the Civil War and the cotton famine were at an end. Cotton prices were rapidly cut in half and fell by two-thirds between 1864 and 1868, forcing the liquidation of most of the new banks and financial institutions that had either speculated in cotton or had financed the speculation of their officers, shareholders, and clients. Even the Bank of Bombay had to be reorganized after writing off more than R. 20 mill. on the R. 35 mill. of loans it had made, including R. 7 mill. on R. 13 mill. of loans made to the leading promoter and speculator, Premchund Roychund (1831–1906) and his associates. The shares of the bank, which had reached R. 2,900 at the height of the mania, received R. 100 in the ensuing liquidation. Another group of speculators and promoters, the "gunpowder trio," led by a British expatriate physician, failed with liabilities of about R. 25 mill., not less than 4 percent of India's annual national product. The fate of the land reclamation companies, which had done hardly any reclaiming, was similar, the price of the shares of the Backbay Company, the largest, falling from a peak of R. 55,000 to virtually zero.

155. This section is essentially based on two short books by D. E. Wacha, *A Financial Chapter in the History of Bombay City,* 1910, and *Premchund Roychund,* 1913. Wacha's books, though as colorful as the episode they describe, are free from economic analysis.

156. This figure is based on the estimate that Bombay Presidency accounted for nearly one-tenth of the national product of India. This ratio in turn is on the order of the Bombay Presidency's share in population and in land revenue.

available only for a few sectors, or for parts of them, such as business corporations and the central government, indirect methods of estimation must be used for most sectors.[170]

In the case of India before independence the construction of a national balance sheet is particularly difficult because of the lack of most of the statistics that could be directly incorporated into them. It is therefore practically impossible to construct balance sheets for the main sectors of the Indian economy and to obtain the national balance sheet as the combination of the sectoral balance sheets. The best that can be hoped for is an aggregate unsectored national balance sheet that provides figures, usually not more than very rough estimates, for the national totals of the main types of tangible assets, such as land, structures and equipment, and inventories, which constitute the real infrastructure, and for the main constituents of the financial superstructure, such as paper money, non-monetary claims against financial institutions, other short- and long-term credits, debt securities of the government and of corporations, and corporate stock.

In the present state of the relevant basic statistics, any national balance sheet for India before 1950 can at best claim to indicate orders of magnitude of the items shown, their relationships to each other and to national product, and their movements over the half century before World War I, the very rough nature of many of the estimates being indicated by the use of round numbers. Even a balance sheet that is qualified and limited to the four benchmark years 1860, 1875, 1895, and 1913[171] provides a picture of the development of India's financial superstructure in quantitative terms that is difficult to obtain by other means.

The main conclusions that can be drawn from the national balance sheet shown in table 1-28, making allowance for the probable margins of error in the estimates of the various components of financial and of tangible assets, are summarized below.[172]

The financial superstructure, measured by the size of all financial assets for which figures exist or for which at least rough estimates can be made, increased in current values in the half century before World War I from R. 3 bill. to R. 13 bill., that is, by about 330 percent, or by 2.8 percent per year, whereas the rate of increase in constant prices was reduced to 120 percent, or 1.5 percent per year.

As the size of the financial superstructure increased somewhat more rapidly than national product for the period as a whole—namely, by 2.8 percent a year against 2.3 percent—the ratio of financial assets to national product rose from 0.49 to 0.63 after having dipped to 0.44 and 0.51 in 1875 and 1895, respectively, reflecting the relatively slow growth of the financial superstructure in the last three decades of the nineteenth century. By this test, therefore, the relative expansion of the financial superstructure began only in the late 1890s.

Considerable changes occurred during the period from 1860 to 1913 in the structure of the financial superstructure as well as in that of the real infrastructure of national wealth.

In the financial superstructure the main changes concern the growth of financial assets in which a Western-type financial institution is the debtor or the creditor and those in which neither party belongs to this group. Although the assets of modern financial institutions (including paper money) increased from only R. 120 mill. in 1860 to about R. 2 bill. in 1913, or on the average by about 5½ percent per year, the volume of other financial assets, which can be estimated only very roughly, expanded only from about R. 3 bill. in 1860 to R. 11 bill., or slightly more than 2

170. The skepticism expressed in the late 1920s by Vakil and Muranjan (p. 529)—"Even an approximately correct estimate of the magnitudes of credit operations in India is not possible. The available statistics are too meagre and imperfect for the purpose"—is still justified. But the adage that half a loaf is better than no bread has seemed applicable here too.

171. The years 1875 and 1895 have been chosen because estimates for some items exist for these years, whereas they are not available for other years within the period.

172. The total for financial assets shown in table 1-28 is probably somewhat too low—disregarding errors of estimation in the enumerated components, which may overstate some of them—because it omits gold coins in circulation, corporate debentures, deposits with nonfinancial corporations, and securities of provincial, municipal, and other government authorities. All of these items, with the exception of gold coins, are, however, known to be small.

It is not unlikely that this debacle and its memories were a factor in limiting public demand for corporate shares for several decades, but no economic historian, Indian or foreign, seems to have addressed this problem.

e. Financing the Railways[157]

One of the few points on which Indian and British historians, as well as Karl Marx, seem to agree is the crucial importance of the Indian railway system to the country's economic development during the second half of the nineteenth century. Some historians have even gone so far as to declare, in effect, "No railways, no modern India."[158,159]

Railway construction started early in the 1850s, less than a generation later than in Europe and North America, and proceeded rapidly until near the end of the century, with a net average annual rate of expansion of 10 percent between 1860 and 1890. From 1890 until 1913 the pace slowed down considerably to an average annual rate of expansion of only 3.3 percent, resulting in a network of about 35,000 miles at the beginning of World War I. This development can be followed decade by decade in table 1-27. Although India at the end of this period probably possessed the most developed railway system in Asia and Africa, with the possible exception of Japan, the system had been expensive to build, it contained a substantial mileage constructed primarily for strategic reasons, and it suffered from lack of uniformity in operation and even in the gauge of the track.

During its first sixty years the railway system passed through three phases, which also differed in methods of financing. During the first phase, which lasted from the early 1850s to 1868, all lines were built and operated by about a dozen private companies incorporated and financed in Great Britain, with the government of India furnishing the required land free of charge, guaranteeing the companies a 5 percent return on their capital, receiving one-half of surplus profits, and retaining the right to take over the companies at the end of twenty-five years. Although this method kept the cost of financing well below the level of most other less developed countries, it did not encourage economy in costs of construction and operations, entailed substantial payments by the government, that is, the Indian taxpayers (up to 1870 about R. 230

157. This section is based on the extensive literature on Indian railways, mostly by Indian authors, which usually pays relatively little attention to the financial aspects. Use has primarily been made of the following publications: H. Bell, *Railway Policy in India*, 1894; T. B. Desai, *Economic History of India Under the British 1757–1947*, 1968; V. Dubey, "Railways" in V. B. Singh, ed., *The Economic History of India, 1857–1956*, 1965; K. V. Iyer, *Indian Railways*, 1929; L. Jenks, *The Migration of British Capital to 1875*, 1927; W. J. Macpherson, "Investment in Indian Railways, 1845–1875," *Economic History Review*, 8, no. 2 (1955–56), and "Economic Development of India Under the British Crown, 1858–1947" in A. J. Youngson, ed., *Economic Development in the Long Run*, 1972; A. Prasad, *Indian Railways*, 1960; V. V. Ramanadham, *Indian Railway Finance*, 1956; J. N. Sahni, *Indian Railways: One Hundred Years, 1853 to 1953*, 1953; N. Sanyal, *Development of Indian Railways*, 1930; R. D. Tiwari, *Railways in Modern India*, 1941; D. E. Wacha, *Indian Railway Finance*, 1912.

158. This consensus, of course, is no guarantee against the appearance of an Indian Fogel, who will deny the crucial role of the railways in the economic development of India and will contend that the same effects could have been obtained by the expansion of river and canal transportation.

159. Many Indian authors have been very critical of the railway policies followed by the British government in India, particularly the use of private guaranteed companies. Thus Tiwari, writing around 1940, noticed the "lack of active economic and energetic management" and charged that "local needs of trade and commerce were sacrificed to strategic considerations" and that the guarantees "placed a heavy burden upon the Indian taxpayer" (1941, pp. 53–56). In the same vein Prasad asserted that "early history of railway development in India is a record of miscalculation, vacillation and lack of planning. The interests of the foreign capitalist and political and defense considerations dominated railway policy" (p. 402). What these authors forget is the fact that except for the guarantees, including the moral guarantee of the British government for the debt of the government of India, and for the trustee status of these securities in Great Britain, India by 1913—or for that matter by 1947—would either have had a much smaller and technically poorer railway system or that the cost of financing the system would have been much higher. Consideration of the extent and cost of providing countries like Turkey, Persia, Egypt, and China, or even most of the Latin American republics, with a railway system will suffice as evidence. They also forget the low rate of profits made by Indian railroads, equal for the period from 1853 to 1913 to an average of 3 percent (Krishnaswami, five pages after table 8).

TABLE 1-27. Railway Development and Finance, 1860–1913

Date[a]	Miles of lines open (1)	Capital outlay (R. bill.)		Capital outlay: gross national product (percent)[c] (4)
		Period (2)	Cumulated[b] (3)	
1860	838	0.27	0.27	
1870	4771	0.63	0.90	0.34
1880	8996	0.39	1.29	0.67
1890	16404	0.85	2.14	0.37
1900	24752	1.16	3.30	0.71
1910	32099	1.09	4.39	0.68
1913	34656	0.56	4.95	0.93

[a]End of calendar year except for 1913 figures, which refer to March 31, 1914.   [b]Cumulated from 1853 on.   [c]Period ending with year indicated, starting with 1853.

SOURCES: **Col. 1:** Sahni, pp. 187–88.   **Cols. 2 and 3:** Krishnaswami, table 6.

mill., or more than one-half of the companies' total gross earnings and slightly more than their net earnings during the period), and proved to be time consuming and complicated.

This system did not produce financial instruments held or traded in India (Indian investors contributed only 1 or 2 percent of the funds raised by the railways).[160] Because about two-fifths of the funds raised were spent in England on rails and rolling stock and most of the rest on wages and coal in India, direct stimulation to Indian industry was very limited. As a result of the low profits, the roads' retained earnings were very small, and virtually all capital expenditures were defrayed out of the proceeds of stocks and debentures sold in England,[161,162] which at times constituted an important outlet for British savings.[163]

The guarantee system was abandoned in the late 1860s, and during the second phase, from 1869 to 1882, the railway network was expanded by lines constructed and operated by the government, particularly strategic and unprofitable lines in northwest India, and was financed primarily by the issuance of government securities in London as well as in India. As a result, state lines accounted for nearly two-thirds of capital expenditures from 1869 to 1881 and for about one-fourth of total expenditures since 1853, retained earnings making only a secondary contribution.[164]

In the third phase, from 1882 to the mid-1920s, private British companies were again used to construct and finance part of the Indian railway system, although construction by the government continued on a substantial scale.[165] This time, however, the guarantee was limited to 3½ percent; the government was entitled to three-fourths of the profits beyond that level; and, as

160. Sanyal (p. 45): up to 1869 "less than one percent was subscribed in India, i.e., less than R. 10 million." Macpherson (p. 165) puts the participation of Indian investors in the offerings of Indian railway shares at 1 percent.

161. Among the British purchasers of the stocks, "the middle classes predominated," whereas the railways' debentures, which acquired trustee status in 1882, were largely purchased by financial institutions, particularly British banks and insurance companies (Macpherson, p. 181).

162. In 1868 there were nearly 50,000 British holders of Indian railway shares or debentures with average holdings of about £1,500 for a total of about R. 750 mill. (Jenks, p. 220).

163. In 1905 and 1914 the capital of foreign (mostly British) registered companies operating entirely in India, chiefly railroads, was slightly larger than that of companies registered in India (Buchanan, p. 154).

164. Government payments under the guarantees continued to the end of the century, when the government's share in surplus earnings began to exceed guarantee payments, from 1901 through 1913 to the extent of nearly R. 250 mill., still leaving a net subsidy payment of about R. 500 mill. for the entire period from the mid-1850s to 1913 (Sanyal, p. 377).

165. From 1870 to 1891 the government of India spent about R. 700 mill. on state railways, of which six-sevenths came from borrowing at rates between 3 and 4 percent (Bell, p. 25).

under the old guarantee, the government was entitled to take over the companie[s] five years.[166]

Because of the virtual cessation of railroad expansion during World War I, t[h] 1922, when the network's total mileage was only 10 percent greater than it had b[een] earlier, may be taken as representative of that of 1913. At that time the governn[ent] owned nearly three-fourths of the total mileage, operating about one-fourth directly through the companies that had originally constructed the lines. Indian native st[ate] operated, and financed about one-eighth of the system. Although private companies operated the remaining 15 percent of the system, two-fifths thereof consisted of br[oad] many of which received government subsidies, and the companies depended on g[overnment] subsidy or guarantee for practically all other lines. The dominant role of the central g[overnment] is equally evident in its share in investment of fully three-fourths of the total of R. 6[?] During this phase, and particularly after the turn of the century, retained earnings finance a substantial proportion of capital expenditures.[168]

Capital expenditures on railways, including imported material as well as outlays[?] constituted a substantial proportion of total capital expenditures in India throughout m[ost of the] period from 1860 to 1913 and were far from negligible in comparison to national[?] Expenditures rose, as table 1-27 indicates, from an annual average of about R. 60 mil[l.] 1860s to R. 85 mill. in 1880 and to about R. 120 mill. in the period from 1891 to 1913[,] short decline to only R. 40 mill. in the 1870s. For the four last decades of the nineteenth [century] the railroads' gross capital expenditures of about R. 3.3 bill. accounted for about one-sixt[h of] national total of gross fixed investment, using the very rough estimate of the latter shown i[n table] 1-9 (p. 19). From 1901 through 1913 the railroads' capital expenditures of about R. 1.[?] represented one-ninth of total gross capital formation. For the period as a whole, total [capital] outlays of the railroads, of which only a fraction was spent in India, were equal to about t[hree] fourths of 1 percent of gross national product, fluctuating on a decadal basis between 0.4 pe[rcent] in the 1880s and 0.9 percent in the 1890s. The absolute and relative volume of domestic f[unds] absorbed by the railways was, however, considerably lower than these figures indicate, bec[ause] practically all the railway capital outlays of private companies and part of those of the gove[rn] ment were financed in London.[169]

7. THE NATIONAL BALANCE SHEET OF INDIA, 1860–1913

A national balance sheet, that is, the combination, or the summation, of the balance sheets of al[l] economic units, such as business enterprises, governmental organizations, and households[,] within the national territory, provides an overview at benchmark dates of the size and structure of a country's financial superstructure and of its relation to the infrastructure of national wealth, as well as of changes over time in these relationships. Because actual balance sheets are usually

166. Iyer, p. 33.

167. In 1902 government-owned lines accounted for four-fifths of total railway capital of R. 3.5 bill.; the remaining few guaranteed lines for less than one-tenth; and native state lines for 5 percent (Sanyal, p. 198).

168. The available statistics unfortunately do not permit a more specific statement, let alone the compiling of even a rudimentary sources- and uses-of-funds statement for the railway sector.

169. As well over one-half of central governments' total investment was accounted for by the railroads in the period from 1898 to 1913 (table 1-11), one might regard at least R. 250 mill. of the total increase in the domestic public debt as attributable to the railroads. This would be equal, for the period from 1901 to 1913, to less than 0.5 percent of gross national product but to about 3 percent of total national net saving if we accept the estimate of table 1-10. It would also be equal to about 15 percent of the period's capital outlay on railroads. The data available for the last four decades of the nineteenth century are too scanty to permit even a rough estimation for that period of the proportion of domestic saving absorbed directly or indirectly by the railroads.

TABLE 1-28. National Balance Sheet, 1860–1913 (R. Bill.)

	1860 (1)	1875 (2)	1895 (3)	1913 (4)	Rate of increase 1861–1913 (percent) (5)
I. Tangible assets	20.15	34.40	51.14	86.45	2.8
1. Land	5.00	10.00	18.00	40.00	4.0
2. Structures and equipment	6.70	12.50	17.50	24.25	2.5
3. Inventories	1.35	2.10	2.30	3.40	1.8
4. Livestock	1.10	1.80	3.34	6.80	3.5
5. Gold and silver[a]	6.00	8.00	10.00	12.00	1.3
II. Financial assets	3.02	4.49	6.46	13.04	2.8
1. Money (notes)	0.04[b]	0.10	0.21	0.51	4.9
2. Claims against financial institutions	0.08	0.20	0.43	1.50	5.7
3. Agricultural debt	1.25	1.75	2.50	5.00	2.7
4. Nonfarm household debt	0.25	0.35	0.50	1.00	2.7
5. Bank debt	0.04	0.09	0.22	0.68	5.5
6. Trade credit	0.70	1.15	1.15	1.70	1.7
7. Government securities[c]	0.60	0.70	1.10	1.70	2.0
8. Corporate stock	0.06	0.15	0.35	0.95	5.3
III. Net foreign assets	−0.50	−2.00	−3.50	−7.00	5.1
IV. National wealth (I + III)	19.65	32.40	47.64	79.45	2.7
V. National assets (I + II)	23.17	38.89	57.60	99.49	2.8

[a]Including gold and silver coins.   [b]1862.   [c]Rupee issues only.

SOURCES: Line I-1: Based on the estimates shown in table 1-24. No separate allowance is made for the value of non-agricultural land, as information is lacking and it is certain to be small compared to that of agricultural land. Lines I, 2–5: 1913, *BR*. Line I, 2: 1860–95, figure for 1900 (*BR*), extrapolated on assumption that ratio of structures and equipment to gross national product (1.49 in 1900) declined by 0.01 per year. Line I-3: 1860–95, figure for 1900 (*BR*), extrapolated on assumption that ratio of inventories to gross national product (18 percent in 1900) increased by 0.1 percent per year. Line I-4: 1875, 1895, estimate by Atkinson, p. 271; 1860, assumed to bear same ratio to gross national product as in 1875. Line I-5: Refers to stock of metal in coins as well as that hoarded in form of bullion or ornaments. Estimates are derived from data on quantities (Prakash, p. 275) and prices (Prakash, p. 291; *BMS*, pp. 960 ff.). The quantity data given for Indian Union are shifted to undivided India by adding 17 percent (Prakash, p. 278). Figures are rounded to nearest R. bill. Line II-1: *BMS*, pp. 651–55. Figure in col. 1 refers to 1862. Up to 1875 to notes issued; for 1895 and 1913 to notes in circulation. Line II-2: Deposits of banks and cooperatives (*BMS*, p. 7), plus total assets of insurance companies. Line II-3: Based on estimates discussed in section 6b. Line II-4: Estimated at one-fifth of line II-3. Line II-5: Estimated at one-half of bank assets (cf. table 1-13). Line II-6: Estimated at one-half of inventories (line I-4). Line II-7: *BMS*, pp. 880–81. Figures refer to April 30 or March 31 (beginning with 1895) of the year following. Line II-8: Paid-up capital of corporations (*BMS*, p. 781) plus 25 percent for reserves to approximate book value of stock. Line III: Rough estimates based on figures discussed in section 3.

½ percent per year, the rate of increase being about the same for the most important single component, agricultural debt to moneylenders, as for the sum of all other financial assets in this group. As a result, the share of financial assets (including paper money) in which a Western-type financial institution was either the debtor or the creditor in total financial assets rose from one-eighth in 1875 to one-third in 1913. This involved a rise in the ratio of the assets of modern financial institutions to national product from about 3 percent in 1875 to nearly 9 percent in 1913, and to an advance compared to national wealth from less than 1 percent to 2½ percent. The sharp increase in the absolute and the relative size of modern financial institutions represents the most important change in the financial superstructure of India in the period from 1860 to 1913.

Rural debt to moneylenders, partly on mortgage and partly on personal security, remained by far the largest type of financial asset, precarious as the estimates of the size of this item may be. Notwithstanding the rapid expansion of Western-type financial institutions, the share of rural

TABLE 1-29. National Wealth and Assets in Relation to Gross National Product, 1860–1913

	1860	1875	1895	1913
I. Tangible assets	3.17	3.43	4.05	4.04
1. Land	0.79	1.00	1.42	1.87
2. Structures and equipment	1.06	1.25	1.38	1.13
3. Inventories	0.22	0.21	0.18	0.16
4. Livestock	0.17	0.18	0.26	0.32
5. Gold and silver[a]	0.94	0.80	0.79	0.56
II. Financial assets	0.48	0.45	0.51	0.66
1. Money (notes)	0.01	0.01	0.02	0.02
2. Claims against financial institutions	0.01	0.02	0.04	0.07
3. Agricultural debt	0.20	0.17	0.20	0.23
4. Nonfarm household debt	0.04	0.03	0.04	0.05
5. Bank debt	0.01	0.01	0.02	0.03
6. Trade credit	0.11	0.11	0.09	0.08
7. Government securities[b]	0.10	0.07	0.09	0.08
8. Corporate stock	0.01	0.02	0.03	0.05
III. Net foreign assets	−0.08	−0.20	−0.28	−0.33
IV. National wealth	3.09	3.23	3.77	3.71
V. National assets	3.65	3.87	4.56	4.64

[a]Including gold and silver coins.   [b]Rupee issues only.

SOURCES: Tables 1-3 and 1-28.

debt in all financial instruments remained in the neighborhood of two-fifths. However, the ratio of rural debt to the value of agricultural land declined, if the rough estimates can be trusted, from about one-fourth in 1860 to one-eighth in 1913.

Government internal (rupee) securities held by Indian investors lost somewhat in importance. Their share in all financial assets declined from about one-fifth in 1860 to one-eighth in 1913. Their relation to national product, however, declined less, from 10 to 8 percent. The role of corporate securities in the financial superstructure remained secondary until at least the turn of the century. Issues of corporate debentures were quite small. Corporate stocks increased their share in total financial assets from 2 percent in 1860 to 3½ percent in 1875, to 5½ percent in

TABLE 1-30. Share of Western-type Financial Institutions in
All Financial Assets, 1875–1913 (Percent)[a]

	1875	1895	1913
Treasury paper currency	2.6	4.7	5.1
Presidency banks	3.3	3.3	3.8
Exchange banks[b]	0.3	1.6	2.4
Commercial banks	0.1	1.0	2.2
Savings banks	0.4	1.5	1.8
Insurance companies	—	0.3	0.5
Pension funds[c]	—	0.2	0.5
Total	6.7	12.6	16.3

[a]Excludes indigenous bankers and moneylenders and some small financial institutions.   [b]Indian deposits only.   [c]Claims against Treasury of state provident funds.

SOURCES OF BASIC DATA: Tables 1-13 and 1-28.

TABLE 1-31. Structure of National Wealth and Assets, 1860–1913 (Percent)

	1860	1875	1895	1913
I. Tangible assets	87.0	88.5	88.8	86.9
1. Land	21.6	25.7	31.3	40.2
2. Structures and equipment	28.9	32.1	30.4	24.4
3. Inventories	5.8	5.4	4.0	3.4
4. Livestock	4.7	4.6	5.8	6.8
5. Gold and silver	25.9	20.6	17.4	12.1
II. Financial assets	13.0	11.5	11.2	13.1
1. Money (notes)	0.2	0.3	0.4	0.5
2. Claims against financial institutions	0.4	0.5	0.7	1.5
3. Agricultural debt	5.3	4.5	4.3	5.0
4. Nonfarm household debt	1.1	0.9	0.9	1.0
5. Bank debt	0.2	0.2	0.4	0.7
6. Trade credit	3.0	3.0	2.0	1.7
7. Government securities[a]	2.6	1.8	1.9	1.7
8. Corporate stock	0.3	0.4	0.6	1.0
III. Net foreign assets	−2.2	−5.1	−6.1	−7.0
IV. National wealth	84.8	83.4	82.7	79.9
V. National assets	100.0	100.0	100.0	100.0

[a]Rupee issues only.

SOURCE: Table 1-28.

1895, and to more than 7 percent in 1913, measured by the paid-in capital and roughly estimated reserves of corporations, low ratios in international comparison.

Probably the most important trend, from the point of view of financial analysis, is the sharp and fairly regular increase, although on a very low level, in the share in total financial assets of Western-type financial institutions, thus excluding native quasi bankers and moneylenders. Their share rose from less than 5 percent in 1860 and 7 percent in 1875 to 10 percent in 1895 and to more than 15 percent in 1913. This movement reflected to a substantial extent the expansion of the stock of money (paper currency and demand deposits), particularly in the first part of the period.

The changes in the structure of national wealth reflect primarily the fact that the price of land, which had been very low before the British occupation because of the narrowness of the market, rose considerably more rapidly in the period from 1860 to 1913, namely, by more than 4 percent a year, than the general price level, which advanced at an average rate of only 1½ percent per year. As a result, the share of land in the current value of all tangible assets rose sharply from one-fourth in 1860 to nearly one-half in 1913, a movement contrary to that observed in developed countries, for example, the United States, where the share of the current value of land in national wealth has generally shown a declining tendency over the nineteenth and twentieth centuries.[173] Partly for the same reason, the share of structures and equipment appears to have declined from 33 to 28 percent. The share of livestock rose from 5½ to 8 percent, whereas that of inventories showed a downward trend, a result partly of the method of estimation used. Because of the very rough methods used in estimating these items not too much importance should be attached to minor movements. Although the size of gold and silver hoards by their very nature is subject to a large error of estimation, though probably not larger than that

173. Cf. for the United States, Goldsmith (1952, p. 310), which indicates a decline in the share of land in national wealth from more than one-half in 1805 to 15 to 20 percent in 1950, depending on the scope of the definition of national wealth used.

TABLE 1-32. Capital-Output Ratios, 1860–1913[a]

	Broad (1)	Intermediate (2)	Narrow (3)
1860	3.28	2.47	1.49
1875	3.37	2.39	1.61
1895	4.20	2.72	1.90
1913	4.16	2.23	1.66

[a]Numerator is total tangible assets (table 1-28, line 1) for col. 1; reproducible assets including gold and silver (lines 2 through 5) for col. 2; and reproducible assets excluding gold and silver (lines 2 through 4) for col. 3. Denominator for all three columns is gross national product (table 1-3, col. 1).

SOURCES: Tables 1-3 and 1-28.

affecting some other items, there is little doubt that their high share in total national wealth and their decline from three-tenths in 1860 to one-seventh in 1913 is not a statistical artifact but a characteristic of the Indian economy well into the twentieth century.[174]

The figures also permit the calculation of various versions of the capital-output ratio, which are shown in table 1-32. The narrow version, limited to structures, equipment, and inventories, rises from 1.5 to 1.7, an indication that the Indian economy became slightly more capitalized during this half century, if the estimates can be trusted.

Probably more informative are the level and the movements of the financial interrelations ratio and the ratio of financial to tangible assets, which can be followed in table 1-33.

It is worthwhile to factor the financial interrelations ratio (FIR) into its main components, even if this can be done only roughly. The formula used is[175]

$$FIR = \tau \left[(\delta + \phi)\, \alpha\beta^{-1}\, (1 + v) \right] + \frac{F_{t-n}}{W_t} (1 + v')$$

where δ and ϕ are the net period's issue ratios of domestic nonfinancial issues; α is the new issue multiplier (i.e., the inverse of the rate of growth of gross national product in current prices); β is the capital-output ratio at the end of the period; v is an adjustment factor reflecting valuation gains on equity securities; τ is the truncation ratio (ratio of sum of geometric series for n years to infinite series increasing at same rate); F_{t-n} is the value of financial assets at the beginning of the period; and W_t is the value of tangible assets at the end of the period. Neglecting v and v', which must have been very small for the period studied, and deriving the issue ratios of financial instruments as well as the capital-output ratio from the national balance sheet, we obtain

$$FIR = 0.51\, [\, 0.017 \times 54 \times 0.24] + 0.051 = 0.163$$

treating gold and silver hoards as tangible, rather than financial, assets. This is reasonably close to the ratio of 0.151 derived directly from the national balance sheet for 1913, given the

174. Cf. the estimates of Prakash, pp. 272 ff. Keynes wrote in 1913 that "during the past sixty years India is supposed to have absorbed . . . more than £300,000,000 of gold (apart from enormous quantities of silver)" and felt that "India, as we all know, already wastes far too high a proportion of her resources in the needless accumulation of precious metals" (pp. 69–70). This may be a man's view. To Indian women, their gold and silver ornaments have always been of particular importance, constituting virtually the only property of their own. Net gold and silver imports from 1861 to 1913, totaling over R. 8 bill., were equal to a little more than 1 percent of India's gross national product in the period. This may look like a rather small figure, but it is very substantial when compared to net investment during the same period, as it may well have amounted to one-third of the latter.

175. Cf. Goldsmith, 1969. chap. 2 and p. xxxii.

TABLE 1-33. Financial Interrelations Ratios, 1860–1913

Numerator Denominator	Financial assets including gold and silver Tangible assets excluding gold and silver	Financial assets excluding gold and silver Tangible assets including gold and silver
1860	0.637	0.150
1875	0.473	0.131
1895	0.400	0.126
1913	0.336	0.151

SOURCE: Table 1-28, lines I, I-5, and II.

numerous simplifying assumptions involved in the formula. The factoring shows that the very low value of the financial interrelations ratio in 1913, low in international comparison as well as with later Indian values, is due primarily to the very low value of the new issue ratio of financial instruments of 0.017. The multiplier (54), on the other hand, is high, reflecting a low rate of growth of national product in current prices. The output-capital ratio of 0.24, finally, is of a commonly found order.

The financial interrelation ratio, derived from the usual definition of financial assets, that is, line II of table 1-28, fails to show a trend, standing at 0.15 at the beginning as well as at the end of the period. Under Indian conditions, it is possible, however, to argue for inclusion of the gold and silver hoards with the financial rather than the tangible assets, as they fulfill at least one of the functions of such assets, namely, the provision of liquidity. If gold and silver hoards are included in financial assets, the levels of the ratio of financial assets to gross national product are sharply raised, namely, to 0.64 in 1869, 0.47 in 1875, 0.40 in 1895, and 0.34 in 1913. They then show a continuous and substantial decline rather than an increase over the period as a whole.

The more significant stock dimension ratio of financial assets to tangible assets, that is, the conventional financial interrelations ratio, followed a similar path, standing close to 15 percent at the beginning as well as at the end of the period, after a substantial decline in the 1870s and 1880s (col. 2 of table 1-33). If, however, gold and silver are included in financial assets, the ratio, moving at a considerably higher level, declines sharply and continuously from 64 to 34 percent (col. 1 of table 1-33), the decline reflecting the decreasing importance of precious metal hoards in the national balance sheet.

Table 1-34 summarizes the national balance sheet estimates through ten ratios, the substance of which has already been discussed.

TABLE 1-34. National Balance Sheet Ratios, 1860–1913

Numerator	Denominator	1860	1875	1895	1913
Financial assets	Tangible assets	0.15	0.13	0.13	0.15
Claims	Financial assets	0.98	0.96	0.95	0.93
Claims against \	Financial assets	0.04	0.07	0.10	0.15
financial institutions[a] /	Gross national product	0.02	0.03	0.05	0.10
Corporate stock	Financial assets	0.02	0.03	0.05	0.07
Land	Tangible assets	0.25	0.29	0.35	0.46
Tangible assets	Gross national product	3.28	3.37	4.20	4.16
Reproducible assets[b]	Gross national product	2.47	2.39	2.72	2.24
Financial assets	Gross national product	0.49	0.44	0.51	0.63
Net foreign assets	Tangible assets	−0.02	−0.06	−0.07	−0.08

[a]Including bank notes.   [b]Including gold and silver hoards; excluding them, the ratios are, starting with 1860: 1.49, 1.61, 1.90, 1.66.

SOURCES: Tables 1-3 and 1-28.

2   India between the Wars, 1914–1946

Four major developments characterize the history of India in the three decades between the beginning of World War I in 1914 and the partition of the subcontinent and creation of the Indian Union in 1947. (Although actually covering a time span from the start of World War I to a few years after World War II, this period will be referred to as the interwar period.)

First, external events, over which neither the British government of India nor the Indian people themselves had control, namely, the two world wars of 1914–18 and 1939–45 and the Great Depression of 1930–33—events whose aftermath crucially influenced developments throughout most of the 1920s, 1930s, and 1940s—dominated both the economic and the political development of India.

Second, a slow but fairly steady Indianization of both the economic and political structure of the country was occurring, in large part as a consequence of the wars. More and more Indians rather than Britishers were occupying the country's "commanding heights," and policy was being determined increasingly by elected Indian representatives than by the British Parliament.

Third, the very slow rate of economic growth that characterized the preceding half century continued.

And fourth, the country's financial superstructure expanded rapidly, in both absolute and relative terms, without basic changes in its institutional makeup except for the addition of a central bank in the mid–1930s.

The thirty-three-year span (1914–47) is divided into subperiods when necessary; a periodization based on political or economic events is little different from one based on financial events, as used here. There is little doubt that the two world wars and their immediate aftermath, that is, the years 1914–20 and 1940–46, constitute two such subperiods, financially characterized by rapid, imported inflation. The use of the start of the Great Depression as the divider within the remaining years from 1921 through 1939 appears to be equally evident, the first subperiod being dominated by readjustments to the changes in the national and international situation brought about by World War I, and the second by the Great Depression and its consequences. This yields four subperiods of between seven and ten years each: 1914–20, 1921–29; 1930–39; and 1940–46.

1. THE INFRASTRUCTURE

a. Population

Between 1913 and 1947 the population of Undivided India increased from 305 million to 415 million, or by 36 percent, equal to an average annual growth rate of 0.9 percent. The rate of growth thus was more than double the average of the preceding four decades (table 1-1). The acceleration was due primarily to a beginning of the secular decline in death rates, from 4.3

percent in 1901–11 to 3.1 percent in 1931–41, which was to have its explosive effect on the country's population in the following decades. The reported birth rates hardly declined at all. Population growth was extremely small between the censuses of 1911 and 1921, chiefly because of the increased mortality resulting from the Bengal famine and the influenza epidemic near the end of the decade. In the 1930s the population growth rate already averaged nearly 1½ percent, about three times the 1871–1911 average.

Urbanization began to accelerate, the proportion of the population living in towns rising from not much more than 10 percent in 1911 to 14 percent in 1941. The growth of the larger cities, that is, those with more than 100,000 inhabitants, was even more marked, their share in total population doubling from 2½ to more than 5 percent. This period thus experienced for the first time, as far back as the statistics go and probably as far back as the Mughal empire, a definite trend toward increasing urbanization.

A similar break in trend is evident in the movement of the literacy rate, which rose sharply from 7 percent of the population in 1911, a rate hardly higher than that reported two decades earlier, to 15 percent in 1941. This marked progress, particularly in the 1930s, though at a level far below that of Western countries or Japan, suggests some improvement in the quality of the labor force, at least of its urban component.

b. National Product

For the period as a whole, aggregate real national product continued its slow growth. The average rate of growth, however, is somewhat uncertain as one estimator (Sivasubramonian) puts it at 1.2 percent, another (Maddison) allows only 0.7 percent, and a third (Heston) returns to 1.1 percent—these are the only three series covering the entire period on an annual basis (table 1-2). The differences become crucial in the estimation of the more meaningful growth rate of real national product per head, which ranges between +0.3 and −0.2 percent a year. As in the preceding half century, if any increase occurred in real national product per head—the least unsatisfactory summary measure of economic welfare—it was very small, small enough not to be noticed by the average Indian who lived his adult life during these three decades.[1]

Decadal rates of growth (table 1-2) showed considerable variations in terms of the average real national income per head. They were negative—by 0.1 and 0.9, respectively, in the two series—for the 1911 to 1920 decade; quite high in the 1920s, reaching a rate of 1.7 percent a year in Sivasubramonian's estimate and 0.8 percent in Maddison's series; and slightly negative in the 1930s and 1940s. Decadal averages, however, mask the effect of business cycles. From that point of view, calculations should cover entire cycles, either from trough to trough or from peak to peak. Choosing the latter approach and omitting possible smaller recessions, the turning points would be located in the years 1913, 1920, 1933, and 1946. The average growth rates of real income per head for the three periods thus determined would be −0.01, 0.68, and 0.00 percent according to Sivasubramonian's estimates: −0.99, 0.31 and −0.36 percent following Maddison; and −0.70, 0.93, and −0.22 according to Heston. All three estimates thus agree that for three-fifths of the period, namely, 1914–20 and 1934–46, the average growth of real national product was zero or negative, and that although it was positive during the 1920s, the average net rate of growth for the trough-to-trough cycle 1920–33 was small—0.9 percent according to Heston, 0.7 percent following Sivasubramonian, and only 0.3 percent according to Maddison. Financial development thus took place against the background of a slow and irregular economic growth, with total real aggregate national product per head declining in nearly every second year of the 1914–46 period.

1. Three other estimates also yield low growth rates of real national income per head. Mukherjee (*NII*, p.61) puts the increase between 1911/19 and 1941/49 at below 0.6 percent per year, whereas Arora and Iyengar and K. Mukherji obtain annual average rates of growth between 1906/14 and 1941/49 of 0.1 percent. (Mukherji, p. 59, using col. 9 of his table 2.4, which combines the two sets of estimates and is apparently regarded as the best way of reflecting them.)

It has been estimated that between 1900 and 1946 the combined factor input in the Indian economy increased at a rate of only 0.5 percent a year, the rate being close to 0.4 percent both for labor and for capital, although population grew at a rate of 1.0 percent. The increase in output per unit of input was 0.7 percent a year, a not insignificant, although in international comparison modest, rate of economic progress. All the improvement occurred in the nonagricultural sector, where output per unit of input rose at the rate of 1.2 percent a year, whereas the increase was essentially zero in agriculture.[2]

Notwithstanding slow overall growth, a number of changes occurred during the three decades of the interwar period in the rate of growth and in the share in total national product of the main sectors.[3] The most important structural change was the decline in the share of the primary sector, that is, essentially agriculture, measured by each sector's contribution to the national product in constant prices, from around three-fifths in 1913 to either about 55 percent (Heston and Maddison) or even to 45 percent (Sivasubramonian) by the end of the period. This decline reflected the fact that the real income of the primary sector increased between 1910/14 and 1942/46 only by 0.4 percent per year compared to rates of growth of about 2 percent for the secondary and tertiary sectors. Because the share of agriculture in the total working force remained at close to 70 percent throughout the period,[4] one would deduce from these figures, if they could be trusted, a more rapid increase in productivity (i.e., product per member of the working force) in the nonagricultural sectors of the economy than in agriculture. In absolute terms the increase in agricultural output by only 7 percent between 1913/15 and 1944/46, or by 0.2 percent a year, failed by a substantial margin to keep up with the population growth of nearly 1 percent, and annual fluctuations, depending mainly on the monsoon, continued to be large. Thus the output index fell by more than 10 percent below the 1913–15 level in seven years (1918, the year of the Bengal famine; 1920; 1923–27), notwithstanding the increase in population. The situation was even less satisfactory for food grains, the output of which increased at an annual rate of less than 0.2 percent. Although the output of other crops expanded at an average of 0.6 percent a year, it too failed to match the increase of population.[5]

The share of secondary industries in real gross national product, which includes most of the modern sector of the economy, increased only by 2 to 3 percentage points over its starting value of 12 or 14 percent in 1913. It was thus still very low—about one-seventh to one-sixth of total national product—at independence. The core of that sector, manufacturing, however, increased its share in national product sharply from close to 4 percent at the beginning of the period to 6 percent near its midpoint (1929) and to more than 7 percent at its end, as a result of the increase in the manufacturing industries' real net output at an average annual rate of 3.8 percent.[6] The influence of the two world wars is evident in the shares of manufacturing of more than 8 percent in 1920 and of 15 percent in 1943, reflecting the opportunities provided to Indian industry by the unavailability of many imported goods and the military demand for others as well as indicating the impossibility of maintaining these peak levels under normal conditions. The average rate of increase over the period as a whole of nearly 4 percent, and thus almost 3 percent per head of the population, as well as the near doubling of the share of manufacturing in national product and the tripling of its share in the labor force, from 0.8 percent in 1911 to about 2.3 percent in 1946, constitute significant progress in the process of industrialization, even at this as yet low level.

2. Mukherjee, 1973, p. 138.

3. The three sets of estimates available differ substantially, although the trends are similar.

4. Cf. J. B. Sinha's estimate of 68 percent in 1911 and 70 percent in 1941 (pp. 112–13) and that of D. and A. Thorner (1960) of about 72 percent in 1911 as well as thirty years later.

5. Figures in this paragraph are based on Blyn's modified annual series for British India (p. 349). Use of his all-India index (p. 251) yields an average annual growth rate for all crops of 0.25 percent and one of zero for food grains, and hence shows an even more unsatisfactory picture.

6. Sivasubramonian, p. 226.

TABLE 2-1. Annual Data on Income, Production, Prices, and Bank Rate, 1913–1946

	Gross national product (R. bill.) (1)	Real income per head[a] (2)	Agricultural production[a] (3)	Industrial production[a] (4)	National income deflator[a] (5)	Wholesale prices[a] (6)	Cost of living[a] (7)	Bank rate (percent) (8)
1913	20.76	100	100	100	100	100	100	5.95
1914	22.08	103	110	103	103	103	100	5.45
1915	22.31	104	113	111	103	115	106	5.69
1916	23.54	108	118	109	104	132	103	6.78
1917	24.56	107	117	106	110	149	104	6.03
1918	28.70	95	84	101	146	181	120	5.54
1919	36.53	105	116	107	166	202	166	5.62
1920	34.72	100	90	115	167	209	171	6.06
1921	35.76	104	109	118	163	185	168	6.20
1922	34.63	109	112	117	150	181	157	6.00
1923	32.63	107	105	99	142	177	143	6.22
1924	36.43	112	106	129	150	178	141	6.25
1925	35.74	111	106	133	147	164	148	5.50
1926	35.54	112	106	151	143	153	151	4.50
1927	35.05	112	103	171	140	153	146	5.67
1928	35.02	112	110	136	139	149	143	6.00
1929	34.00	116	112	170	129	145	138	6.50
1930	27.21	113	114	154	104	120	113	5.67
1931	24.08	111	110	162	93	99	99	7.00
1932	23.14	110	112	175	89	94	93	5.50
1933	21.92	109	118	166	84	90	87	3.56
1934	22.81	109	111	188	86	92	89	3.50
1935	22.99	108	110	203	87	94	90	3.46
1936	23.83	110	119	237	87	94	92	3.00
1937	24.66	109	117	268	89	105	93	3.00
1938	24.89	108	104	276	90	98	91	3.00
1939	27.35	110	115	280	96	111	96	3.00
1940	29.38	110	116	337	101	124	98	3.50
1941	35.55	109	111	337	121	137	111	3.50
1942	50.31	110	116	409	168	170	151	3.50
1943	69.40	109	126	401	232	229	266	3.50
1944	71.97	114	118	433	228	253	260	3.50
1945	72.08	116	114	432	222	256	261	3.50
1946	72.50	109	115	342	234	280	281	3.50

[a]1913 = 100.

SOURCES: **Col. 1:** Sivasubramonian (p. 337), raised by 10 percent to shift from net to gross national product.   **Col. 2:** Ibid., p. 338.   **Col. 3:** Blyn, p. 349.   **Col. 4:** Sivasubramonian, p. 226; net output of manufacturing industries.   **Cols. 5–7:** Ibid., pp. 336, 339.   **Col. 8:** *BSM*, p. 690; average rate of Bank of Bengal 1913–19, Imperial Bank 1920–46.

The share of the mixed tertiary sector in real national product rose, but to an entirely different degree in the two estimates: by only 2 percentage points, or only 5 percent of its 1913 value, according to Maddison, but by nearly 11 percentage points, or no less than 40 percent of its 1913 level, according to Sivasubramonian, the sharp increase being due mainly to an increase in government services which expanded, in constant prices by 240 percent, or nearly 4 percent per year between 1910/14 and 1942/46.[7]

The diversity in natural resources, the capabilities of the population, the accumulated

7. Sivasubramonian, p. 350.

TABLE 2-2. Regional Distribution of Income and Public Expenditures, 1938–1939

Area	National income (R. bill.)	Population (mill.)	Income per head (R.)	Public expenditure (R. mill.)
Madras	24.9	21.8	113	22.9
Bombay	15.9	9.3	168	18.2
Central Provinces	9.4	7.5	124	6.7
United Provinces	21.5	24.6	86	18.2
Bihar	9.9	16.2	60	7.0
Orissa	3.8	3.9	95	2.6
Assam	4.2	4.6	91	4.2
East Punjab	4.5	4.3	103	8.3
West Bengal	5.9	7.8	73	11.9
Indian Union territory				
Percent	100.0	100.0	100	100.0
Amount	14.82[a]	219.4	68	70.4

[a]This is low compared with R. 24.9 bill. for the gross national product of Undivided India shown in table 2-1.

SOURCE: Natarajan, pp. 15, 47.

capital, and the economic structure of the large regions that constitute the Indian subcontinent are reflected in wide differences in income per head, near the end of the interwar period (table 2-2). The differences in income per head range from an estimated 40 percent below the national average (Bihar) to nearly 70 percent above the average (Bombay). The absence of comparable estimates for earlier years (except one for 1922)[8] prevents a determination of whether regional differences in per head income increased or narrowed during the interwar period. Fragmentary information suggests, however, that the differentials reflect basic differences in the natural endowment of the regions and in the characteristics of their population, along with accidents in their history.

Turning to national product in current prices, the picture is one of a rapid increase, reflecting mainly the sharp rises in the price level during both world wars. Between 1914 and 1946 national product rose by 250 percent, or, at an average annual rate of 3.9 percent. The annual data show that the increases occurred primarily during the two world wars. National product in current prices rose by more than 75 percent between 1913 and 1919 and by 145 percent between 1940 and 1944. These sharp increases, at annual rates of 10 and 25 percent, respectively, accounted for more than the total increase of current national product between 1913 and 1946. These increases, as well as periods of shorter and less pronounced rises, were partly offset by the decline in the current value of national product by 35 percent, or on the average by 10 percent a year, between 1929 and 1933. The financial development of India during this period thus took place against the backdrop of two periods of rapid, imported inflation and of one period of very sharp contraction, all of which had their origins outside the country.

2. MONEY, PRICES, AND INTEREST RATES

a. The Money Supply

India ended the period as it had begun it, on a sterling exchange standard, at the rate of 16 pence per rupee until 1917 and at one of 18 pence beginning with 1927. Although in the intervening decade, both the value of the rupee, in terms of sterling or gold, and the country's

8. Shah and Kambata.

TABLE 2-3. Components of Money Supply, 1913–1946

	Notes (1)	Rupee coins (2)	Gold coins (3)	Bank demand deposits (4)	Total (5)
		I. Level (R. bill.)			
1913	0.51	1.90	0.55	0.58	3.54
1920	1.43	2.64	—	1.40	5.47
1929	1.72	1.58	—	1.20	4.50
1939	2.25	0.63	—	1.55	4.43
1946	12.25	1.67	—	8.04	21.96
		II. Distribution (percent)			
1913	14.4	53.7	15.5	16.4	100.0
1920	26.1	48.3	—	25.6	100.0
1929	38.2	35.1	—	26.7	100.0
1939	50.8	14.2	—	35.0	100.0
1946	55.8	7.6	—	36.6	100.0
		III. Relation to GNP (percent)			
1913	2.4	8.9	2.6	2.7	16.5
1920	4.1	7.6	—	4.0	15.5
1929	5.6	5.2	—	3.9	14.7
1939	7.9	2.2	—	5.5	15.6
1946	16.9	2.3	—	11.1	30.3
		IV. Average annual change (percent)			
1914–20	15.9	4.8	—	13.4	6.4
1921–29	2.1	−8.8	—	−1.7	−2.1
1930–39	2.7	−5.5	—	2.6	−0.2
1940–46	27.4	14.9	—	26.5	25.7
1914–46	10.1	−0.4	—	8.3	5.7
		V. Distribution of change over period (percent)			
1914–20	48	38	−28	43	100
1921–29	−30	109	—	−21	100
1930–39	−757	1357	—	−500	100
1940–46	57	8	—	37	100
1914–46	64	−1	−3	41	100
		VI. Relation of change to period's GNP (percent)			
1914–20	0.48	0.38	−0.28	0.43	1.00
1921–29	0.09	−0.34	—	−0.06	−0.31
1930–39	0.22	−0.39	—	0.14	−0.03
1940–46	2.49	0.26	—	1.62	4.37
1914–46	1.02	−0.02	—	0.65	1.60

SOURCES: **Col. 1:** *BMS*, pp. 655 ff., 678 ff.　　**Cols. 2 and 3:** See text.　　**Col. 4:** A fraction, declining from 55 to 50 percent (see text) of total deposits with commercial banks (*BMS*, p. 7).

exchange rate policy underwent many movements and changes, they appear to have had little influence on financial developments and on changes in the country's financial structure.[9]

Because silver rupees constituted the largest component of the money supply at the beginning of the period, the difficulties were bound to occur when the world price for silver exceeded the level at which the market value of the silver content of rupee coins equaled their face value, that is, when it would become profitable to melt down rupee coins and sell the resulting silver bullion as a commodity. This level, reached in 1917, was surpassed by a wide margin during the following years. The Indian government, therefore, had to increase the

9. For descriptions of Indian currency and exchange during the interwar period, cf., e.g., Anstey, chap. 15; Jain, passim, and Malhotra and Minocha, chaps. 5–10.

amount of sterling it was willing to offer for rupees or let the rupee-sterling rate find its own level and thus introduce a floating exchange regime. In fact, the value of the rupee was increased to 17d in mid-1917 and to 18d in the spring of 1918. Thereafter, the now floating rate rose to 29d late in 1919. As a result of a sharp fall in the world price of silver and an adverse balance of trade in India, the rupee then declined precipitously, notwithstanding attempts by the government to stabilize the exchange rate at 24d per rupee, and reached a low of 15d in the spring of 1921. From then on the rupee, now again freely floating, rose slowly and erratically, reaching 18 pence in the fall of 1924. At that level the rupee was stabilized, by returning to the mechanism of the prewar sterling exchange standard. As a result of this tie, the rupee was devalued in 1931 together with the pound sterling by about 30 percent against gold.

The violent movements of the value of the rupee in terms of sterling and of gold had pronounced effects on the circulation of silver rupees and on the hoarding of precious metals. These unfortunately cannot be followed in detail or with confidence in the absence of statistics of rupee coin circulation and, of necessity, of the changes in gold and silver hoards. The only relevant and fairly reliable statistics refer to annual figures for gold and silver imports and exports (table 2-4).

Any assessment of the trends in the money supply and of the velocity of circulation in India during the 1913–46 period is seriously hampered and reduced to rough guesses by the lack of official or unofficial estimates of the volume of circulation until very near the end of the period, namely 1943. The situation is thus even worse than for the last three decades prior to 1913 when semiofficial estimates of the volume of silver coins in circulation were available.

The only component of the money supply for which fairly exact figures exist are bank notes—before the mid-thirties those of the Treasury and thereafter those of the Reserve Bank of India. Note circulation increased from about R. 0.5 bill. in 1913 to R. 12.3 bill. in 1946, or at an annual average of 10 percent. Most of the expansion, however, occurred during World War II when note circulation shot up from R. 2.3 bill. in 1941 to R. 12.1 bill. in 1945, or by an average annual rate of 40 percent. The increase had also been very rapid during World War I, namely at an annual average of 34 percent during the years 1916–19. During the two decades from 1920 through 1940 the net increase was small—2.4 percent per year—as were annual fluctuations, including the years of the Great Depression.

Unfortunately, the movements of note circulation cannot be used as even a rough indicator of changes in total money supply. It is therefore necessary to estimate, even if very roughly, the movements of the other components of the money supply, that is, gold, silver, and small coins, and the check deposits of commercial banks.

Small coins may be disregarded, as the increase in their circulation is put at only R. 0.8 bill. for the period as a whole, seven-eighths of the increase occurring during the years 1939–46.

It may be assumed that gold coins disappeared from circulation during World War I. Any later net imports of sovereigns, shown in the monetary statistics at about R. 50 mill. for the period from 1914 to 1923 and then disappearing, may be regarded as having gone into hoards rather than into circulation.[10]

Demand deposits of commercial banks are not separately reported before 1935, when they constituted about one-half of total deposits of all scheduled banks. In the absence of indications of possible changes in this proportion during the two decades before 1935 and because the ratio seems to have been only slightly higher in 1913, a fraction, declining from 55 to 50 percent of total deposits of scheduled banks, has been regarded as part of the money supply for the 1914–46 period.

There are two benchmarks for estimating the circulation of silver rupees during this period, a semiofficial estimate of R. 1,900 mill. for 1912 and an official estimate of about R.

10. *BMS*, p. 665.

TABLE 2-4. Annual Financial Data, 1913–1946 (R. Bill.)

	Money in circulation		Bank deposits (3)	Assets of financial institutions (4)	Central government debt		Gold and silver imports or exports(-) (7)	Corporate stock outstanding (8)	Stock prices (1927 = 100) (9)
	Rupee coins (1)	Notes (2)			Total (5)	Funded rupee (6)			
1913	1.90	0.51	1.21	2.14	4.45	1.46	0.36	0.77	
1914	1.79	0.45	1.12	2.05	4.63	1.51	0.17	0.81	
1915	1.85	0.51	1.15	2.17	4.63	1.56	0.04	0.85	
1916	2.14	0.67	1.34	2.57	4.60	1.63	0.32	0.91	
1917	2.38	0.79	1.82	3.26	6.49	1.70	0.44	0.99	
1918	2.78	1.35	1.88	3.92	6.64	1.99	0.62	10.7	
1919	2.94	1.66	2.44	4.75	6.71	2.19	0.65	1023	
1920	2.64	1.43	2.67	4.97	6.38	2.57	0.09	1.64	
1921	2.49	1.63	2.62	5.14	6.82	3.05	0.12	2.31	
1922	2.35	1.63	2.47	5.04	7.16	3.40	0.60	2.60	
1923	2.38	1.73	2.40	3.21	7.47	3.59	0.48	2.65	
1924	2.37	1.70	2.55	5.36	8.42	3.70	0.94	2.75	
1925	2.24	1.80	2.62	5.58	8.55	3.68	0.52	2.77	
1926	2.00	1.66	2.72	5.70	8.63	3.74	0.39	2.77	
1927	1.92	1.77	2.78	5.92	9.90	3.72	0.32	2.77	100
1928	1.84	1.85	2.89	6.24	10.34	3.92	0.31	2.79	100
1929	1.58	1.72	2.90	6.17	10.96	4.05	0.23	2.86	99
1930	1.32	1.54	3.00	6.23	11.42	4.17	0.23	2.83	87
1931	1.31	1.73	2.88	6.37	11.92	4.23	0.58	2.86	68
1932	1.19	1.58	3.13	6.64	11.90	4.45	0.68	2.86	64
1933	1.14	1.63	3.28	6.90	12.05	4.35	0.63	3.01	83
1934	1.07	1.68	3.40	7.23	12.20	4.38	0.58	3.04	100
1935	0.93	1.72	3.59	7.78	11.91	4.26	0.38	3.03	110
1936	0.86	1.90	3.80	8.10	11.79	4.38	0.14	3.11	111
1937	0.75	1.81	3.89	8.28	11.75	4.39	0.15	2.79	125
1938	0.58	1.80	3.86	8.33	11.79	4.39	0.11	2.90	106
1939	0.63	2.25	4.07	9.41	11.70	4.51	−0.34	3.04	107
1940	0.92	2.29	4.22	10.08	12.06	5.77	−0.15	3.10	117
1941	0.95	3.15	4.73	11.69	11.52	6.15	−0.08	3.25	129
1942	1.35	5.70	6.10	15.91	12.98	7.52	−0.09	3.36	130
1943	1.31	8.41	8.54	21.96	14.15	10.12	0.02	3.53	172
1944	1.42	10.10	10.66	28.81	16.39	12.19	0.24	3.89	196
1945	1.50	12.11	12.93	36.32	19.79	14.99	0.07	4.24	211
1946	1.67	12.25	14.23	38.24	21.85	15.42	0.33	4.79	265

SOURCES: **Col. 1:** 1913–42, see text; 1943–46, *BMS*, p. 679.　　　**Col. 2:** *BMS*, pp. 665 ff.　　　**Col. 3:** *BMS*, pp. 7 ff. **Col. 4:** *BMS*, pp. 10–16, 237, 368–69, 384, 410, 422, 448, 476, 504, 881, 922.　　　**Cols. 5 and 6:** *BMS*, p. 881.　　　**Col. 7:** *BMS*, pp. 961 ff., 981 ff.　　　**Col. 8:** *BMS*, pp. 703 ff.　　　**Col. 9:** *BMS*, p. 733.

1,400 mill. for 1944.[11] Interpolation between these two dates is difficult, as the statistics of the absorption of rupee coins show a net increase of about R. 1,100 mill. compared to a net decrease by about R. 600 mill. between the two benchmarks. If one regards the difference as representing, apart from wear and tear of the stock, a shift from monetary to non-monetary use; and if one further assumes that the difference was equally distributed over the period, rough guesses can be made of the volume of silver rupees in circulation, and hence of the total money supply. The resulting figures are shown in table 2-3 for the five benchmark years of 1913, 1920, 1929, 1939, and 1946 and on an annual basis in table 2-4.

11. *BMS*, p. 680.

Taking the plunge into this sea of statistical uncertainties, and trusting mainly to the estimates of 1913 and 1946 because they are less infirm than those for the benchmarks 1920, 1929, and 1939, we find in table 2-3 a marked modernization of the money supply of India. This is indicated by the increase in the share of the two types of scriptural money from only 30 percent of the total money supply in 1913 to more than 90 percent in 1946 and by the complementary decline in the proportion of metallic money from nearly 70 percent to only 8 percent. Indeed, the change was so radical that the absolute amount of the metallic part of the circulation was reduced from about R. 2.5 bill. in 1913 to R. 1.7 bill. in 1946, although the total money supply increased by no less than R. 18 bill. Although little confidence can be put into the estimates for the intervening three benchmarks, it would appear that they correctly reflect the movements of the money supply during these three decades, namely, a continuous decline in the share of metallic money, which was particularly pronounced in the 1920s and 1930s.

We also find a striking contrast between the very rapid increase in the money supply during the two world wars and the generally deflationary policy followed during the 1920s and 1930s. During the war years large surpluses in the balance of trade led to the accumulation of huge sterling assets in the Treasury and the Reserve Bank because wartime shortages and exchange controls prevented the transformation of the surplus into imports, whereas during the twenties and thirties monetary authorities chose a deflationary policy because of their conviction that such deflation was good for the soul and possibly for prestige in the international financial community, even if not for the welfare of the population. The policy was only too successful in India. The price level was reduced by about two-fifths, bringing it back for most of the 1930s to or below the niveau prevailing in 1913, which was probably regarded as the touchstone of normality, and real product per head stagnated.

We find, in addition, relatively small fluctuations, mostly downward, in the ratio of the money supply to national product, that is, a modest increase in the income velocity of money until the late 1930s, followed by a sharp increase in that ratio from about two months' national product to well over three months', indicating a decline in annual income velocity from about 6 to less than 4. This accumulation of Indian money in the hands of households and business enterprises (data are lacking for an allocation of the total money supply among sectors) is the counterpart to the accumulation of London funds by the Reserve Bank. These developments, of course, are similar to those observed in many other countries, fully belligerent, marginally belligerent like India, or neutral.

b. Prices

For the period as a whole, prices show a marked though irregular upward trend, which can be followed on a period basis in table 2-5 and on an annual basis in table 2-1. The national

TABLE 2-5. Price and Wage Movements, 1914–1946 (Percent Per Year)

	National product deflator (1)	Cost of living (2)	Wholesale prices (3)	Wages	
				Rural, field (4)	Urban, skilled (5)
1914–20	+7.6	+8.0	+11.1	+10.1	+7.6
1921–29	−2.8	−2.4	−4.0	+0.1	+3.5
1930–39	−3.0	−3.6	−2.6	−4.9	−3.1
1940–46	+13.6	+16.6	+14.1	+20.0	+10.5
1914–46	+2.6	+3.2	+3.2	+4.7	+3.7

SOURCES: **Col. 1:** Sivasubramonian, pp. 337–39.   **Cols. 2 and 3:** Table 2-1.   **Cols. 4 and 5:** Sivasubramonian, p. 240; rural wages refer to up-country areas in Bombay province.

income deflator more than doubled and the wholesale price and cost-of-living indices almost trebled, implying an average annual growth rate of slightly more than 3 percent. This, however, was the net result of sharply divergent movements for subperiods. Thus the national income deflator as well as the cost-of-living index rose from 1913 to 1920 by about 70 percent, an average annual rise of about 8 percent, which reflected the imported inflation of World War I.

For the following thirteen years the trend of prices was downward, slowly during the 1920s but precipitously from 1929 to 1933, again reflecting an extraneous event, the Great Depression. The national income deflator declined at a rate of nearly 3 percent from 1921 to 1929 but by an average of 5 percent a year in the following four years. As a result, the price level of 1933 was actually lower than that of 1913. This is a vivid indication of the extent of the deflations following World War I and accompanying the Great Depression, a movement that was sharper in India than in most other countries.[12]

Prices rose moderately during the remainder of the 1930s. The imported inflation of World War II led to the sharpest rise in the price level that India had experienced for at least a century, the national income deflator advancing at an annual rate of nearly 14 percent to reach a level in 1946 that was about two-and-one-half times as high as that of 1913. The paths of the wholesale price and the cost-of-living indices differed slightly, but both stood in 1946 at about three times their levels on the eve of World War I.

c. Interest Rates

All quoted interest rates must be taken with several grains of salt in a country in which the money and capital markets were as little developed as in India in the interwar period, in which many interest rates have conventional features and do not often change; in which charges additional to the interest rate are common; and in which silent credit rationing is not rare. These reservations are of more importance in evaluating the effective level of interest rates and the exact amount of change in rates than for determining the direction of interest rate movements and the order of magnitude of the changes. They are, of course, also less applicable to the short-term money market than to other rates.

Interest rates moved generally upward during the first part of the period and downward during the second half, the early 1930s generally representing the watershed. The downward movement was considerably more pronounced than the preceding upward swing, so that the level of interest rates was substantially lower at the end of the period than at its start. As in other countries, the reduction of demand for loans during the Great Depression and the easy money policies followed by the authorities during most of the 1930s and 1940s were the main factors in reducing quoted short-term rates by 1946 to probably the lowest level ever experienced for any protracted period. The movement of practically all rates for which continuous quotations are available between the six benchmark years 1913, 1920, 1929, 1933, 1939, and 1946 can be followed in table 2-5; annual quotations for the discount rate of the central bank or of its predecessors' will be found in table 2-1.

Between 1913 and 1920 all short- and long-term rates, for which information is at hand, advanced, the rise being larger for the only available long-term market rate, the central government's undated 3½ percent paper (2.3 percent or by nearly two-thirds of the starting value), than for the short-term market rates and the rates paid by banks to their depositors. Movements during the 1920s were mixed and in general relatively small. The decline between 1929 and 1933 was precipitous in the case of short-term market rates, which fell within four years by between one-half and three-fifths. In marked contrast, though not in conflict with common experience, long-term rates, as well as the rates paid depositors by banks and presumably also the rates charged by

12. The price level of 1933, measured by the national product deflator, was about 20 percent above that of 1913 in the United States (U.S. Bureau of the Census, *Historical Statistics,* 1960, p. 139) and more than 35 percent in Great Britain (B. R. Mitchell and P. Deane, *Abstract of British Historical Statistics,* Cambridge University Press, 1962, p. 368).

TABLE 2-6. Interest Rates, 1913–1946 (Percent; Annual Averages)

	1913	1920	1929	1933	1939	1946
I. *Short-term rates*						
1. Bank[a]	5.92	6.35	7.00	3.50	3.50	3.50
2. Call money[b]	·	·	4.00	1.13	1.38	0.50
3. Hundi rediscount[c]	6.50	8.00[h]	7.00	3.50	3.50	3.52
4. Bazaar	·	7.50	8.25	3.38	5.31	5.38
5. Treasury bills[d]	·	6.00	6.23	2.58	1.94	0.44
6. Deposits with commercial banks	3.53[g]	3.92	3.96	3.36	1.75	1.50
7. Post Office Saving System[e]	2.83	3.80	2.89	3.21	1.78	1.74
II. *Long-term rates*						
1. 3½% undated rupee paper of government of India	3.66	5.98	5.00	4.22	3.77	3.38
2. Loans by agricultural cooperative societies[f]	·	9.38	10.94	10.15	9.38	7.82

[a]Bank of Bombay 1913 and 1920; Imperial Bank 1929 and 1933; Reserve Bank of India 1939 and 1946.   [b]Bombay.
[c]End of year rate; Bank of Bombay 1913 and 1920; Imperial Bank 1929 to 1946.   [d]Three months' bills of central
government; end of year.   [e]Year ended June; Bombay.   [f]Obtained by dividing interest credited by average deposit
balance (*BMS*, p. 369).   [g]1914.   [h]1921.

SOURCES: Lines I, 1–5, 7 and II, 1 and 2: *BMS*, pp. 369, 690 ff. Line I-6: Ramana, p. 31.

banks to borrowers, proved to be sticky, the reduction being on the order of only one-tenth to
one-fifth of their level in 1929. Changes during the rest of the 1930s were small and tended in
different directions except for the near-halving of the rates paid by banks to their depositors.
From 1939 to 1946, some rates were frozen and others declined, most of them falling to levels
more commonly associated with rich than with poor countries.

3. THE BALANCE OF PAYMENTS AND FOREIGN INVESTMENTS

a. *The Balance of Payments*

The basic structure of India's balance of payments during the first half of this period,
particularly during the 1920s, was similar to that of the half century before 1914. A substantial
excess of commodity exports over imports was more than offset by net expenditures on service
account, particularly for interest and pensions, and by substantial gold and silver imports. The
difference was provided by net capital imports, which totaled more than R. 3½ bill. for the
1920s, or slightly more than 1 percent of national product. In the 1930s the depression led to

TABLE 2-7. Balance of Payments, 1921–1946[a]

	1921–29	1930–39	1940–46	1921–46
	I. Amounts (R. bill.)			
Commodity trade	5.84	2.26	2.04	8.85
Services	−6.73	−4.47	17.21	5.35
Net gold movement	−2.54	3.36	0.13	0.93
Capital movement	3.43	−1.15	−19.38	−15.35
	II. Relation to gross national product (percent)			
Commodity trade	1.9	0.9	0.5	0.9
Services	−2.1	−1.8	4.3	0.5
Net gold movement	−0.8	1.4	0.0	0.1
Capital movement	1.1	−0.5	−4.8	−1.6

[a]Fiscal years.

SOURCE OF I: Gurtoo, p. 51.

large net gold exports—nearly R. 3½ bill. for the decade—in part the result of people in distress parting with some or all of their gold and silver hoards. These exports were considerably in excess of the negative balance on current account of fully R. 2 bill., as continuing large net payments on service account were no longer compensated by the relatively small net commodity exports and thus permitted a net outflow of foreign funds by nearly R. 1½ bill, or 0.6 percent of national product. World War II led, as World War I had done, to a very large excess of credits on current account, this time however mostly in the form of services rather than of commodities, an excess that altogether totaled for 1940–46 about R. 19 bill., or nearly 5 percent of gross national product. This was balanced, in the absence of substantial gold movements, by a massive repatriation of foreign investments, particularly of the direct or guaranteed sterling debt of the central government. As the balance of payments surplus at the beginning of the period was far in excess of the total foreign investment that could be liquidated, that is, primarily Indian government securities held in Great Britain, the surplus led to the accumulation of large short-term London funds concentrated in the Reserve Bank and made India a net creditor on international account, although a relatively small block of foreign investments in India, now predominantly private, survived the war.

b. Foreign Investments[13]

Foreign, that is, primarily British,[14] investments in India increased moderately and irregularly in aggregate value between 1913 and 1929 and possibly until the beginning of World War II, but they did not keep up fully with the growth of national product and national wealth. From then on to independence, foreign gross investments declined both in absolute terms and in relation to national product, and net foreign investments were drastically reduced. Holdings of government securities continued to represent the largest component of foreign investment, although their share in total foreign investment declined. Considering both quantitative and qualitative criteria, the dependence of India on foreign capital and entrepreneurship was substantially reduced.

These are about the only generalizing and imprecise statements that can be made in view of the divergence, the lack of comparability, and the absence of detail in the numerous estimates of the flow and stock of foreign investments.[15] Three of these estimates, providing some information on the structure of foreign investments in India at the bench-mark dates 1921, 1929, and 1939, approximately decadal intervals, are reproduced in table 2-8.[16]

In combining a series of not obviously incompatible estimates, it would appear that the value of foreign investments in India in 1921, about R. 7 bill. was very close to that of 1913, and that it continued to increase slowly by between R. 2 and 3 bill. in each of the following decades, reaching a value of possibly R. 12 bill. in 1939.[17,18] Because no estimates exist for 1946, the official 1948 estimate of foreign investments in the Indian Union,[19] which is considerably better

13. For a description as well as statistical treatment, cf. Bose, pp. 485–527. Most of the studies of the balance of payments also discuss foreign investments, e.g., the books of Banerjee and Gurtoo cited in footnotes 14 and 15.

14. The share of Great Britain has been put at as much as 90 percent in 1938, only a slight decline in predominance from 93 percent in 1921 (Banerjee).

15. Gurtoo (p. 55) lists and discusses nine estimates for seven benchmark dates, and there are others, the ratio of different estimates for the same or neighboring years being in the order of 2 to 1.

16. More detailed information on foreign investment in Indian securities can be found in Gurtoo (pp. 51 ff.), according to whom it was practically the same in 1920 and 1946, namely about R. 5 bill., equal to 14 percent of national product in 1920 but to only 7 percent in 1946.

17. If Soni (p.175) is correct in asserting that there is "no doubt whatever that British investments in India amount to nearly £800 million at the present time [i.e., around 1930], and those of foreign countries to more than £100 million," the estimates for other dates would have to be substantially increased.

18. A set of estimates that has the advantage of being comparable over time but is limited to long-term investments and moves at a considerably lower level than most other estimates is that of Gurtoo (p. 69), which puts foreign long-term investments at R. 4.4 bill. early in 1921, R. 8.6 bill. in 1930, R. 8.2 bill. in 1940, and R. 4.7 bill. in 1947.

19. *RBIB*, 1957, pp. 1191 ff.

TABLE 2-8. Foreign Investments, 1921–1948 (R. Bill.)

	1921 (1)	1929 (2)	1939 (3)	1948 (4)
Government securities[a]				
Sterling[a]	3.7	5.3	5.4	
Rupee	1.6	0.1	1.2	
Companies registered in India		0.6	1.3	
Companies registered abroad operating in India		3.6	3.0	
Unincorporated business and land		0.6	1.5	
Others	1.8	—	—	
Total, R. bill.	7.1	10.2	12.4	6.2
Total, percent of national product	20	33	44	7

[a]Including municipal and port trusts and railway securities.

SOURCES: **Col. 1:** Banerjee.   **Cols. 2 and 3:** Rao (for 1929) and B. R. Shenory (for 1939) as adapted by Bose, pp. 496, 499.   **Col. 4:** Estimate for Indian Union in mid-1948 (*RBIB*, 1957, p. 1191) increased by about one-fifth to cover Pakistan, assuming no substantial changes in 1947 and 1948. Another estimate cited by Gurtoo (p. 56) yields about R. 7 bill.

founded than earlier figures, may be used as a measure of foreign investment in Undivided India before independence, adding, on the basis of population, about one-fifth for foreign investments in that part of Undivided India that became Pakistan. This would put foreign investments in 1946 at about R. 6 bill. This is undoubtedly considerably less than foreign investments in 1939 and is also probably below the level of foreign investments in 1913, even disregarding the much higher price level of 1946.

If foreign investments are related to annual gross national product, the ratios are approximately one-third in 1913, one-fifth in 1920, nearly 30 percent in 1929, more than two-fifths in 1939, and, finally, less than one-tenth in 1946. These figures, however, greatly exaggerate the width of the swings in the ratio, because they compare foreign investment estimates, which are mostly on an original cost or face value basis, with national product figures, which move with the price level. The ratios, however, should correctly show the direction of the actual movements and indicate the generally downward trend in the ratio.

There is no doubt that foreign investments declined considerably in comparison to national wealth, the ratio falling from nearly one-tenth in 1913 to about 5 percent in 1929 and 6 percent in 1939, and further declining to less than 2 percent in 1946. Although the reduction in the ratio is again overstated because of the failure to use market values for direct investments, there is no doubt that the reduction in the share of Indian national wealth that can be statistically regarded as foreign owned was radical and that it occurred mainly after the beginning of World War II. The reduction would be even more spectacular if based on net, rather than on gross, foreign investment, that is, after deduction of India's then substantial foreign assets from its foreign liabilities. In that case, India's net foreign investment position in 1946 is positive to the extent of about R. 18 bill., or more than 4 percent of tangible assets, compared with a negative position of 8 percent in 1913.

Securities issued or guaranteed by the government of India, denominated in sterling or rupees, have always represented the largest single component of foreign investment and have accounted for the majority of it. Their share, however, declined from more than four-fifths in 1913 to about one-half in 1929 and 1939 and had almost disappeared in 1946 as the large surpluses in the balance of payments permitted the repatriation of most of the government bonds in British hands. Private foreign investments in companies registered in India or abroad, in branch plants, and in real estate showed an upward trend at least until the Great Depression.

4. CAPITAL FORMATION AND SAVING

a. Gross and Net Investment[20]

The ratio of gross investment to gross national product failed to show a definite trend during the last three decades of the British Raj and thus stayed at the low level of the first decade of the twentieth century. For the entire period from 1914 through 1946 gross capital formation averaged slightly more than 7 percent of gross national product and increased in current prices only from 5.7 percent in 1912–14 to 6.2 percent in 1945–47. Net capital formation averaged only 2¼ percent for the entire period with only moderate differences among subperiods.

Fluctuations of the fixed capital formation ratio appear to have been moderate, five-year averages within the period lying within the relatively narrow range of 6.7 and 9.0 percent of gross national product, and even annual figures fluctuating only between 4.9 percent (1925) and 9.8 percent (1937). The two world wars, which generated a sharp rise in the price level, do not appear to have had a stimulating effect on capital formation. In fact, the average ratios for the years 1914–20 and 1940–46 at slightly above 7 percent are well below that of the 1930s though above that of the 1920s. These ratios are low in comparison with both the rates for the then leading Western countries and the rates reached in India and in many other poor countries after World War II.

For the period as a whole, construction accounted for nearly two-thirds of total gross capital formation and machinery and equipment for less than one-third, the share actually declining from 31 percent in the first half of the period to 29 percent in the second half, contrary to what one would expect in an industrializing country. Inventories are reported to have absorbed 5 percent of gross capital formation with violent annual fluctuations in the estimates.

Public capital formation accounted for nearly one-fourth of the total gross capital formation for the entire period, about three-fifths thereof attributable to the central government, reaching a peak in the 1920s and the lowest share during World War II. Of private investment, the rural areas accounted for the entire period for less than 30 percent, their share estimated to have declined continuously from 38 percent in World War I to 23 percent during World War II. Because the division of public investment between rural and urban areas is not known, it is not possible to allocate total national capital formation to these two sectors. There is no doubt, however, that the share of the rural areas was far below their share in population, labor force, and national product. Capital formation per head was extremely low in both rural and urban areas. In the 1914–46 period gross capital formation averaged R. 10 per head for the country as a whole and in rural areas may have been, on the average, as low as R. 2 (about 70 cents) per head.

The shifts in the distribution of total capital formation reflect the differences in the growth rate of its various components. Thus the rate of growth in constant prices of gross fixed capital formation of 1.2 percent was much larger than that of investment in machinery and equipment with only 0.3 percent and considerably below the population growth rate of 1.0 percent. The growth rate of total gross capital formation was so low that net capital formation actually declined at the rate of 0.4 percent per year between the beginning and the end of the interwar period. The trend was also downward for public capital formation, which declined substantially at a rate of 0.8 percent per year. Because private rural capital formation increased only very slowly, most of the increases in total investment occurred in the private urban sector, where capital formation expanded at a rate of fully 2 percent per year.

The net reproducible capital stock in current prices is estimated to have increased from R. 34 bill. in 1913 to R. 138 bill. in 1946, or at a rate of fully 4 percent per year. Most of the increase, however, was due to the rise in the price level, so that the rate of growth of the

---

20. This section is based on the most recent and detailed estimates of capital formation in India in the interwar period of Dr. Bina Roy, who kindly made her dissertation available.

TABLE 2-9. Distribution and Relation of Capital Formation and Saving to Gross National Product, 1914–1946

	Distribution (percent)					Ratio to GNP (percent)				
	1914–20	1921–29	1930–39	1940–46	1914–46	1914–20	1921–29	1930–39	1940–46	1914–46
Gross fixed capital formation	96.5	88.5	96.7	98.6	95.0	6.81	4.39	9.05	7.20	6.42
Construction	64.7	57.2	67.5	70.2	65.1	4.56	2.84	6.31	5.12	4.39
Rural	25.6	19.4	19.4	14.1	18.6	1.81	0.96	1.81	1.03	1.26
Urban	39.1	37.8	48.1	56.1	46.5	2.75	1.88	4.50	4.09	3.14
Machinery and equipment	31.7	31.3	29.2	28.5	29.9	2.23	1.55	2.73	2.08	2.02
Rural	2.5	2.9	3.5	4.6	3.5	0.18	0.14	0.33	0.33	0.24
Urban	29.2	28.4	25.7	23.9	26.4	2.05	1.41	2.40	1.75	1.78
Inventories	3.5	11.5	3.3	1.4	5.0	0.25	0.57	0.30	0.10	0.34
Gross domestic capital formation	100.0	100.0	100.0	100.0	100.0	7.06	4.96	9.35	7.30	6.75
Depreciation	65.0	58.7	69.6	71.0	66.3	4.58	2.91	6.51	5.18	4.48
Net domestic capital formation	35.0	41.3	30.4	29.0	33.7	2.48	2.05	2.84	2.12	2.27
Capital inflow	12.0	−9.9	−4.3	−15.6	−7.1	0.85	−0.49	−0.40	−1.14	−0.48
Net domestic saving	23.0	51.2	34.7	44.6	40.7	1.63	2.55	3.24	3.26	2.75
Gross capital formation										
Public	26.3	30.0	22.2	18.0	23.7	1.86	1.49	2.08	1.32	1.60
Rural	28.1	22.2	22.9	18.7	22.1	1.99	1.10	2.14	1.36	1.49
Urban	45.6	47.8	54.9	63.3	54.2	3.22	2.36	5.13	4.62	3.66
Gross domestic capital formation (R. bill.)	13.58	25.16	22.72	29.27	90.73					

SOURCE OF BASIC DATA: BR.

TABLE 2-10. Reproducible Net Capital Stock, 1913–1946 (R. Bill.)

	1913	1920	1929	1939	1946
		I. Current prices			
Fixed assets	24.24	55.34	55.08	53.00	102.02
Livestock	6.79	14.74	11.14	8.36	22.13
Inventories	3.36	7.52	6.25	5.29	14.32
Total	34.39	77.60	72.47	66.65	138.47
		II. Constant (1951) prices			
Fixed assets	92.86	104.74	120.22	137.95	151.79
Livestock	30.10	31.36	33.95	33.30	34.60
Inventories	14.88	16.07	19.06	21.07	21.76
Total	137.84	152.17	173.23	192.32	208.15
		III. Distribution (current prices; percent)			
Fixed assets	70.5	71.3	76.0	79.5	73.7
Livestock	19.7	19.0	15.4	12.5	16.0
Inventories	9.8	9.7	8.6	7.9	10.3
Total	100.0	100.0	100.0	100.0	100.0
		IV. Capital output ratio (current prices)			
Fixed assets	1.13	1.57	1.78	1.87	1.41
Livestock	0.32	0.41	0.42	0.30	0.30
Inventories	0.16	0.22	0.20	0.18	0.20
Total	1.61	2.20	2.40	2.35	1.91

SOURCE: *BR*, increased in I and II by 20 percent to shift from Indian Union to undivided India.

aggregate real net reproducible capital stock was only 1¼ percent per year, and the increase in the stock per head at 0.3 percent per year was almost imperceptible. The growth in the stock was, however, sufficient to raise the capital-output ratio from 1.7 to 1.9 after having reached a level of slightly above 2 in the 1920s and 1930s.

Changes in the structure of the capital stock in current prices were minor or erratic, the distributions at the beginning and the end of the period being quite similar. In constant prices the share of fixed assets increased slightly, from 67 to 73 percent, at the expense of the share of livestock.

Changes in the hoards of precious metals constitute in India a not negligible component of investment (or disinvestment) and of saving (or dissaving). For the entire period the net changes do not seem to have been large enough to affect the level or the rate of investment or saving substantially. Thus for the years 1914 to 1946 the net increase in the stocks of gold and silver, at an original cost of about R. 4 bill., was equal to less than 0.4 percent of national product compared to a net capital formation ratio of 2¼ percent. For the subperiods the changes in the hoards of precious metals are, however, more important. They were equal to about two-fifths of capital formation during World War I and in the 1920s, but small in comparison to net capital formation during World War II. In the 1930s, dishoarding equal to 1½ percent of national product supplemented net capital formation of nearly 3 percent.

b. Savings

The estimation of aggregate domestic saving can be approached either on the basis of investment by the deduction of net capital imports or more directly from the financial side by the estimation of changes in financial assets and liabilities of the nonfinancial sectors of the economy, eliminating changes that represent valuation changes rather than fund flows.

Because India's balance of payments showed an outward net capital movement of more than R. 5 bill. for the years 1920 to 1946,[21] equal to about one-half of 1 percent of national

21. The estimate of net capital movements used by Dr. B. Roy in her calculation of total investment and saving. Another estimate, derived as part of a calculation of the balance of payments (table 2-7), gives much higher figures—more than R. 15 bill. for the years 1920 to 1946.

product, the national saving ratio for the entire interwar period at 2¾ percent is considerably above the net investment ratio of 2¼ percent, but still very low.

Although the capital formation ratio showed only minor fluctuations among subperiods, at least for fixed capital, net foreign investment varied greatly. A substantial surplus, that is, a net acquisition of foreign assets, during World War I was followed by net imports of slightly more than 1 percent of national product during the 1920s, small exports in the 1930s, and finally a surplus equal to nearly 5 percent of national product in the years 1940–46. In particular the surplus during the World War II period is large enough to affect decisively national saving during that period, raising it from 2.1 to 3.3 percent of national product.

Theoretically, this indirect approach to the estimation of saving can be continued, by deducting from aggregate national saving estimates of government saving, such as those discussed in section 6a, and estimates for corporate saving, to yield as a residual estimate of saving of the household sector, including unincorporated business activities inside and outside of agriculture. However, in the absence of estimates for corporate saving, the method cannot be applied to India in the interwar period. The most that can be done is to give an indication of the magnitudes involved for the interwar period as a whole.

It then appears that government saving amounted to approximately R. 7 bill. gross and R. 2.6 bill. net for the 1920s and 1930s, equal to slightly more than 1 percent and slightly less than 0.5 percent of the period's national product.[22] Corporate saving, according to the very rough estimate of section 6c(ii), may have been on the order of 0.3 percent of national product on a gross basis and 0.1 to 0.2 percent on a net basis. This would leave approximately 2 percent of national product for saving of the household sector broadly defined, excluding saving in the form of precious metals. Both estimates would be about one-fourth higher in relation to personal income. An attempt will be made in sections 6c and 6d to estimate the saving of agricultural and nonagricultural households by the alternative method of combining estimates for the various tangible and financial components of saving and dissaving, that is, the changes (excluding those reflecting price changes) in the household sector's assets and liabilities.

5. THE DEVELOPMENT OF FINANCIAL INSTITUTIONS

The three decades between the start of World War I and independence witnessed a substantial expansion of the superstructures of financial institutions without fundamental changes in the types of institutions in existence or in the nature of their operations except for the creation of the Reserve Bank of India in the mid-1930s. The following subsections discuss briefly the development of each major type of financial institution, and the concluding subsection presents an overview of the development of all financial institutions.

a. The Reserve Bank of India[23]

Proposals for the establishment of a central bank for India were first introduced in the late nineteenth century. Keynes produced one such proposal for the Indian Currency Commission before World War I. In 1926 a central bank was recommended in the report of the Hilton Young Commission and active preparations began. The first two bills proposed by the government were submitted early in 1927 and 1928 but were not implemented. The third bill, introduced in September 1933, was more successful, partly as a result of the experience during the Great Depression, and was enacted in March 1934. And on April 1, 1935, the bank began operations.

Following the then prevailing practice, the bank was orgainzed as a joint stock company whose shares were privately held. Because a wide distribution of the banks shares was regarded

---

22. Thavaraj, pp. 220, 228.

23. A detailed description of the origin of the Reserve Bank and its operations during the period covered in this chapter is provided by Simha in the semiofficial *History of the Reserve Bank of India, 1935–51*.

TABLE 2-11. Assets of Financial Institutions, Annually, 1913–1946 (R. Mill.)

	Total (1)	Reserve Bank[a] (2)	Imperial Bank (3)	Exchange banks (4)	Commercial banks		Postal saving (7)	Cooperatives (8)	Insurance companies (9)	Pension funds (10)
					All (5)	Class A-1 (6)				
1913	2143	661	498	310	262	242	232	53	65	62
1914	2051	616	533	302	228	210	149	77	77	69
1915	2163	677	510	336	238	223	153	89	82	78
1916	2570	864	573	380	309	293	166	104	88	86
1917	3258	998	829	534	373	358	166	123	94	141
1918	3944	1535	688	619	488	466	188	144	92	190
1919	4743	1745	873	744	696	666	214	176	98	197
1920	4968	1662	938	748	852	821	229	214	106	219
1921	5136	1748	828	752	936	893	223	264	109	276
1922	5038	1747	822	734	768	723	232	311	118	306
1923	5219	1859	1012	688	596	542	248	355	127	334
1924	5651	1842	913	715	700	632	295	576	162	448
1925	5585	1933	942	706	697	651	272	482	149	404
1926	5702	1841	913	715	752	705	295	576	162	448
1927	5931	1849	942	698	766	719	327	679	177	493
1928	6234	1880	974	711	787	740	345	767	233	537
1929	6174	1772	909	667	790	743	371	827	256	582
1930	6223	1608	954	681	810	752	370	895	277	628
1931	6365	1781	863	675	795	743	382	919	300	650
1932	6643	1769	871	731	898	846	435	927	329	683
1933	6896	1772	923	708	901	840	522	958	377	735
1934	7228	1861	929	714	960	894	583	957	421	803

(continued)

TABLE 2-11. (continued)

				Commercial banks					
Total (1)	Reserve Bank[a] (2)	Imperial Bank (3)	Exchange banks (4)	All (5)	Class A-1 (6)	Postal saving (7)	Cooperatives (8)	Insurance companies (9)	Pension funds (10)
1935	7870	2193	909	762	1044	977	673	969	458	862
1936	8092	2245	906	752	1230	1057	747	1001	505	706
1937	8276	2277	929	732	1289	1110	775	1016	559	697
1938	8428	2248	934	672	1380	1094	819	1030	620	725
1939	9406	2802	998	741	1568	1133	783	1066	695	752
1940	10078	3205	1080	853	1732	1260	595	1070	763	780
1941	11692	4061	1210	1067	2081	1570	521	1093	848	812
1942	15914	6665	1757	1169	2865	2197	522	1124	972	840
1943	21952	9826	2269	1402	4643	3723	642	1211	1072	887
1944	28810	13864	2502	1652	6511	5099	802	1322	1227	930
1945	36323	18283	2719	1837	8513	6489	1151	1466	1383	971
1946	38238	18140	2944	1813	9787	7708	1424	1640	1515	976

[a]Treasury note issues to 1934.

SOURCES: Cols. 2–6: BMS, pp. 12–16, 237. Figures refer to total assets in col. 2; in col. 3 from 1921; and in cols. 4 and 5 from 1936; otherwise, to sum of capital, reserves, and deposits, but in col. 4 to Indian deposits only. Banks or branches in Burma are generally included until 1936. Figures in col. 2 for 1914–20 represent sum of capital, reserves, and deposits of three Presidency banks.   Col. 5: Includes class A-1 and B banks from 1913 on; also class A-2 banks beginning with 1936; class C and D and reporting nonscheduled banks from 1939 on.   Col. 7: BMS, pp. 368–69; deposits as of March 31 of the following year.   Col. 8: BMS, pp. 384, 410, 422, 448, 476, and 504; figures refer to working capital, generally as of June 30, which is slightly below total assets. Land mortgage banks excluded from 1938 on. Burma included through 1937.   Col. 9: BMS, p. 924, assets of Indian companies only. Premium income of foreign life insurance companies operating in India was 88 percent of that of Indian companies in 1929, 28 percent in 1939, and 22 percent in 1946 (BMS, p. 922).   Col. 10: Claims against Treasury of state provident funds (BMS, p. 881).

as desirable, its capital of R. 50 mill. was divided into shares of R. 100 and the number of votes any one shareholder could exercise was limited. As a result of the initial offering, which was heavily oversubscribed, the bank's shares were distributed among 130,000 shareholders—considerably more than any other Indian joint stock company—who on the average owned fewer than four shares.[24] Although the government held no shares and great importance was attached to the bank's independence, the government's influence was nevertheless substantial and was reflected mainly in its power to appoint half of the members of the board of directors as well as the bank's governor and two deputy governors.

British example was followed in the division of the bank into an Issue Department and a Banking Department. The main function of the Issue Department was to issue notes backed by gold, silver rupees, government of India rupee securities, and certain sterling securities, particularly those issued by the British government. The initially much smaller Banking Department derived its funds primarily from government and bankers' deposits, part of which represented the reserves that scheduled commercial banks had to keep with the bank to the extent of 5 percent of their demand and 2 percent of their time liabilities.

Of the four main functions of the bank, as of most other central banks, two, namely, the issuance of notes and the maintenance of the exchange rate, were transferred from the Treasury, which had exercised them for more than a half century. The other two functions, acting as the banker for the government and for other bankers, were taken over from the Imperial Bank and its predecessors, the three Presidency banks.

Until World War II, a period designated by the bank's historian as "the formative years,"[25] the bank did not substantially extend its operations, and its main assets and liabilities (table 2-12) remained close to those in total size as well as in distribution taken over from the Treasury and the Imperial Bank in 1935. Notes provided fully four-fifths of the bank's funds, and deposits, mostly from the government, fluctuated around one-eighth. Foreign assets (including gold) accounted on the average for about one-third of total assets, rupee coins for about one-fourth, and Indian government securities for about one-third. Advances and discounts were of negligible size.

World War II and the large surpluses on India's current international account, which accompanied it and which have already been discussed in section 3, led to a sharp increase in the bank's assets and to a radical change in their distribution. Between the end of 1938 and that of 1945 total assets increased from not much more than R. 2 bill., only one-tenth above the opening balance sheet of April 1935, to more than R. 18 bill., equivalent to an average annual rate of increase of 30 percent. The sharpest increases occurred from 1942 to 1944 with an average of 50 percent. The rise in the ratio of the bank's assets to national product from less than one-tenth in 1938 to one-fourth in 1945 indicates that only a relatively small part of the eightfold expansion of the bank's assets reflects an increase by over 150 percent of the price level.

This extraordinary expansion was caused primarily by the increase in foreign assets, mostly British government securities, from R. 0.6 bill. to R. 16.7 bill., an average annual rate of increase of more than 60 percent. As a result, foreign assets, which had accounted for not much more than one-fourth of the bank's total assets in 1938, became completely dominant in 1945 with a share of slightly more than 90 percent. Holdings of Indian government securities rose slowly and irregularly and thus declined from 17 percent of total assets in 1938 to less than 5 percent in 1945. These holdings represented in both years approximately 5 percent of the Indian government's total rupee debt, whereas the increase in holdings of about R. 500 mill. was equal

24. The shares were retired at R. 118 a share on the occasion of the nationalization of the Reserve Bank in 1947. Because the dividend of the shares had been limited to 5 percent, whereas the Indian price level had more than doubled since the mid-1930s, the experience of original shareholders who had retained the shares for more than a decade was rather disappointing.

25. Simha, p. xi.

TABLE 2-12. Structure of Assets and Liabilities of Reserve Bank of India, 1934–1948
(Percent of Total Assets or Liabilities)

| | Liabilities | | Assets | | | | |
| | | | Foreign | Coins | Government securities | Advances and discounts | Total (R. mill.)[a] |
End of year	Notes	Deposits					
1934[b]	82.2	12.9	29.8	24.6	23.7	0.0	2032
1935	78.5	16.1	38.4	26.1	14.0	0.0	2193
1936	84.6	10.1	37.4	28.5	13.2	0.4	2245
1937	81.3	13.7	36.8	27.5	14.8	0.9	2277
1938	83.6	10.8	27.0	31.2	16.9	4.2	2248
1939	84.2	11.2	40.4	22.9	16.0	3.7	2802
1940	75.3	20.5	58.9	9.3	17.6	0.0	3205
1941	82.6	13.8	67.7	8.5	12.4	0.1	4061
1942	85.6	11.9	71.4	2.1	19.3	0.2	6665
1943	85.6	12.4	87.1	1.3	6.7	0.1	9826
1944	72.8	25.3	89.9	1.1	5.3	0.2	13864
1945	66.2	32.5	91.2	0.8	4.6	0.5	18283
1946	67.5	31.1	89.5	1.2	5.4	0.0	18140
1947	69.8	28.9	86.5	2.1	8.6	0.1	17560
1948[c]	72.8	25.5	84.7	2.4	10.0	0.1	18130

[a]Includes other assets and other liabilities including capital and reserves.   [b]April 5, 1935.   [c]June 25, 1948.

SOURCE OF BASIC DATA: *BMS*, pp. 562 ff.

to about 4 percent of the increase in the debt. Advances and discounts remained negligible, hardly astonishing in view of the plethora of funds available to business during World War II.

The extraordinary expansion of assets was matched by an equally marked increase in the two types of liabilities—notes and deposits—that together accounted for about 95 percent of the total. Notes issue increased from less than R. 2 bill. in 1938 to more than R. 12 bill. in 1945, an average annual rate of increase of 30 percent. As this rate was nearly twice the average rate of expansion of national product, the ratio of notes to gross national product advanced sharply from less than 8 percent in 1938 to nearly 17 percent in 1945. Although these ratios point to a marked increase in the liquidity of the Indian economy, they overstate the extent of improvement in liquidity because other forms of money and other liquid assets increased much more slowly. Deposits expanded even more rapidly, from less than R. 250 mill. to nearly R. 6 bill., an average annual rate of about 50 percent, and an advance in relation to national product from 1 to more than 8 percent. Although the government's and the bankers' deposit were of approximately equal size in 1938, the share of government deposits had risen to about seven-eighths by 1945, and at that date were equal to considerably more than one-fourth of all sources of funds of the Reserve Bank.

Changes between the end of 1945 and mid-1948, when the bank's business was formally divided between India and Pakistan, were small. Total assets were practically identical at both dates, which meant a considerable reduction in their relation to national product. However, holdings of foreign assets were drawn down by about R. 1.3 bill., or nearly one-tenth, a process that was to be continued after 1948 at a greatly accelerated speed in the Indian Union.

When the Reserve Bank was organized it became immediately the largest financial institution in India with about one-third of the assets of all financial institutions, relegating the Imperial Bank to second place. As the Reserve Bank was the first recipient of a large part of the sterling funds that had accumulated as the result of balance of payments surpluses during World War II, its position among financial institutions was even stronger in 1946, when its assets were almost equal to those of all other financial institutions combined.[26]

b. The Imperial Bank

World War I, with its accompanying large export surplus, led under the monetary system then in force to an accumulation of foreign assets in the hands of the Treasury and of the banking system, particularly those banks whose business was most closely related to exporting regions. Although the figures to prove it are not available, it seems likely that the increase in size (measured by capital, reserves, and deposits) of the three Presidency banks by nearly 90 percent between 1913 and 1920 was to a good extent due to this imported inflation, as the ratio of the three banks' assets to gross national product rose only insignificantly from 2.4 to 2.7 percent. Cash balances rose by nearly 70 percent, and investments, mainly government securities, were increased by nearly 110 percent. Other assets, consisting chiefly of loans and discounts, nearly doubled. Thus, changes in the structure of assets were relatively small, as were shifts in the distribution of total assets among the three banks, the share of the Bank of Bombay advancing from 28 to 35 percent at the expense of the share of the Bank of Bengal, which declined from 50 to 45 percent.[27]

There apparently are no continuous statistics about the origin of the private deposits of the Presidency banks. Around 1915 about one-sixth of total deposits came from other banks, attesting to their function as bankers' banks. Of the remaining five-sixths, about one-fourth belonged to European, presumably mainly British, depositors and three-fourths to Indian business and private depositors. There were considerable differences in the structure of deposits of the three banks.[28] Thus the Bank of Bombay had the highest share of bankers' deposits, a reflection of the position of Bombay as the leading financial center; and the share of European deposits was highest in the Bank of Madras.

Because India lacked a central bank and the three Presidency banks fulfilled two functions usually exercised by a central bank, namely, acting as the government's and other bankers' bank, the first more completely than the second, it is not astonishing that from time to time suggestions were made to amalgamate them and possibly to develop the merged institution into a full-fledged central bank. All these suggestions came to nought, because of opposition, sometimes by the government, which was afraid of too much concentration of financial power in one hand; sometimes by the three banks themselves; and sometimes by other banks or by business. Influenced by the experiences of World War I, the three banks themselves after the end of the war proposed a merger, a proposal that was accepted by the government. The bill providing for the merger of the three Presidency banks into the Imperial Bank of India was introduced in the Indian Legislative Council in March 1920, passed in September 1920, and became effective in January 1921.[29]

The Imperial Bank, continuing as the government's bank and in many respects also as a bankers' bank, was at its formation by far the largest financial institution in India. With assets of more than R. 900 mill. in 1920, it accounted for nearly one-fifth of the assets of all reporting financial institutions. Its seventy-odd offices represented one in six of the offices of all reporting commercial banks.[30] The Imperial Bank was a privately owned joint stock company, much of its stock owned by British investors living in India or Great Britain; most of the top and middle management were also British, two characteristics inherited from the Presidency banks.

26. The ratios are slightly reduced if account is taken of the relatively small assets of indigenous bankers and in 1935 also of class D and unscheduled Indian joint stock banks.
27. *BMS,* p. 10.
28. Ghose, p. 26.
29. Much of this paragraph is based on the discussion in Simha, chap. 1.
30. *BMS,* pp. 7 ff.

The Imperial Bank continued to be the largest financial institution in India until 1935 when the Reserve Bank began operations—at that time the assets of the Reserve Bank were more than twice as large as those of the Imperial Bank, and it remained the largest commercial bank throughout the period. In 1939 the assets of the Imperial Bank were three times as large as those of the largest other Indian joint stock bank (table 1-15); and they were slightly larger than the assets of all scheduled Indian joint stock banks or those of all exchange banks. Nevertheless, the Imperial Bank could not fully maintain its original share in the assets of all commercial banks or of all financial institutions. Thus the Imperial Bank's share in the assets of all commercial banks declined from nearly 40 percent in 1920 and 1929 to 30 percent in 1939 and to 20 percent in 1946, mainly because of the very rapid increase in the number and assets of Indian joint stock banks.

In the 1920s the assets of the Imperial Bank declined by only 3 percent and thus held up better than those of the exchange or Indian joint stock banks. They began to lag in the 1930s when they increased by only 6 percent, and particularly between 1939 and 1946; although the bank's assets trebled in seven years, while those of the Indian joint stock banks increased by over 500 percent. Compared to the assets of all reporting financial institutions, the share of the Imperial Bank declined even more sharply from 30 percent in 1920 to about 20 percent in 1929, 11 percent in 1939, and 8 percent in 1946. Similarly, the share of the Imperial Bank in the offices of all commercial banks fell from between one in six in 1920 and one in four in 1929 and 1940 to one in eleven in 1946; although the bank built up its network of branches from 72 in 1920 to 383 in 1940, it failed to expand it substantially during the following six years when the Indian joint stock banks opened nearly 3,500 new offices.

Between 1920 and 1946 the Imperial Bank came to rely increasingly on private deposits (its government deposits were transferred to the Reserve Bank in 1935) as its capital and reserves declined from 8 to 4 percent of liabilities. As a result, private deposits, which had been around 80 percent from 1920 to 1934, contributed 95 percent of total funds in 1946. No information seems to be available on the origin and size distribution of the Imperial Bank's private deposits.

The outstanding change in the structure of assets was the continuous and sharp increase in the share of government securities from less than one-seventh in 1920 to nearly two-fifths in 1939 and to slightly more than one-half in 1946. The share of most other assets fell considerably, that of cash declining between 1920 and 1946 from 30 to 13 percent and that of loans of all types from slightly more than one-half to about 30 percent.[31]

c. The Exchange Banks[32]

Restricted as they were to large cities and concentrating on the financing of India's foreign trade, the exchange banks participated during part of the period only to a limited extent in the rapid expansion of the country's banking system.

The exchange banks expanded rapidly during World War I in line with the sharp increase in India's exports, their Indian deposits rising from not more than R. 300 mill. in 1913 to R. 750 mill. in 1920. No further expansion occurred in the following two decades. In the 1939–46 period assets increased sharply, though less than those of the rest of the banking system. As a result, the share of the exchange banks in the deposits of all commercial banks decreased from almost one-third in 1913, 1920, and 1929 to one-fourth in 1939 and to less than one-sixth in 1946. The decline of the share of the exchange banks' assets in those of all financial institutions is still more pronounced, namely from approximately one-fourth in 1913 and 1920 to less than

31. *BMS*, pp. 32 ff.

32. The statistical information on the exchange banks is very deficient, reports being limited to the main types of their assets and liabilities in India (*BMS*, pp. 7, 192 ff). Most of the exchange banks were also operating in other countries, which makes it difficult, if not impossible, to determine the part of the banks' capital and reserves attributable to their Indian business. Similar difficulties prevent allocation of the excess of Indian deposits over Indian assets to specific types of foreign assets.

one-tenth in 1939 and to only 5 percent in 1946. Although the expansion of the exchange banks was much slower than that of the rest of the banking system in the 1930s and 1940s, it sufficed to increase the relation of their deposits to gross national product from 1.5 percent in 1913 to 2.5 percent in 1946.

Similar tendencies are shown in the development of the exchange banks' branch network. Although the number of offices doubled, from about 40 in 1916 to more than 80 in 1929 and 1940, their share in all commercial banking offices in India declined from nearly one in six in 1916 to only one in twenty-five in 1939. Between 1939 and 1946 the number of offices was reduced by ten and the exchange banks' share in the national total, which nearly trebled during this period, fell precipitously to less than 1½ percent.

Little is known quantitatively about the structure of the assets and liabilities of the exchange banks, because statistics begin only in 1935 and even then are limited to a few broad components. The main trend among deposits is the decline of the share of time deposits from more than two-fifths in 1935 to less than one-sixth in 1946. Although the direction of the movement is the same as that observed in the case of Indian scheduled commercial banks (about 45 percent in 1935 and 30 percent in 1946), the decline is much more pronounced for the exchange banks. This may reflect the presumed lower share of individual deposits as compared to business deposits among the sources of funds of the exchange banks. Changes in the structure of assets were small and limited to the 1939–46 period, a slight decline of the share of advances at the expense of an increase in the share of deposits with the Reserve Bank. Although no direct evidence is available, the movement of the excess of Indian deposits over reported Indian assets (from about R. 330 mill. in 1935 to R. 180 mill. in 1939 to R. 920 mill. in 1946) suggests a substantial absolute and relative decline in the excess, which may be regarded as an indicator of the net funds made available by the Indian branches of the exchange banks to their main office or to other offices outside India, between 1935 and 1939, followed by a large increase in the 1940–46 period.

d. Indian Joint Stock Banks[33]

Although all financial institutions, with the exception of indigenous bankers (and rural moneylenders, if they be regarded as financial institutions), expanded rapidly during the three decades following 1913, both in absolute terms and in relation to the size of the Indian economy, the Indian commercial joint stock banks may be said to have come into their own. By the end of World War I, or even in the late 1930s, Indian commercial banking had been well established in a pattern, often criticized as not well adapted to foster the country's rapid economic development, that in its essential features continued throughout the first two decades after independence.

(i) ASSET EXPANSION. At the beginning of the period the reporting Indian commercial joint stock banks ranked third among the six main groups of financial institutions, measured by total assets, behind both the three Presidency banks and the dozen exchange banks and only slightly ahead of the Post Office Saving System. They accounted for more than one-sixth of the assets of all financial institutions and their assets were equal to less than 1.5 percent of national product. Three decades later these banks constituted the second largest group of financial institutions, outranked only by the Reserve Bank; they held more than one-fourth of the assets of all financial institutions and in 1946 their assets were equal to nearly 14 percent of national product, almost ten times the 1913 relationship.[34]

33. For basic statistics, cf. BMS, pp. 96 ff.

34. The available statistics include until the mid-1930s in addition to the Imperial Bank only the so-called class A-1 and B banks, that is, the large and medium-sized institutions. Because the assets of the much more numerous class C and D banks as well as the unscheduled banks then amounted to only 15 percent of those of class A and B banks, their omission from the statistics for the earlier part of the period cannot significantly affect the overall picture. Most of the class C and D and unscheduled banks may be presumed to have been relatively young in 1935. It is, therefore, likely that the growth rate of all Indian commercial banks during the first two decades of this period was slightly higher than indicated by the available

TABLE 2-13. Determinants of Commercial Bank Asset Expansion, 1914–1946 (Percent Change Per Year)

	1914–20	1921–29	1930–39	1940–46	1914–46
Total assets[a]	18.3	−0.8	−7.1	29.9	11.6
Gross national product	7.6	−0.3	−2.2	14.9	3.9
Ratio of assets to GNP	9.9	0.5	8.1	13.1	7.4
Number of banks	5.1	3.3	7.9	10.6	5.5
Number of bank offices	14.5[b]	4.8	8.3	23.4	10.9[c]
Average assets per bank[a]	14.2	−4.3	−2.1	19.2	3.8
Average assets per bank office[a]	13.1[b]	−5.7	−2.6	10.3	0.9[c]

[a]Based for 1913–40 on capital, reserves, and deposits.   [b]1916–20.   [c]1916–46.

SOURCE OF BASIC DATA: *BMS*, pp. 7 ff.

The increase of the assets of Indian commercial banks between 1913 and 1946 from about R. 0.3 bill. to nearly R. 10 bill., an average annual growth rate of fully 11 percent, is due primarily to three factors: First, the growth of the Indian economy, reflected in the increase of national product at an average annual rate of somewhat less than 4 percent; second, an increase in the monetization ratio, which cannot be exactly measured but which hardly can have exceeded one-tenth of total national product, equivalent to at most one-half of 1 percent per year; and third, and obviously most important, an increase in the ratio of commercial banks' assets to total or monetized income. The increase in the third component, in turn, can be ascribed to, first, an increase in the number of banks and bank offices, and, second, to the rise in the average assets per bank or per office.

Most of the growth of the assets of Indian commercial banks, in fact about 90 percent, occurred during the two periods of war inflation, 1914–20 and 1940–46. The rate of expansion was, however, more rapid in 1940–46, with 30 percent a year, than in 1914–20 when it averaged 17 percent a year. In both cases the rate of expansion was approximately twice as rapid as that of national product. Neither bank assets nor gross national product showed any substantial change between the benchmarks of 1921 and 1929. The contrast was most pronounced during the 1930s, when bank assets increased at the substantial rate of nearly 6 percent a year, although national product showed a downward trend and in 1939 was still 20 percent below the 1929 level.[35] We are thus left with a nineteenfold increase in bank assets compared with a less than fourfold increase of national product; in particular, with a full trebling of bank assets and an increase of national product by less than 70 percent in the 1914–20 period; a doubling in bank assets in the face of a decline of national product by one-fifth in the 1930s; and a more than sixfold expansion of bank assets compared with an increase of national product by 165 percent during the 1940–46 period.

(ii) ORGANIZATIONAL EXPANSION. During the period the number of Indian commercial banks, as well as that of their branches, increased considerably. This process, which involved an increase in the number of bank offices in territory already having such offices at the beginning of

statistics. However, even on the extreme assumption that all class C and D and all unscheduled banks first reporting in 1935 had been organized after 1913, the average annual growth rate of all Indian commercial banks for the 1913–46 period would have been less than 1 percent above the rate of 9 percent applying to the Imperial Bank and class A and B banks.

35. The discrepancy in the trend of bank assets and national product during the 1930s is due mainly to developments in 1930–33. During these four years bank assets, represented by deposits of class A and B banks, increased by 15 percent, whereas national product declined by 36 percent. Most of the discrepancy occurred in 1932 when bank assets expanded by 15 percent, although national product shrank by 4 percent. During the other three years, changes in bank assets were small, notwithstanding decreases in national product by 20 percent in 1930, 11 percent in 1931, and 5 percent in 1933. These discrepancies are not easy to explain, in particular because money supply did not change much over the four years.

the period as well as the penetration into areas, mostly urban but to a limited extent also rural, that had formerly been without a bank office, must have accounted for part of the increase in the ratio of bank assets to national product. Its effects, however, cannot be statistically separated from other factors, particularly the spread of the "banking habit," that is, the propensity of business enterprises and households to keep part of their assets, particularly their financial assets, in the form of bank deposits and their propensity to lend to and to borrow from Indian commercial banks compared with other possible channels of financing.

Because fairly complete statistics of the smaller institutions start only in 1939, the number of commercial banks operating at the beginning of the period is unknown. The number of large and medium-sized Indian banks (i.e., class A and B), other than the Presidency banks, rose from 41 in 1913 to 58 in 1920.[36] It is doubtful that the number of small banks showed the same movement, because many of them, as well as some larger ones, regionally concentrated in western India and particularly the Punjab, were eliminated by a wave of bank failures in 1914 and, on a smaller scale, in 1915 and 1916. Most of the victims had been organized during the preceding decade, particularly in connection with the Swadeshi movement, and many of the failures were the result of excessive credits to unsuccessful industrial or commercial enterprises sponsored by or affiliated with the bank.[37] The story for the 1920s is similar. The number of class A and B banks increased from 58 to 78, but failures, the most serious in 1923, eliminated more than 130 institutions, again mainly small firms. The organization of new banks accelerated during the following two decades, the number of class A and B banks more than doubling from 78 to nearly 170 during the 1930s and doubling again to 340 in the 1940–46 period. The number of smaller banks (class C and D and unscheduled) declined during the early 1940s, the first period for which statistics are available, from nearly 1,200 to about 1,000. This decline resulted from mergers as well as failures, which continued at an average rate of about 50 per year, again mainly affecting very small institutions, as is evidenced by the average paid-up capital of the failing banks, of only R. 20,000 for 1940–46. This continuous run of bank failures points to a basic weakness, particularly among smaller institutions, and to insufficient bank supervision.

From the point of view of the penetration of the banking system, the number of bank offices is more important than the number of banks. At the beginning of the period the network of bank offices was still very wide-meshed. Class A and B banks had fewer than 200 offices, or only 1 per 1.7 million inhabitants; less than half of them had branch offices and those that did averaged about nine branches per bank. The smaller banks, for which no comparable data exist, would probably have added only slightly to the number of offices, and even less to their resources.[38]

Expansion of the class A and B banks' branch networks proceeded at a fair pace through the 1920s and 1930s. By 1940 these banks had increased the number of offices more than six times since 1913, or at an average annual rate of 8 percent. As a result, the number of inhabitants per branch fell from 1.7 to 0.3 million. The expansion was due primarily to the increase in number of banks and only secondarily to the rise in the proportion of banks having branches from 44 to 58 percent or to an increase in the average number of branches per system from about nine to twelve.

The broadest expansion of the banks' branch network occurred, however, in the closing

36. *BMS*, pp. 6 ff.

37. Statistics show for 1914–1919 89 failures with a paid-up capital of R. 16 mill. (*BMS*, p. 279). The average size of paid-up capital of R. 180,000 suggests that the failures concerned mainly small institutions, although they included two medium-sized banks, People's Bank and Amritsar Bank (Lokanathan, pp. 238, 251). In the absence of information on the number and capital of all India commercial banks, it is not possible to ascertain the share of the failed institutions in the number or capital of all banks. That it must have been substantial is indicated by the fact that the paid-up capital of the banks failing in the 1914–20 period of R. 16 mill. compares with a total capital of class A banks of R. 23 mill. in 1913.

38. The class C banks had only 145 offices in 1946, the first year for which their number is reported (*BMS*, p. 282), or 8 percent of those of the class A and B banks. Those of the class D and unscheduled banks were hardly more numerous. Most of the unreported offices were undoubtedly of very small size.

TABLE 2-14. Development of Branch Network of Commercial Banks, 1916–1946

	All banks (1)	Banks with branches			Offices		Percent of banks with branches (7)	Deposits per office (R. mill.) (8)
		Number (2)	Offices (3)	Offices per bank (4)	Total (5)	Per million inhabitants (6)		
I. Imperial Bank of India[a]								
1916[a]	3	3	65	21.7	65	0.21	100	7.68
1920[a]	3	3	72	24.0	72	0.24	100	11.99
1929	1	1	187	187.0	187	0.56	100	4.24
1940	1	1	383	383.0	383	0.99	100	2.51
1946	1	1	443	443.0	443	1.07	100	6.13
II. Exchange banks								
1916	12	10	45	4.5	47	0.15	83	8.09
1920	15	15	55	3.7	55	0.18	100	13.60
1929	18	18	86	4.8	86	0.26	100	7.76
1940	20	17	87	5.1	90	0.23	85	9.48
1946	15	15	77	5.1	77	0.19	100	23.55
III. Class A and B banks								
1916	48	21	182	8.7	209	0.60	44	1.23
1920	58	34	335	9.9	359	1.10	59	2.05
1929	78	51	521	10.2	548	1.65	65	1.27
1940	177	103	1244	12.1	1318	3.22	58	0.95
1946	339	265	4570	17.2	4644	11.12	78	1.56
IV. All large and medium-sized commercial banks								
1916	63	34	292	6.6	321	1.05	54	3.54
1920	76	54	462	8.6	486	1.59	71	4.83
1929	99	72	763	10.6	821	2.46	73	2.58
1940	198	121	1714	14.2	1791	4.70	61	1.71
1946	355	281	5090	18.1	5164	12.44	79	1.93

[a]Presidency banks in 1916 and 1920.

SOURCE: **Cols. 1–3, 5, and 8:** *BMS,* pp. 7 ff. and 282.

years of the period. In the five years from 1941 through 1946 the number of branches, now also including the class C banks, more than tripled, corresponding to an average annual growth rate of more than 23 percent and increasing the number of bank offices per million inhabitants from four to twelve. This time the growth in the number of offices was due chiefly to the rise in the number of banks in operation and the increase in the number of branches per bank with branches and only secondarily, particularly if class C banks are included, in the proportion of banks having any branches.

e. Structure of Assets and Liabilities

Probably the most serious obstacle to an analysis of the Indian banking system in the interwar period is the absence of any sufficiently detailed breakdown of assets and liabilities, even for the larger class A and B banks. As a matter of fact, before 1935 the statistics provide only one item of information for the scheduled banks and exchange banks, that is, cash in hand and at banks. Even for the last decade of the period the statistics distinguish only five items (cash, required and excess reserves with the Reserve Bank, advances, and inland bills discounted), items that fail to break down about one-half of total assets in 1935. (The slightly less unsatisfactory information on the Imperial Bank has already been discussed in subsection b.) Thus we can calculate that cash constituted 23 percent of capital and deposits in 1913, 27 percent in 1920, and 14 percent in 1929, hardly enough for even the roughest analysis of these banks'

Calcutta in the first two decades of the century. The position of Madras increased, but even in 1946 its share in check clearings was only 5 percent of all centers, compared with 39 percent for Bombay, 41 percent for Calcutta, and 8 percent for all other places. As an indication of the financial development of India, bank clearings rose from 16 percent of national product in 1900 to 28 percent in 1913, 57 percent in 1929, and 93 percent in 1946.

g. Concentration

Although the degree of concentration in Indian commercial banking has always been high, both among Indian joint stock banks and among a broader group that includes the Presidency banks and the exchange banks, it began to decline during the interwar period.

Starting with the Indian joint stock banks, a considerable number of class C and D and unscheduled banks are included, the share of the nine largest banks, which since the 1930s constituted less than 1 percent of the number of all banks, exceeded one-half from 1913 to 1939 but declined to not much more than one-third in 1946. The largest single bank (the Allahabad Bank in 1913, the Central Bank of India in 1929 and 1946) held more than one-fourth of the deposits of all banks in 1913, one-sixth in 1929, and one-eighth in 1946. The corresponding shares for the three largest banks were more than two-fifths in 1913, one-half in 1929, but only one-fourth in 1946.

The picture is quite different if the scope is enlarged to include the three Presidency banks (in 1913), the Imperial Bank (in 1929, 1939, and 1946), and the exchange banks, in order to cover the entire field of commercial banking, although necessarily including the limited central banking activities of the Presidency banks or the Imperial Bank. In that case concentration is much more pronounced but does not increase. The two to three dozen largest banks, out of a total of about 1,400 in 1939 and 1946 and of a substantially smaller number at earlier benchmark dates, particularly 1913, held approximately nine-tenths of total bank deposits from 1913 to 1939 but less than two-thirds in 1946. Within this leading group, however, positions changed rapidly. The share of the Imperial Bank (or its predecessors), always the largest private bank in the country, which was around two-fifths from 1913 to 1929, fell sharply to only one-fifth in 1946. Similarly, the share of the exchange banks, fluctuating in number between twelve and twenty, most of which were large institutions, remained in the neighborhood of one-third from 1913 to 1929 but dropped to one-seventh in 1946. In contrast, the nine largest Indian joint stock

TABLE 2-16. Concentration in Banking, 1913–1946[a]

	1913	1920	1929	1939	1946
All banks, percent	100	100	100	100	100
Main groups, percent					
Imperial Bank[b]	43	37	37	30	21
Exchange banks	32	32	31	25	14
Indian joint stock banks	25[c]	31	32	44	64
Class A	23	30	30	34	54
Class B	2	1	2	3	3
Classes C and D	·	·	·	2	1
Unscheduled	·	·	·	5	6
Nine large banks[d]	14	·	27	31	28
All banks (R. bill.)	0.98	2.35	2.12	2.93	12.66
Reserve Bank (R. bill.)[e]	—	—	—	2.12	17.44
Treasury (R. bill.)[f]	0.51	1.43	1.72	—	—

[a]Based on total deposits.   [b]In 1913 and 1920 three Presidency banks.   [c]Only class A and B banks.   [d]For individual banks, cf. table 1-15.   [e]Notes and deposits.   [f]Notes.

SOURCE OF BASIC DATA: *BMS*, passim.

banks increased their share from one-seventh in 1913 to more than one-fourth in 1929 and 1946. Table 2-16 thus illustrates the shift of the balance within the commercial banking system from the foreign, that is, essentially British-owned and managed, banks to institutions managed and owned predominantly by Indian bankers and shareholders.[41],[42]

h. The Post Office Saving System

The increase in deposits with the postal saving system was relatively slow with an annual average rate of increase for the entire period from 1914 through 1946 of 5.7 percent. This was due in part to the wave of withdrawals after the start of World War I, which required almost a decade to offset. The growth of deposits accelerated to nearly 8 percent a year during the 1930s, possibly influenced by the greater confidence in the system during the Great Depression. The rate of growth advanced further to nearly 9 percent in the 1940–46 period.

The growth in aggregate deposits was due until the late 1930s primarily to the increase in the number of accounts. Between 1913 and 1939 the number of accounts almost tripled and thus raised the proportion of depositors from a little more than 0.5 percent of the population to nearly 1.2 percent, most of the increase occurring during the 1930s, in international comparison still a very low figure, which reflects the country's poverty. The average balance per account increased slowly, from 1913 through 1939 at an average annual rate of only 0.6 percent. If allowance is made for the rise in the price level, the average deposit was practically the same in 1939 as it had been in 1913. During the 1939–46 period the statistics show a decrease in the number of accounts by 13 percent, concentrated in the year 1940 during which the deposit balance fell by nearly one-fourth, which continued at a much slower rate during the following two years. The reason for this movement is not clear; it may have been connected with the sales of government bonds issued to finance war expenditures. Although the average balance per account more than doubled between 1939 to 1946, the increase was not sufficient to offset the rise in the price level, so that the average balance in constant prices declined by nearly 20 percent.

For the period as a whole the share of Post Office Saving System in the assets of all financial institutions declined sharply from more than 16 to less than 4 percent. The losses occurred during the two periods of war inflation, paralleled during World War II by the experience of credit cooperatives, whereas the share of the savings banks increased moderately during the 1920s and almost retained its position during the 1930s.

Notwithstanding this downward trend, the system's deposits increased for the period as a whole more rapidly than national product, namely, from slightly more than 1 to 2 percent. Here again the increase was concentrated in the 1930s, when the ratio reached its peak with nearly 3 percent of national product, and declined substantially during both war inflation periods.

The growth of deposits from not much more than R. 0.2 bill. to R. 1.4 bill. was accompanied by substantial changes in their regional aspects. The outstanding feature was the doubling of the share of the Punjab from 13 percent in 1914 to 26 percent in 1946, which was offset by a substantial reduction in the share of Bombay and a smaller reduction in that of Bengal. In the absence of figures on regional product or income it is difficult to say to what extent these shifts reflected differences in the trend of personal income or changes in saving habits. It is likely, however, that the latter were more important than the former in explaining the observed changes in the regional distribution of deposits.

41. If the scope is further broadened to include the Treasury's note issuing department for the 1913, 1920, and 1929 benchmarks and the Reserve Bank for 1939 and 1946, the picture changes again. The Reserve Bank and its partial predecessor, the Treasury's note issuing department, and the Imperial Bank and its predecessor, the three Presidency banks (i.e., four units in 1913 and 1929, two from 1939 on), accounted for slightly more than three-fifths of the assets of all banks broadly defined (but still excluding the Post Office Saving System and cooperative banks) throughout the period.

42. A more detailed picture of the degree of concentration among Indian commercial banks and the Imperial Bank can be derived from *BMS*, pp. 17 ff. It permits the inference that the share of the top 5 percent of banks in the total assets of the group was in the neighborhood of two-thirds in 1915 and 1940, after having been somewhat below that level in 1920 and above it in 1930. No substantial change appears to have occurred between 1940 and 1946.

Regional differences in average deposits per office, per account, and per inhabitant remained large and even increased in some respects. Possibly the most interesting figure is that of average deposits per inhabitant, which varied in 1940 from less than R. 0.50 in Madras and Bihar to R. 2.25 in Bombay compared to a national average for British India of R. 2. Whereas the average deposit per inhabitant increased in the provinces where the average had been well below the national average in 1910, it declined in the provinces with the highest averages, thus somewhat reducing interregional differences.[43]

i. The Cooperative Credit System[44]

At the beginning of the period the cooperative credit system was still in its infancy, having been started less than a decade before. It consisted essentially of about 19,000 local societies, most of which were very small, as evidenced by an average working capital (capital, reserves, deposits, and borrowings) of only about R. 6,000[45] and working capital of only R. 90 per member.

In the following three decades the system expanded rapidly, particularly during the first half of the period. By 1929 the number of local societies was close to 100,000 with 4 million members, three-fourths of them located in rural areas. There existed in addition 10 state cooperative banks and nearly 600 central (district) banks. The local societies were still very small with an average working capital of about R. 3,600 for rural and R. 14,000 for urban societies. Even the central banks had on the average a working capital of only R. 0.5 mill., whereas that of the state banks averaged R. 8 mill. The limited degree of penetration of the rural societies is indicated by the fact that only one out of seven villages had a local society and their 3 million members represented only somewhat above 5 percent of all rural families. The total working capital of the system of fully R. 800 mill. in 1929 (including state and central, i.e., district banks) was, however, equal to more than one-eighth of the total assets of all financial institutions and to nearly 2.5 percent of national product. Both ratios are considerably reduced if the substantial duplications caused by deposits and borrowings within the system are eliminated.

Expansion of the cooperative system continued throughout the 1930s, although at a considerably slower pace, particularly during the Great Depression. Between 1929 and 1939 the number of local societies increased by nearly one-fourth, the expansion being much more pronounced for urban societies (59 percent) than for rural ones (12 percent). With an increase in the number of members by less than one-third, to 5¼ million, penetration of rural India remained limited.

Total assets of local societies grew by more than one-fourth, but the increase was limited to urban societies whose assets doubled during the 1930s. Average assets per rural society fell to only R. 3,000. The share of the cooperative credit system in the assets of all financial institutions declined from about 13 to 11 percent, as the system failed to expand as rapidly as other types of financial institutions, particularly the Indian joint stock banks and the Post Office Saving System, a development that points to some doubts of the rural population about the safety of credit cooperatives. The ratio of the assets of the cooperative credit system to national product nevertheless increased from 2.5 percent in 1929 to 4 percent a decade later, reflecting the sharp rise in the ratio of the assets of all financial institutions to national product.[46]

43. For basic data, cf. BMS, pp. 370 ff.

44. All the figures used in this section cover noncredit as well as credit societies, because the statistics readily available (e.g., BMS, pp. 384 ff.) do not give separate information for the members and the assets and liabilities of credit societies. In terms of number of societies, credit cooperatives have always been predominant. In 1916, for example, they represented 98 percent of all individual societies, 99 percent of rural and 83 percent of urban societies. By 1946 their share had declined considerably, to 77 percent for all cooperatives and to 84 percent and 32 percent, respectively, for rural and urban societies. The figures in the text thus somewhat overstate the growth of credit cooperatives.

45. BMS, pp. 384 ff.

46. If account is taken of duplications within the cooperative credit system, its assets would be smaller by one-fourth to one-third.

During World War II the cooperative credit system resumed the rapid absolute and relative expansion that had characterized the 1914–29 period and was to continue after independence. Between 1939 and 1946 the number of local societies increased by more than 40 percent, this time without a large difference between rural and urban societies; and the number of members rose by more than two-thirds to about 9 million. The system's total working capital, however, increased by only slightly more than 50 percent, and the entire increase took place outside the rural societies, whose average working capital as a result fell from R. 3,000 to R. 2,250 and average loans to members declined from about R. 100 to not much more than R. 50 in the face of an increase in agricultural income by 170 percent.[47] It is probably the relative, and short-lived, prosperity of at least part of the Indian peasantry that explains the failure of the cooperative system to increase its credit to agriculture during World War II.

Possibly the main characteristic of the combined statement of the cooperative system shown in table 2-17 is the large, though relatively declining, extent of upstream and downstream loans and deposits, which reflects the triple layering in the system. Thus loans and deposits from other members of the system provided nearly two-fifths of total working capital in 1916, 1920, and 1929 but only about one-fourth in 1939 and less than one-fifth in 1946. Similarly, loans within the system represented throughout the period about two-fifths of total loans, that is, they were equal to two-thirds of loans to individual members.

No information appears to be available on assets other than loans. They must, however, have been substantial during the later part of the period because total loans represented only a little more than 70 percent of capital, reserves, deposits, and borrowings in 1939 and slightly less than one-half in 1946, compared to ratios of four-fifths and over in 1913, 1920, and 1929. The remaining assets probably consisted of liquid items, such as government securities, to a good extent, particularly in 1946 when demands for loans were relatively low.

In view of the variations in physical, social, and economic characteristics among the regions of the Indian peninsula, it is not astonishing that the extent of penetration by credit cooperatives is far from uniform. Thus in the late 1920s, when about 5 percent of all rural families in India may be estimated to have belonged to cooperatives, the ratio varied between 36 percent in Coorg, 15 percent in Ajmer-Merwara (both small regions), 10 percent in the Punjab, and 8 to 9 percent in Madras and Bombay, and as little as 2 to 4 percent in Bengal, Bihar and Orissa, the Central Provinces, and the United Provinces.[48] Another illustration of the unevenness of the penetration of agricultural cooperatives is provided by the ratio between the number of members of agricultural and urban cooperatives in the different regions with their total population. In some provinces the share in the national total for membership is much higher than their share in population. This was the case for Madras, West Bengal, and the Punjab. These three provinces, which account for less than one-third of the population in the territory of the present Indian Union, had about one-half of all members of rural cooperative societies. On the other hand, the United Provinces, the Central Provinces, and Bihar and Orissa with about two-fifths of the population had only about one-fifth of the membership of rural cooperatives. As no estimates of regional income exist for the interwar period, it is not possible to say whether these differences could be explained by variations in income per head.[49]

47. Based on Sivasubramonian's estimate of agricultural income, p. 162.

48. Indian Central Banking Enquiry Committee, *Report,* 1931, I-1:113. Figures are given only for eleven regions, which do not cover the entire peninsula.

49. Use of an estimate of national income of nine regions in 1938–39 (Natarajan, p. 15; cf. table 2-2) indicates a closer correspondence between the shares of the various provinces in national income and in membership of agricultural cooperatives than between the latter and the distribution in population, but some of the differences remain, that is, the higher share of membership than of national income in the Punjab and in West Bengal and the lower share in the United Provinces. This suggests that the penetration of the cooperative banking system was influenced by factors other than income, but closer study might well indicate that income per head was the most important single factor.

TABLE 2-17. Development of Cooperative System, 1916–1946[a,b]

June 30	1916	1920	1929	1939	1946
	I. Number of societies and members (thou.)				
Number of societies	18.75	38.96	97.75	120.84	170.80
Agricultural	17.73	36.30	87.99	105.31	146.96
Nonagricultural	1.02	2.66	9.76	15.53	23.84
Number of individual members	865	1514	3996	5267	8936
Agricultural	717	1175	3004	3560	5501
Nonagricultural	148	339	992	1707	3435
	II. Assets and liabilities (R. mill.)				
Working capital	103	214	827	1066	1640
Capital and reserves	26	52	193	319	475
Loans and deposits from					
Individuals and others	40	78	316	402	687
Cooperative societies	3	7	35	39	137
Central and state cooperative banks	33	73	266	245	251
Government	2	4	18	12	15
Loans to individuals	56	105	382	470	469
Loans to banks and societies	36	80	278	291	325
	III. Distribution (working capital = 100)				
Working capital	100.0	100.0	100.0	100.0	100.0
Capital and reserve	25.2	24.3	23.3	29.9	29.0
Loans and deposits from					
Individuals and others	38.8	36.5	38.2	37.7	41.9
Cooperative societies	2.9	3.3	4.2	3.7	8.4
Central and state cooperative banks	32.0	34.1	32.2	23.0	15.3
Government	1.9	1.9	2.2	1.1	0.9
Loans to individuals	54.3	49.1	46.2	44.1	28.6
Loans to banks and societies	35.0	37.4	33.6	27.3	19.8
	IV. Working capital				
Per society (R. thou.)	5.5	5.5	8.4	8.8	9.6
Per member (R.)	119	141	206	202	184

[a]Includes noncredit societies, but excludes state and central banks in I.   [b]Includes Burma through 1929.

SOURCE: *BMS,* pp. 384 ff.

Even in 1946 when there were about 170,000 local societies (147,000 of them agricultural) with nearly 9 million members (5.5 million of them belonging to rural societies) and loans to individual members were close to R. 0.5 bill., most of these figures being ten or more times as large as they had been in 1916, the cooperative system, and particularly its agricultural wing, was still far from maturity. This is evident not only in the low degree of penetration of the countryside—only one in five villages had a cooperative society; only about 8 percent of rural families were members; and the loans outstanding constituted only a small fraction of total rural indebtedness, probably on the order of 2 percent—but also in many organizational and operational deficiencies, such as the high proportion of loans overdue and the lack of adequate accounting. In the late 1920s a witness before the Indian Central Banking Enquiry Committee summed up his opinion by asserting that "the fundamental principle of cooperation is lacking. Overdues are highly excessive. Audit is defective. Control in inefficient."[50] It is unlikely that the situation had changed much by 1946, for similar complaints were voiced after independence.[51]

50. Indian Central Banking Enquiry Committee, *Report,* 1930, I-1: 132. The witness was the managing governor of the Imperial Bank.
51. Cf. chap. 3, sec. 4d, and particularly Thorner.

j. Indigenous Bankers

Quantitative information on the activities of urban indigenous bankers, as distinct from rural moneylenders, is missing for this period as it was for the half century before 1913.[52] Consequently, not much can be added to what has been said in chapter 1, section 5a.

There is little doubt that the relative importance of indigenous bankers declined considerably in the period from 1913 to 1946, during which the assets of their main competitors— commercial banks and urban credit cooperatives—shot up from not much more than R. 1 bill. to more than R. 15 bill. The absolute amount of indigenous bankers' resources may well have increased, but there is no statistical evidence. By the end of the period, and probably even earlier, indigenous bankers had been reduced to a minor component in the country's financial structure except in a few cities, such as Bombay and Ahmadabad, and for certain types of borrowers. As early as 1931 the Indian Chamber of Commerce in Calcutta went so far as to say that "the position today is that the indigenous bankers in India are like Lilliputians who [in] despite of their numbers are helpless in tackling the financial problems of the country,"[53] symbolic, though probably correct, language, but without statistical foundation. The order of magnitude of the operations of indigenous bankers, however, is indicated by the fact that in Bengal slightly more than 3,000 firms were registered in the late 1930s under the Bengal Moneylenders Act of 1937, of which 350 were in Calcutta and 2,800 in the rest of Bengal, most of the latter probably operating as rural moneylenders rather than as urban indigenous bankers, and that the resources of indigenous bankers in Calcutta were estimated at only R. 20 mill.[54,55] On that basis the resources of indigenous bankers in all of India can hardly have exceeded a few hundred mill. R. in the late 1930s when the assets of commercial banks were in excess of R. 3 bill. and even those of urban cooperatives approached R. 300 mill.

k. Insurance Organizations

Insurance, at least life insurance, was still in its infancy at the beginning of the period. The 60-odd life or mixed companies, including two dozen foreign firms, were with few exceptions quite small, as indicated by the fact that the assets of 35 reporting Indian companies averaged less than R. 2 mill. and totaled only R. 65 mill., or about 3 percent of the assets of all financial institutions and 0.3 percent of national product. Penetration had hardly scratched the surface as the number of policies of Indian companies was probably not much in excess of 100,000, or one policy for about every 2,500 inhabitants.

The growth of life insurance accelerated from the 1920s on. By 1929 the assets of Indian reporting companies exceeded R. 250 mill., four times the 1913 level; their share in the assets of all financial institutions had risen to 4 percent; the ratio of their assets to national product had climbed to 0.8 percent, although still a very low level; and the number of their policies was approaching 500,000, still less than 1 in 1,300 Indians, with an average face value of about R. 1,700 and an average reserve of not much more than R. 120.

Approximately the same rate of growth was maintained during the 1930s. Assets of Indian companies increased at an annual rate of 10.5 percent compared with a rate of 9.4 percent in the 1920s, reaching in 1939 a level of more than 7 percent of the assets of all financial institutions and of 2.5 percent of national product. By 1938 the number of policies exceeded 1.2 million,

52. In 1931 the members of the Indian Central Banking Enquiry Committee said in their report, "We are greatly struck by the absence of published statistics in regard to the operation of indigenous bankers" (I-1:431), but the situation did not change for another four decades.

53. Indian Central Banking Enquiry Committee, 1930, *Report*, I-1:529.

54. Another source (Ghose, p. 337) gives the paid-up capital of 208 banking and loan companies in Bengal in 1921 at R. 19 mill. and that of 1,043 companies with R. 73 mill. in 1936. The average paid-up capital thus declined from R. 91,000 in 1921 to R. 41,000 in 1936.

55. Such a figure is compatible with the fact that around 1970 the resources of the most important group of indigenous bankers came to about R. 800 mill. (chap. 3, sec. 4j).

TABLE 2-18. Development of Life Insurance, 1913–1946[a]

	1913	1920	1929	1939	1946
1. Number of reporting Indian companies	35	43	73	196	227
2. Total assets (R. mill.)	65	106	256	696	1515
3. Assets per company (R. mill.)	1.86	2.46	3.51	3.55	6.68
4. Average rate of growth (percent)					
Total assets	—	7.2	10.3	10.5	11.8
Assets per company	—	4.1	4.0	0.1	9.5
5. Number of policies (thou.)	150[b]	200[b]	484	1402	2655
6. Assets per policy (R.)	510[b]	530[b]	529	496	570
7. Face value of policies (R. mill.)	244[c]	311	813	2324	5394
8. Face value per policy (R.)	1470[b,c]	1555	1681	1658	2032
9. Assets as percentage of					
Assets of all financial institutions	3.0	2.1	4.2	7.4	4.0
Gross national product	0.3	0.3	0.8	2.5	2.1
10. Post Office life insurance policies (thou.)	25	33	71	101	93
11. Face value of Post Office life insurance (R. mill.)	34	49	137	200	189
12. Post Office life insurance assets (R. mill.)[d]	2	2	7	11	12
13. Provident society policies (thou.)	—	—	—	70[e]	82
14. Face value of provident societies (R. mill.)	—	—	—	20[e]	31
15. Provident society assets (R. mill.)	—	—	—	8[e]	10

[a]Indian companies only in lines 1–9.　　[b]Rough estimates.　　[c]1914.　　[d]The figures refer to 1912, 1918, 1932, 1939, and 1947, respectively.　　[e]1941.

SOURCES: Lines 1 and 2: *BMS*, p. 924. Line 5: *BMS*, p. 921. Lines 7 and 8: 1914–20, Ray, p. 36; 1929–46, *BMS*, p. 924. Lines 10–15: *BMS*, pp. 926–27.

still less than 1 in about every 350 inhabitants. A good deal of the growth during this decade is attributable to the organization of many small companies, the number of Indian companies reporting almost trebling. The effect is seen in the failure of assets per company to increase at all, the reduction of the amount of assets per policy by 6 percent, and the unchanged face value of the average policy.

In monetary terms, the growth of life insurance further accelerated during World War II, with assets more than doubling in seven years and increasing at an average rate of nearly 12 percent between 1939 and 1946. The purchasing power of these assets, and hence of beneficiaries' equity, however, decreased, as the price level rose in the same interval by nearly 150 percent.

Government securities dominated the portfolios of Indian life insurance companies throughout the period as they had done prior to 1914. The only substantial enduring changes in portfolio structure were the decline of the share of Indian municipal, port, and improvement trust and similar bonds from about 15 percent of total assets from 1913 to 1929 to only 5 percent in 1946; the increase of the share of corporate bonds and shares from 2 percent in 1913 and 1920 to 10 percent in 1946, most of the increase occurring in the 1930s and 1940s; and the rise of cash from 2 to 6 percent of total assets. Policy loans fluctuated at the benchmark dates between 4 and 8 percent, averaging 6.5 percent.

Up to the end of the 1930s the number of companies, of their policies, of business in force as well as the value of their assets in absolute terms or in relation to the assets of all financial institutions or to national product, all increased rapidly. The inflation of the early 1940s, however, brought a setback, as inflation usually does for life insurance companies, if not in the absolute value of assets or in the number and face value of policies, then in the relation of the value of life insurance companies' assets to the assets of all financial institutions, personal income, and national product. As a result, the share of life insurance in all financial institutions' assets was only slightly higher in 1946 than it had been more than three decades earlier; and the

TABLE 2-19. Structure of Assets of Life Insurance Companies, 1913–1946
(Percent of Total Assets)

	1913	1920	1929	1939	1946
Cash	2.2	2.6	3.8	3.8	5.8
Government securities	64.3	59.1	52.0	53.8	61.9
Municipal securities[a]	15.4	14.2	14.5	8.1	5.0
Company and cooperative securities	1.7	2.1	3.3	6.8	10.1
Mortgages	0.3	3.0	3.7	2.9	1.1
Policy loans	5.2	7.7	7.1	9.0	4.0
Other loans	0.6	0.9	1.8	0.8	0.7
Foreign government securities	—	—	2.5	1.1	0.9
Receivables[b]	2.6	1.8	3.8	3.8	4.7
Real property	4.9	5.9	5.0	6.7	3.6
Other assets	2.8	2.7	2.6	3.2	2.2
Total assets (percent)	100.0	100.0	100.0	100.0	100.0
Total assets (R. mill.)	65.0	105.6	256.3	695.8	1515.4
Number of companies	35	43	73	196	227

[a]Includes port and improvement trust and similar securities.   [b]Agents' balances, outstanding premiums, interest, etc.

SOURCE OF BASIC DATA: *BMS*, p. 924.

ratio of assets to national product, although much higher than in 1913, was slightly below the level reached in 1939. It is worth noting that average assets per policy, as well as average face value per policy, increased only very slowly over three decades during which the price level rose almost threefold. This was the result of the combination of the usual lag of life insurance protection behind the price level; the need to reach less affluent sectors of the population as the number of policyholders increased rapidly; and the decreasing age of the average policy, which again reflects a rapid growth in new business, from about 100,000 policies a year in the late 1920s to nearly 600,000 in 1946.

Notwithstanding the proliferation of new Indian life insurance companies, the older companies continued to dominate the industry. Thus Oriental, in 1945 the oldest, and before 1913 by far the largest company, held considerably more than one-third of the life fund of all Indian companies, followed at a large distance by four companies (Hindustan, Empire, National, and Bombay Mutual), which together held considerably more than one-fifth. The next five companies, each with life funds of more than R. 20 mill., together accounted for another one-eighth, bringing the share of the 10 largest companies, out of more than 200, close to three-fourths of the total life funds of all Indian companies.[56]

Although comprehensive information on the Indian business of foreign life insurance companies is apparently not available outside of India, it may be inferred, from data on the number of and face value of policies, on premium receipts, and on assets, that their business in the mid-1940s amounted to about one-fourth of that of all Indian life insurance companies, that share being about equally divided among a number of British insurance companies, on the one hand, and the Sun Life of Canada, on the other. It is also evident from these data that foreign companies tended to do business, on the average, with more affluent, or less indigent, people, the average face value of their policies being about twice as high as those of Indian companies.

In additon to life insurance companies, life coverage is also provided, on a much smaller scale and to only limited groups of the population, by the Post Office and by provident societies. At the end of the interwar period the face value of the policies sold by these two groups of insurers amounted to less than 2 percent and their assets to less than 1 percent of those of life

56. *Indian Insurance Yearbook,* 1945, pp. 3, 11, and 117 ff.

insurance companies. The assets of Post Office life insurance were in the form of an unfunded claim on the government, whereas somewhat more than one-half of the assets of provident societies were in government or semigovernment securities. Before independence, therefore, these two groups of institutions played only a negligible role as an outlet for individual saving or as a source of financing.

The interwar period also witnessed a considerable increase, although still on a rather small scale, of public and private pension (provident) funds. The claims of public provident funds against the Treasury, which constituted the funds' only asset, rose from R. 62 mill. in 1913 to R. 197 mill. in 1920, R. 582 mill. in 1929, R. 752 mill. in 1939, and R. 976 mill. in 1946, an average rate of growth of nearly 9 percent. Thus, although they were about as large as the funds of life insurance companies at the beginning of the period, they grew more slowly and at the end of the period were equal to less than two-thirds of life insurance companies' assets. The new issue ratio of these provident funds averaged 0.8 percent for the entire period (0.7 percent for 1914–20, 1.2 percent for 1921–29, 0.7 percent for 1930–39, and 0.6 percent for 1940–46), compared with 1.0 percent for life insurance companies. Their share in the assets of all financial institutions was on the order of nearly 3 percent at the beginning as well as at the end of the period. Inclusion of private provident funds, for which statistics are lacking, would somewhat increase these figures, especially at the end of the period.

Table 2-20 shows the information on the number and capital of financial joint stock companies, which is derived from statistics independent from those of the various groups of financial institutions on which the discussion in this section has been based. As is to be expected,

TABLE 2-20. Number and Capital of Financial Joint Stock Companies, 1920–1946

March 31 of following year	Total	Banking and loan				Insurance		
		Banking	Loan	Investment and trust	Nidhis and chit funds	Life, fire, and marine	Provident funds	Other
I. Number								
1920	829	351	131	40	213	52	38	4
1925	1062	463	228	8	282	52	16	13
1933	2972	1236	621	119	152	394	431	19
1939	2849	1369	575	160	113	203	414	15
1946	2624	1137	527	441	130	198	167	24
II. Paid-up capital (R. mill.)								
1920	217	107	8	68	23	12	0	0
1925	199	98	28	17	29	30	0	0
1933	347	142	13	141	19	27	1	3
1939	304	131	23	95	13	35	2	6
1946	624	345	28	143	2	88	4	13
III. Paid-up capital (percent)								
1920	100.0	49.2	3.7	31.2	10.6	5.5	0.0	0.0
1925	100.0	49.2	14.1	8.5	14.6	15.1	0.0	0.0
1933	100.0	41.0	3.8	40.8	5.5	7.8	0.3	0.9
1939	100.0	43.0	7.6	31.2	4.3	11.5	0.7	2.0
1946	100.0	55.4	4.5	22.9	0.3	14.1	0.6	2.1
IV. Paid-up capital per unit (R. 000)								
1920	262	305	61	170	108	231	—	—
1925	187	212	123	2125	103	577	—	—
1933	116	115	21	1185	125	69	2	168
1939	107	96	40	594	115	172	5	367
1946	238	303	53	324	15	444	26	624

SOURCE OF I AND II: *BMS*, pp. 784 ff.

these two sets of statistics do not always agree, but the second set provides some information not available from other sources, such as the number of all banks before the mid-1930s and the number and capital of five minor groups of financial institutions—loan companies, investment and trust companies, nidhis and chit funds (two types of small neighborhood quasi-cooperative credit organizations popular in southern India), and provident funds. The total paid-up capital of these five groups, which represents a large fraction of their total assets, amounted to R. 100 mill. in 1920, the first date for which the information is available, and to about R. 180 mill. in 1946. Their share in the total assets of all financial institutions is not likely to have exceeded 5 percent of the assets of all financial institutions in 1920 and 1 percent in 1946, so that their ommission from the statistics used cannot affect the overall picture.

l. All Financial Institutions

(i) OVERVIEW. The progress made by modern financial institutions in India (i.e., excluding indigenous bankers and moneylenders for whom statistics are lacking) during the interwar period may be summarized in five figures: The assets of financial institutions increased at an average annual rate of 9 percent from 1914 through 1946 compared with a rate of less than 5 percent for the 1871–1913 period; the new issue ratio for the period advanced to slightly more than 3 percent of national product compared with less than 1 percent in the preceding four decades; the ratio of the assets of financial institutions to national product increased from about one-tenth in 1913 to more than one-half in 1946; the ratio of financial institutions' assets to national wealth rose from 0.03 in 1913 to 0.10 in 1946; and the share of financial institutions in all financial assets outstanding doubled from 0.18 to 0.36. Table 2-21 shows these five basic ratios for each of the four subperiods, both for the entirety of all financial institutions and for its most important component, the banking system.

It is evident from table 2-21 that the rate of growth was rapid over the period as a whole, for both the banking system and all financial institutions and in both current and constant prices. In current prices the average annual rates of growth were on the order of 9 percent, and after adjustment for the rise of the price level, they still amounted to a very respectable 6 percent a year.[57]

The rates differed widely between the two war periods, on the one hand, and the 1920s and 1930s, on the other, particularly in current prices, but remained positive for all four subperiods and on either price basis. The rate of growth in constant prices accelerated from the first to the fourth subperiod, from nearly 5 percent in World War I to nearly 8 percent in World War II for all financial institutions and even more steeply from 5 to nearly 12 percent for the banking system alone.

(ii) THE PATH OF GROWTH RATES. For the period as a whole, only three groups deviated substantially from the average of 9 percent of all modern financial institutions. The laggards were the Imperial Bank, the exchange banks, and the Post Office Saving System with a rate of about 5½ percent each. Whereas the low average growth rate of the latter is explained by its lag during two war inflations, that of the Imperial Bank and that of the exchange banks is due to a decline of the share of the large port cities in the country's banking business and in the increasing competition offered by the Indian commercial banks. On the other hand, the average rate of growth of the monetary authorities, the Indian commercial banks, and cooperative credit institutions was about 2 percent higher than the average. This seemingly small margin will build up to

57. If it is assumed that indigenous bankers' assets rose from R. 0.1 bill. to R. 0.3 bill. between 1913 and 1946, probably as low a level and rate of growth as is worth consideration, the average annual growth rate of financial institutions, including indigenous bankers, would be reduced by only about 0.1 percent compared to the 9.1 percent for the total, which excludes them. The difference, however, is radical if, in addition, rural and urban moneylenders are included, rough as the estimates of their resources may be. In that case, the growth rate is reduced to below 7 percent in current, and to about 3 percent in constant, prices.

TABLE 2-21. Growth of Financial Institutions, 1914–1946

	1914–20	1921–29	1930–39	1940–46	1914–46
	I. Rate of growth of assets (percent a year)				
All financial institutions	12.8	2.4	4.3	22.2	9.1
Banking system[a]	13.5	0.2	4.0	27.1	9.3
Price level[b]	7.6	−2.8	−2.9	13.6	2.6
	II. New issue ratio (percent of GNP)				
All financial institutions	1.47	0.38	1.33	7.19	3.14
Banking system[a]	1.28	−0.02	0.81	6.63	2.69
	III. Ratio of assets to GNP (percent)[c]				
All financial institutions	14.1	20.2	33.1	52.7	52.7
Banking system[a]	11.9	13.5	21.5	45.1	45.1
	IV. Ratio of assets to national wealth[c]				
All financial institutions	0.029	0.034	0.052	0.092	0.096
Banking system[a]	0.023	0.023	0.033	0.079	0.084
	V. Ratio of assets to all financial assets[c]				
All financial institutions	0.18[d]	0.18	0.20	0.36	0.36
Banking system[a]	0.14[d]	0.12	0.14	0.32	0.32

[a]Reserve Bank, Imperial Bank, exchange banks, and commercial banks, including, before 1935, the Treasury's note issue department.   [b]Gross national product deflator.   [c]End of period.   [d]1913: 10.0 in line III-1 and 8.1 in line III-2; 0.027 in line IV-1 and 0.22 in line IV-2; 0.18 in line V-1 and 0.15 in line V-2.

SOURCES OF BASIC DATA: Table 2-11; table 2-1 for line I-3.

TABLE 2-22. Assets of Financial Institutions, 1913–1946
(R. Mill.)

	1913	1920	1929	1939	1946
Reserve Bank	661[a]	1662[a]	1772[a]	2802	18140
Imperial Bank	498	938	909	998	2944
Exchange banks	310	748	667	741	1813
Commercial banks	262	852	790	1568	9787
A-1 and A-2	242	821	743	1222	8485
B	20	31	47	115	409
C, D, and unscheduled	·	·	·	231	893
Post Office Saving System	232	229	371	783	1424
Cooperative societies	53	214	827	1066	1639
State banks	·	24	80	129	249
Central banks	·	64	287	294	451
Agricultural societies	·	96	324	316	330
Nonagricultural societies	·	29		272	526
Land banks, central	—	—	—	53	46
Land banks, primary	—	—	—	53	37
Insurance organizations	127	325	838	1448	2491
Insurance companies	65	106	256	696	1515
Pension funds	62	219	582	752	976
All financial institutions	2143	4968	6174	9406	38238

[a]Treasury paper money in circulation.

SOURCE: *BMS*, passim.

very substantial differences in the share of these groups in the assets of all financial institutions over a period of more than thirty years.

The ranking and proportions of the growth rates of the different types of institutions naturally varied from subperiod to subperiod. These fluctuations can be followed in table 2-23, but do not need detailed discussion. What clearly emerges from this table, however, is that the growth rates for the three types of thrift institutions tended to be well below the average for all financial institutions during inflationary periods but to exceed it during noninflationary periods. The only exceptions are cooperative credit institutions and the pension funds in their formative period during World War I. The banking system generally shows the opposite relationship, that is, more of an increase during inflationary periods and less of an increase during periods of recession.

(iii) DISTRIBUTION AMONG GROUPS OF FINANCIAL INSTITUTIONS. The difference in the growth rate of assets of the different groups of financial institutions is reflected in changes in the distribution of the aggregate assets of the sector. The relevant figures are shown in table 2-24, including the Treasury's note issue department for 1913, 1920, and 1929. The discussion is based on the broader definition.

At all benchmark dates the monetary authorities have constituted the largest single institution, a sign of the relative financial backwardness of India throughout the period. Their share was relatively stable from 1913 to 1939, at close to 30 percent of the total for all financial institutions. It then advanced sharply to nearly one-half, an increase commonly found in inflationary periods. The share of the commercial banks (Imperial Bank, exchange banks, and Indian joint stock banks) suffered a downward level shift in the 1920s, their share declining from one-half in 1913 and 1920 to somewhat more than one-third from 1929 to 1946. The movements of the share of the thrift and insurance institutions were erratic and greatly affected by the two war

TABLE 2-23. Growth of Assets of Financial Institutions, 1914–1946
(Percent Per Year)

	1914–20 (1)	1921–29 (2)	1930–39 (3)	1940–46 (4)	1914–46 (5)
Treasury note issue department	14.1	6.6	4.7	—	10.6
Reserve Bank	—	—		20.0	
Imperial Bank	9.5	−0.4	0.9	16.7	5.5
Exchange banks	13.4	−1.3	1.1	13.6	5.5
Commercial banks[a]	18.3	−0.8	7.1	29.9	11.6
A	19.0	−1.1	5.1	31.9	11.1
B	6.5	−4.7	9.4	19.5	9.6
C, D, and unscheduled	·	·	·	19.0	·
Post Office Saving System	−0.2	5.5	7.8	8.9	5.7
Cooperative societies	22.1	16.2	2.6	6.3	11.0
State banks	·	14.3	4.9	9.9	·
Central banks	·	18.1	0.2	6.3	·
Agricultural societies	·	14.5	−0.2	0.6	·
Nonagricultural societies	·	24.7	7.2	9.9	·
Land banks, central	·	·	·	1.9	·
Land banks, primary	·	·	·	1.9	·
Insurance organizations	14.4	11.3	7.3	8.1	9.4
Insurance companies	7.2	10.3	10.5	11.8	10.0
Pension funds	19.8	11.5	2.6	3.8	8.7
All financial institutions	12.8	2.4	4.3	22.2	9.1

[a]Coverage was more complete in 1939 and 1946 than before; hence the figures in cols. 3 and 5 are slightly overstated.

SOURCE OF BASIC DATA: Table 2-11.

TABLE 2-24. Distribution of Assets of Financial Institutions, 1913–1946 (Percent)

	1913 (1)	1920 (2)	1929 (3)	1939 (4)	1946 (5)
Reserve Bank[a]	30.8	33.4	28.7	29.4	47.4
Imperial Bank	23.2	18.9	14.7	10.4	7.7
Exchange banks	14.5	15.0	10.8	7.7	4.7
Commercial banks	12.2	17.1	12.8	16.2	25.6
A-1 and A-2	11.3	16.5	12.0	12.7	22.2
B	0.9	0.6	0.8	1.2	1.1
C, D, and unscheduled	—	—	—	0.7	0.3
Post Office Saving System	10.8	4.6	6.0	8.2	3.7
Cooperative societies	2.5	4.3	13.4	11.1	4.3
State banks	·	0.5	1.3	1.3	0.7
Central banks	·	1.3	4.7	3.1	1.2
Agricultural societies	·	1.9	5.3	3.2	0.9
Nonagricultural societies	·	0.6	2.2	2.8	1.4
Land banks	·	—	—	0.6	0.2
Insurance organizations	5.9	6.5	13.6	16.9	6.6
Insurance companies	3.0	2.1	4.2	7.3	4.0
Pension funds	2.9	4.4	9.4	9.6	2.6
All financial institutions	100.0	100.0	100.0	100.0	100.0

[a]Treasury notes in cols. 1–3.

SOURCE OF BASIC DATA: Table 2-11.

inflations. Thus their share fell from 19 percent in 1913 to 15 percent in 1920; then, having rapidly climbed to more than 30 percent in 1929 and to more than 35 percent in 1939, their share fell back sharply during World War II to 15 percent in 1946, the level it had already reached three decades earlier. These aggregates, however, hide considerable differences among the three component groups. The share of the Post Office Saving System followed an irregular downward trend and ended the period with a share of less than 4 percent, one-third of that of 1913. That of insurance organizations increased throughout most of the period, from nearly 6 percent in 1913 to 16 percent in 1939, reflecting a structural upward trend in the country's financial system, but then could not withstand the effects of World War II inflation, which cut its share by two-fifths. Cooperative societies followed an intermediate path, increasing their share sharply from 1913 to 1929 but losing most of the advance in the 1930s and, like all thrift institutions, particularly during World War II. Their share at the end of the period was nevertheless considerably above that at the beginning.

(iv) THE NEW ISSUE RATIO. The new issue ratio of all financial institutions (including the note issue department of the Treasury) was highest during the two periods of war inflation, 1914–20 and particularly in 1940–46. It was lowest for the 1920s but even so was almost as high as it had been in the 1901–13 period, the highest level reached until then. For the period as a whole, it was slightly in excess of 3 percent.[58]

The components of the ratio showed considerable differences between the four sub-periods, although the banking system predominated in all of them. The two war inflations are characterized by high values of the issue ratio of the monetary authorities (the Treasury's note issuing department in 1914–20, the Reserve Bank in 1946) and to a smaller extent of the commercial banks. These two groups were responsbile for more than nine-tenths of the ratio for all financial institutions in both periods of war inflation. In contrast, their share was much

58. Inclusion of indigenous moneylenders would raise the new issue ratio for the entire interwar period to about 4½ percent.

TABLE 2-25. New Issue Ratios of Financial Institutions, 1914–1946
(Percent of Gross National Product)

	1914–20	1921–29	1930–39	1940–46	1914–46
Reserve Bank[a]	0.52	0.03	0.42	3.82	1.52
Imperial Bank[b]	0.23	−0.01	0.04	0.49	0.21
Exchange banks	0.23	−0.03	0.03	0.27	0.13
Commercial banks	0.31	−0.02	0.32	2.05	0.83
A-1 and A-2	0.30	−0.02	0.20	1.82	0.71
B	0.01	0.01	0.03	0.07	0.03
C, D, and unscheduled	.	.	0.10[c]	0.17	0.08
Post Office Saving System	0.00	0.05	0.17	0.16	0.10
Cooperative societies	0.08	0.19	0.07	0.14	0.14
State banks	0.01[c]	0.02	0.02	0.03	0.02
Central banks	0.03[c]	0.07	0.00	0.04	0.03
Agricultural societies	0.04[c]	0.07	−0.00	0.00	0.02
Nonagricultural societies	0.01[c]	0.03	0.06	0.06	0.04
Land banks	—	—	—	0.01	0.00
Insurance organizations	0.10	0.17	0.25	0.26	0.21
Insurance companies	0.02	0.05	0.18	0.20	0.13
Pension funds	0.08	0.12	0.07	0.06	0.08
All financial institutions	1.46	0.38	1.33	7.19	3.15

[a]Treasury paper currency until 1935.   [b]Presidency banks until 1920.   [c]1917–20; assuming zero assets in 1929.

SOURCE OF BASIC DATA: Table 2-11.

smaller in the 1920s and 1930s, when the thrift institutions (Post Office Saving System, cooperatives, and insurance companies) contributed nearly four-fifths and two-fifths, respectively, of the new issue ratio of all financial institutions. Among the thrift institutions, insurance companies showed the largest and most regular increase, their issues rising from only 0.02 percent of national product in 1914–20 to 0.20 in 1940–46.

The period averages of the new issue ratios of financial institutions necessarily hide year-to-year or cyclical fluctuations, which are not shown here. Brief comments will be limited to the movements of the ratio for all financial institutions.

One of the main characteristics of the annual ratios is their irregularity, even for the aggregate ratio of all financial institutions. A doubling or halving of the ratio from one year to the next is not rare, occurring in 15 of the 32 pairs, including changes between positive and negative values. Nevertheless, some movements seem to have a cyclical character.[59] These are, using trough-to-trough dating, the years 1914–19; 1919–22; 1924–27; 1927–29; 1929–33 (remarkable because the peak occurs in 1932, a depression year for the economy), 1933–38, and 1940–46. Thus all but two years of the thirty-three-year period can be classified as belonging to seven cycles. In the absence of a business cycle chronology for India after the mid-1920s, the dating of peak and trough years is based on average real national income per head. A comparison of the turning points in the new issue ratio with those in real national income per head and, until 1925, Thorp's cycle chronology shows that the correspondence between that chronology and the new issue ratio is quite satisfactory, with three of the six turning points occurring in the same year and the difference in the other three being only one year. The same cannot be said of the comparison between the new issue ratio and real national product per head, partly because of the low cyclical sensitivity of the estimates of the latter. Up to the late 1920s all but one cycle can be matched, the new issue ratio lagging at six of the eight turning points, usually by one year. The

59. Cf. the chronology in Thorp, pp. 338–40.

TABLE 2-26. Relation of Assets of Financial Institutions to Gross
National Product, 1913–1946

	1913 (1)	1920 (2)	1929 (3)	1939 (4)	1946 (5)
Reserve Bank[a]	3.1	4.7	5.8	9.8	25.0
Imperial Bank[b]	2.3	2.7	3.0	3.5	4.1
Exchange banks	1.5	2.1	2.2	2.6	2.5
Commercial banks	1.2	2.4	2.6	5.5	13.5
A-1 and A-2	1.1	2.4	2.4	4.3	11.7
B	0.1	0.1	0.2	0.4	0.6
C, D, and unscheduled	—	—	—	0.8	1.2
Post Office Saving System	1.1	0.7	1.2	2.8	2.0
Cooperative Societies	0.2	0.6	2.7	3.8	2.3
State banks	—	0.1	0.3	0.5	0.3
Central banks	—	0.2	0.9	1.0	0.6
Agricultural societies	—	0.3	1.1	1.1	0.4
Nonagricultural societies	—	0.1	0.4	1.0	0.7
Land banks, central	—	—	—	0.2	0.1
Land banks, primary	—	—	—	0.2	0.1
Insurance organizations	0.6	0.9	2.7	5.1	3.4
Insurance companies	0.3	0.3	0.8	2.5	2.1
Pension funds	0.3	0.6	1.9	2.7	1.3
All financial institutions	10.0	14.1	20.2	33.1	52.7

[a]Treasury notes in cols. 1–3.   [b]Presidency banks in cols. 1 and 2.

SOURCE OF BASIC DATA: Table 2-11.

match is also satisfactory for the last three cycles, which cover the years 1933 to 1946. In this period turning points are synchronous in three of the seven cases; the issue ratio lags by one year at two turning points but leads at the remaining two turning points by one or two years. Matching is difficult or impossible for the early 1930s. Hence, all that can be suggested is, first, that the aggregate new issue ratio seems in the interwar period to have shown cyclical movements similar to those in the general economy and, second, that a slight tendency for a short lag of the new issue ratio may have existed. More can hardly be claimed until an intensive study of the problem can be made, a study that would require many data beyond those now available.

(v) THE ASSET/GNP RATIO. The cumulative result of new issues, taking account of changes in national product, appears in the ratios of the assets of financial institutions to national product. Their movement can be followed in table 2-26.

In 1913 the assets of all modern financial institutions amounted to only 10 percent of the year's national product. The ratio rose slowly but steadily through the 1920s, reaching a level of nearly one-fifth of national product by 1929. From then on the ratio accelerated sharply, reaching more than one-third of national product in 1939 and fully one-half in 1946. The rise during the 1930s was the result of a substantial increase in the assets of financial institutions, which climbed at an annual average rate of 4.6 percent in the face of a substantial decline in the current value of national product. In the 1940–46 period, on the other hand, the rise was due to a very rapid expansion of the assets of financial institutions, which averaged 22 percent a year, an expansion that exceeded the 15 percent rate of increase in national product.[60]

The increase in the ratio of assets to national product was largest, in absolute terms, for the monetary authorities, rising from a little more than 3 percent in 1913 to 5 percent in 1929,

60. If rural and urban moneylenders are included among financial institutions the ratio is much higher—close to two-fifths in 1913 and approximately four-fifths in 1946—but shows a smaller relative increase over the period.

TABLE 2-27. Assets of Financial Institutions and National Wealth, 1913–1946 (Percent)[a,b]

	1913	1920	1929	1939	1946
Reserve Bank	0.84[e]	0.95[e]	0.97[e]	1.54	4.39
Imperial Bank	0.64[f]	0.55[f]	0.50	0.55	0.71
Exchange banks[c]	0.40	0.44	0.36	0.41	0.44
Commercial banks	0.34	0.50	0.43	0.86	2.37
Savings banks	0.30	0.13	0.20	0.43	0.34
Cooperatives	0.07	0.13	0.45	0.58	0.40
Insurance companies	0.08	0.06	0.14	0.37	0.37
Pension funds[d]	0.08	0.13	0.32	0.41	0.24
Total	2.74	2.90	3.38	5.16	9.25

[a]Excludes indigenous bankers and moneylenders and a few small financial institutions.   [b]Excluding gold and silver.
[c]Indian deposits only.   [d]Claims of state provident funds against Treasury.   [e]Treasury currency notes.   [f]Presidency banks.

SOURCES OF BASIC DATA: Tables 2-11 and 2-40.

doubling during the 1930s, and reaching a level of one-fourth of national income in 1946. The commercial banks' ratio rose at a similar rate for the period as a whole. However, it only advanced from 5 to 7 percent between 1913 and 1929 and remained practically unchanged over the 1920s but then rose rapidly to reach one-eighth of national product in 1939 and one-fifth in 1946. The increase in the ratio of the assets of thrift institutions (including insurance) to national product was limited to the 1920s and 1930s, rising in these two decades from 2 percent in 1920 to 12 percent in 1939. The ratio actually declined, not unexpectedly, during the inflation of World War II, losing about one-third of its value at the beginning of the period.

(vi) THE ASSET/WEALTH RATIO. Because the assets of financial institutions have the dimension of stocks rather than of flows, the dimensionally appropriate comparison is between the assets of financial institutions and either all financial assets outstanding or all tangible assets or, preferably, national wealth, that is, tangible assets less net foreign balance.

The increase in the ratio of the assets of modern financial institutions to all financial assets, the margin of estimation error being much larger in the latter than in the former, from about one-sixth in 1913 to more than one-third in 1946, is an indication of the increasing importance of financial institutions in the country's financial structure and continues a trend that began during the half century prior to World War I. The movement during the interwar period was, however, irregular, with small increases between 1913 and 1939 that were followed by a sharp rise, from 20 to 36 percent, during the inflation that accompanied World War II, and concentrated its effect on a rapid increase in the share of the banking system from less than one-tenth of all financial assets outstanding in 1939 to one-fifth in 1946.

Table 2-27, showing the relation between the assets of the main types of financial institutions and the value of national wealth, does not provide much additional information, as the ratios are related via the capital-output ratio to the asset-national product ratios. Continuing a trend already evident in the 1860–1913 period, the ratio increased from nearly 3 percent of national wealth in 1913 and 1920 to more than 5 percent in 1939 and doubled again during World

61. The ratio of the assets of financial institutions to national wealth in the United States was close to one-fifth—more than twice the Indian ratio of 1946—as far back as 1900 (Goldsmith, Lipsey, and Mendelsson, 2:72–73). To reach a ratio as low as one-fifth, one would have to go back to about 1880 (Goldsmith, 1969, p. 549, and 1973, p. 36), a time at which real product per head was undoubtedly far higher in the United States than it was in India in 1946. In comparison to the level of real national product per head, India in 1946 had a statistically larger financial superstructure than the United States had in 1880, which, of course, does not mean a more sophisticated, more specialized, more effective, or better integrated superstructure.

TABLE 2-28. Share of Financial Institutions in All Financial Assets, 1913–1946 (Percent)[a]

	1913	1920	1929	1939	1946
Reserve Bank	4.9[d]	5.9[d]	5.1[d]	6.1	16.9
Imperial Bank	3.7[e]	3.3[e]	2.6	2.2	2.7
Exchange banks[b]	2.2	2.7	1.9	1.6	1.7
Commercial banks	1.9	3.0	2.3	3.4	9.1
Savings banks	1.7	0.8	1.1	1.7	1.3
Cooperatives	0.4	0.8	2.4	2.3	1.5
Insurance companies	0.5	0.4	0.7	1.5	1.4
Pension funds[c]	0.5	0.8	1.7	1.6	0.9
Total	15.8	17.6	17.9	20.5	35.5

[a]Excludes indigenous bankers and moneylenders and some small financial institutions.   [b]Indian deposits only.
[c]Claims against Treasury of state provident funds.   [d]Treasury paper currency.   [e]Presidency banks.

SOURCES: Tables 2-11 and 2-40.

War II to reach a level of more than 9½ percent in 1946, a ratio still very low in international comparison.[61]

(vii) THE FINANCIAL INTERMEDIATION RATIO. A rough measure of the position of financial institutions in an economy's financial structure is provided by the ratio of financial institutions' assets to all financial instruments outstanding. Financial development is generally characterized by an increase in this ratio, indicating an increasing degree of institutionalization of the financial structure.

This movement continued a trend already at work, though even more parlous to measure, between 1860 and 1913. The figures also show that up to 1946 most of the ratio was accounted for by the central and commercial banking system rather than by thrift institutions and indeed largely reflected the increasing degree of monetization of the Indian economy.

6. FINANCING THE NONFINANCIAL SECTORS OF THE ECONOMY

a. Financing the Government

As the central government's activities expanded only slowly during the interwar period, the share of its expenditures in national product, combining central and state governments, declined from more than 5 percent, a level maintained with relatively small fluctuations in the four decades before World War I, to about 3½ percent in the 1920s, 1930s, and 1940s. Although considerable military expenses were shouldered by the government in both wars, they did not lead during World War II to a sharp increase in the portion of national product absorbed by the government's current expenses nor to a large amount of deficit financing.

In the 1920s and 1930s the financial relations between the central and provincial governments were fundamentally changed by the Montagu-Chelmsford reforms of 1919, which enlarged the scope of revenues and expenditures of the provinces. However, the structure of the central government's revenue or expenditures did not show large changes.[62] Customs duties remained the main source of revenue, furnishing about one-half of total revenues, and the personal income tax contributed about one-fifth of total revenues, which amounted to hardly 1 percent of total personal income. A corporate income tax was introduced only in the mid-1930s. Military expenses absorbed about one-half of total expenditures, a remarkably high ratio in a period without hostilities, civil administration slightly more than one-tenth, and debt service

62. *BMS*, pp. 875 ff, and 882.

TABLE 2-29. Finances of Central Government, 1914–1946

| | Current account | | Capital account | | Capital advanced | | |
	Revenue	Deficit	Debt receipts	Capital outlay	Total[a]	To railways	To states
			I. Amounts (R. bill.)				
1914–1920	9.40	0.37	2.78	2.46	·	·	·
1921–1929	8.55	0.31	3.39	2.49	2.81[b]	2.14[b]	0.64[b]
1930–1939	8.49	0.24	1.29	0.42	−0.12	0.01	−0.18
1940–1946	17.09	6.06	15.11	4.99	0.31	0.78	−0.68
1914–1946	43.54	6.97	22.55	10.32	3.00[c]	2.93[c]	−0.22[c]
			II. Relation to gross national product (percent)				
1914–1920	4.88	0.19	1.45	1.28	·	·	·
1921–1929	2.72	0.10	1.08	0.79	1.14[b]	0.88[b]	0.26[b]
1930–1939	3.50	0.10	0.53	0.17	−0.05	0.00	0.07
1940–1946	4.26	1.51	3.77	1.24	0.08	0.19	−0.17
1914–1946	3.78	0.61	1.96	0.90	0.34[c]	0.33[c]	−0.02[c]

[a]Includes advances to commercial departments of central government other than railways.   [b]1923–29.   [c]1923–46.

SOURCE OF I: *BMS*, pp. 872 ff. and 882.

about 15 percent. The revenues of the provincial governments averaged about 3 percent of national product between 1921 and 1946 without large differences among the subperiods. The land tax remained the main source of revenue of the provinces, whose budgets were about equal in size to that of the central government, but its share declined from one-half to one-third. Security (police) expenditures accounted for about one-third of the total.[63]

During World War II revenues and expenditures of the central and provincial governments increased sharply from an annual average of R. 1.7 bill. during the 1930s to R. 3.3 bill. in 1940–46. The increase hardly kept government revenues and expenditures in step with the expansion of national product, and as a result, their ratio to national product declined from nearly 8 percent to below 7 percent, the ratio falling by about one-half of 1 percent for the central as well as for the provincial governments. The structure of revenues, however, underwent substantial changes, whereas that of expenditures did not, notwithstanding an increase of military outlays by more than 250 percent. On the revenue side the main change was a sharp increase of the share of income taxes from about one-fifth to two-fifths and a decrease of the share of customs from more than one-half to one-fifth.

According to the budget figures (table 2-29), total capital outlays of the central government from 1914 through 1946, R. 10 bill., were equal to slightly less than 1 percent of national product and on the order of one-eighth of total capital formation. A more detailed independent study summarized in table 2-30, which also covers provincial and local government, but omits the war years and ends with 1937, puts total gross public investment from 1919 through 1937 at about R. 11 bill. This figure, substantially higher than the budget figures, is equal to about one-third of the period's total public expenditures, to nearly 2 percent of its national product, and to more than one-fourth of gross fixed capital formation. Finally, a much more recent estimate (table 2-9) puts total gross public capital expenditures for the entire interwar period at more than R. 21 bill., equal to nearly one-fourth of total capital formation and to nearly 2 percent of national product.

The central government continued to be the dominant factor in public investment throughout the period, although its share declined from more than three-fifths in the 1920s—and

63. *BMS*, pp. 874–75.

TABLE 2-30. Public Investment and Saving, 1919–1937

Fiscal years ending March 31 following	Gross public investment								Gross public saving
	Central government	Provincial government	Municipal government	District and local government	Total	Railways	Irrigation	Other[a]	
	I. Amounts (R. bill.)								
1919–20	0.94	(0.24)	0.05	0.07	1.30	0.70	0.07	0.53	0.49
1921–29	3.80	1.85	0.33	0.32	6.30	3.00	0.77	2.53	3.80
1930–37	1.55	1.28	0.23	0.27	3.33	0.89	0.55	1.89	2.78
1919–37	6.29	3.37	0.61	0.66	10.93	4.59	1.39	4.95	7.07
	II. Distribution (percent)								
1919–20	72	18	4	6	100	54	6	41	38
1921–29	61	29	5	5	100	58	12	40	60
1930–37	47	38	7	8	100	27	17	57	93
1919–37	57	31	6	6	100	42	13	45	65
	III. Relation to gross national product (percent)								
1919–20	1.32	0.34	0.07	0.10	1.83	0.98	0.10	0.75	0.69
1921–29	1.21	0.59	0.10	0.10	2.00	0.95	0.24	0.80	1.21
1930–37	0.81	0.67	0.12	0.14	1.75	0.47	0.29	0.99	1.46
1919–37	1.09	0.59	0.11	0.11	1.90	0.80	0.24	0.86	1.23

[a]Mostly roads and buildings.

SOURCE: Thavaraj, pp. 221 ff.

probably four-fifths or more before World War I—to about one-half in the 1930s, a result primarily of the rise of the share of the provinces after the Montagu-Chelmsford reforms.

In line with the cessation of extensive growth in the country's railroad system, the share of the railways in public investment declined from about one-half in the 1920s, the level of the 1898–1913 period, to not much more than one-fourth in the 1930s. Although expenditures on irrigation increased their share, the main difference between the 1930s and earlier decades was the sharp rise in the absolute level and in the share of expenditures on roads, reflecting in part the effects of the introduction of automotive transportation.

The regional distribution of public investment was uneven. Thus about one-third of public investment took place in the Central Provinces, which had only about one-eighth of the population, and one-fourth in northwestern India, which had one-eighth of the population. On the other hand, the northeastern provinces, with nearly three-fifths of the country's population, received less than 30 percent of total public investment.[64]

For the period from 1919 to 1937 as a whole nearly two-thirds of total gross public investment was internally financed, mainly by the central government, leaving less than R. 4 bill., or about 0.7 percent of the period's national product, to be financed externally. The share of internal financing was somewhat higher in the 1930s with more than four-fifths of total gross public investment than in the 1920s when the share amounted to three-fifths, partly the result of very low internal financing ratios in the depression of 1920–22.[65] The ratio of internally financed public investment to national product was in the neighborhood of 1¼ percent in both periods, whereas externally financed public investment declined sharply from 0.8 to 0.3 percent of national product.

The changes in total public debt, the bulk of which was contracted by the central government, reflect mainly the developments in the surplus or deficits on current account and in the volume of public investment, changes in government cash balance having in general been minor except during World War II when they rose from R. 0.3 bill. to R. 4.6 bill.[66] The total debt of the central government quintupled between 1913 and 1946, rising from R. 4.5 bill. to R. 22 bill. Most of the increase took place in the 1920s and during World War II. The movement of the ratio of debt to national product may seem more astonishing as it declined during both wars, slightly from 1913 to 1920 and substantially from 1940 to 1946, which is indicative of India's position as a marginal participant. The ratio doubled from nearly one-third to over two-fifths of national product during the 1920s and 1930s; the rise in the 1920s resulted mainly from an increase of the debt by more than 70 percent, whereas the rise in the 1930s resulted from a combination of a very small increase in debt and a sharp decline in the current value of national product, which was due mainly to the precipitous fall in the price level. These movements were the result of a new issue ratio of not much more than 1½ percent for the period as a whole, fluctuating between 1.0 and 2.5 percent during the two war periods and between 1.7 and 0.3 percent during the 1920s and 1930s.

The Indian government had formerly done the majority of its borrowing in the London market with the result that in 1913 sterling securities, part of which had been repatriated, represented three-fifths of its total debt. World War I introduced a sharp break in this policy. The large balance of payments surpluses permitted the government to reduce its sterling debt by R. 0.75 bill., or by more than one-fourth, whereas it increased its rupee debt by R. 2.67 bill., an amount equal to 1.4 percent of national product. About one-half of the total increase was in the form of floating debt, which reached R. 1.34 bill. in March 1921, mostly in Treasury bills introduced in 1918, nearly one-half of which was held in the Treasury's Paper Currency Reserve. The increase in funded rupee debt could thus be held to R. 1.11 bill., including two issues

64. D. L. Dubey, p. 17.
65. For details, cf. *BMS*, p. 883.
66. *BMS*, p. 879.

TABLE 2-31. Central Government Debt, 1913–1946

	Total debt	Rupee debt				Other		Sterling debt
		Total	Funded	Treasury bills	Total[a]	Post Office Saving	State provident funds	
I. Amounts (R. bill.)								
1913	4.45	1.80	1.46	—	0.34	0.23	0.06	2.65
1920	6.38	4.47	2.57	1.05	0.85	0.28	0.22	1.91
1929	10.96	6.08	4.05	0.65	1.38	0.72	0.58	4.88
1939	11.71	7.28	4.51	0.55	2.22	1.35	0.75	4.43
1946	21.85	21.26	15.42	0.78	5.06	2.68	0.98	0.59
II. Ratio to gross national product (percent)								
1913	20.8	8.4	6.8	—	1.6	1.1	0.3	12.4
1920	18.1	12.7	7.3	3.0	2.4	0.8	0.6	5.4
1929	35.8	19.9	13.2	2.1	4.5	2.4	1.9	15.9
1939	41.3	25.7	15.9	1.9	7.8	4.8	2.6	15.6
1946	30.1	29.3	21.3	1.1	7.0	3.7	1.4	0.8
III. New issue ratio (percent of GNP)								
1914–20	1.00	1.39	0.58	0.55	0.27	0.03	0.08	−0.38
1921–29	1.45	0.51	0.47	−0.13	0.17	0.14	0.11	0.94
1930–39	0.31	0.49	0.19	−0.04	0.35	0.26	0.07	−0.19
1940–46	2.53	3.48	2.72	0.06	0.71	0.33	0.06	−0.96
1913–46	1.51	1.69	1.21	0.07	0.41	0.21	0.08	−0.18
IV. Distribution of net issues (percent)								
1914–20	100.0	138.3	57.5	54.4	26.4	2.6	8.3	−38.3
1921–29	100.0	35.2	32.3	−8.7	11.5	9.6	7.9	64.8
1930–39	100.0	160.0	61.3	13.3	85.4	84.0	22.7	−60.0
1940–46	100.0	137.9	107.6	2.2	28.1	13.1	0.6	−37.9
1913–46	100.0	111.8	80.2	4.5	27.1	14.1	5.3	−11.8
V. Distribution of outstanding debt (percent)								
1914	100.0	40.4	32.8	—	7.6	5.1	1.3	59.6
1920	100.0	70.1	40.3	16.5	13.5	4.4	3.4	29.9
1929	100.0	55.5	37.0	5.9	12.6	6.6	5.3	44.5
1939	100.0	62.2	38.5	4.7	18.9	11.5	6.4	37.8
1946	100.0	97.3	70.6	3.6	23.1	12.3	4.5	2.7

[a]Also includes other unfunded debt.

SOURCE OF I: *BMS*, pp. 881, 884.

in 1917 and 1919 of R. 125 mill. and R. 213 mill., respectively, equal to 0.5 and 0.6 percent of the year's national product.

During the 1920s the old borrowing pattern was restored. About two-thirds of net borrowing took place in London, more than doubling the sterling debt outstanding and bringing it to 45 percent of total debt, about midway between the ratios of 60 percent in 1913 and 30 percent in 1920. Total rupee debt increased by only R. 1.6 bill. or 0.6 percent of national product, mostly in funded debt. Changes in the volume and the composition of central government debt during the 1930s were small. The small decrease in the sterling debt is worth notice for its symptomatic nature rather than for its size.

Developments during World War II were dramatic, not so much because of the near doubling of the central government's total debt, although the new issue ratio reached a peak with 2.5 percent, as for the slashing of the sterling debt by seven-eighths, reducing it to practical insignificance by 1946, that is, to less than R. 600 mill., or less than 3 percent of the total debt and 0.8 percent of national product. This was the result of maturities, calls, and open market purchases, all made possible by the large balance of payments surpluses of the World War II period. In contrast, rupee debt almost trebled, the new issue ratio reaching 3.5 percent of national product. Outstandings of more than R.21 bill. in 1946 were equal to 30 percent of a year's national product. Of the total increase of R. 14 bill., nearly R. 3 bill. was furnished by government pension and other funds, reducing the increase in funded debt to R. 11 bill., or 2.7 percent of the period's national product. Even this amount, although low in international comparison, was unprecedented in size for India.[67]

The available statistics do not permit us to ascertain the distribution of these large amounts of government securities among Indian financial institutions and other sectors except for the holdings of the monetary authorities. These holdings increased from R. 0.10 bill. in 1913 to R. 0.36 bill. in 1934 (nearly 6 percent and 5 percent of total rupee debt) when they were transferred to the Reserve Bank. Holdings were little changed during the remainder of the 1930s but increased rapidly during World War II. They reached a peak, on the basis of annual averages, in 1943 with R. 1.39 bill. but declined in the following years. The 1946 holdings, averaging R. 0.58 bill., represented less than 3 percent of total rupee securities outstanding.[68]

The holdings of Indian insurance companies were too small to have contributed a substantial outlet for government securities, rising from R. 0.04 bill. in 1913 to R. 0.37 bill. in 1939 and R. 0.94 bill. in 1946. The breakdown of these totals into rupee and Indian or British sterling securities is not known. But even if they had consisted exclusively of rupee securities, the increases in holdings would have absorbed only about 7 percent of total net issues of Indian government rupee securities in the 1914–39 period and about 5 percent from 1940 through 1946.

Although a lack of data thus prevents an analysis of the absorption of government rupee securities, it would appear that these securities, notwithstanding their nearly twelvefold increase between 1913 and 1946, lost in importance in the portfolios of most holder groups. They were equal in 1913 to more than four-fifths of the assets of all financial institutions (including the Treasury's note issue department), a relationship that rose to nearly 100 percent in 1929. By 1946, however, the volume of government rupee debt had fallen to only 55 percent of the assets of financial institutions. A comparison of the net issue ratios illustrates this development and shows the decline of the new issue ratio of government rupee securities compared with that of financial institutions in the 1930s and 1940s.

b. Financing the Railways

During the interwar period, particularly the second half, capital expenditures on railways and railway financing in India, as in most other countries, lost much of the leading role they had played during the preceding half-century.[69]

The length of the railway network remained practically stable throughout the period. The book value of invested capital, however, increased by R. 3.4 bill., or fully 70 percent of its 1913 value, mainly as a result of improvement in track and an increase in rolling stock. A direct estimate of government gross capital expenditures on railways puts them at R. 4.6 bill. for the years 1919–37 (table 2–30), which would have to be increased to about R. 5.5 bill. to cover the entire period. This would be equal to about one-tenth of total gross fixed capital formation in

67. Discussion of provincial debts has been omitted because of their small size (R. 1.68 bill. in 1939 and R. 1.63 bill. in 1946, or 14 and 7 percent, respectively, of the central government's debt) and the fact that a large part of them (73 percent in 1939 and 34 percent in 1946) consisted of loans by the central government, reducing the remainder to R. 0.45 bill. in 1939 and R. 1.08 bill. in 1946, amounts insufficient to be of noticeable effect in the capital market (*BMS*, p. 883).

68. In the case of the Imperial Bank, total holdings of government securities have been reported regularly, but the breakdown between rupee and sterling securities, either those of the Indian or the British government, does not seem to have been published. As the bank's total holdings of government securities amounted to only R. 0.38 bill. at the end of 1939 and to R. 1.44 bill. seven years later, the increase, even if it had consisted entirely of Indian government rupee securities, would have represented less than 8 percent of the total net issues of such securities. Information appears to be entirely lacking on exchange and Indian joint stock banks.

69. *BMS*, pp. 876 ff.

India during the period and to about two-fifths of total public gross capital expenditures. However, although the ratio was as high as one-seventh of national capital formation and more than one-half of government capital expenditures during the 1920s, it declined to about 5 percent of national gross capital formation and to one-third of government capital expenditures during the 1930s, the absolute level of railway gross capital expenditures during the 1930s being less than one-third of that of the 1920s when the price level was higher.

By the end of the period the railway system was state-owned and managed in almost its entirety, compared to the situation in 1921 when private companies or native states still owned more than one-fourth and managed about four-fifths of the mileage. The financial accounts of the government railways were an integral part of the central government's budget until they were separated in 1925. It was only then that depreciation was introduced into the railway accounts and reserve funds were set up. These funds remained small, standing at the end of the period at R. 1.08 bill. for the depreciation fund, equal to about one-eighth of the capital-at charge, and at R. 0.38 bill. for the reserve fund.

The financing of the railways during the interwar period was handled almost entirely by the central government; the funds were raised by the sale of government securities, which were not distinguished from its other borrowings.

c. Financing Nonagricultural Business

Because nothing is known in quantitative terms about the development of unincorporated enterprises in manufacturing, where they played only a secondary role, as well as in handicrafts, trade, and services, where they predominated, the discussion must be limited to corporations outside of agriculture and finance. And even within this restricted field comprehensive or continuous statistics are limited to the information on the number and paid-up capital of joint stock companies incorporated in India, which are summarized in table 2-32. No comparable data are available for corporations operating in India but incorporated abroad, that is, mainly Great Britain. Occasional information indicates that the share of these enterprises in the total assets or sales of all nonagricultural corporations was relatively low, although not insignificant, and was concentrated in a few industries.

(i) TRENDS IN PAID-UP CAPITAL OF CORPORATIONS. The available statistics, limited as they are, leave little doubt that during the interwar period the corporate form of business became common and that nonfinancial corporations grew more rapidly than the Indian economy as a whole. The number of nonfinancial corporations, below 2,000 in 1913, increased rapidly, although not uniformly, to more than 19,000 in 1946. The decline of the average paid-up capital per corporation during the 1930s and 1940s, as well as the fact that average capital at the end of the period was considerably smaller than it had been at the beginning, notwithstanding the substantial rise in the price level and the expansion of the Indian economy, shows that the corporate form was extended to many medium-sized enterprises. In international comparison, corporate density remained low, however: one nonfinancial corporation for every 22,000 inhabitants in 1946.

The paid-up capital of all nonfinancial corporations, the only comprehensive measure of their size available, increased between 1913 and 1946 by more than six times, or at an annual rate of nearly 6 percent. Growth was most rapid during the two war periods, averaging about 11½ percent in 1914–20 and close to 7 percent from 1940 through 1946, and slowed down to a rate of only 0.6 percent during the 1930s. Corporations grew more rapidly than national product throughout the period. Paid-up capital was equal to not much more than 3 percent of national product in 1913 but to nearly 6 percent in 1946.

For financial analysis, one of the most interesting figures is the new issue ratio of stock of nonfinancial corporations, which is approximated by the ratio of the change in paid-up capital to national product. This ratio kept close to 0.35 percent for all subperiods, twice the level of the 1901–13 period, except during the depressed 1930s when it fell to 0.08 percent.

TABLE 2-32. Number and Capital of Nonfinancial Joint Stock Companies, 1913–1946

March 31 of following year	All companies	All nonfinancial	Trading and manufacturing	Mills and presses	Other
		I. Number			
1913[a]	2744	1978	902	518	558
1920	4708	3879	1869	717	1293
1929	6919	4894	2541	761	1592
1939	11372	8523	5027	1017	2479
1946	21853	19229	12609	1825	4795
		II. Paid-up capital (R. mill.)			
1913	766	682	192	295	195
1920	1645	1428	438	465	525
1929	2863	2578	923	716	939
1939	3037	2733	1093	718	922
1946	4795	4171	1776	1062	1333
		III. Paid-up capital (percent)			
1913	100.0	89.0	25.1	38.5	25.5
1920	100.0	86.8	26.6	28.3	31.9
1929	100.0	90.0	32.2	25.0	32.8
1939	100.0	90.0	36.0	23.6	30.4
1946	100.0	87.0	37.1	22.1	27.8
		IV. Paid-up capital per company (R. thou.)			
1913	279	345	213	569	349
1920	349	368	234	649	405
1929	414	527	363	941	590
1939	267	321	217	706	372
1946	219	217	141	582	278
		V. New issue ratio (percent of GNP)			
1914–1920	0.45	0.39	0.12	0.08	0.17
1921–1929	0.39	0.37	0.15	0.08	0.13
1930–1939	0.07	0.08	0.07	0.00	−0.01
1939–1946	0.44	0.36	0.17	0.08	0.10
1913–1946	0.35	0.30	0.14	0.07	0.10

[a]A few native states omitted.

SOURCE OF I AND II: *BMS,* pp. 780 ff.

Within nonfinancial corporations, the main change was the decline of the share of the cotton and jute mills, the two leading old industries, from nearly two-fifths to less than one-fourth of aggregate paid-up capital. This was offset primarily by the increasing importance of trading and manufacturing companies, among which the latter appear to have predominated, from less than 25 percent to less than 40 percent of the total.

(ii) SOURCES OF FUNDS.[70] The amount of funds raised by nonfinancial corporations through stock issues should have been in the neighborhood of the R. 3.5 bill. increase in paid-up capital because the agio above par on some issues was offset, to an unknown extent, by noncash issues in mergers and on the occasion of the transformation of unincorporated businesses into corporations. There is, however, no comprehensive information about other sources of funds, and most of the fragmentary data available relate to the cotton industry, which may well not be representative of all nonfinancial corporations.

70. The most useful discussions on the financing of corporations in the interwar period are still two books originally published more than forty years ago, D. R. Gadgil's *The Industrial Evolution of India in Recent Times* (1st ed. 1924; 5th, 1971) and P. S. Lokanathan's *Industrial Organization in India* (1935).

There is little doubt that nonfinancial corporations retained part of their profits; issued relatively small amounts of debentures; borrowed from banks as well as, to a certainly much smaller extent, from indigenous bankers; used trade credit; and in some cases received deposits from the public, but there is no information on the relative importance of these sources of funds or on possible and even probable changes in the structure of internal and external financing.

Almost the only relevant statistics refer to 120 cotton mills in Bombay and Ahmadabad in 1930.[71] These mills accounted for about two-fifths of the capital of all incorporated cotton mills and they used about 6 percent of the capital of all nonfinancial corporations, so that the relations shown by this group of firms can hardly be regarded as applying to the universe of nonfinancial corporations.[72] Thus public deposits, which supplied one-fifth of total sources of funds (the statistics are incomplete as they do not provide information on retained earnings or on trade accounts payable), were hardly known outside the cotton mill industry; and managing agents, who furnished another one-fifth, are probably of considerably less importance in most other industries. Hence bank borrowings, which accounted for only 8 percent of all funds reported and for about one-eighth of all debt other than accounts payable, almost certainly were of greater importance for the aggregate of nonfinancial corporations.

Debentures furnished only a small proportion of total external financing. Near the end of the 1930s the joint stock companies listed on the Bombay and Calcutta stock exchanges, which accounted for about two-fifths of the paid-up capital of all corporations, had only R. 105 mill. of debentures outstanding.[73] Because large companies rather than small ones are more likely to use this form of financing, it is doubtful that all corporate debentures then outstanding exceeded R. 200 mill. This would be equal to about 7 percent of the paid-up capital of all nonfinancial corporations. Assuming that most of these debentures were issued after 1913, their net issue ratio for the period 1914–39 would come at most to 0.3 percent of national product.

Unfortunately, an indirect approach to measuring some of the sources of funds of corporations, namely, by information available from the lenders' records, is not feasible in India in the interwar period, as the banking statistics do not break down advances by type of borrower. An idea of the order of magnitude involved may be obtained, however, if it is assumed that the proportion of bank loans to corporations' paid-up capital was similar to that prevailing in the 1950s, namely, about three-fourths. This would put nonfinancial corporations' bank borrowings in 1946 at slightly above R. 3 bill., or somewhat more than two-thirds of total advances of scheduled commercial banks.[74] This is not an unreasonable figure, given the fact that in 1947 industry, which operates predominantly in corporate form, accounted for one-third of total bank loans, and trade, chiefly wholesale, for nearly one-half of them.

No information appears to exist on either the amount of profits, dividends, or retained profits of nonfinancial corporations during the interwar period or for substantial parts of it. All that is available are some indicators of the movement of corporate profits. An index of profits (coverage unknown) shows that they fell by nearly three-fourths between 1928 and 1931, stayed close to two-thirds of the 1928 level from 1934 through 1938, and exceeded that level only from 1941 on,[75] and very substantially so for some important industries like cotton, sugar, paper, and iron and steel. This suggests that retained earnings were in the 1930s well below the level of the 1920s but substantially above it during World War II, even though Indian companies appear to

71. *Report of the Central Banking Inquiry*, 1:278.

72. If nothing else, the substantial differences in the relative importance of the main sources of funds between the Bombay and the Ahmadabad cotton mills should cast doubt on the general applicability of the cotton industry ratios.

73. Basu, 1950, p. 114.

74. *BMS*, pp. 96 ff.

75. The Economic Advisor's index of industrial profits (Office of the Economic Advisor, *Statistical Summary of the Social and Economic Trends in India in the Interwar Period*, 1945, p. 32). The index unfortunately covers only the years 1928 through 1941.

have followed the policy of paying out most of declared profits rather than stabilizing dividends.[76]

The same tendencies are reflected in share prices. World War I led to a sharp, although very unequal, increase, the boom lasting until the spring of 1920. At that time an unweighted index of the shares of 265 nonfinancial companies stood at fully 250 percent of its level of the spring of 1914 and at nearly 170 percent of that of mid–1917.[77] No index is available for most of the 1920s, but it may be assumed that the trend was downward, reflecting a substantial decline in corporate profits from the level of World War I. The effect of the Great Depression is evident in the decline of a stock price index between 1928 and 1932 by more than one-third, which was considerably less than the decline in profits during the same period.[78] Stock prices recovered their 1927 level in mid-1934, but by mid-1942 they had risen by only 25 percent above it. Prices more than doubled in the next four years, reflecting exceptional wartime profits, but by the end of 1948 they had fallen back to only 60 percent above the level reached twenty years earlier, although the price level had more than quadrupled.

These data are hardly sufficient for an estimate of corporate saving in the interwar period. One is, therefore, forced either to abandon the attempt or to resort to the assumption that relations between corporate saving and corporate paid-up capital or national product observed in the 1950s may also be applied to the interwar period. These two approaches unfortunately yield quite different estimates of corporate retained earnings during the entire interwar period, namely about R. 4½ bill. (0.4 percent of gross national product) and approximately R. 1½ bill. (one-half of average paid-up capital).[79] It is, therefore, an act of faith to use the average of these two figures, namely, R. 3 bill., as a rough estimate of corporate saving during the interwar period, with the mental reservation that this figure is more likely to be too high rather than too low.

Putting these rough estimates together in the way of piling Ossa on Pelion, the following very rough picture of nonfinancial corporations' financing during the interwar period is obtained, still omitting net trade credit:

Retained earnings	R. 3 bill.
Stock issues	R. 3½ bill.
Debentures	R. ¼ bill.
Bank borrowing	R. 3 bill.
Total funds	R. 9¾ bill.

Total funds raised by nonfinancial corporations of about R. 9 bill. (deducting about R. 0.5 bill. for stock of financial corporations still included above) would have been equivalent to about 0.8 percent of the gross national product of the interwar period, approximately the same ratio as for the 1950s and is, therefore, probably to be regarded as the upper limit of the estimate. Possibly more valid than the estimates of the level of the several sources of funds in the interwar period, and more interesting for financial analysis, is the indication that retained earnings, stock issues, and bank borrowing may have provided approximately equal shares of the total funds raised by nonfinancial corporations.

(iii) MANAGING AGENCIES. The Indian corporate scene was characterized in the interwar period, as it had been in the preceding half century, by the managing agencies, a form of organization specific to the subcontinent.[80] Because the statistics. though plentiful, generally

---

76. Samant and Mulky, pp. 171–73.

77. Derived from data in Muranjan, p. 386.

78. *BMS*, pp. 733 ff.

79. These estimates are based on average paid-up capital for the interwar period taken from *BMS*, pp. 781 ff., and for the 1950s from Kulkarni, p. 140.

80. The literature on managing agencies listed in footnote 147 of chapter 1 generally also deals with the interwar period.

refer to the number of companies controlled by managing agencies rather than to more relevant criteria like capital or assets, they provide only an imperfect picture of the level and the changes in the actual importance of managing agencies within the nonfinancial corporate sector. The statistics, notwithstanding their defects, should, nevertheless be able to support two conclusions. First, the scope of activities of managing agencies increased during the interwar period, both absolutely and probably also in relation to all nonfinancial corporations. Thus the number of companies reported as controlled by a good dozen of the largest agencies increased from 165 in 1911 to nearly 250 in 1931 and to 350 in 1951.[81] Second, the area of control of Indian managing agencies increased much more rapidly than that of British agencies, particularly since the 1930s. As a result, at the end of the interwar period the capital of companies controlled by eleven large British agencies, whose histories in many cases go back to the ninteenth century, was well below that of the three leading Indian agencies, Tata, Birla, and Dalmia.[82]

(iv) DISTRIBUTION OF STOCK OWNERSHIP. Because the extent of foreign ownership of shares of Indian corporations is of interest not only for financial analysis but also as the subject of often impassioned political debate, it is astonishing that information on the distribution of stockownership during the interwar period is not only scarce but frequently unsystematic, with the available data often contradictory. Actually, the probably most comprehensive statistics on the share of foreign-controlled enterprises in large-scale industry are not based on shareownership but on employment. According to these statistics the share of foreign owners decreased in four out of eight industries between 1915 and 1937 and in five out of nine industries, primarily the same ones, from 1937 to 1944.[83] Even in 1944 the proportion of foreign ownership in these large corporations was still high, the median for ten industries being in excess of one-half. This figure, of course, substantially overstates the share of foreign ownership in all Indian nonfinancial corporations, as it excludes small and medium-sized firms in which foreign ownership was very small. That share would, on the other hand, be increased if the corporations working in India but incorporated abroad were included.

A similar picture of foreign ownership in Indian corporations is provided by a calculation based on a sample of more than one-half of the capital of all public companies registered in Bombay. This calculation shows a substantial decline in the share of British owners from 31 percent in 1912 to 22 percent in 1935, followed by a proportionally sharper fall to only 9 percent in 1944, the decline being even more pronounced in terms of the corporations' assets, namely, from 43 percent in 1912 to 10 percent in 1935 and 4 percent in 1948.[84] British influence apparently declined more sharply in western India than in Bengal, the chief area of concentration of British managing agencies.

The scattered data thus seem to agree on two points: first, a sharp decline in the share of foreign ownership in Indian corporations from the late 1930s on and second, the retention of substantial foreign holdings of stock in some large Indian corporations at the end of the interwar period.[85]

Although hardly anything is known in quantitative terms about the Indian buyers of the new shares issued or the methods of distribution, the descriptive literature leads to the conclusion that a large part of the shares was acquired by managing agencies or by close associates of the management or was disposed of by a rights offering to shareholders, as the country's investment banking machinery was poorly developed, impermanent, and not geared to the distribution of large issues to the general public. An incorporated investment bank, the Tata Industrial Bank,

81. M. M. Mehta, pp. 282, 295, and 309.
82. Lokanathan, p. 237.
83. Gokhale Institute, *Notes on the Rise of Business Communities in India,* 1957, cited by Islam, p. 171.
84. Estimates of A. Brimmer, cited in Meyers, p. 22.
85. Soni estimated, the basis of his calculations being far from clear, that foreigners in the middle 1920s owned ''at least one-third'' (a few lines later ''one- half'') of the capital of Indian joint stock companies, p. 172.

started in the midst of the war boom in 1918 by the largest Indian corporate group, had to be liquidated in the mid-1920s as the bank could not find enough acceptable clients.[86] If an estimate of underwriting commissions of between 2 and 5 percent, generally nearer to the upper boundary,[87] correctly reflects the situation, the cost of stock flotation was relatively low and close to the levels then prevailing in developed countries.

Needless to say, there is no comprehensive information, or even a rough estimate, of the number of stockholders in Indian corporations or of the shape of the distribution of stockholdings by size. Near the end of the period eight large corporations had on the average about 13,000 shareholders, the numbers ranging from fewer than 3,000 to more than 22,000. Although shareholdings classified as "small and middle class" constituted on the average 93 percent of the total number of holdings, they represented only between 2 and nearly 60 percent of the shares outstanding with an average and median of 40 percent.[88,89] No broad conclusions can be drawn from this minuscule sample, of course. However, the picture of concentrated ownership in many large corporations resulting from the managing agency system and in almost all small and medium-sized corporations, where family or small group control is usual, and the consequent small number of Indian shareholders—even in the mid-fifties probably not more than 500,000, or 1 in about every 150 families—correspond to the impression conveyed by the descriptive literature.

d. Financing Agriculture

Because agriculture provided in the interwar period slightly more than one-half of national income[90] and employed more than two-thirds of the labor force, it stands to reason that, even taking account of its considerably lower per head income, it should have accounted for a very substantial part of investment and saving of the entire household sector. Indeed, in view of the fact that a much higher but statistically indistinguishable proportion of agricultural households were at the same time engaged in productive activities, herein similar to households of most nonagricultural entrepreneurs, the share of agricultural households in total investment and saving of the household sector ought to have exceeded their share in that sector's income.

(i) CAPITAL FORMATION. Private gross fixed capital formation in agriculture has been estimated for the interwar period at slightly more than one-fifth of the national total. This would be equal to nearly 3½ percent of agricultural income and to only 1½ percent of national product. No estimate of net fixed capital formation in agriculture appears to have been made for the period as a whole. In view of the slow rate of increase of the volume of gross capital expenditures of only about 0.3 percent per year between 1913 and 1946,[91] and of the rate of increase between 1920 and 1945 of an index of durable physical capital in agriculture of only 0.3 percent per year,[92] the ratio of net private fixed capital expenditures to agricultural income must have been very low, probably on the order of 1 percent. To this would have to be added the increase in farm inventories, but these do not seem to have been large. They are, however, likely to raise the ratio

86. Lokanathan, pp. 257–59.

87. Lokanathan, p. 237.

88. Thomas, 1948, passim.

89. Among 50 companies, large shareholders, generally managing agencies, owned off record on the average 50 percent of the stock outstanding, but the amount actually controlled may have been higher because of nominee holdings (derived from figures in Lokanathan, pp. 185–86, which in turn were attributed to the *Mirror of Investment*, edited by P. Lovett, a publication not accessible for this study). Because the share was below 20 percent in only 6 companies, most of the companies can be regarded as having been under working control by managing agencies.

90. Sivasubramonian, p. 352.

91. BR.

92. Shukla, p. 104. The number of bullocks is estimated to have increased between 1920 and 1945 by 21 percent, or by 0.2 percent per year (p. 234).

TABLE 2-33. Gross Private Fixed Capital Formation in Agriculture, 1914–1946[a]

	1914–20	1921–29	1930–40	1941–46	1914–46
		I. Amounts (R. bill.)			
Construction	2.83	4.17	4.44	3.84	15.28
Machinery and equipment	0.80	1.18	1.24	1.08	4.30
Total	3.64	5.34	5.69	4.92	19.58
		II. Distribution (percent)			
Construction	78.0	77.9	78.2	78.0	78.0
Machinery and equipment	22.0	22.1	21.8	22.0	22.0
Total	100.0	100.0	100.0	100.0	100.0
		III. Share in total gross capital formation (percent)			
Construction	32.2	29.0	25.8	20.6	25.8
Machinery and equipment	18.6	15.0	16.7	14.3	15.8
Total	27.7	24.0	23.0	18.6	22.7
		IV. Relation to agricultural income (percent)			
Construction	1.47	1.32	1.63	1.03	1.33
Machinery and equipment	0.42	0.37	0.46	0.29	0.37
Total	1.89	1.69	2.09	1.32	1.70

[a]Includes livestock, but not crop inventories.

SOURCE OF I: *BR*.

of total net capital formation somewhat above 1 percent of agricultural income, although almost certainly not beyond 2 percent.[93]

(ii) SAVING THROUGH FINANCIAL INSTRUMENTS. Estimates of the saving of agricultural households through financial assets are even more precarious. Members' deposits in agricultural cooperatives, the only relevant reported item for which a fairly firm basis exists, are too small to be used as an indicator, as they increased by less than R. 30 mill. during the entire interwar period, or only 0.03 percent of agricultural income.[94] Because commercial banks hardly penetrated the countryside, only a very small percentage of the large increase in commercial bank deposits can be allocated to agriculture. The sector's share in deposits with the Post Office Saving System, which increased during the period by about R. 1.20 bill., was certainly larger than in the case of commercial bank deposits, although still probably only a moderate proportion of the total. Rural saving through life insurance and corporate securities may safely be neglected. Saving through the acquisition of government securities was certainly small, although not entirely negligible. This leaves saving in the form of bank notes as the most important form of agricultural saving through financial instruments. Because the increase in the volume of notes held by the entire household sector exceeded R. 9 bill. for the interwar period (table 2-39), the division of this total between agricultural and nonagricultural households is crucial to any estimate of agricultural saving through financial assets, but there is hardly any basis for such a division except the share of agriculture in population or personal income. Using the latter ratio of about one-half, agricultural saving through notes would have been on the order of R. 4 bill. to R. 5 bill., or about 0.8 to 1 percent of agricultural income. It is, therefore, difficult to estimate agricultural saving through financial assets as being much in excess of 1 percent of agricultural income for the entire interwar period. Most of this would have to be allocated to the 1940–46 period, when agricultural saving through financial assets would have amounted to more than 2

93. Shukla (pp. 151–55) provides estimates for four variants of gross and net capital formation in agriculture for the last decade of the interwar period, all in constant prices, none of which seems to include residential and nonresidential structures on farms.

94. *BMS*, p. 448. Based on Sivasubramonian's estimates of agricultural income.

percent of agricultural income if two-fifths of the total increase in note circulation, or one-half of the increase attributed to all households, are allocated to farm households. For the preceding period of 1914 to 1939, on the other hand, the ratio of saving through financial instruments to agricultural income can hardly have exceeded one-half of 1 percent.

The most elusive component of the saving and dissaving of the rural population, but unfortunately a very important one, is the change in their holdings of precious metals in the form of coins, bullion, or ornaments. In view of the obvious absence of any direct measurement, all that can be obtained is an idea of the order of magnitude involved. This estimate is derived by using the statistics of imports and exports of gold and silver, incomplete as they are because of probably substantial unrecorded movements during certain parts of the period, and adjusting them for domestic production of gold and for changes in the holdings of the banking system or the Treasury and of nonagricultural households. The estimates are not an exact measure of the absorption of precious metals by Indian households because they make no allowance for unrecorded imports and exports, for wear and tear and losses, and for changes in the holdings, particularly of silver coin, by financial institutions other than the monetary authorities, business enterprises, and the central and local governments. They should nevertheless correctly indicate at least the direction of the changes and their order of magnitude. Because these items, other than the unrecorded movements of precious metals, are likely to have been positive, actual absorption by agricultural households probably was smaller than the rough estimates used here.

The absorption of precious metals by the household sector then appears to have been slightly in excess of R. 4 bill. for the entire interwar period, four-fifths in the form of silver, equal to not quite 0.5 percent of the period's personal income. This was the result of substantial hoarding in World War I and during the 1920s, totaling almost R. 6 bill., or nearly 1.5 percent of personal income, and heavy distress dishoarding in the 1930s, totaling nearly R. 3 bill., or again 1.5 percent of income. Although these estimates certainly have to be used cautiously, they are sufficient to indicate that the accumulation or decumulation of precious metals constituted an important element in total saving or dissaving of Indian households and were in some periods larger than their total financial saving.

The allocation of the estimated absorption of precious metals by the household sector among its rural and urban parts can be done only in a rough and partly arbitrary way. The

TABLE 2-34. Estimate of Absorption of Gold and Silver by Households, 1914–1946
(R. Bill.)

	1914–20	1921–29	1930–39	1940–46	1914–46
1. Gold production	0.23	0.22	0.28	0.26	0.99
2. Net imports (+) or exports (−) of					
a. Gold	0.88	2.49	−3.52	0.05	−0.10
b. Silver	1.55	1.42	0.13	0.40	3.50
3. Change in supply of					
a. Gold	1.11	2.71	−3.24	0.30	0.88
b. Silver	1.55	1.42	0.13	0.40	3.50
4. Change in Reserve Bank holdings of					
a. Gold[a]	−0.05	0.08	0.09	—	0.12
b. Silver[a]	0.49	0.34	−0.30	−0.49	0.04
5. Estimated absorption by households[b] of					
a. Gold	1.16	2.63	−3.33	0.30	0.76
b. Silver	1.06	1.08	0.43	0.89	3.46
c. Gold and silver	2.22	3.71	−2.90	1.19	4.22
6. Percent of GNP	1.15	1.18	−1.19	0.30	0.37

[a]Paper Currency Reserve in cols. 1 and 2.   [b]At original cost.

SOURCES: Line 1: *BMS*, p. 938. Lines 2a, 2b: *BMS*, pp. 945 ff. Lines 4a, 4b: *BMS*, pp. 562, 573, and 647.

TABLE 2-35. Rough Estimate of Agricultural Saving, 1914–1946
(Percent of Agricultural Income)[a]

| | Capital formation[b] | | Financial assets | Gold and silver | Agricultural debt | Total gross | Total net |
	Gross (1)	Net[c] (2)	(3)	(4)	(5)	(6)	(7)
1914–20	3.7	1.2	0.5	1.3	2.9	3.0	0.1
1921–29	4.0	1.3	0.3	1.6	2.5	3.2	0.7
1930–39	4.6	1.5	0.4	−1.5	5.9	0.4	−5.5
1940–46	2.8	0.9	2.7	0.4	0.0	4.0	4.0
1914–46	3.7	1.3	1.2	0.5	2.4	3.0	0.6

[a]Estimate of Sivasubramonian.   [b]Excluding inventories.   [c]Assumed at one-third of col. 1.

SOURCES: **Col. 1:** *BR* and table 1-9.   **Col. 3:** Obtained by allocating to agricultural household one-half of the change in holdings of notes by the household sector, two-thirds of members' deposits with cooperatives, and a small proportion of lines 2 to 5 and 7 to 9 of table 2-39.   **Col. 4:** Assumed equal to three-fifths of total absorption by households (table 2-34).   **Col. 5:** Table 2-37.   **Col. 6:** Cols. 2 + 3 + 4.   **Col. 7:** Cols. 2 + 3 + 4 − 5.

population and the income of the two subsectors or a combination of them appear to be the best allocators available, ignoring possible differences between the two subsectors in hoarding per head or family or in the ratio of hoarding to income, as well as changes in these differences. On that basis between one-half (income basis) and two-thirds (population basis) should be allocated to agriculture, that is, for the period as a whole between R. 2 bill. and R. 3 bill., or from 0.4 to 0.5 percent of agricultural income. This is a substantial item because it compares with gross saving through financial assets of probably not much more than 1 percent of agricultural income and would bring agricultural financial saving close to 2 percent of income and that of total agricultural saving before allowance for changes in debt to about 3 percent.

The inclusion of accumulation or decumulation of precious metals would have even more influence on agricultural financial saving over shorter spans. Thus it would greatly increase the saving ratio for the 1914–29 period, when hoarding apparently was far in excess, indeed possibly three times as large as saving through financial instruments. In the 1930s the heavy dishoarding would certainly far exceed any financial saving. During World War II, on the other hand, hoarding appears to have been small enough to increase total financial saving only marginally.

This discussion, inconclusive as it is, should suffice to show that the level and direction of agricultural saving cannot even be approximated without considering the hoarding and dishoarding of precious metals.

(iii) AGRICULTURAL DEBT. Changes in agricultural debt have undoubtedly been the decisive element in determining the volume of financial saving or dissaving of many agricultural households. Such changes, however, do not seriously affect the total or the financial saving of agriculture, nor a fortiori that of the entire household sector, because they are offset by changes in the opposite direction of lenders' financial positions, and most of the lenders also belong to the agricultural or more rarely to the nonagricultural part of the household sector. It is only agricultural debt to financial institutions, nonfinancial corporations, and the government that should be entered as an item of negative saving of agriculture, and this part of agricultural debt should have been rather low in the interwar period. This is suggested by the fact that even in 1951 only about one-tenth of agricultural debt was owed to government or institutional lenders.[95]

95. Reserve Bank of India, *All-India Rural Credit Survey,* vol. 1, pt.2, and *BMS,* p. 448.

Although all estimates of agricultural debt during the interwar period are conjectural, there exists at least one somewhat firmer anchor for the end of the period, the amount of agricultural debt of R. 15½ bill. derived for the Indian Union from the first rural credit survey of the Reserve Bank for the beginning of the 1950s.[96] To obtain an estimate for Undivided India in 1946, this figure would have to be stepped up, using population as base, by about one-fifth and would have to be reduced to take account of the increase in net debt during the years 1946–50. This would lead to an estimate of agricultural debt in Undivided India in 1946 on the order of R. 18 bill.

Only rough estimates exist of agricultural indebtedness at the beginning of the interwar period. In chapter 1, section 6b, arguments have been presented for a range of between R. 4 bill. and R.7 bill. For purposes of the present discussion, a figure of R. 5 bill. with a margin of error of at least R. 1 bill. of either side is used. Acceptance of these figures leads to putting the increase of agricultural debt between 1913 and 1946 at about R. 13 bill., or 260 percent of its 1913 level, an average annual increase of 4 percent.[97] In terms of constant prices, the increase, however, amounted to only 30 percent, or 0.8 percent per year.

The statistical material is insufficient to establish the movements of agricultural debt within the interwar period with confidence. A few estimates exist, for example, one by Darling of about R. 8 bill. in 1924; one by Thomas of about R. 11½ bill. in 1928–29 derived from Indian Central Banking Enquiry Committee material; another one of more than R. 15 bill. in 1933; and one of R. 18 bill. in 1939 by the Agricultural Credit Department of the Reserve Bank.[98] These estimates, which differ in method and reliability, are compatible with the estimates used here for the beginning and end of the interwar period. They also permit the inference that the volume of debt increased fairly rapidly until the late 1930s but did not change much during the World War II period, which was a very prosperous one for Indian agriculture.

As one might expect in a country of India's diversity, there were substantial regional differences in the burden of agricultural debt. These differences can be followed in table 2-36 for British India, which accounted for about three-fourths of the population of the subcontinent at the end of the 1920s. These data may be regarded as reasonably reliable for interregional comparisons, much as the level of the estimates derived from material collected by the Indian Central Banking Enquiry Committee may be subject to a substantial margin of error. Thus the debt per agriculturalist and the ratio of debt to the value of principal crops were almost three times or twice as high, respectively, as the country averaged in the Punjab, whereas the two ratios were relatively low in Bengal and the Central Provinces. For an appraisal of relative debt burden figures for the ratio of debt to land values would be needed, but they are not available for the interwar period. It is likely, however, that land values per acre were higher in the Punjab than in most of the other regions.

How does the increase in agricultural debt compare with other relevant characteristics of agriculture, particularly the trend in agricultural prices, in agricultural incomes, and in farmland prices? Table 2-37 is intended to provide a basis for answering these questions. The answer may be summed up in the statement that the burden of debt, measured by its relations to farm income and farmland prices, was substantially reduced during World War I; increased moderately during the 1920s and advanced sharply during the 1930s as a result of a substantial rise of debt in the face of a protracted decline in prices; but fell sufficiently as a result of the inflation during World War II to bring the burden of debt back to the level of more than three decades earlier. Thus the debt burden of Indian agriculture at the end of the interwar period was moderate, if attention is

96. Loc. cit.

97. If margins of error of R. 1 bill. on either side are allowed in the estimates for 1913 and 1946, the annual rate of increase in agricultural debt might be as low as 3.2 percent and as high as 4.8 percent.

98. See listings in Cirvante, pp. 19, 48; in Jathar and Beri, chap. 9; also Thomas, 1939, chap. 9. Estimates referring to British India have been stepped up.

TABLE 2-36. Regional Distribution of Agricultural Debt, 1928–1929[a]

Provinces	Total debt (R. bill.) (1)	Share of mortgage debt (percent) (2)	Debt per agriculturalist[b] (rupees) (3)	Ratio of debt to principal crops (4)	Debt (5)	Debt per agriculturalist[b] (6)	Ratio of debt to principal crops (7)
Madras	1.50[c]	50	50	.83	19	156	86
Bombay	0.81	28–36	49	.67	10	153	69
Bengal	1.00	45	31	.43	13	97	44
United Provinces	1.24	56	36	.88	16	113	91
Central Provinces	0.36	28	30	.52	5	94	54
Punjab	1.35	43	92	1.75	17	288	180
Bihar and Orissa	1.55	40	31	1.15	20	97	119
Total[a]	7.81	44	32	.97	100	100	100

[a]Covers ca. 95 percent of British India.   [b]The country total appears to be too low in comparison to the provincial totals.   [c]Includes some nonagricultural debt.

SOURCES: **Cols. 1, 3 and 4:** Thomas, 1934, p. 11 (from report of Indian Central Banking Enquiry Committee).   **Col. 2:** Nanavati and Anjaria, p. 302.

TABLE 2-37. Indicators of Burden of Agricultural Debt, 1913–1946

	1913	1920	1929	1939	1946
	I. Amount or ratio				
1. Debt, capital (R. bill.)	5.0	8.0	11.5	18.0	18.0
2. Debt, annual service (R. bill.)	0.90	1.44	2.07	3.24	3.24
3. Income, current prices (R. bill.)	11.5	17.0	16.3	12.8	34.8
4. Prices received (1938 = 100)	116	172	148	113	307
5. Farmland prices (1913 = 100)	100	200	250	250	445
6. Farmland value (R. bill.)[a]	36	74	94	95	175
7. Debt					
Annual income ratio	0.43	0.47	0.71	1.41	0.52
Land value ratio	0.14	0.11	0.12	0.19	0.10
8. Service: income ratio	0.08	0.08	0.13	0.25	0.09
	II. Movements (1913 = 100)				
1. Debt, capital (R. bill.)	100	160	230	360	360
2. Debt, annual service (R. bill.)	100	160	230	360	360
3. Income, current prices (R. bill.)	100	148	142	111	303
4. Prices received (1938 = 100)	100	148	128	97	265
5. Farmland prices (1913 = 100)	100	200	250	250	445
6. Farmland value (R. bill.)	100	206	260	263	481
7. Debt					
Annual income ratio	100	116	165	328	121
Land value ratio	100	78	88	136	71
8. Service: income ratio	100	100	163	313	113

[a]Includes nonagricultural land.

SOURCES: Line 1: See text. Line 2: Assumed at 18 percent of debt. Lines 3 and 4: Sivasubramonian, pp. 162–63; price index is implicit deflator, basis 1938. Lines 5 and 6: Table 2-38.

TABLE 2-38. Estimated Value of Agricultural Land, 1913–1946

Year	Crop acreage[a] (1)	Land prices[a] (2)	Value of agricultural land	
			(3)[b]	(4)[a]
1913	100	100	36	100
1920	103	200	74	206
1929	104	250	94	260
1939	105	250	95	263
1946	108	445	175	481

[a]1913–14 = 100.   [b]R. bill.

SOURCES: **Col. 1:** Blyn, pp. 316–17. It has been assumed that movement for Undivided India parallels that for British India.   **Col. 2:** Values for 1920–39 based on indices of land prices in Punjab (Mukerji, pp. 529 ff., and Singh and Calvert, p. 13) adjusted to fit into relation of 1913 and 1940 values of col. 3, allowing for increase in acreage.   **Col. 3:** Tables 1-24 (for 1913) and 3-34 (for 1946) stepped up by 20 percent to shift from Indian Union to Undivided India, reducing both estimates by about one-tenth to exclude nonagricultural land and for 1949 by another one-tenth to allow for price rise between 1946 and 1949. Values for 1920, 1929, and 1939 obtained by applying product of cols. 1 and 2 to R. 36 bill. in 1913.

focused on all agricultural households rather than on smaller groups or areas. The debt was on the order of one-tenth of the value of farmland and of six months' agricultural income; and debt service is not likely to have absorbed more than one-tenth of agricultural income, even at the high rates charged by rural moneylenders.[99] The situation of many of the debtors was, of course, worse and often considerably so; and one may assume that those debtors were chiefly owners of very small holdings or landless peasants as well as farmers who had suffered crop failures or incurred particularly high expenses as a result of illness or ceremonial obligations.[100] The burden of agricultural debt thus constituted a serious social problem, although the debt cannot in the aggregate be regarded as excessive by economic and financial standards.

e. The finances of the Nonagricultural Household Sector

The estimation of nonagricultural household saving, including unincorporated nonfarm business, is almost as difficult and the results are almost as uncertain as for the thirty to fifty years before World War I. No wonder, therefore, that no attempt at such an estimation seems to have been made. To overcome this deficiency would require much more intensive study and much larger resources than are available here. All that can be done is to obtain an idea of the orders of magnitude involved.

There are two possible approaches. The first is to estimate nonagricultural household saving as the residual of total gross capital formation and of five subtrahends, namely, depreciation, net capital imports or exports, government saving, corporate business saving, and agricultural saving. This approach, which yields only one figure aggregating all forms of non-

99. No comprehensive information exists on rates effectively charged, i.e., making allowance for defaults, on rural debt. The report of the Indian Central Banking Enquiry Committee put the "general" rate charged by village moneylenders on unsecured loans in the United Provinces at 24 percent and that on mortgages at 12 percent (I-1: 80–81). Table 2-37 uses the average of these two rates.

100. The burden of debt is naturally much higher if compared with the value of land actually mortgaged or with the income of its proprietors. If it is assumed that about one-half of total debt is mortgage debt (cf. Indian Central Banking Enquiry Committee, I-1:302) and that about one-eighth of the land is mortgaged (if the Punjab is indicative, the proportion of land that was mortgaged did not substantially change between 1916 and 1929, the median for twelve districts remaining in the neighborhood of 11 percent, according to Calvert, p. 268) the burden resting on this land would be four times as heavy as it was for all agricultural land. This would mean that even after the *seisachtheia* of World War II the ratio of mortgage debt to the value of the pledged land would be on the order of two-fifths; that the debt would be equal to two years' income of the cultivator; and that the debt service/income ratio would be on the order of one-third of income. The mortgagees, and the borrowers without mortgage security as well, would indeed be in a fairly serious position.

TABLE 2-39. Some Components of Household Financial Saving, 1914–1946

Item	Assumed share of household sector (percent)	Estimated saving				
		1914–20	1921–29	1930–39	1940–46	1914–46
		I. Amounts (R. bill.)				
1. Notes	80	0.74	0.23	0.42	8.00	9.39
2. Deposits with commercial banks						
Demand	30	0.23	−0.05	0.08	1.35	1.61
Time	50	0.21	0.07	0.19	2.29	2.76
3. Post Office Saving System						
Deposits	100	−0.02	0.16	0.41	0.64	1.19
Certificates	100	—	—	0.60	0.55	1.15
4. Cooperative societies	100	0.06	0.24	0.09	0.29	0.68
5. Life insurance[a]	100	0.03	0.09	0.33	0.60	1.04
6. State provident funds	100	0.16	0.36	0.17	0.22	0.93
7. Corporate stock	75	0.66	0.91	0.14	1.32	3.03
8. Total: 1–7	—	2.07	2.01	2.43	15.26	21.78
9. Gold and silver	100	2.22	3.71	−2.90	1.19	4.22
10. Total: 8 + 9	—	4.29	5.72	−0.47	16.45	26.00
		II. Distribution (percent)				
1. Notes	—	36	11	17	52	43
2. Deposits with commercial banks						
Demand	—	11	−2	3	9	7
Time	—	10	3	8	15	13
3. Post Office Saving System						
Deposits	—	− 1	8	17	4	5
Certificates	—	—	—	25	4	5
4. Cooperative societies	—	3	12	4	2	3
5. Life insurance[a]	—	1	4	14	4	5
6. State provident funds	—	8	18	7	1	4
7. Corporate stock	—	32	45	6	9	14
8. Total: 1–7	—	100	100	100	100	100
9. Gold and silver	—	107	185	−119	8	19
10. Total: 8 + 9	—	207	285	−119	108	119
		III. Relation to personal income (percent)[b]				
1. Notes	—	0.48	0.09	0.22	2.49	1.02
2. Deposits with commercial banks						
Demand	—	0.15	−0.02	0.04	0.42	0.18
Time	—	0.14	0.03	0.10	0.71	0.30
3. Post Office Saving System						
Deposits	—	−0.01	0.06	0.21	0.20	0.13
Certificates	—	—	—	0.31	0.17	0.12
4. Cooperative societies	—	0.04	0.10	0.05	0.09	0.07
5. Life insurance[a]	—	0.02	0.04	0.17	0.19	0.11
6. State provident funds	—	0.10	0.14	0.09	0.07	0.09
7. Corporate stock	—	0.43	0.36	0.07	0.41	0.33
8. Total: 1–7	—	1.36	0.80	1.26	4.75	2.35
9. Gold and silver	—	1.44	1.47	−1.49	0.37	0.46
10. Total: 8 + 9	—	2.80	2.27	−0.23	5.12	2.81

[a]Net of policy loans.   [b]Assumed at 80 percent of gross national product.

SOURCES: Line 1: *BMS*, pp. 562 ff., 655 ff. Line 2: *BMS*, pp. 96 ff. Line 3: *BMS*, pp. 377, 399. Line 4: *BMS*, p. 384. Line 5: Life insurance and other insurance funds, less policy loans; *BMS*, p. 924. Line 6: *BMS*, p. 881. Line 8: *BMS*, pp. 780 ff. Line 9: Table 2-34.

agricultural household saving, was tried but abandoned, because the cumulative margin of error in the components of the subtrahend, for most of which there is no directly relevant information, became excessive. The alternative is to build up nonagricultural household saving from estimates of the numerous forms of saving and dissaving. The tentative estimates so obtained are shown in table 2-39 for the aggregate and for the main forms of financial saving.

The nine types of financial saving for which the national totals are fairly reliable, although the share of all households, and still more that of nonagricultural households, is subject to a substantial margin of error in most of them, totaled close to R. 22 bill. for the interwar period, equal to nearly 2½ percent of personal disposable income. The ratio was in the neighborhood of 1 percent from 1914 through 1939 but shot up to nearly 5 percent during World War II. This increase, as well as the fact that the ratio was higher during World War I than during the 1920s and 1930s, is in line with expectations.

For the entire interwar period, currency (notes) was the most important of the nine instruments of financial saving by households, accounting for more than two-fifths of the total. Deposits, more than one-fourth of the total, were next. Life insurance and provident funds each accounted for 5 percent. The share of corporate stock, one-seventh of the total, was relatively high.

The distribution of aggregate financial saving is, however, different for the war periods, on the one hand, and for the 1920s and 1930s, on the other. During the two war periods the share of notes, in which an inflation manifests itself most rapidly, was much higher than in the intervening two decades. In contrast, thrift deposits, insurance, and pension funds accounted for a substantially higher proportion of the total in the 1920s and 1930s than they did in World War I or in World War II.

This still leaves unaccounted a number of financial instruments that may be assumed to have accounted for not negligible amounts of household saving or dissaving, namely, among assets, Indian government securities and corporate bonds; deposits with corporations, indigenous bankers, nidhis and chit funds; and provident funds outside the government; and among liabilities, borrowings from banks and indigenous bankers, the borrowings on life insurance policies already having been deducted from the life insurance fund that constitutes one of the components of financial saving shown in table 2-39. Another very important item, rural mortgage and unsecured debt, affects aggregate saving or dissaving of the nonagricultural household sector only to a very small extent, as it may be assumed that the share of urban lenders was small enough to be neglected. The same reasoning applies to most urban mortgage debt as well as to other loans among nonagricultural households. Statistical information is lacking for all these items. Some of them are probably small enough, for example, corporate debentures, so that their omission will not seriously affect the picture. This, however, is certainly not true of the hoarding or dishoarding of precious metals; for the saving or dissaving in the form of Indian government securities; and for the household sector's borrowing from financial institutions. Hence, an effort must be made to ascertain at least the order of magnitude of these four items.

In the case of the hoarding of precious metals it appears that the absorption by nonagricultural households may be very roughly put at less than R. 2 bill. for the entire postwar period, or approximately one-half of 1 percent of personal income and on the order of one-tenth of financial saving. Because hoarding by nonagricultural households has been derived as a fixed percentage of total hoarding, it shows the same movements as for agricultural households, namely, a substantial accumulation of precious metals during World War I and the 1920s and considerable dishoarding in the 1930s. If the estimates are at least of the right order of magnitude, the hoarding of precious metals was as large as financial saving from 1914 to 1920, offset all financial saving during the 1930s, and was almost insignificant in comparison to financial saving during World War II.

Nonagricultural household saving in the form of the acquisition of Indian government securities presents a rather puzzling picture. In 1913, when holdings by domestic and foreign investors were reported separately, Indian investors were credited with R. 0.80 bill. of central government securities.[101] Although the proportion owned by individual investors is not known, it should have been fairly high, the only reported institutional holdings being R. 100 mill. in the Paper Currency Reserve and about R. 40 mill. in the portfolios of life insurance companies.[102] The holdings of commercial banks, not separately reported, should have been of the same order of magnitude. This would have left, at most, R. 0.50 bill. for Indian private investors. An estimate on the order of R. 0.40 bill. appears more likely so as to leave room for corporate and other nonindividual Indian holdings. In 1950, the first date for which any estimate is available, the holdings of government securities by the household sector were put at R. 0.64 bill.[103] Because these figures refer to the Indian Union only, and because total rupee funded debt decreased between 1946 and 1951 by 6 percent, the figures for Undivided India in 1946 should have been in the neighborhood of R. 0.80 bill., practically all of which would have to be allocated to nonagricultural households and attributed to the World War II period. It thus appears that the nonagricultural household sector's saving in the form of Indian government securities was very small, namely, on the order of R. 0.40 bill. for the entire interwar period. This would be about 3 percent of total financial saving by households and on the order of 0.1 percent of their income. There is no way of estimating household saving through Indian government securities for the four subperiods. Nor is this necessary, because it is fairly clear that Indian government securities constituted only a small fraction of household financial saving throughout the interwar period.

Direct information on the size of movements of household debt other than agricultural debt but including the debt of nonagricultural unincorporated businesses is lacking except for borrowing from cooperative societies and for policy loans, which have been treated as an offset to saving through life insurance. The first available estimate of institutional borrowing by the entire household sector refers to 1950 and the Indian Union and puts the debt at R. 4.4 bill., about two-thirds in the form of bank borrowing and nearly one-fifth in borrowing from credit cooperatives.[104] Raising the figure by one-fifth to cover the territory of Undivided India, reducing it by one-fourth because of the increase in borrowing between 1946 and 1951, and further reducing it by one-tenth to allow for the institutional debt of agricultural households, an estimate of about R. 3½ bill. is obtained for nonagricultural households' borrowing in Undivided India at the end of 1946. This total would have been equal to about one-eighth of nonagricultural households' income in 1946. If it is assumed that the ratio of borrowings to income was the same at earlier benchmark dates, they would have amounted to about R. 1.00 bill. in 1913 and to about R. 1.70 bill. in both 1920 and 1930, an assumption that, even if correct for a long-time average, is almost certain to understate cyclical movements. For 1939 a more relevant extrapolator is available in the movement of total advances of Indian scheduled banks, [105] which leads to an estimate of nonagricultural households' borrowings of approximately R. 1.10 bill.

The result of these hazardous calculations is an estimate of net financial saving of nonagricultural households, including the accumulation of precious metals, of between R. 15 bill. and R. 20 bill. for the interwar period as a whole. This would be equal to about 4 to 5 percent of their income. The ratio appears to have been considerably lower than the period average in the 1930s and considerably above the average during World War II.

The nonagricultural household sector has, of course, had substantial gross saving in tangible assets, chiefly in the form of dwellings and the structures, equipment, and inventories of unincorporated, mostly quite small business enterprises, but no estimate separating these items from total gross fixed capital formation appears to exist. Net saving in these forms, although

101. Vakil, p. 557.
102. *BMS,* pp. 647, 924.
103. V-S, pp. 134–35.
104. Ibid.
105. *BMS,* pp. 156, 174.

probably small, given the low growth rate of nonagricultural capital formation in the interwar period, cannot have been negligible, given a doubling of the nonagricultural population.[106]

f. Total Saving

As a minimum of control, the very rough estimates of the saving of the nonfinancial sector discussed in this section must be compared with the estimates of national net saving obtained by deducting net capital imports from net capital formation shown in table 2-9, which puts it at 2¾ percent for the entire interwar period. It then appears that the sum of the saving ratio for the four sectors for which these rough estimates were attempted, too rashly perhaps, is somewhat in excess of the estimate derived from capital formation, namely, between 3 and 4 percent, a relationship usually found when comparing estimates of net saving derived by these two methods. It also appears that corporate saving contributed only a small proportion of the total, probably less than one-tenth, whereas public saving may have accounted for as much as one-fifth. The bulk of the total saving was, as it almost always is, contributed by the household sector, apparently in about equal proportions by farm and nonfarm households, although the share of nonfarm households may have been slightly larger. In that case the sectoral distribution of saving would be quite similar to that estimated, somewhat less recklessly, for the postwar period.

7. THE NATIONAL BALANCE SHEET OF INDIA, 1913–1946

a. National Balance Sheets

Because a national balance sheet that shows the value of the main tangible assets and financial instruments is one of the best ways to obtain an overview of a country's financial superstructure, an attempt has been made to construct such balance sheets for the benchmark dates of 1913, 1920, 1929, 1939, and 1946. It is hardly necessary to stress again the unavoidable roughness of the estimates for most components and the consequent wide margins of error. Notwithstanding these limitations, the balance sheet should give a reasonably correct picture of the orders of magnitude involved and of the direction of changes within the interwar period. Almost all estimates could have been improved if more time and resources had been available, and estimates of a few small items now omitted, for example, securities of local governments, corporate debentures, and deposits with non-bank corporations, could have been added. It might then also have been possible to distribute the national totals among the main sectors—households, corporate business, and government—a task beyond the possibilities of this study. But even then, the margins of error would remain large, both because of methodological differences and of unavailability of sufficiently relevant and accurate data. Table 2-40 shows, therefore, the absolute figures combined for all sectors, all values supposed to reflect market prices, or in the case of claims, face values, at the date of the balance sheet. The structure of the balance sheets is shown in table 2-41 by expressing each component as a percentage of national assets, whereas table 2-42 relates each balance sheet item to gross national product. It seems best to let these tables speak for themselves and to limit discussion here to a few remarks on relevant ratios and on changes in them during the interwar period, which are shown in tables 2-43, 2-44, and 2-45.

Over the period almost all the ratios move in a way consonant with a financial superstructure that is expanding more rapidly than the country's real infrastructure, although substantially affected by two periods of inflation during World War I and II, and by two periods of deflation, that is, most of the 1920s and 1930s. Thus, the financial interrelations ratio nearly doubled during the interwar period, with most of the increase occurring during the 1930s when the current value of national product declined by one-fifth, whereas financial assets grew by nearly one-fourth, in part reflecting the increasing monetization of the economy. The ratio of financial

---

106. Increase refers to towns and is derived from table 1-1.

TABLE 2-40. National Balance Sheet, 1913–1946 (R. Bill.)

	1913 (1)	1920 (2)	1929 (3)	1939 (4)	1946 (5)
I. *Tangible assets*	86.5	178.5	195.5	195.7	395.4
1. Land	40.0	84.0	107.0	109.0	203.0
2. Structures and equipment	24.2	55.3	55.1	53.0	102.0
3. Inventories	3.4	7.5	11.1	5.3	14.3
4. Livestock	6.8	14.7	6.3	8.4	22.1
5. Gold and silver	12.0	17.0	16.0	20.0	54.0
II. *Financial assets*	13.0	28.2	37.1	45.9	106.6
1. Money: notes	0.5	1.4	1.7	2.3	12.3
2. Money: demand deposits	0.6	1.4	1.2	1.6	8.0
3. Other claims against financial institutions	1.0	2.2	3.3	5.5	17.9
4. Agricultural debt	5.0	8.0	11.5	18.0	18.0
5. Nonfarm household debt	1.0	1.7	1.7	1.1	3.6
6. Bank debt	0.7	1.7	1.3	1.7	4.4
7. Trade credit	1.7	3.8	5.6	2.7	7.2
8. Government domestic debt	1.7	5.0	8.0	9.0	23.2
9. Corporate stock	1.0	3.0	2.8	4.0	12.0
III. *Net foreign assets*	−7.0	−7.0	−9.6	−12.4	18.0
IV. *National wealth (I + III)*	79.5	171.5	185.9	183.3	413.4
V. *National assets (I + II)*	99.5	206.6	232.6	241.6	502.0

SOURCES: Col. 1: Table 1-28.   Cols. 2–5: Line I-1, table 2-38, increasing value of agricultural land by between 12 and 16 percent; lines I-2 and I-3, *BR*, increased by 20 percent to shift from Indian Union to Undivided India; lines I-4 and I-5, same as for table 1-28, lines I-4 and I-5. lines II-1 and 2, table 2-31; line II-3, assets of financial institutions (table 2-11) less lines II-1 and II-2; line II-4, see discussion in section 6e; line II-5, assumed at one-fifth of line 2-4; line II-6, sum of advances of scheduled banks (*BMS*, pp. 96 ff. for 1939 and 1946; roughly estimated for earlier dates) and of loans to members by cooperatives (*BMS*, p. 385); line II-7, estimated at one-half of inventories; line II-8, for 1939 and 1946 rupee debt of central and provincial governments (*BMS*, pp. 881, 883); for 1920 and 1929 rupee debt of central government plus rough allowance for provincial debts; line II-9, for 1929 to 1946 estimated on the assumption that average price of stocks in 1927–28, the basis of the stock price index (*BMS*, pp. 734 ff.), was equal to par (table 2-4); rough estimate for 1920. Line III, estimates of foreign investments in India for 1921, 1929, and 1939 in Bose, pp. 496, 499; rough estimate for 1946 based on estimate for Indian Union of R. 15 bill. as of June 30, 1948 (*RBIB*, 1957, pp. 1191 ff.).

TABLE 2-41. Structure of National Balance Sheet, 1913–1946 (National Assets = 100)

	1913	1920	1929	1939	1946
I. *Tangible assets*	86.8	86.4	84.0	81.0	78.8
1. Land	40.1	40.7	46.0	45.1	40.4
2. Structures and equipment	24.4	26.8	23.7	21.9	20.3
3. Inventories	3.4	3.6	4.8	2.2	2.8
4. Livestock	6.8	7.1	2.7	3.5	4.4
5. Gold and silver	12.1	8.2	6.9	8.3	10.8
II. *Financial assets*	13.2	13.6	16.0	19.0	21.2
1. Money: notes	0.5	0.7	0.7	1.0	2.5
2. Money: demand deposits	0.6	0.7	0.5	0.7	1.6
3. Other claims against financial institutions	1.0	1.1	1.4	2.3	3.6
4. Agricultural debt	5.0	3.9	4.9	7.5	3.6
5. Nonfarm household debt	1.0	0.8	0.7	0.5	0.7
6. Bank debt	0.7	0.8	0.6	0.7	0.9
7. Trade credit	1.7	1.8	2.4	1.1	1.4
8. Government debt[a]	1.7	2.4	3.4	3.7	4.6
9. Corporate stock	1.0	1.5	1.2	1.7	2.4
III. *Net foreign assets*	−7.0	−3.4	−4.1	−5.1	3.6
IV. *National wealth (I + III)*	79.9	83.0	79.9	75.9	82.4
V. *National assets (I + II)*	100.0	100.0	100.0	100.0	100.0

[a]Rupee issues only.

SOURCE: Table 2-40.

TABLE 2-42. National Balance Sheet Compared to Gross National Product, 1913–1946

	1913	1920	1929	1939	1946
I. Tangible assets	4.04	5.06	6.39	6.90	5.45
1. Land	1.87	2.33	3.50	3.84	2.80
2. Structures and equipment	1.13	1.57	1.80	1.87	1.41
3. Inventories	0.16	0.21	0.36	0.19	0.20
4. Livestock	0.32	0.42	0.21	0.30	0.30
5. Gold and silver	0.56	0.48	0.52	0.70	0.74
II. Financial assets	0.61	0.80	1.21	1.62	1.47
1. Money: notes	0.02	0.04	0.06	0.08	0.17
2. Money: demand deposits	0.03	0.04	0.04	0.06	0.11
3. Other claims against financial institutions	0.05	0.06	0.11	0.19	0.25
4. Agricultural debt	0.23	0.23	0.38	0.63	0.25
5. Nonfarm household debt	0.05	0.05	0.06	0.04	0.05
6. Bank debt	0.03	0.05	0.04	0.06	0.06
7. Trade credit	0.08	0.11	0.18	0.10	0.10
8. Government debt	0.08	0.14	0.26	0.32	0.32
9. Corporate stock	0.05	0.09	0.09	0.14	0.17
III. Net foreign assets	−0.33	−0.20	−0.31	−0.44	0.25
IV. National wealth (I + III)	3.71	4.87	6.07	6.46	5.70
V. National assets (I + II)	4.65	5.86	7.50	8.52	6.92

SOURCE: Table 2-40.

TABLE 2-43. National Balance Sheet Ratios, 1913–1946

		Value of ratio				
Numerator	*Denominator*	*1913*	*1920*	*1929*	*1939*	*1946*
Financial assets	Tangible assets	0.15	0.16	0.19	0.24	0.27
Claims	Financial assets	0.92	0.89	0.92	0.91	0.89
Claims against	Financial assets	0.16	0.18	0.17	0.20	0.36
financial institutions[a]	Gross national product	0.10	0.14	0.21	0.33	0.53
Corporate stock	Financial assets	0.08	0.11	0.08	0.09	0.11
Land	Tangible assets	0.46	0.47	0.55	0.56	0.51
Financial assets	Gross national product	0.61	0.80	1.20	1.62	1.47
Net foreign assets	Tangible assets	−0.08	−0.04	−0.05	−0.06	0.05

[a]Including bank notes.

SOURCES: Tables 2-1 and 2-40.

TABLE 2-44. Capital-Output Ratios, 1913–1946[a]

	Broad (1)	Intermediate (2)	Narrow (3)
1913	4.04	2.17	1.61
1920	5.06	2.68	2.20
1929	6.39	2.89	2.37
1939	6.90	3.06	2.35
1946	5.45	2.65	1.91

[a]Numerator is tangible assets for col. 1; reproducible assets including gold and silver for col. 2; and reproducible assets excluding gold and silver for col. 3. Denominator for all three columns is gross national product.

SOURCES: Tables 2-1 and 2-40.

TABLE 2-45. Financial Interrelations Ratio, 1913–1946

Numerator	Including	Excluding	Including	Excluding
		gold and silver		
Denominator	Including gold and silver		Excluding gold and silver	
	(1)	(2)	(3)	(4)
1913	0.289	0.150	0.336	0.174
1920	0.253	0.158	0.280	0.175
1929	0.272	0.190	0.296	0.207
1939	0.337	0.235	0.375	0.261
1946	0.406	0.270	0.470	0.312

SOURCE OF BASIC DATA: Table 2-40.

assets to national product more than doubled from 1913 to 1946, the increase again being concentrated in the 1930s. The rise in the ratio of financial institutions' assets to all financial assets from 0.16 to 0.36, which implies that financial institutions participated as holders or issuers in more than two-thirds of all issues of financial instruments in 1946 against a share of only about one-third in 1913, is an indication of the growing institutionalization of the financial process. The preponderance of claims over corporate equities declined from 12 to 1 to 8 to 1, reflecting the increasing importance of corporations in the economy.

Table 2-41 also provides information on some characteristics of the real infrastructure, which are relevant to the structure and development of the financial superstructure. Thus the ratio of all tangible assets, as well as that of reproducible assets, to national product showed an upward trend, although only through the 1930s, partly because the actual national product was then below the potential national product. Contrary to the trend observed in most countries, the share of land in national wealth was similar, and very high, at the beginning and the end of the interwar period, which was possibly due to the uncertainties about the actual movements of land prices. The share of net foreign assets to national wealth, finally, declined from a range of −4 and −9 percent between 1913 and 1939 to 4 percent in 1946, a radical change, which reflects the heavy positive balance of trade and services during World War II, but a change that proved to be ephemeral.

Finally, an attempt may be made to explain the observed financial interrelations ratio (FIR) of 0.24 for 1939 in terms of a simple algebraic approach, as was done for 1913 at the end of chapter 1.[107] The formula is

$$FIR = \frac{F_t}{W_t} = \tau[\alpha \beta^{-1} (\delta + \phi)(1 + \nu)] + \frac{F_{t-n}}{W_t} (1 + \nu')$$

where τ is the truncation ratio, α is the inverse of the growth rate of gross national product, δ and ϕ are the net issue ratios of nonfinancial sectors and of financial institutions, respectively, which refer to averages for the period 1914 to 1939; F_{t-n} stands for the value of financial assets in 1913 and W_t for that of tangible assets in 1946; β is the capital-output ratio in 1939. The adjustment for the effect of price changes in equity securities (ν and ν') has been very roughly estimated. Insertion of the previously developed values into the formula yields

$$FIR_{1939} = 0.24 \times 94.5 \times 0.14 \times 0.044 + 0.07 = 0.21$$

which is reasonably close to the observed value of 0.23 in view of only approximative character of the formula and the roughness of many of the underlying figures. The structure of the formula

107. Cf. Goldsmith, 1969, p. 83 and chap. 2.

indicates that the low value, in international comparison, of FIR for 1939 is the result mainly of low new issue ratios for the issues of financial institutions and the nonfinancial sectors.

b. New Issue Ratios of Financial Instruments

One of the main uses of the estimates assembled for the national balance sheet is the derivation of issue ratios for the various financial instruments shown in table 2-46. Such a derivation involves the simplifying assumption that the net issues of a debt instrument are equal to the difference between the amounts, that is, the face values, estimated as outstanding at the end and the beginning of the period. In the case of corporate stock, the difference in the paid-up capital of joint stock companies is taken as the measure of net new issues, a procedure that would underestimate actual net new issues if offerings at a price substantially in excess of par had been common. Before proceeding to a discussion of table 2-46, it is necessary to stress again the unavoidably very rough character of some of the estimates (particularly of lines 4, 5, and 7) and the omission of several smaller types of financial instruments. On the other hand, the failure to eliminate claims and liabilities among financial institutions leads to a small overstatement of the totals.

Starting with the issue ratios for the entire interwar period, which are probably somewhat more reliable than those for the four subperiods, we find a new domestic issue ratio for all financial instruments of about 8 percent, made up a ratio of 3 percent for instruments issued by financial institutions, contributed, in turn, in about equal proportions by monetary and nonmonetary claims against financial institutions, and a ratio of 5 percent for the issues of nonfinancial sectors. The fact that the issue ratio for financial institutions comes to about three-fifths of that of the ratio for nonfinancial issuers points to a relatively high degree of institutionalization of the financial process, even though the ratio is actually somewhat overstated because of the failure to eliminate interfinancial issues and of the omission of some smaller types of instruments issued by nonfinancial sectors. Although these issue ratios are low in international comparison, the progress made by India is evident from a comparison of the aggregate new issue ratio for the interwar period of about 8 percent with that of the half century before World War I of well below 2 percent, and even with that of the 1896–1913 period of 2¼ percent, and from the fact that the relation of the issue ratio of financial institutions to that of the nonfinancial sectors rose sharply to more than three-fifths in the interwar period from about one-fifth in 1861–1913 as well as in 1896–1913.

The fact that the aggregate new issue ratio is higher for the two periods of war inflation, particularly for the years 1940 to 1946, than it is in the 1920s and 1930s is in accord with

TABLE 2-46. Net New Issue Ratio of Financial Instruments, 1914–1946
(Percent of Gross National Product)

	1914–20	1921–29	1930–39	1940–46	1914–46
1. Money: notes	0.47	0.10	0.25	2.49	1.03
2. Money: demand deposits	0.42	−0.06	0.16	1.60	0.64
3. Nonmonetary claims against financial institutions	0.62	0.35	0.91	3.09	1.47
4. Agricultural debt	1.56	1.11	2.68	0.00	1.13
5. Nonfarm household debt	0.36	0.00	−0.25	0.62	0.23
6. Bank debt	0.52	−0.13	0.16	0.67	0.32
7. Trade credit	1.10	0.57	−1.19	1.12	0.48
8. Government domestic debt	1.71	0.95	0.41	3.54	1.87
9. Corporate stock	1.04	−0.06	0.49	1.99	0.96
10. Total	7.80	2.83	3.62	15.13	8.13

SOURCE OF BASIC DATA: Table 2-40.

expectations, as are the relatively high level of the issue ratio of financial institutions, compared to that of nonfinancial sectors, in World War II and the relatively low ratios in the 1920s and 1930s. Similarly, the net issue ratio of government securities is highest in the two war periods. The low issue ratios of bank debt, trade credit, and nonfarm household debt, the latter two little more than guesses, in the 1920s and 1930s reflect the depressions that dominated the first years of these two decades. The figure most difficult to explain is the high ratio for agricultural debt in the 1930s, which may be due, in part, to errors in the estimates, even though they are based on contemporary sources; distress borrowing is at least a partial explanation.

3   Independent India, 1947–1977

1. DEVELOPMENT OF THE INFRASTRUCTURE

a. This period has a clear beginning, the declaration of independence on August 15, 1947, but not yet a definite end. From the point of view of financial structure, the two most important turning points are, first, 1956, when the beginning of the second five-year plan gave the country's economic development a definite lift, and, second, 1969, when the large commercial banks were nationalized, bringing, together with the earlier nationalization of the Reserve Bank in 1949, the State Bank of India (formerly the Imperial Bank) in 1955, and all life insurance companies in 1956, all important parts of the country's financial structure under the control of the central government. The two most important political events of the first three decades after independence, Indira Gandhi's temporary constitutional dictatorship of June 1975 and the temporary establishment of the first non-Congress administration in the spring of 1977, do not seem to have had a far-reaching influence on financial developments.

b. No major subperiods clearly marked by differences in the rate and character of the growth of the Indian economy or by business cycles of the Western type can be easily identified during these three decades, except possibly the break at the end of the first five-year plan in 1955. It seems justified, therefore, to divide the three decades merely chronologically into five periods of five years each—1951–55, 1956–60, 1961–65, 1966–70, and 1971–75—and to treat the first three years after independence as well as the few years after 1975 as additional periods insofar as comparable data are available for them. This periodization has the advantage that the first three periods coincide with the first three five-year plans and that the second to fourth periods are almost coterminous with the span between the two financial turning points of 1956 and 1969.

c. The development of the real infrastructure of the Indian economy during this period of three decades is characterized by five major trends, some of which can be followed in table 3-1: (1) a high, and until the mid-1950s accelerating, rate of growth of population; (2) the continued predominance of agriculture, notwithstanding the rapid progress of industrialization from a low basis;[1] (3) a rate of growth of national product per head of 1½ percent per year, which, though well above that of the preceding decades, remains moderate if considered in the light of its extremely low absolute level and in comparison to the goals of the government, the expectations of the population, and the experience of many other poor countries; (4) the gradual, but fairly continuous, increase in the share of the government, and here primarily the central government, in economic activities outside agriculture and particularly in capital formation and in finance; and (5) a "near superstitious respect of the holy trinity of collectivism, democracy and equality"[2] and an almost unbounded confidence in the need for, and beneficial effect of, detailed

---

1. An indication of the persisting dominant position of agriculture is the continued use of the distinction made between the "busy season" from November through April, when the major crops are moved, and the "slack season" from May through October.

TABLE 3-1. Growth of Real Infrastructure, 1951–1975 (Percent Per Year)

	1951–55	1956–60	1961–65	1966–70	1971–75	1951–75
1. Real gross national product						
a. Total	3.45	4.03	2.90	4.82	3.00	3.63
b. Per head	1.87	1.89	0.60	2.40	0.89	1.53
2. Population	1.53	2.10	2.39	2.23	2.10	2.07
3. Agricultural production	4.22	3.80	−1.39	6.65	2.39	3.10
4. Industrial production	8.00	7.16	9.06	3.43	3.60	6.22
5. Labor force	1.21	1.51	1.97	2.40	—	1.78[a]
6. Capital stock	3.70[b]		5.77			4.93[c]
7. Area under cultivation	2.74	1.12	0.30	1.24	0.60	1.20

[a]1951–70.   [b]1950–60.   [c]1950–70.

SOURCES: Line 1: Table 3-3. Line 2: *IFS*, various issues. Lines 3 and 4: Table 3-3. Line 5: Malenbaum, p. 109. Line 6: Choudhury, 1955. Line 7: *Basic Statistics of the Indian Economy*, New Delhi, 1975, table 8-9 (Ministry of Agriculture data).

centralized planning, both attitudes attenuated, but only temporarily and in limited areas,[3] it would seem, since the second half of the 1960s. As a result of these developments, a large proportion, if not most, of the modern part of the Indian economy had been actually or potentially nationalized and centrally planned, and political power concentrated in the hands of the prime minister.

    d. Between 1948 and 1977 the population of the Indian Union increased from about 350 million to about 640 million, thus adding about 290 million, or much more than the entire present population of the United States or the Soviet Union, or at an average rate of 2 percent per year. The rate of growth, however, accelerated from 1.5 percent in the early 1950s to nearly 2¼ percent during the 1960s and 1970s. The contrast to the pre-independence period was even greater, the average for the years from 1921 to 1950 being only 1.2 percent a year, or less than one-half the present rate.[4] India's "population explosion" was the result, as in other less developed countries, of a dramatic decline in the death rate, from 2.7 percent in the 1940s and considerably more than 4.0 percent before 1920 to 1.6 percent in the 1960s, whereas the birth rate declined slowly and in the 1960s was still close to 4 percent. The burden that an annual increase of India's population by more than 2 percent, or now by more than 12 million persons a year, puts on capital formation and its financing is obvious. Even at a marginal capital-output ratio of only 2, a net investment of approximately 5 percent of national product is required just to prevent a decline in the already exiguous reproducible capital stock per head. Urbanization continued, but even in 1971 only about one-fifth of the population lived in towns, one-half of which was concentrated in cities of more than 100,000 inhabitants, compared to shares of 17 and 7 percent in 1951. A substantial increase in the qualifications of the population is indicated by the doubling of the literacy rate from 15 percent in 1941 to nearly 30 percent in 1971 and by the sharp increases in attendance at secondary schools and colleges. Even in 1969, however, less than one-fifth of the population of 14–17 years attended secondary schools and only 3 percent of the population of 17–23 was at a college or a university.[5]

    2. Hanson, p. 37.

    3. The literature on Indian planning, official and unofficial, indigenous and foreign, popular and professional, is so immense that whoever cannot afford to specialize on this subject must limit himself to a few authorities. I have relied primarily on Bhagwati and Desai; Hanson (*The Process of Planning* and his contribution to *CIP*); Myrdal (part 4 and appendix 4), and Reddaway. For a more critical view than that taken in the text, cf. Bauer.

    4. In the late 1950s, in one of the most intensive studies of India's population, Coale and Hoover (p. 35) estimated the 1976 population at 601 million, very close to the actually reported population of 610 million.

    5. *SOI*, 1972–73, p. 124.

    e. Notwithstanding the more rapid growth of industry and of most other sectors, agricul-
ture continued to dominate the Indian economy throughout the period. The share of agriculture in
employment declined between 1951 and 1961 by less than 3 percentage points (from 72.2 to
69.5) and in 1971 was still in excess of two-thirds.[6] Agriculture's share in national income,
however, fell from about one-half in 1950 and 1960 to not much more than two-fifths in 1975.
This relatively small decline in the share of agriculture was due to the substantial increase in
agricultural output that occurred since independence. Thus, (using three-year moving averages
to reduce the influence of weather), the index of agricultural production more than doubled
between 1949 and 1976, equivalent to an annual rate of increase of 2.7 percent for the period.
The increase in agricultural output was well ahead of population growth in the 1950s, matched it
in the 1960s, stayed slightly ahead of it in the first half of the 1970s, and for the nearly three
decades together exceeded it by 0.7 percent a year. The difference between the two decades is
due in part to the fact that the increase in land under cultivation and the increase in the
agricultural labor force were considerably larger in the 1950s than in the 1960s. Thus the area
under principal crops (food grains, cotton, sugar, groundnuts, and oilseeds) expanded by 21
percent between 1950 and 1960 but only by 7 percent in the following decade.[7] As a result of
these differences, as well as of the operation of other factors (increases in irrigation and the use
of fertilizer and higher yielding varieties), the index of agricultural productivity rose with about
the same speed during the 1950s and 1960s, the annual increase averaging about 1½ percent.
The expansion of agricultural output was achieved with a relatively modest amount of investment. Thus capital outlays in agriculture have accounted for less than one-sixth of total gross
investment in the 1960–72 period, about half of which was contributed by the government.[8]

    f. Industrialization, in the sense of rapid expansion and the achievement of self-sufficien-
cy in heavy industry, particularly steel, machinery, chemicals, and power, has been the chief
goal of Indian economic policy and until recently even outranked *garibi hatao* (elimination of
poverty). A very substantial proportion of domestic and foreign resources under the control of
the central government, as well as of total gross fixed investment, has been allocated to it since
the second five-year plan, for example, about one-fourth of all public capital outlays.[9] As a
result, the volume of industrial production more than quintupled between 1948 and 1977, rising
at an average annual rate of 5.8 percent. The rate of growth, however, slowed down from 7.6
percent in the 1950s to 6.2 percent in the 1960s and to 4.7 percent for the first seven years of the
1970s, which is not astonishing in view of the very low base at independence. The index
increased in every single year after 1950 with the exception of the two years 1966 and 1967,
which were affected by drought. The emphasis on heavy industry is evident in the differential
growth rates. Compared to an annual increase between 1951 and 1976 of 6½ percent for all
industries, production rose by about 8 and fully 9 percent in basic and capital goods industries,
whereas consumer goods industries expanded by only about 4 percent. As a result of this fairly
rapid expansion, the share of factory industry in national income rose between 1950 and 1975
from 6 to 10 percent.[10] If small manufacturing enterprises are included, however, the share
hardly increased at all.

    g. Total real gross national product increased between 1948 and 1971 by 170 percent, or
at an annual rate of 3.6 percent per year. The rate of growth was about equal in the 1950s and
1960s, with about 3.8 percent each, but considerably above this average if five-year periods are
considered in the second half of the 1950s (4.0 percent) and the 1960s (4.8 percent). Growth was

    6. *PEI*, 1971, p. 23.
    7. *PEI*, 1972, p. 242.
    8. *NAS*, 1960/61–1973/74, pp. 36–37.
    9. Inclusion of investment in power plants, financed almost exclusively by the government, would add approx-
imately another tenth of total gross investment, raising the share of these two modern sectors to more than one-third of total
gross capital outlays.
    10. Shetty, p. 186.

TABLE 3-2. Industrial Origin of National Income, 1950/51 to 1975/76 (Percent)[a]

Fiscal years (April/March)	1950 (1)	1955 (2)	1960A (3)	1960B (4)	1965 (5)	1970 (6)	1975 (7)
Agriculture	50.2	44.0	47.0	49.1	45.8	46.9	40.8
Forestry and fishing	1.1	1.3	1.5	1.9	2.0	1.8	2.1
Mining and quarrying	0.7	1.0	1.1	1.1	1.1	1.0	1.5
Manufacturing	15.4	17.5	17.3	13.9	14.8	13.6	15.7
Factories	5.8	7.8	9.4	8.0[c]	8.9	8.5	9.8
Small enterprises	9.6	9.7	7.9	5.9[c]	5.9	5.1	5.9
Construction	[d]	[d]	[d]	4.6	4.5	5.5	5.6
Electricity, gas, water	[d]	[d]	[d]	0.5	0.7	0.9	1.0
Communication[b]	2.3	3.0	3.0	2.4	2.5	15.9	17.9
Other commerce and transport	14.7	15.0	12.5	11.6[e]	11.5[e]		
Organized banking and insurance	0.7	0.9	1.1	1.2	1.6	1.8	2.9[f]
Private services	10.6	11.6	10.3	9.7[f]	10.7[f]	7.9[f]	7.1
Government services	4.5	5.7	6.4	4.0	4.8	4.7	5.3
Total[g]	100.0	100.0	100.0	100.0	100.0	100.0	100.0

[a]National income for cols. 1–3; net domestic product at factor cost for cols. 4–7.   [b]Registered and unregistered sector, respectively.   [c]Railways, post, telegraph, and telephone.   [d]Included with other sectors (probably chiefly 4).   [e]Real estate and ownership of dwellings and other services.   [f]Trade, storage, hotels, and restaurants.   [g]Includes net earned income from abroad.

SOURCES: Central Statistical Office, *Estimates of National Income 1948–1949 to 1962–1963* for cols. 1–3; *Estimates of National Product 1960/61–1969/70* for cols. 4 and 5; and *NAS*, 1970/71–1975/76 for cols. 6 and 7.

slower, 3.2 percent, for the first seven years of the 1970s. Real national product declined, in only three years (1957, 1965, and 1972) and increased by more than 6 percent in only six years (1958, 1960, 1964, 1967, 1969, and 1975). Because of the high rate of population growth real national product per head increased by only 1.4 percent a year between 1948 and 1977, the average falling from about 1.9 percent in the 1950s to 1.5 percent in the 1960s and to 1.0 percent for the 1971–77 period. Real national product per head actually declined in nine of the twenty-nine years between 1948 and 1977, including the drought year of 1965, and every second year in the 1970s. Although these rates of growth may seem moderate, they are, of course, well above those experienced before independence. National product per head in 1973, about R. 1,000 (equivalent to $130 at the exchange rate, although to considerably more, possibly to as much as $400 in purchasing power in 1973 and approximately $450 in 1977), was still very low in international comparison.[11] In this situation the financing of a large-scale investment program without impairment of the standard of living was obviously a very difficult task, even with substantial foreign assistance.

h. India's income is not only low, it is also unequally distributed. It has been estimated, although all calculations of this type are extremely hazardous, that the top fifth of spending units received about one-half of total pretax income, whereas the bottom fifth had to make do with 7 percent.[12] These ratios are not very different from those found in other countries. Whether personal income distribution has become more or less equal since independence is impossible to determine with any degree of confidence. The only feature reasonably certain is that a higher degree of inequality occurs in urban than in rural areas.

i. Notwithstanding a relatively slow rate of growth of real national product per head and a very low level of real income per household, the capital formation ratio has increased considerably during the period, primarily in the public, but also in the private, sector. The overall gross

11. The 1970 ratio of 3.35 of the rupee's purchasing power to its exchange rate is taken from Kravis et al., p. 10.
12. Myrdal, appendix 14, pp. 2181–85.

TABLE 3-3. National Product and Prices, Annual Data, 1948–1977

| | Gross national product[a] | | | | Personal disposable monetary income (R. bill.) (5) | Agricultural production (6) | Industrial production (7) | Wholesale prices (8) | Consumer prices (9) | GNP deflator (10) |
| | Current prices (R. bill.) (1) | Constant (1975) prices | | | | | | | | |
		Total (R. bill.) (2)	Change (percent) (3)	Per head (R.) (4)						
1948	89.2	306.2	+4.8	875	62.3	69.9	37.7	73.1	72.0	75.5
1949	93.0	312.5	+2.1	883	65.0	71.3	37.1	75.6	74.0	77.2
1950	98.4	313.4	+0.3	875	69.1	67.1	37.1	82.3	75.0	81.4
1951	108.5	322.5	+2.9	895	72.4	68.1	43.3	90.6	78.0	83.2
1952	101.6	335.2	+3.9	915	72.1	72.1	43.6	79.3	77.0	78.6
1953	108.2	355.5	+6.1	953	78.5	82.1	45.9	78.6	79.8	78.9
1954	100.8	364.6	+2.6	961	73.5	82.8	48.9	75.1	75.9	71.7
1955	105.0	371.3	+1.8	960	76.9	82.5	54.5	69.1	72.3	73.3
1956	118.2	389.4	+4.9	988	85.0	87.4	59.3	77.5	78.9	78.7
1957	120.4	385.8	-0.9	959	84.8	81.2	61.7	82.1	83.3	80.9
1958	132.7	412.9	+7.0	1005	93.5	94.3	63.8	83.8	87.2	83.4
1959	132.2	420.6	+1.9	1002	96.8	91.9	69.3	87.0	91.7	82.5
1960	149.5	452.3	+7.5	1054	108.0	99.4	77.0	92.8	92.9	85.7
1961	158.8	468.3	+3.5	1067	114.7	99.5	84.2	95.1	94.9	87.9

Year	1	2	3	4	5	6	7	8	9	10
1962	169.9	481.1	+2.7	1067	119.9	97.8	92.3	96.0	97.3	91.6
1963	195.4	506.8	+5.3	1097	136.7	100.0	100.0	100.0	100.0	100.0
1964	229.0	545.3	+7.6	1155	160.7	111.1	108.9	110.4	114.0	108.9
1965	239.5	521.7	−4.3	1088	165.2	92.7	118.8	119.4	124.1	119.1
1966	274.3	527.4	+1.1	1079	190.4	91.7	118.0	133.5	138.1	134.8
1967	320.4	570.6	+8.2	1131	223.5	113.4	117.1	153.8	157.4	145.5
1968	330.2	586.8	+2.8	1138	234.5	111.6	124.5	153.2	161.3	145.9
1969	365.8	624.2	+6.4	1184	260.4	119.0	133.6	156.4	164.0	152.0
1970	401.8	660.3	+5.8	1225	284.7	127.9	140.6	166.2	172.3	157.8
1971	432.7	667.9	+1.2	1212	300.0	127.5	146.2	172.5	178.0	168.0
1972	477.6	660.1	−1.2	1173	319.2	117.3	154.5	185.8	187.2	187.4
1973	588.6	694.5	+5.1	1209	397.7	128.9	157.1	216.5	220.5	219.8
1974	697.6	705.4	+1.6	1203	488.3	124.8	160.2	278.0	281.8	260.3
1975	727.0	765.6	+8.5	1280	508.9	143.9	167.8	289.0	297.6	261.6
1976	769.4	775.7	+1.3	1271	538.6	134.3	184.4	283.5	274.4	273.3
1977	854.0	822.0	+6.0	1313	597.8	150.0	193.8	304.3	297.6	286.2

ᵃYears starting April 1.

SOURCES: **Col. 1**: 1948–51, Mukherjee's estimate (*NII*, p. 330), linked in 1959; 1960–70, *IFS*, May 1978, p. 199; 1971–76, *NAS*, *1970/75*, *1975/76*; 1977, Commerce Bureau estimate.   **Col. 2**: 1948–59, as for col. 1; 1960–75, *IFS*, May 1978, pp. 198–99; 1976, *IFS*, January 1979, p. 182; 1977, extrapolated at 6 percent above 1976.   **Col. 4**: 1948–76, col. 2 divided by mid-year population (*IFS*, 1972 Supplement, p. 242; May 1978, pp. 198–99; January 1979, p. 182).   **Col. 5**: 1948–73, communication from Venkatachalam (superseding figures in *RBIB*, 1972, p. 95); 1974–77, estimated at 70 percent of col. 1, the 1971–73 ratio.   **Col. 6**: 1948–77, *RBIB*, 1978, p. 453.   **Cols. 7–9**: 1948–52, *SAIU*, various issues; 1953–77, *IFS*, May 1978, pp. 196–97; January 1979, p. 180, shifting for 1975 to 1963 basis.   **Col. 10**: 1948–77, derived from cols. 1 and 2.

capital formation ratio rose from 12 percent in 1947–50 and 14 percent of gross national product in 1951–55 to between 18 and 20 percent from the mid-1950s to the mid-1970s. Most of the increase occurred in the public sector, whose gross capital formation sharply advanced from not much more than 2 percent of national product in 1947–50 to 8½ percent in the first half of the 1970s. The private gross capital formation ratio, in contrast, rose only from nearly 10 percent in 1947–50 to 11½ percent in 1971–75. The volume and composition of national capital formation and investment and their relation to national product will be discussed in section 3, and we will return to the financing of capital expenditures and the sources and uses of funds of the main sectors of the economy in section 5.

j. As a result of the increasing share of capital formation in national product, the reproducible capital stock available to the Indian economy increased fairly rapidly, particularly since the mid-1950s when the second five-year plan started. The rate of growth in constant prices rose from less than 4 percent a year in the 1950s to close to 6 percent in the 1960s. The aggregate reproducible capital stock of 1970 was about 2½ times as large as that of 1950, and even the stock per head rose by more than a third, or at an annual average rate of nearly 1½ percent. Because real national product increased over the same period at a rate of more than 3½ percent, the reproducible capital-output ratio increased from 2 to 2½.

k. The increasing role of the government in the Indian economy is indicated, as far as aggregate statistics are able to do so, in the rising share of the government in national product, capital formation, and saving. Thus the share of the public sector in domestic product rose from not much more than 7 percent in 1948 to 12 percent in 1960 and to 16 percent in 1972, all of the increase occurring in government enterprises rather than in government administration, whose share in net national product stayed about 5 percent.[13] Possibly more significant from the financial point of view is the increase in the share of the government in gross capital formation from less than one-fifth in 1947–50 to more than two-fifths in 1971–75. The share of the government in total domestic saving, on the other hand, after increasing from less than one-fifth in 1950 to less than one-fourth in 1960, fell back to below one-fifth in the early 1970s. The public sector, although employing in 1970 only 1.7 million people, or about 7 percent of the total nonagricultural work force, accounted for about 60 percent of the labor force in the "organized," that is, modern and large scale, sectors of the economy.[14]

l. The ambitious investment projects that constitute the essence of the five-year plans, together with substantial food import needs in years of poor crops and with the low elasticity for most of India's exports, made the balance of payments an almost continuous problem and represented one of the most important limitations on economic expansion from the mid-1950s, when the second five-year plan went into effect and the large sterling balances that had accumulated during World War II were exhausted, to 1975. To overcome this constraint, India had to rely primarily on intergovernment grants and loans, because the economic policy of the government did not permit it to offer foreign investors terms that would have attracted private capital on a large scale. From 1949 through 1975 India had an unfavorable balance on goods and services of about R. 110 bill., equal to fully 1½ percent of the period's gross national product. Because transfers were small and net, though not gross, private capital imports were almost negligible, most of this deficit had to be covered by foreign aid and by the government's foreign borrowing, which on a net basis totaled nearly R. 75 bill., or 1.1 percent of gross national product and more than one-tenth of total domestic saving. The deficit on current account, however, showed a declining tendency, falling from nearly 3 percent of gross national product in 1956–60 to not much more than 1 percent in 1971–75. Because of the development of a substantial export surplus and of large increases in net income from invisibles, particularly workers' remittances,

13. Cf. table 3-2.
14. Commerce Research Bureau, *Commerce Yearbook of the Public Sector*, 1971, p. 16.

TABLE 3-4. Sectoral Distribution of Public Sector Plan Outlays (Percent)

	Bombay group, 1944			Actual				Targets	
	1st	2nd	3rd	1st 1951–53	2nd 1956–60	3rd 1961–65	Annual plans 1966–68	4th 1969–73	5th 1974–78
	(1)	(2)	(3)	(4)	(5)	(6)	(7)	(8)	(9)
Agriculture }	14	14	11	15	12	13	17	16	12
Irrigation				16	9	8	7	9	9
Industry[a] }	57	53	38	5	24	23	25	20	26
Power				14	10	15	18	18	18
Communication[b]	8	11	9	26	27	25	18	20	18
All others	21	22	42	24	18	15	15	18	17
Total	100	100	100	100	100	100	100	100	100

[a]Organized industry and mining, plus village and small industries, the share of the latter being 2, 4, 3, 2, 2, and 2 percent for cols. 4–9, respectively.   [b]Transport and communication for cols. 4–9.

SOURCES: **Cols. 1–3:** Thakurdas, p. 59.   **Cols. 4–9:** *RCF,* 1976–77, pp. 104–05.

the balance of payments even became favorable from 1976 to 1978, which permitted an increase in international reserves by about R. 35 bill.

m. Since the early 1950s the five-year plans have constituted the focus of Indian economic policy and have had a crucial effect on economic development. Although they have centered on physical planning and the financial side of the plans has been one of their weakest aspects, both with respect to the sophistication of planning techniques and to the differences between plan and reality, the plans have necessarily greatly influenced developments in the financial superstructure, if only because they set the targets for capital formation and saving in the main economic sectors and for the methods of financing the large plan outlays. Their effect, of course, has been much greater in the government than in the private sector. The plans are probably the clearest expression of Nehru's dream of creating a specific Indian form of socialism through a combination of a Soviet-type centrally planned economy and a Western-type democratic political system.[15] The impossibility, or at least the great difficulty, of this combination became evident in June 1975 when the second leg was temporarily removed, in fact if not in law.

n. The first plan, which covered the years 1951 to 1955, was produced rapidly, kept to a modest scale, and did not imply fundamental changes in the Indian economy. It was therefore labeled by Nehru "a modest approach to planning."[16] The definitive break came with the second plan for 1956–60, which was strongly influenced by a group of left-wing socialist economists and administrators, among whom Professor P. C. Mahalanobis was probably the most influential. It has been called a Soviet-type plan[17] because of its underlying philosophy of industrialization *à outrance,* with primary emphasis on heavy industry, and the achievement of industrial independence and central-government control of the crucial sectors of the economy in the shortest possible time. Nehru himself claimed that it was "the first organized attempt at real planning in India."[18] The difference between the first and second plans is possibly best indicated by the facts that outlays under the second plan equaled more than 7 percent of gross national product compared with less than 4 percent under the first plan and that the share of organized

15. Hanson, p. 43.
16. Bauer, p. 30.
17. Hanson, loc. cit.
18. Bauer, loc. cit.

industry in plan outlays was increased from 3 to 20 percent of the total, whereas that of agriculture (including irrigation) was reduced from 31 to 21 percent. The third plan for 1961–65, as well as the draft of the fourth plan, continued the basic assumptions and goals of the second plan. Total outlays under the third plan were stepped up, though less rapidly, to nearly 9 percent of gross national product, but the allocation of outlays among the main sectors was little changed, except that the share of agriculture was slightly increased at the expense of that of communications. This reflected the fact that in the judgment of one of the most intensive studies of the Indian planning process, the Planning Commission had "developed a collection of orthodoxies, which have become less and less relevant to Indian socioeconomic situations and less and less helpful to the cause of planned growth."[19] The fourth plan was derailed near its start by the severe droughts of 1965 and 1966 and the industrial depression and balance of payments crisis that accompanied them. As a result, three ad hoc annual plans, similar in structure though of slightly smaller relative size (outlays equal to about 7 percent of national product), were substituted and a revised fourth plan to cover the years 1969 to 1973 was drawn up. The fifth plan, covering the years 1974–78, continued the policies of the second to fourth plans, with emphasis on rapid industrialization, self-sufficiency, socialization of crucial sectors, and large central government deficits.

o. The nature of the real infrastructure and its development since independence show, of course, considerable regional differences, which are to be expected in a country where many of the constituents (the states) have a population equal to the larger European countries. Table 3-5 brings together some of the most important available indicators of these differences, expressing in most cases the values for each of the sixteen states as percentages of the total or of the average for the Indian Union. From an economic point of view, possibly the most important indicators are the differences in income per head and one of its main determinants, the proportion of the labor force in agriculture.

p. In the mid-seventies the differences in income per head among the sixteen states, large and often far from homogeneous units but the only ones for which regional data are available, ranged from about 60 percent of the Union average for Bihar, a notoriously poverty-stricken area, to 144 percent for the Punjab, which had been most rapid in accepting the "green revolution." Apart from the two extremes, two states (Haryana, formerly a part of Punjab, and Maharashtra, which includes Bombay) had an average income that was more than 20 percent in excess of the Union average, and two states (Madhya Pradesh and Orissa) fell by more than 20 percent below the average. Differences in the growth rate of population over the 1950s and 1960s were substantial, reflecting mainly differences in birth and death rates and secondarily interstate migration. Compared with a Union average of 2.1 percent, state growth rates ranged from 1.6 percent in Tamil Nadu to 3.2 percent in Assam. The rate kept within the range of 1.8 to 2.4 percent in seven states, accounting for considerably more than two-fifths of the total population of all sixteen states.

The financial structure of the different regions is considerably influenced by two financial flows, one through the central government's budget and the other through the transfer of funds by financial institutions. The two streams generally flow in opposite directions. The budget as a rule transfers funds from richer to poorer regions, whereas the net fund flows of financial institutions go in the opposite direction. It has been estimated[20] that in 1969–70 the ratio between budget receipts and expenditures was well below unity in some of the wealthier states, for example, 0.81 in Punjab and 0.82 in Uttar Pradesh, but well above it in some, though not all, poorer states, such as Orissa with 1.28, Rajasthan with 1.34, and the very poor, small border regions with much higher ratios. In the case of institutional fund flows the ratios were high for

19. Hanson, p. 35. This judgment is essentially shared by Bhagwati and Desai.
20. Gulati and George, pp. 1391 ff.

TABLE 3-5. Changes in Basic Regional Characteristics, 1960–61 and 1974–75

State	Per head domestic product (R. of 1960–61)		Share in domestic product (percent)		Income share of primary sector (percent)	
	1960–61	1974–75	1960–61	1974–75	1960–61	1974–75
Andhra Pradesh	90	96	7.4	8.0	112	121
Assam	82	84	2.5	2.2	84	138
Bihar	70	60	7.4	6.9[d]	110	111[d]
Gujarat	118	95	5.5	5.1	80	73
Haryana	107	122	1.8	2.3	120	124
Jammu and Kashmir	88	95	0.7	0.7	129	124
Karnataka	78	95	5.0	4.3	118	145
Kerala	84	88	3.2	3.4	107	117
Madhya Pradesh	85	75	6.2	6.4	121	131
Maharashtra	133	134	12.0	11.9	80	71
Orissa	71	71	2.8	2.8	120	147
Punjab	113	144	2.9	3.7	109	129
Rajasthan	93	81	4.2	3.9	109	131
Tamil Nadu	109	88	8.3	6.2	99	71
Uttar Pradesh	82	74	13.8	13.1	115	123
West Bengal	127	112	10.0	8.5	81	96
Indian Union[b]						
Percent	100	100	100.0	100.0	100	100
Amount	307	345	—	—	52.5[e]	48.5[e]

[a]Rate of growth of product per head in 1960–61 prices.   [b]Includes territories and states not shown separately.   [c]1960–61 to 1969–70.   [d]1969–70.   [e]Unweighted average of states.

SOURCES: RBIB, 1978, pp. 283 ff.; NAS, 1960/61–1973/74, p. 6; 1970/71–1975/76, pp. 10–11.

most of the richer states, for example, 1.62 for Gujarat, 1.80 for Haryana, 2.14 for Maharashtra, and 2.22 for Punjab; whereas they were low for most of the poorer states, for example, 0.42 for Bihar, 0.43 for Madhya Pradesh, and 0.46 for Orissa. Taking both flows together, there was still in general a transfer of resources from the poorer regions. Thus the ratio was 1.27 for five upper-income states, 1.01 for six middle-income states, and 0.70 for four lower-income states, but 2.84 for six small, poor, and peripheral territories. A similar picture appeared in the regional credit/deposit ratios. Thus the ratios were, compared with 0.68 for the entire country, 1.14 for Tamil Nadu, 1.03 for Haryana, 0.78 for Punjab, and 0.73 for Maharashtra, but 0.41 for Bihar, 0.51 for Orissa, and 0.52 for Uttar Pradesh.

2. MONEY, PRICES, INTEREST RATES, AND THE BALANCE OF PAYMENTS

a. Money[21]

Throughout the period India has lived under a regime of inconvertible paper money. The rupee was linked at a fixed rate first to the pound sterling, then to the dollar, and again to the pound sterling, but reduced twice (in 1949 by nearly 30 percent and in 1966 by 38 percent) and after the devaluation of the dollar in 1971 was slightly increased in several steps, ending the period at slightly more than R. 8 per dollar compared to R. 3.3 at independence.[22] Except for the

21. The statistics used in this section are generally derived from various issues of IFS, RBIB, and RCF. For a survey of the literature on the demand for money, cf. Vasudevan pp. 58–83.

22. The second devaluation of 1966, which was long delayed, gave rise to extensive discussions, and its effects remain somewhat controversial. The most intensive analysis is provided in Bhagwati and Srinivasan.

first few years, when the large sterling balances accumulated during World War II could be drawn down, the Reserve Bank of India has had to operate until 1975 on a very modest amount of international reserves, and the supply of money has varied primarily on the basis of central government securities sold directly by the Treasury to the Reserve Bank, there being hardly an open market in such securities, or of advances to commercial and cooperative banks, because the volume of commercial bills discounted has been relatively small.

The monetary policy of the Reserve Bank of India and of the government, which controlled it to an increasing extent, was directed primarily to assist in the economy's reaching the goals set by the plans, except during the first few years after independence when more traditional policies, oriented toward stable prices and international solvency, prevailed.[23] The results of these changing policies are evident in the character of the assets of the Reserve Bank, which will be reviewed in section 4b. In 1948 nearly two-thirds of the bank's assets consisted of foreign reserves, whereas government securities constituted not much more than one-third, and advances to banks were very small. Between 1948 and 1955 total assets remained fairly stable, although the share of foreign reserves declined to slightly below one-half and that of government securities increased to fully one-half. The sharp break came, however, during the second and third plans, which implied large deficits by the government, a considerable part of which had to be financed by the banking system. As a result, net foreign assets declined between 1955 and 1965 from nearly R. 8 bill. to not much more than R. 2 bill., or from nearly one-half to only 6 percent of total assets, whereas claims on the government increased from less than R. 9 bill. to nearly R. 32 bill., or from one-half to about seven-eighths of total assets. The absorption of government securities has continued on a substantial scale until the present time; but thanks first to foreign aid and then to a large surplus of invisibles, international reserves increased from their critically low level of the mid-sixties, particularly since 1975, and advances to the banking system expanded substantially. At the end of 1977 claims on the government constituted nearly three-fifths of the assets of the Reserve Bank and nearly one-third of international reserves.[24]

As a result of this expansion of the Reserve Bank's assets and the concomitant increase in the volume of the bank's liabilities, the volume of money in circulation increased sharply and far in excess of the growth of real national product from the mid-1950s on, after having approximately kept in step with it from 1949 to 1955. The relevant figures are shown in table 3-6 for five-year periods and in table 3-7 on an annual basis.

For the entire period from 1951 through 1977 money narrowly defined (currency in circulation plus demand deposits) increased at an average rate of 8½ percent, whereas under a broader definition, which includes time deposits with banks, the rate was in excess of 10 percent. This average, however, hides the sharp difference between the 1950s, when the rate averaged a little more than 4 percent for the narrow definition of money, and the 1960s, during which it was close to 10 percent for the decade, as well as during its two halves, compared to a rate of growth of real national product of well under 4 percent. The pattern was similar for money more broadly defined, although the acceleration in the second half of the 1950s was more pronounced and continued during the 1960s. Both rates increased sharply during the 1970s, reaching in 1976 and 1977 17 percent for the narrower definition and 20 percent for the broader in the face of an increase of real national product of not much more than 3 percent.

This sharp expansion was accompanied by substantial changes in the distribution of money broadly defined among its main components, changes that reflect differences in their rate of growth. As a result, the share of currency declined from nearly three-fifths in the first half of the 1950s, a high ratio typical of a country with a little-developed banking and credit system, to

23. In the absence of a thorough study by outsiders covering the entire post-independence period, cf. annual reports of the Reserve Bank: Simha, 1970; M. Joshi, *The Monetary Policy of the Reserve Bank of India,* 1964; Pendharkar and Narasimhan; and Shrivastava.

24. Cf. table 3-21.

TABLE 3-6. Growth of Money Supply, 1951–1977

	1951–55	1956–60	1961–65	1966–70	1971–75	1976–77	1951–77
	I. Rate of growth (percent per year)						
Currency	2.68	6.27	7.81	7.79	9.16	14.35	7.26
Demand deposits	1.31	4.44	13.43	12.47	17.15	19.90	10.39
Money A	2.29	5.87	9.72	9.58	12.52	17.01	8.49
Time deposits[a]	8.12	20.10	6.87	15.26	20.90	25.21	14.89
Money B	3.21	8.74	8.89	11.19	15.29	20.41	10.22
	II. Distribution (percent)[b]						
Currency	57.6	50.8	48.7	41.0	31.2	28.1	28.1
Demand deposits	24.1	19.4	24.0	25.8	28.0	27.8	27.8
Money A	81.7	70.2	72.7	66.8	59.2	55.9	55.9
Time deposits[a]	18.3	29.8	27.3	33.2	40.8	44.1	44.1
Money B	100.0	100.0	100.0	100.0	100.0	100.0	100.0
	III. Ratio of money stock to national product (percent)[c]						
Currency	12.9	12.8	11.2	10.1	8.8	9.5	9.5
Demand deposits	5.6	4.9	5.5	6.2	7.1	9.4	9.4
Money A	18.5	17.7	16.8	16.3	16.3	18.9	18.9
Time deposits	4.1	7.5	6.3	7.8	11.3	14.9	14.9
Money B	22.6	25.2	23.0	24.1	27.6	33.8	33.8
	IV. Ratio of net money issues to national product (percent)[d]						
Currency	0.34	0.78	0.90	0.77	0.91	1.22	0.85
Demand deposits	0.07	0.22	0.66	0.66	1.11	1.56	0.92
Money A	0.41	1.00	1.56	1.43	2.02	2.78	1.77
Time deposits	0.29	1.05	0.45	0.96	1.74	2.95	1.54
Money B	0.70	2.05	2.01	2.39	3.75	5.73	3.31

[a]"Quasi money" as defined by *IFS*.   [b]End of period; figures for 1950: 59.1; 26.4; 85.5; 14.5.   [c]End of period; figures for 1950: 12.4; 5.5; 17.9; 3.0; 20.9.   [d]Net increase during calendar-year period divided by sum of gross national product for fiscal years.

SOURCES: *IFS*, 1972 Supplement, pp. 192–93; January 1979, p. 180.

about one-half in the first half of the 1960s and about three-tenths in the 1970s. From 1950 to 1977 the share fell annually by 1¼ percentage points, or by 3 percent of its starting value. The decline was even more pronounced for coin, whose share in total currency shrank from about one-seventh in 1950 to one-twelfth in 1970. The share of demand deposits in total money in circulation remained fairly stable at about one-fourth except for a slump around 1960, whereas that of time deposits, the monetary character of part of which is doubtful, rose sharply from less than one-fifth to more than two-fifths of the total.

The income velocity of money in the narrower definition showed an irregular upward movement from 5.3 in 1950 to 6.0 in 1975. On the broader definition the trend was irregularly downward from 4.6 to 3.5 because of the very rapid rate of increase of time deposits, which averaged 14 percent for the quarter century, or almost twice the rate of growth of national product. If short-term fluctuations are reduced by using five-year averages, the velocity of money in the narrower definition was in the neighborhood of 5¾ in the first half of the 1950s as well as twenty years later, whereas in the broader definition it showed a substantial decline from 4.7 to 3.6. From 1974 to 1977, however, both velocities declined by about one-fifth. Thus, the movements are far from radical for an economic and financial environment that has been changing as rapidly as it has been in India since independence.

A measure less influenced by year-to-year changes is provided by the money issue ratio, that is, the quotient of the net increase in the volume of the different types of money outstanding between the beginning and the end of the period and the period's aggregate gross national product. For the entire period 1951–77 this ratio averaged 1.8 percent on the narrower definition

TABLE 3-7. Money, Bank Deposits, and Bank Credit, Annual Data, 1948–1977 (R. Bill.)

| End of | Money | Quasi money | Post Office saving deposits | Domestic credit[a] | | | Foreign assets (net) |
				Total	Government	Private sector	
1948	19.61	3.87	0.28	12.23	7.97	4.26	10.54
1949	17.93	2.90	0.43	12.84	8.54	4.30	8.32
1950	18.54	3.12	0.63	14.45	9.73	4.72	8.39
1951	17.90	3.17	0.69	15.28	9.32	5.96	8.21
1952	17.06	3.54	0.89	15.31	9.81	5.50	7.46
1953	17.40	3.69	1.00	15.42	9.95	5.47	7.63
1954	18.58	4.08	1.21	16.86	10.70	6.16	7.71
1955	20.65	4.61	1.56	19.40	12.36	7.04	7.82
1956	22.02	5.10	1.91	23.68	14.84	8.84	6.61
1957	22.96	6.91	2.08	29.82	19.66	10.16	4.15
1958	23.69	9.21	2.25	34.27	23.88	10.39	3.09
1959	25.36	11.58	2.46	37.79	26.15	11.64	3.31
1960	27.40	11.52	2.85	40.29	26.45	13.84	2.70
1961	28.42	11.75	3.22	43.43	27.52	15.91	2.68
1962	31.12	12.91	3.40	48.52	30.49	18.03	2.15
1963	35.41	13.28	3.66	54.76	33.76	21.00	2.23
1964	39.05	14.22	4.08	59.13	36.17	22.96	2.13
1965	43.00	16.06	6.12	66.26	39.97	26.29	2.19
1966	46.81	18.88	6.70	74.75	44.20	30.55	3.20
1967	51.03	20.80	7.15	81.28	47.00	34.28	3.76
1968	53.89	24.79	7.78	87.97	48.87	39.10	4.03
1969	60.36	28.94	8.41	97.14	51.55	45.59	6.10
1970	67.91	32.68	9.12	106.74	54.13	52.61	6.49
1971	77.06	41.40	9.88	128.79	64.48	64.31	7.67
1972	86.96	49.92	10.37	148.51	75.85	72.65	10.25
1973	101.62	61.58	11.31	178.55	88.57	89.98	10.96
1974	111.96	70.46	11.62	205.34	99.44	105.90	12.94
1975	122.33	84.39	11.66	239.29	107.39	131.90	17.69
1976	147.25	109.57	14.34	280.13	111.47	168.66	27.26
1977	167.48	132.30	15.23	336.32	147.91	188.41	43.71

[a]Reserve Bank, commercial and cooperative banks.

SOURCES: *IFS*, 1972 Supplement, pp. 244–45; May 1976, pp. 192–93; January 1979, pp. 180–81.

and slightly more than 3¼ percent on the broader concept, currency contributing more than four-fifths of 1 percent, demand deposits nearly 1 percent, and time deposits 1½ percent. Both ratios more than doubled between the first and the second half of the 1950s; increased much more slowly during the 1960s, the broader ratio actually declining; but again increased sharply during the 1970s. In 1976 and 1977 the narrower ratio was seven times and the broader ratio eight times as high as in the first half of the 1950s, an indication of the rapid monetization of the Indian economy. Year-to-year fluctuations in the money issue ratio, however, were considerable. Thus the narrow ratio shows peaks, with more than 2 percent in 1955, 1963, 1971–73, and 1976–77, and troughs of less than 1 percent in 1957–58, 1961, and 1968, disregarding the transition period of 1949–53. There is no obvious relation between the troughs and peaks and the rates of growth in nominal or real national product.

The reasons for these developments are far from clear. They occurred primarily in the household sector, which accounts for the bulk of currency outstanding and of savings deposits and for fully one-half of time deposits, although for only a relatively small fraction of demand deposits, which declined from three-tenths in 1951 to a good fifth in 1972. Most of the household sector's holdings of currency and a considerable part of its holdings of demand deposits may be assumed to represent transactions balances and therefore to move more or less parallel to monetized disposable household income. In fact, currency and demand deposits attributed to the household sector amounted to 17 and 6 percent of monetized personal disposable income in 1950, to 17 and 5 percent in 1960, and to 14 and 7 percent in 1970, the combined ratio being practically identical at slightly above one-fifth at the three dates.[25] One might think, therefore, that income suffices to explain the volume of these two types of money held by the household sector. Econometric analysis has shown, however, that some other factors are also of influence. Time deposits have, on the contrary, shown a definite upward trend, their ratio to monetized disposable personal income rising from 3 percent in 1950 to 8 percent in 1970, a rise that can be attributed in part to the effect of interest rates, both on time deposits themselves and apparently also on the yield of one of the competing uses of funds, industrial stocks.[26]

With rates of increase of the money supply so far in excess of the growth of real national product since the mid-fifties, a substantial rise in the price level was bound to occur. For the period from 1955 through 1977 the money supply (narrower definition) increased at an average annual rate of 10 percent and velocity remained unchanged, whereas real national product grew at a rate of 3.7 percent. During the same period the price level (gross national product deflator) advanced by 6.4 percent a year and the indices of wholesale and consumer prices both rose by nearly 7 percent a year. Although it is often impossible to disentangle the relationships between changes in the money supply, liquidity preferences of the different public sectors, and the factors affecting real national product, such as the supply of the factors of production and their productivity, there seems little doubt that the quadrupling of the Indian price level between the middle 1950s and the middle 1970s was due primarily to the expansion of the money supply. Indeed, the exact equality of the rise in the price level and the sum of the rates of expansion of real national product and of the money supply may be to some extent a coincidence. This expansion, in turn, was to a large extent the result of the large deficits that the government incurred in financing development plans, which put a very severe strain on economic resources, even with substanial foreign assistance. In view of the limited amount of voluntary financial saving in the private sectors of the Indian economy and of the unattractive terms on which government securities were offered to the public, such deficits had to be financed in large part by the banking system. Thus the Reserve Bank absorbed nearly R. 80 bill. and the commercial and cooperative banks another R. 70 bill, equal together to nearly 2 percent of the period's national product, or more than 70 percent of the total increase in the central government's domestic debt from 1956 through 1977 of R. 210 bill.

The expansion of domestic bank credit, shown in table 3-8, proceeded at a rate considerably in excess of that of money, particularly in the narrower definition, as the assets of commercial and cooperative banks grew considerably more rapidly than those of the Reserve Bank. In 1948 the assets of commercial and cooperative banks were smaller by more than 30 percent than those of the Reserve Bank; in 1977 they were nearly 160 percent larger. For the entire period 1949–77 the rate of expansion of domestic bank credit was above 12 percent and was most rapid, with nearly 16 percent, during the second plan period and, with 18 percent, in the 1970s. Expansion was considerably in excess of the growth of national product during the 1950s with

25. These figures are derived from the estimates of Venkatachalam and Sarma (p. 134) of currency and bank demand deposits held by the household sector, and the statistics for total currency outside banks and of demand deposits with banks are from *IFS*, 1972 Supplement, pp. 242–43. If the amounts of demand deposits of the banking statistics are used (cf. table 3-28), the ratios are considerably lower, around 2 percent of personal disposable monetized income, but are also practically identical in 1951 and 1971.

26. Cf. Divatia and Venkatachalam, pp. 948–56; and Laumas (pp. 614–18), who claims to have provided evidence that "the [money demand] function was stable during the period considered, 1950/51–1965/66," notwithstanding increasing monetization. Cf. also Madagli, pp. 46–72.

TABLE 3-8. Expansion of Domestic Bank Credit, 1951–1977[a]

	1951–55	1956–60	1961–65	1966–70	1971–75	1976–77	1951–77
	I. Rate of growth (percent per year)						
Total	6.1	15.7	10.5	10.0	17.5	18.6	12.4
To government[b]	4.9	16.4	8.6	6.3	14.7	17.4	10.6
To private sector[c]	8.3	14.5	13.7	14.9	20.2	19.5	14.6
	II. Distribution (percent)[d]						
To government[b]	63.7	65.6	60.3	50.6	44.9	44.0	44.0
To private sector[c]	36.3	34.4	39.7	49.4	55.1	56.0	56.0
	III. Relation to gross national product (percent)[e]						
Total	18.5	26.9	27.7	26.3	32.9	39.4	39.4
To government[b]	11.8	17.7	16.7	13.3	14.8	17.3	17.3
To private sector[c]	6.7	9.2	11.0	13.0	18.1	22.1	22.1

[a]Reserve Bank, commercial and cooperative banks.   [b]Net government securities only.   [c]Includes credits to government companies and to government in forms other than securities.   [d]End of period; figures for 1950: 67.3; 32.7.   [e]End of period; figures for 1950: 9.9; 4.8; 14.7.

SOURCES: *IFS*, 1971 Supplement, pp. 242–43; January 1979, pp. 180–81.

the result that the ratio of domestic bank credit to national product rose from less than 15 percent in 1950 to 27 percent in 1960. During the 1960s credit expansion kept more or less in step with national product, but in the 1970s it again far exceeded the growth of national product, raising the ratio to 33 percent in 1977.

In view of the increase in the share of the government in economic activities throughout the period, particularly in capital expenditures, it is remarkable that its share in total domestic bank credit declined steadily from about two-thirds during the 1950s and the first half of the 1960s to well below one-half in the mid-1970s. This, however, is in part due to the statistical convention that the figures for credit to government are limited to the acquisition of government securities, whereas loans to government companies are included in credits to the private sector. It is also in part a reflection of the relatively slow growth of the assets of the Reserve Bank, which makes a very high proportion of its funds available to the government, and of the declining share of government securities and advances in the assets of commercial and cooperative banks.

No mention has hitherto been made of gold. This seems to be justified by the fact that although considerable quantities of gold[27] continued to be absorbed by India, notwithstanding the legal prohibition against imports, gold has been an object of thesaurization and adornment and a reserve against hard times, the last two chiefly on the part of women, but has hardly been used at all as a medium of exchange.

27. This is a touchy subject, which Indian officials are generally unwilling to discuss and on which obviously no statistics exist except for the relatively small amounts of gold intercepted by the customs authorities. One unofficial Indian estimate puts the import of gold for 1950–61 at close to R. 3 bill., or about R. 250 mill. per year. Much higher estimates can, however, be found, indeed as high as $200 mill., i.e., about R. 1 bill. per year (Green, chap. 9, which contains a description of "The Golden Route to India," mainly via Dubhai). The total of hoarded gold has been estimated by the Reserve Bank at 105 million ounces in 1958, then $3.7 bill., or about R. 18 bill. at the official exchange rate, but at R. 30 bill. March 31, 1957, at the higher Indian market price for gold by Prakash (p. 273). Green's guess (p. 171) puts it at considerably more than $5 bill., then about R. 40 bill., at the end of 1967, implying an annual net import, disregarding valuation changes, of nearly R. 70 mill. from 1959 to 1967, compared to Saravane's estimate (1971, p. 75) of smuggled gold of R. 350 mill. a year for 1958–61 and of about R. 150 mill. a year for 1950–57. Hirsch (p. 210) ventures a "roughest guess" of $8 bill., or R. 38 bill. for the mid-1960s. Weighing hearsay and estimates of the type just cited, it does not seem unreasonable to put the average gold imports for the 1960s at least at R. 500 mill. This would be equivalent to about 0.2 percent of national product and to about 2 percent of national net saving. For 1950–58 V. V. Bhatt (*RBIB*, March 1960) put the ratios at 0.2 percent of national income and 3.6 percent of the household sector's saving. An indirect piece of evidence is the amount of gold imported by Dubhai, most of which is supposed to be destined for India. This was put for 1971 at $425 mill. (*Indian Express*, January 5, 1972), or more than R. 3 bill. at the official exchange rate. If this figure is even

TABLE 3-9. Price and Wage Movements, 1949–1977
(Average Annual Rate of Change, Percent)

	1949–50	1951–55	1956–60	1961–65	1966–70	1971–75	1976–77	1949–77
1. GNP deflator	3.84	−2.07	3.18	6.80	5.79	10.61	4.60	4.70
2. Wholesale prices	6.11	−3.44	6.08	5.17	6.84	11.70	2.61	5.04
3. Consumer prices	2.06	−0.73	5.14	5.96	6.78	11.55	0.00	5.02
4. Stock prices	−12.00	2.54	2.56	−2.28	4.62	−1.34	4.45	0.43
5. Wage rates	4.96	3.71	3.36	2.09	5.45	13.45	0.53[a]	5.38[b]

[a]1976.   [b]1949–76.

SOURCES: Lines 1-3: Table 3-3, col. 10. Line 4: *RBIB*, passim; figures refer to years starting April 1. Line 5: 1951–66, Bhagwati, p. 80; 1967–68, India (Republic), Department of Labour and Employment, *Pocket Book of Labor Statistics*, 1972, p. 30; 1969–76, *Indian Labor Journal*, 1978, p. 90.

b. Prices

For the first decade after independence India showed a considerable degree of price stability compared with many other developed as well as less developed countries. In 1960 the national product deflator was only 14 percent higher than in 1948, and the wholesale and consumer price indices had advanced by only 13 percent. This, however, was the result of fairly rapid advances in 1950 and 1956–58, which were partly offset by fairly sharp declines in 1952 and 1954–55.

The situation changed sharply beginning in the late 1950s, mainly as the result of the strain imposed on the economy by the second and later plans, difficulties that were accentuated by several poor crops and led to a substantial increase in money in circulation. The price level, as well as wholesale and consumer prices, increased between 1960 and 1970 by more than 80 percent, equivalent to average annual rates of increase of more than 6 percent. There were only two years (1968 and 1969) during which prices, helped by excellent crops, did not rise substantially, whereas the average annual rate of increase was close to 10 percent for the general price level in the years 1964 to 1967, which experienced two very poor crops. Another sharp rise in prices occurred in 1974–75, when prices advanced by one-third, although the national product deflator rose by only one-fifth under the influence of international as well as domestic factors, particularly a sharp increase in oil prices and in the volume of money and credit. In contrast to the continued rise in prices in many other countries in 1976 and 1977, Indian prices were fairly stable, in the face of a further large expansion of the supply of money and credit. In these two years wholesale and consumer prices rose by about one-tenth, whereas money and credit expanded by approximately two-fifths and real national product grew by only 7 percent. How these discrepancies, which involve a sharp decline in the velocity of circulation, are to be resolved, is not obvious. Good crops provide only a partial explanation.

The trend of real wages is also in doubt. Although real gross national product grew at an average rate of 1½ percent a year, the index of wages for industrial workers shows an increase of less than 5½ percent, only 0.4 percent a year ahead of the index of consumer prices. Given the substantial margins of error in both indices, it is doubtful whether real industrial wages showed any substantial increase since independence, and it is very likely that the relative position of industrial workers deteriorated.

---

approximately correct and 1971 was not an abnormal year, it would make the clandestine gold imports an important component of Indian saving, as they would amount, including smaller imports from places other than Dubhai, to about more than 1 percent of national product and to more than 5 percent of saving. (Cf. also Chandavarkar, p. 77.) A very recent and probably more reliable but apparently unpublished semiofficial estimate puts the average annual absorption at 60 to 70 tons per year. This would be equal, at the Indian 1977 price, to nearly R. 4 bill. a year, or nearly 0.5 percent of national product.

TABLE 3-10. Interest Rates, 1950–1977

	1950	1955	1960	1965	1970	1975	1977
1. Reserve Bank, discount	3.00	3.50	4.00	5.50	5.00	9.00	9.00
2. Call money	0.62	2.75	5.00	8.25	10.25	10.32	9.28
3. Commercial banks, advances[a]	.	.	4.75	7.25	7.75	13.75	14.50
4. Bazaar rate	8.13	9.75	10.50	13.50	15.00	21.00	.
5. Hundi rate	3.75	4.75	5.88	9.50	9.50	15.25	15.00
6. Government bonds	3.11	3.72	4.07	5.32	5.00	6.34	6.32
7. Industrial debentures	.	3.82	4.09	7.36	8.11	10.53	12.54
8. Corporate shares, yield	.	5.01	4.88	6.53	5.53	4.87	6.47
9. Bank deposits, six months	1.65	3.00	3.49	5.50	4.75	6.00	.
10. Rise in price level	3.8 [b]	−2.1	3.2	6.8	5.8	10.6	4.4

[a]Advance rate of State Bank of India; average of range.   [b]1948–50.

SOURCES: Lines 1 and 6: *IFS*, 1972 Supplement, pp. 244–45; May 1978, pp. 196–97; refers to calendar years. Line 2: *RBIB*, 1975, S 892; 1978, S 443; refers to fiscal years starting in April. Lines 3 and 4: *RBIB*, September 1972, p. 1649 and passim; refers to fiscal years. Line 5: Lakdawala and Mody, p. 89; fiscal year; average of range. Line 7: *RBIB*, September 1972, pp. 1666–67 and passim; refers to fiscal years. Lines 8 and 9: *BMSS*, II, p. 52; *POE*, January 1971, p. 115. *RBIB*, 1978, p. 456. Line 10: Table 3-3, GNP deflator change for period between benchmark dates.

c. Interest Rates

In hardly any other aspect of financial structure is the dual nature of the Indian economy as evident, and even as measurable, as in interest rates, with the stark contrast between the organized market for government and corporate securities and for loans from, and deposits with, banks and credit cooperatives, on the one hand, and the unorganized market extending from the semiorganized bazaar market in large cities to the village moneylender, on the other. Through most of the period the rates in the organized market were rather low, considering the stage of development of the Indian economy, and hardly exceeded those in many developed and semi-developed countries. Thus in 1970 the Reserve Bank's discount rate stood at 5 percent; commercial banks charged about 8 percent for loans; government bonds yielded 5 percent, a virtually fixed rate, and even industrial debentures brought only about 8 percent. On the other hand, the urban hundi rate, probably the lowest rate outside the organized market, was on the order of 10 percent and village moneylenders and occasional other providers of funds charged anywhere from 1½ to 3 percent a month for mortgage or personal loans. In this situation important types of funds, for which rates were set well below market-clearing rates, except possibly in periods of economic depression, particularly the rates charged by the banking system and by government lending institutions, had to be rationed in effect if not in form. This procedure was much facilitated by the fact that since the late 1960s virtually all important organized lenders have been owned or controlled by the government and ultimately depended on the Reserve Bank, and that the bank or the government had far-reaching powers, in law or in fact, over the terms on which corporate securities were offered. These limitations, particularly the increasing direct or indirect influence of the government on the setting of interest rates as we move from the mid-1950s to the early 1970s, must be kept in mind in assessing the movements of interest rates over the past three decades, the most important of which are shown in table 3-10 for seven benchmark dates.

The trend of interest rates since independence has been definitely upward. Most rates, particularly those not tightly controlled by the authorities, were at least twice as high in 1970 as they had been two decades earlier, and most of the increase occurred in the 1960s, particularly in the less controlled rates. Whether this was a reflection of inflation—the national product deflator increased at an annual average rate of 6.3 percent in the 1960s compared with only 0.5 percent in the 1950s—or a change in the supply and demand schedules for funds, reflecting increasing profitability of business or liquidity preferences of the public, it is difficult to say, but the first explanation appears to be more likely. At the rates of inflation that have prevailed during the past decade, the level of real (price adjusted) interest rates was very low, in the 1960s close to or even below zero for borrowers who had access to institutional lenders and particularly for privileged borrowers in the government and private sectors. The necessity of, in effect, rationing credit is therefore not difficult to understand, apart even from the more and more pronounced tendency to give priority in the allocation of credit to plan targets and to social considerations as against market criteria. Almost all rates moved sharply upward in the 1970s, but during the first half of the decade most real rates remained close to zero. In 1977, when inflation abated, real rates, except the manipulated rate on government bonds, were on the order of at least 5 percent.

The rates paid on deposits of financial institutions were also relatively low. They advanced substantially in the early 1950s from the extraordinarily low levels of the 1940s and rose again considerably in 1964 and 1965 with a sharp increase in the differentials between shorter and longer maturities. From the first half of the 1960s to the mid-1970s nominal rates were below the increase in the price level with the result that real rates became negative. Even after the increase of the mid-1960s real rates have been close to zero.

d. The Balance of Payments

Except during the first few years after independence when India could draw on the large sterling balances accumulated during World War II, the balance of payments was a permanent problem until the mid-1970s. Its main effect has been to limit imports, particularly of investment goods, and thus to hold down capital formation. Imports exceeded exports continuously until the mid-1970s, for the period as a whole to the amount of about 2 percent of national product, the deficit reaching 2½ percent in the late 1950s but falling below one-half of 1 percent in the early 1970s. The gap was filled primarily by borrowing and partly by international aid. Although private capital imports were small, the government was a heavy borrower, from the middle 1950s through the 1960s to the extent of nearly 2 percent of national product. The reduction of borrowing in the first half of the 1970s to 1½ percent was less the result of the government's putting into practice its often proclaimed goal of doing without foreign capital than of the difficulty of raising funds in the international market. Even at a level lower than the government would have wished and with large imports of food in poor crop years, which then preempted the country's borrowing capacity to a considerable extent, capital imports made a substantial contribution to India's industrialization. Although not all capital imports were used to import investment goods, an idea of their importance is given by the fact that from 1951 to 1975 the net capital inflow of about R. 100 bill., to which government net borrowing contributed about three-fourths, was equal to about 1½ percent of national product and to one-seventh of total net domestic saving.

3. CAPITAL FORMATION AND SAVING[28]

This section is limited to an overview of the available aggregative estimates of national capital formation and saving; their division among the private and the public sector; and in the case of capital formation, their breakdown into the three main constituents of construction, equipment, and inventories; and of the different sectors' financial surpluses and deficits, that is, the difference between their capital expenditures and their savings. In the present state of the data, official and unofficial, it is unfortunately not possible to give more than this insufficiently detailed picture, and even then consistency over the entire period is not feasible.

28. This section is based primarily on the estimates of capital formation and saving of the Central Statistical Organization; cf. their *Estimates of National Income, 1948/49–1962/63* (1964), and *National Accounts Statistics, 1960/61–1975/76* (1978). For another estimate covering most of the period, cf. Lal. Cf. also Minocha.

TABLE 3-11. Capital Formation, 1947–1975
(Current Prices; Percent of Gross National Product)

Fiscal years (April/March)	1947–50	1951–55	1956–60	1961–65	1966–70	1971–75
Construction[a]	7.30	8.90	11.70	9.24	10.02	9.93
Public	·	·	·	5.47	4.18	4.15
Private	·	·	·	3.77	5.83	5.78
Machinery and equipment	3.30	3.70	5.40	6.89	6.33	6.53
Public	·	·	·	2.43	2.16	2.67
Private	·	·	·	4.46	4.17	3.88
Inventories	1.10	1.30	1.70	1.75	1.54	3.68
Public	·	·	·	0.59	0.53	1.77
Private	·	·	·	1.16	1.01	1.91
Gross capital formation	11.70	13.90	18.80	17.88	17.89	20.14
Public	·	3.30	6.40	8.49	6.88	8.59
Private	·	10.60	12.40	9.39	11.01	11.55
Depreciation	6.70	6.70	6.30	5.12	5.09	5.69
Public	·	·	·	0.89	1.01	1.14
Private	·	·	·	4.24	4.08	4.55
Net capital formation	5.00	7.20	12.50	12.76	12.80	14.45
Public	·	·	·	7.61	5.87	7.44
Private	·	·	·	5.16	6.93	7.01
Errors and omissions	·	·	·	−1.02	−0.61	−0.78
Gross capital formation (R. bill. per year)	10.5	14.5	24.6	35.5	60.6	117.7

[a]Includes dwellings to the extent of 1.65 in 1951–55; 2.13 in 1956–60; 1.82 in 1961–65; and 3.31 in 1966–70 (Lal).

SOURCES: Central Statistical Office, *Estimates of Gross Domestic Capital Formation in India 1948/49–1960/61* (1961); *NFS, 1960/61–1973/74* (1976); *1960/61–1975/76* (1978).

a. Capital Formation

India's capital formation since independence is characterized by at least a half dozen features:

1. A rapid increase in the volume of capital expenditures, in constant as well as in current prices, that was well in excess of the growth of national product until the mid-1950s, and hence resulted in a marked rise in the national capital formation ratio in the first decade after independence. The ratio stablized during the 1960s.

2. A declining ratio of capital consumption allowances to gross capital formation and a substantial decrease in the average age of capital stock, both necessary concomitants of the increase in the capital formation ratio.

3. A substantial rise until the mid-1960s in the share of the government sector in total capital formation.

4. A sharp increase in the proportion of total capital formation going to large-scale industry.

5. A relatively small share of capital formation devoted to agriculture.

6. A moderate increase from the 1960s on in the proportion of gross capital formation that took the form of expenditures on machinery and equipment.

7. A small share of housing in total capital formation.

These trends, most of which can be followed in table 3-11, are of great importance for the financial development of India because they indicate changes in the relative size of the national financing task and in the allocation of that task among sectors and, to the extent that forms of capital expenditures and types of financing are interrelated, among financial instruments and institutions.

The gross capital formation ratio rose from 12 percent of national product in 1947–50, that is, before the plans, to 14 percent in the first plan period, 1951–55, but then increased sharply to 19 percent in the second plan period, 1956–60, which, as so often, constitutes a watershed in Indian postwar economic history.[29] The ratio remained at the higher level throughout the 1960s and rose further to 20 percent in the first half of the 1970s, a respectable rate in international comparison given the low real income per head.

The structure of gross capital formation by forms changed relatively little. In view of the heavy emphasis on industrialization, it is astonishing that the share of machinery and equipment in total gross capital formation only increased from 29 percent in the first plan period to 32 percent in the first half of the 1970s after having reached nearly 39 percent in the second plan period. The share of construction declined from nearly two-thirds in the first decade after independence to one-half in the early 1970s. Dwellings accounted, with considerable fluctuations, for less than one-sixth of total gross capital formation and not much more than one-fourth of total construction, a reflection of the wretched housing conditions of most of the population. Additions to inventories absorbed nearly one-tenth of total gross capital formation in the 1950s and 1960s. Their share in net capital formation fell, however, from one-fifth in 1947–50 to about one-eighth in the late 1960s as a result of the rising net-gross ratio. This, in turn, reflects the accelerating rate of capital formation, but may also be influenced by the method of calculating capital consumption allowances, which probably are strongly influenced and held down by being tied to the original amount of capital expenditures. The sharp increase of the ratio to one-fourth of total net capital formation and more than 3½ percent of national product in 1971–75 may be temporary and may be connected to the acceleration of inflation. It is important from a financial point of view because of the customarily high ratio of inventories financed by bank credit.

By far the most pronounced change occurred, of course, in the shares of the public and private sectors in total capital formation. On a gross basis, the public sector's share increased from less than one-fifth in the late 1940s to nearly one-half during the third plan but declined to two-fifths in the following decade. Equally remarkable, within the public sector's capital expenditures the share of nondepartmental enterprises, that is, mainly the large, new industrial plants, rose from less than one-tenth under the first plan to more than one-third under the third at the expense primarily of the share of departmental enterprise, such as the railroads, the Post Office, and communications.[30]

This set of ratios implies that since the early 1960s on the average financing for fully two-fifths of total capital formation had to be provided by the central government, partly for its direct needs, partly for its own enterprises, and partly for the state governments and their enterprises. It is possibly the best single explanation of the changes that have occurred in the financial super-structure of the Indian economy.[31]

29. Recently published estimates by Lal are considerably lower for the 1950s as shown below (percent of gross national product).

	1951–55	1956–60
Construction	5.84	8.06
Machinery	3.20	4.02
Inventories	0.83	1.81
Gross capital formation	9.87	14.69
Depreciation	3.56	4.69
Net capital formation	6.31	10.00

30. V. Dagli, ed., *Commerce Yearbook of the Public Sector*, 1974, p. 26, citing Lal.

31. An econometric study of the determinants of business investment, concluding that the investment equation had behaved almost autonomously, and had been fairly independent of interest rates, rates of return, liquidity, expectations, and stock prices, ascribed this behavior to "myriad of inefficient economic controls" and claimed that "economic efficiency is at a discount in a highly sheltered, shortage ridden economy" (Johar, pp. 415 ff, particularly pp. 431–32).

TABLE 3-12. Sectoral Distribution of Increase of Net Stock of
Reproducible Tangible Assets, 1950–1970 (1960–61 Prices; Percent)

	Stock			Distribution of change in stock		Rate of growth
	1949	1960	1970	1950–60	1961–70	1950–70
Agriculture	27.1	21.4	18.1	9.8	12.0	2.36
Mining and quarrying	0.6	0.5	0.7	0.4	1.1	5.48
Manufacturing	12.3	16.8	18.7	25.9	20.8	6.50
Of which registered	8.4	11.3	14.4	17.2	19.0	7.22
Electricity	1.3	3.3	5.2	7.2	8.7	11.70
Railways	8.2	9.2	7.9	11.1	6.8	4.50
Other transport	4.7	5.1	4.1	5.9	5.0	4.84
Communications	0.5	0.7	0.9	1.2	1.3	7.85
Trade, hotels, and restaurants	8.9	5.5	4.1	−1.4	1.9	0.6
Banking and insurance	0.3	0.5	0.8	1.0	1.1	8.55
House property	32.8	27.8	24.6	17.7	19.8	3.08
Public administration	3.3	7.6	9.3	16.4	11.5	9.74
Other services	—	1.6	5.0	4.8	10.2	·
Total (percent)	100.0	100.0	100.0	100.0	100.0	4.48
Total (R. bill. of 1960–61)	240.7	359.1	604.5	118.4	245.3	—
Rate of growth (percent)	—	3.70	5.35	—		4.48

SOURCE OF BASIC DATA: Choudhury, "Industrial Breakdown," pp. 152, 155.

In the absence of comprehensive and comparable data for the entire period on gross and net capital formation by sector, recourse must be had to partial and indirect evidence. Thus a comparison based on sectoral national wealth estimates in constant prices for 1950, 1960, and 1970 shows that for these two decades not much more than one-tenth of total net capital formation took place in agriculture, nearly one-fourth in manufacturing and mining, one-twelfth in electric power, about one-seventh in transportation and communication, one-tenth in government administration, and not quite one-fifth in housing.[32] When these figures are compared with the share of the various sectors in national income, it is evident that the share of agriculture in net capital expenditures was considerably below its contribution to national product, indeed, not even as much as one-fourth as large. On the other hand, the share of modern manufacturing in net capital formation was about twice as large as its share in national income. This imbalance was to a considerable degree the result of deliberate government policy. The result of the changing share of the various sectors in net capital formation is evident in the changes in the distribution of capital stock. Sharp increases in the shares of the modern sectors (manufacturing and electricity) and public administration, together from one-seventh to nearly one-third of the total, contrast with significant decreases in the share of the traditional sectors (agriculture and trade) from considerably more than one-third to not much more than one-fifth.

As a result of the acceleration of the rate of capital formation beyond the growth of national product, the average capital-output ratio in constant prices rose from 2.35 in 1949 to 3.10 in 1970 and the marginal ratio advanced even more rapidly from 2.50 to 4.35.[33] Omitting house property, the rise is more rapid, from 1.65 in 1949 to 2.40 in 1970 for the average ratio and from 2.15 to 3.55 for the marginal ratio. These figures reflect a considerable degree of capital deepening in these two decades.

32. Choudhury, p. 155.
33. Op. cit., p. 156.

TABLE 3-13. Total Domestic and Sectoral Net Saving, 1951–1977

	1951–55	1956–60	1961–65	1966–70	1971–75	1976–77
I. Absolute figures (R. bill.)						
Public	5.9	9.1	24.9	26.6	72.3	65.7
Corporate	2.0	2.7	5.8	5.6	21.5	5.8
Household	24.5	39.5	61.5	106.8	270.1	153.3
Financial	8.2	18.1	34.1	51.1	135.9	108.9
Tangible	16.3	21.4	27.4	55.7	134.1	44.4
Total	32.4	51.3	92.2	139.0	363.9	224.8
II. Distribution (percent)						
Public	18.2	17.7	27.0	19.1	19.9	29.2
Corporate	6.2	5.3	6.3	4.0	5.9	2.6
Household	75.6	77.0	66.7	76.9	74.2	68.2
Financial	25.3	35.4	37.0	36.8	37.3	48.4
Tangible	50.3	41.6	29.7	40.1	36.9	19.8
Total	100.0	100.0	100.0	100.0	100.0	100.0
III. Relation to gross national product (percent)						
Public	1.12	1.41	2.51	1.56	2.47	4.04
Corporate	0.38	0.42	0.58	0.33	0.74	0.36
Household	4.64	6.12	6.20	6.28	9.14	9.44
Financial	1.55	2.81	3.44	3.01	4.55	6.71
Tangible	3.09	3.32	2.76	3.28	4.59	2.74
Total	6.14	7.95	9.29	8.17	12.35	13.84

SOURCES OF I: *RCF*, 1970–71, S 10; *NAS, 1970/71–1973/74*, p. 33; *NAS, 1970/71–1975/76*, p. 23; *RBIB*, 1978, p. 267; *RCF*, 1977–78, 1:6–7. According to more recent estimates, values for 1976–77 are considerably higher for tangible and total assets of householder.

b. Saving[34,35]

If attention is limited to total national saving and its distribution among the three main sectors, the saving process in India during the post-independence period is characterized by, as table 3-13 shows for quinquennial periods and table 3-14 for individual years:

1. A substantial rise in the national net saving ratio from not much more than 6 percent of gross national product in the first half of the 1950s to, on the average, fully 8 percent from 1956 to 1970, the ratio reaching a level of 12½ percent in the first half of the 1970s.

2. An irregular upward trend in the share of the public sector's saving, from 1.1 percent of national product in the first half of the 1950s to 2.5 percent of national product in the first half of the 1960s and again in the first half of the 1970s, and to 4 percent in 1976–77. The share of public saving remained slightly below one-fifth, however, much lower than its share in capital formation, except for the third plan period and for 1976–77 when it rose to considerably more than one-fourth.

3. An irregular movement of the corporate saving ratio about the relatively low level of between 0.3 and 0.7 percent of national product, declining from a share of 6 percent of national saving from 1951 to 1965 to only 2½ percent in the first half of the 1970s.

34. The macroeconomic statistics of saving in India are rather unsatisfactory, and no consistent or trustworthy detailed series can be constructed for the entire post-independence period. This is particularly true for household saving through physical assets. For a review of the available figures, cf. Khatkhate and Deshpande.

35. All figures used in this subsection fail to include saving in the form of gold and silver accumulation and the increase in the stock of consumer durables. Although no reasonably accurate figures exist for gold and silver hoarding, it is likely that they would for the entire post-independence period add between 0.25 and 0.50 percent of gross national product to the national as well as to the personal saving ratio, and hence increase these ratios by up to one-twentieth. The net saving through consumer durables seems to have amounted on the average to more than 1 percent of national product, or more than one-tenth. It is also likely, though more doubtful, that this addition had a tendency to rise over the period, particularly in the case of consumer durables.

TABLE 3-14. National and Sectoral Saving, Annual Data, 1950–1977

Fiscal year ending March 31 following year	Total		Public	Private corporate	Households		
					Total	Financial	Nonfinancial
	R. bill.			percent of gross national product			
1950	5.42	5.51	0.98	0.36	4.18	0.18	4.00
1951	5.29	5.11	1.81	0.62	2.70	−0.18	2.88
1952	4.08	4.02	1.00	0.01	3.00	0.44	2.56
1953	5.65	5.22	0.86	0.24	4.13	0.78	3.35
1954	7.64	7.58	0.92	0.50	6.16	3.13	3.03
1955	9.71	9.25	1.06	0.57	7.61	3.71	3.90
1956	10.76	9.10	1.50	0.50	7.12	2.69	4.42
1957	7.98	6.63	1.30	0.15	5.17	2.76	2.42
1958	9.31	7.02	1.04	0.24	5.73	2.49	3.24
1959	11.02	8.34	1.54	0.45	6.37	2.88	3.49
1960	13.27	8.88	2.07	0.78	6.03	3.05	2.98
1961	12.81	8.07	2.29	0.85	4.93	3.08	1.85
1962	15.44	9.09	2.40	0.83	5.86	2.94	2.92
1963	18.25	9.34	2.76	0.76	5.82	3.80	2.02
1964	20.23	8.83	2.67	0.46	5.71	3.12	2.59
1965	25.62	10.70	2.47	0.41	7.81	4.44	3.37
1966	31.18	11.37	1.48	0.39	9.49	3.15	6.34
1967	30.27	9.45	1.11	0.22	8.12	2.94	5.18
1968	31.34	9.49	1.58	0.23	7.68	2.60	5.08
1969	40.22	11.00	1.76	0.40	8.83	2.50	6.33
1970	46.17	11.49	2.00	0.52	8.97	3.41	5.56
1971	50.18	11.60	1.71	0.63	9.26	3.58	5.68
1972	53.48	11.20	1.51	0.53	9.17	4.33	4.84
1973	71.64	12.17	1.83	0.82	9.52	6.05	3.48
1974	88.62	12.71	3.14	1.11	8.45	3.65	4.80
1975	100.02	13.75	3.45	0.51	9.80	5.32	4.47
1976	115.17	14.72	4.16	0.51	10.05	7.69	2.36
1977	109.61	12.83	3.94	0.36	8.53	5.82	2.71

SOURCES OF BASIC DATA: Same as for table 3-13.

4. The predominance of household saving, which supplied nearly three-fourths of total national saving for the quarter century as a whole. The share declined substantially, to two-thirds of the total, only during the third plan period, when the share of public sector saving reached its peak, and in 1976–77. As a result, the ratio of total household saving to national product rose from less than 5 percent in the first half of the 1950s to fully 6 percent in the following quinquennia without a difference between them, and further advanced to more than 9 percent in the 1970s.

5. Within household saving financial saving gained sharply at the expense of net saving through physical assets, the share of financial saving rising from one-third of total net household saving in the first half of the 1950s to, on the average, one-half in the two following decades. Whether the sharp further advance to considerably more than two-thirds in 1976–77 fore-shadows a structural change remains to be seen. This movement must, however, be interpreted with caution because of the roughness of the estimates for household saving through tangible assets. Household saving through financial assets, which can be measured a little more accurately, tripled from 2.2 percent of personal disposable monetized income in the first half of the 1950s to 6.5 percent in the first half of the 1970s, whereas net saving through tangible assets remained at 6½ percent. As a result, the share of financial saving of households rose steadily from 1½ percent of national product, with an interruption only in the second half of the 1960s, to

TABLE 3-15. Sectoral Financial Surpluses and Deficits, 1951–1975

	1951–55	1956–60	1961–65	1966–70	1971–75	1951–75
	I. Absolute figures (R. bill.)					
Financial institutions	0.41	0.94	2.79	3.50	12.78	20.42
Private corporations	−4.16	−8.24	−15.96	−18.07	−29.73	−76.16
Government	−8.82	−28.81	−44.26	−70.18	−123.86	−275.93
Households	8.81	18.49	33.07	45.63	130.74	236.34
Rest of the world	1.40	17.19	20.32	29.02	5.45	73.39
All sectors; absolute	23.60	73.67	116.40	166.40	307.57	682.24
	II. Distribution (percent)					
Financial institutions	1.7	1.3	2.4	2.1	4.2	3.0
Private corporations	−17.6	−11.2	−13.7	−10.9	−9.8	−11.2
Government	−37.4	−39.1	−38.0	−42.2	−40.9	−40.4
Households	37.4	25.1	28.4	27.4	43.2	34.6
Rest of the world	5.9	23.3	17.5	17.4	1.8	10.8
All sectors; absolute	100.0	100.0	100.0	100.0	100.0	100.0
	III. Relation to gross national product (percent)					
Financial institutions	0.08	0.14	0.28	0.21	0.44	0.30
Private corporations	−0.78	−1.25	−1.60	−1.07	−1.02	−1.22
Government	−1.69	−4.35	−4.45	−4.15	−4.24	−4.07
Households	1.69	2.81	3.32	2.70	4.47	3.48
Rest of the world	0.27	2.61	2.04	1.71	0.19	1.08
All sectors; absolute	4.51	11.18	11.67	9.83	10.35	10.15

SOURCES: *RBIB*, March 1967, July 1969, and February 1972; *RCF*, 1974–75, II:78; 1975–76, II:18; 1976–77, II:20; 1977–78, II:6.

5½ percent in the 1970s, or from one-fourth to more than two-fifths of total national saving, indicating an increasing share of financial institutions in the saving and investment process.

6. The saving ratio and its distribution among sectors seem to show considerable year-to-year fluctuations, which can be followed in table 3-14, but must be regarded with caution because of the weakness of some of the underlying estimates. Fairly pronounced peaks are shown at about five-year intervals, namely, in 1955, 1960, 1966, 1971, and 1976, four of which either coincide with years of large increases in real national product (1960) or follow them (1966, 1971, 1976). Because of the upward trend of the ratio, each of the peaks, with the exception of that of 1960, is at a level above the preceding one.

The structure of government, corporate, and household saving will be discussed in section 4 in as much detail as the available data permit.

c. Financial Surpluses and Deficits

For financial analysis, the difference between a sector's saving and its capital formation, that is, its financial surplus or deficit, is possibly more significant than the separate figures for its saving and capital formation, because it is the surplus or deficit that indicates the net amount of funds supplied to or withdrawn from the market. Because the financial surplus or deficit is a single, undifferentiated figure, it must be supplemented by information on the increases or decreases in the holdings of the different forms of financial instruments that together result in the surplus or deficit. This will be done for the main sectors of the Indian economy in section 4. Meanwhile, table 3-15 shows the net financial surplus or deficit for five sectors for the years 1951 to 1975, not only in absolute figures, but also in the more informative form of the sectoral distribution of surpluses and deficits and in that of their ratios to gross national product.[36]

36. For a similar use of flow-of-funds data, cf. Srinivasan.

TABLE 3-16. Balance of Payments, 1948–1976 (Percent of Gross National Product)

	1948–50	1951–55	1956–60	1961–65	1966–70	1971–75	1976
Commodity trade	−1.33	−1.04	−2.52	−1.81	−0.97	−0.38	0.91
Services	0.08	0.37	−0.43	−0.73	−0.89	−0.70	−0.29
Transfers, private	0.32	0.38	0.38	0.16	0.35	0.40	0.90
Transfers, government	0.00	0.21	0.23	0.28	0.13	0.63	0.31
Capital, private	−0.21	−0.04	0.07	0.02	−0.02	0.05 }	1.30
Capital, central government	−1.03	0.08	1.43	1.96	1.85	0.48 }	
Monetary authorities	2.13	0.25	0.98	0.19	−0.33	−0.10	−2.79
Miscellaneous[a]	—	—	0.03	0.00	0.01	0.03	—
Net errors and omissions	0.04	−0.21	−0.17	−0.06	−0.15	−0.41	−0.34

[a]Deposit money banks and allocations of SDRs.

SOURCES OF BASIC DATA: 1948–55, *BMSS*, pt. 2, p. 110; 1956–76, *IFS*, May 1978; February 1979.

The absolute sum of sectoral financial surpluses and deficits, which is a rough measure of the intensity of intersectoral fund flows, rose sharply from 4½ percent of gross national product in the first plan period to fully 10 percent for the two decades starting in the mid-1950s with only small differences among the four five-year periods. This was a result primarily of the sharp increase in the government's financial deficit from not much more than 1½ percent of national product to more than 4 percent, an increase reflecting mainly borrowing to finance rising capital expenditures under the second and later plans. The deficit of private nonfinancial corporations also rose, though only from 0.8 percent to nearly 1½ percent from 1956 to 1965. In the following decade, it fell to not much more than 1 percent, reflecting the declining importance of the private corporate sector in the financing process. The main net supplier of funds was, as in almost all countries and periods, the household sector. The ratio of its net financial surplus to gross national product rose from 1.7 percent in the first plan period to, on the average, nearly 3 percent from 1956 to 1970 and further to 4½ percent in the early 1970s, increasing in terms of personal disposable monetized income from less than 2½ to 6½ percent.[37] In India, however, the role of the rest of the world as a supplier of funds was extraordinarily large from the mid-1950s on, as it averaged about 2 percent of national product from 1956 to 1970 and was equal to nearly two-fifths of the combined financial deficit of the government and corporate business sectors, reflecting large net capital imports and foreign aid. In the early 1970s, however, the financial surplus of the rest-of-the-world sector almost disappeared as the balance of payments improved sharply. These figures show that until the 1970s the financing of the large capital expenditures under the plans was crucially dependent on the funds supplied by the rest of the world, in part in the form of assistance by foreign governments and international organizations on concessionary terms, an assistance that increased in absolute and relative size from the mid-1950s to the late 1960s, quite contrary to the downward pattern envisaged in the plans when originally drawn up.

37. An additional dimension of the various sectors' participation in intrasectoral fund flows is given by the ratio between sources and uses of funds. This ratio was, using the larger of the two components as the denominator and basing the calculation of the ratio on flows during the five years 1971 through 1975 (the higher the ratio the more one-sided the sector's borrowing and lending activities), among net borrowers, 2.8 for private nonfinancial corporations and 3.9 for the government, and among net lenders, 4.2 for households and less than 1.1 for financial institutions.

4. THE DEVELOPMENT OF FINANCIAL INSTITUTIONS

a. Main Trends[38]

(i) The discussion in this subsection, as well as part of the discussion in the other subsections, is based on a set of tables (3-18, 19, and 20) that present the basic information on the size of the assets of the eleven types of financial institutions being distinguished, the distribution of the total assets of financial institutions among the eleven types, the growth rate of their assets, the ratio of their assets to gross national product, and the ratio of the change in their assets to gross national product, that is, the new issue ratio, for seven benchmark years (1950, 1955, 1960, 1965, 1970, 1975, and 1977) or for the six quinquennial periods between them. Information on the total assets of each group on an annual basis will be found in table 3-17. Most of the basic data are taken from periodicals issued by the Reserve Bank of India.

(ii) During the period from 1951 through 1977, the assets of financial institutions increased at an average rate of almost 12 percent per year and thus expanded substantially more rapidly than the price level rose. The average rate of growth in real terms, using the national product deflator, was slightly in excess of 7 percent, or higher than the rate of 3.6 percent at which real national product grew. As a result, the ratio of financial institutions' assets to national product more than doubled from a level of fully one-third in 1950 to more than four-fifths at the end of 1977. Financial institutions thus came to play an increasingly important role in the Indian economy.

(iii) The growth rate of assets, in absolute terms as well as in relation to national product, was, however, far from regular. Reflecting, in part, movements of national product, the assets of financial institutions moved rather irregularly in the first years after independence and in 1953 were only 9 percent higher than they had been in 1948. From then on, however, that is, since the middle of the first plan, the rate of increase averaged in excess of 13 percent a year, fell below 10 percent in only two years (1954 and 1961), and accelerated to nearly 20 percent in 1976–77. In the more significant terms of the ratio of assets to national product, financial institutions gained on the average 2 percentage points a year, equivalent to an average annual increase in the ratio of assets to national product of 4 percent. Increases in the ratio, indicating a growth of financial institutions' assets in excess of national product, were especially pronounced in 1954–55, 1957, 1959, and in the 1970s, particularly 1976 and 1977. In contrast, the ratio kept fairly close to one-half from 1959 to 1967.

The upward trend in the ratio of financial institutions' assets to national product is more clearly visible in the increase in the new issue ratio (the increase in financial institutions' assets divided by national product) from 1.7 percent during the first plan to between 5½ and nearly 9 percent during the following four five-year periods and, finally, to more than 13 percent in 1976 and 1977. Some of the reasons for these fluctuations will appear when the new issue ratio of financial institutions is investigated in subsection k.

(iv) Because the different types of financial institutions grew at a far from uniform speed, the differences reflecting the operation of both market forces and governmental policies, substantial changes occurred in the distribution of the total assets of all financial institutions (table 3-19). The average annual growth of assets between 1950 and 1977 ranged, considering only major institutions or groups of them, from 10½ percent for the banking system (more than 8 percent for the Reserve Bank and nearly 13 percent for the commercial banks) to 12½ percent for the Post Office Saving System, 13½ percent for insurance and pension organizations, 16 percent for the cooperative banks, and 18 percent for term-lending institutions (development banks), in this case starting with 1957 because they were almost nonexistent at the beginning of the period.

As a result, the share of the banking system in the assets of all financial institutions

---

38. Because this subsection constitutes a brief summary of the remainder of the section, specific source references are generally dispensed with.

TABLE 3-17. Assets of Financial Institutions, Annually, 1948–1977 (R. Bill.)

	Reserve Bank (1)	Commercial banks (2)	Cooperative banks (3)	Post Office Saving System (4)	Development banks[a] (5)	ARDC[b] (6)	Finance companies (7)	Unit Trust (8)	Life insurance companies (9)	Other insurance companies (10)	Provident funds (11)	Total (12)
1948	16.81	10.16	1.40	0.23	0.10	—	·	—	2.45	2.45	1.05	32.65
1949	15.60	9.55	1.75	0.43	0.10	—	·	—	2.76	0.22	1.23	31.64
1950	16.76	10.05	1.80	0.63	0.11	—	·	—	2.88	0.23	1.42	33.87
1951	16.94	10.22	2.03	0.69	0.11	—	·	—	3.23	0.27	1.60	35.09
1952	15.78	10.16	2.20	0.89	0.11	—	·	—	3.52	0.29	1.83	34.78
1953	15.54	10.11	2.23	1.00	0.18	—	·	—	3.78	0.32	2.25	35.41
1954	15.71	11.29	2.55	1.21	0.21	—	·	—	3.63	0.35	2.69	37.64
1955	17.24	12.61	2.89	1.56	0.39	—	·	—	3.83	0.37	3.19	42.08
1956	19.30	14.04	3.51	1.91	0.50	—	·	—	4.14	0.44	3.80	47.64
1957	20.70	16.10	4.22	2.08	1.83	—	1.18	—	4.65	0.50	4.52	55.78
1958	21.85	18.25	5.88	2.25	1.95	—	1.24	—	5.05	0.53	5.20	62.20
1959	23.23	20.84	7.21	2.46	2.13	—	1.31	—	5.54	0.58	5.99	69.29
1960	25.14	21.94	8.97	2.85	2.40	—	1.41	—	6.22	0.65	7.05	76.63
1961	26.71	22.34	10.88	3.22	2.70	—	1.47	—	6.96	0.73	8.22	83.23
1962	28.50	24.82	12.86	3.40	3.06	—	1.50	—	7.84	0.83	9.51	92.32
1963	31.06	28.47	14.74	3.66	3.56	—	1.62	—	8.80	0.91	11.06	103.88
1964	33.32	30.54	17.49	4.08	4.00	—	1.62	—	10.05	1.02	12.88	115.00
1965	36.55	34.74	20.35	6.12	4.03	0.05	1.96	0.25	10.95	1.13	14.86	130.99

Year	Col 1	Col 2	Col 3	Col 4	Col 5	Col 6	Col 7	Col 8	Col 9	Col 10	Col 11	Total
1966	40.53	40.40	23.16	6.70	5.52	0.06	2.13	0.27	12.38	1.32	17.05	149.52
1967	43.65	44.81	25.95	7.15	6.39	0.10	2.21	0.35	13.84	1.46	19.59	165.50
1968	45.65	50.77	29.79	7.78	6.49	0.21	2.29	0.50	15.55	1.63	22.34	183.00
1969	51.71	58.30	35.88	8.41	7.25	0.44	2.41	0.67	17.45	1.89	25.86	210.36
1970	56.42	66.08	41.50	9.12	7.84	0.74	2.56	0.92	19.54	2.19	29.93	236.84
1971	64.56	79.45	48.69	9.88	9.05	1.13	1.74	1.05	22.04	2.50	35.01	275.10
1972	69.56	94.47	54.63	10.37	10.45	1.72	1.71	1.25	25.10	2.85	40.24	312.35
1973	84.34	115.98	61.72	11.31	12.06	2.68	1.77	1.52	28.76	3.25	46.27	369.66
1974	95.18	132.75	68.65	11.62	14.56	3.94	2.15	1.49	32.37	3.70	54.14	420.55
1975	109.32	163.35	78.99	11.66	18.46	5.78	2.26	1.67	36.42	4.20	64.84	496.95
1976	122.04	199.81	87.67	14.34	22.23	8.67	2.40	1.93	41.63	4.80	76.00	581.52
1977	141.77	267.96	98.50	15.23	28.68	13.00	2.50	2.55	47.25	5.50	89.00	711.94

aState Finance Corporations, Industrial Finance Corporation of India, Industrial Development Bank of India, and Industrial Credit and Investment Corporation of India.   bAgricultural Refinance and Development Corporation.

SOURCES: **Col. 1:** 1948–71, *IFS*, 1972 Supplement, pp. 242–43; 1972–77, *IFS*, January 1979, p. 180.   **Col. 2:** 1948–71, *IFS*, 1972 Supplement, pp. 242–43; 1972–77, *IMF*, unpublished printout.   **Col. 3:** 1948–76, Reserve Bank of India, *Statistical Tables Relating to the Cooperative Movement in India*, various issues; figures refer to June 30; 1977, extrapolated on basis of trend in 1974–76.   **Col. 4:** 1948–71, *IFS*, 1972 Supplement, pp. 242–43; 1972–77, *IFS*, January 1979, p. 180.   **Col. 5:** 1948–64, *RCF*, various issues; 1965–71, *IFS*, 1972 Supplement, p. 243; 1972–77, *RCF*, 1977–78, II:71 ff.   **Col. 6:** 1965–75, *RCF*, various issues; average of June of indicated and following year; 1976–77, extrapolated on basis of 1973–75 growth rate.   **Col. 7:** 1957–70, Reserve Bank of India, *Financial Statistics of Joint Stock Companies in India*, 1950–51 to 1962–63 and 1960–61 to 1970–71; 1971–75, *RBIB*, April 1975.   **Col. 8:** 1965–69, *Annual Report on the Working of the Unit Trust of India*, various issues; 1970–77, *RCF*, 1977–78, II:77; figures refer to par values as of June 30 of following year.   **Col. 9:** 1948–70, *IFS*, 1978 Supplement, p. 197; 1971–76, obtained by cumulating increase in assets (*IFS*, January 1979, p. 180); 1977, estimated on basis of previous years' changes.   **Col. 10:** 1948–70, *SAIU*, various issues; 1971–77, estimated on basis of 1966–75 average increase.   **Col. 11:** 1950, 1960, 1967–71, *V-S*, p. 134; 1948–49, 1951–59, 1961–66, 1972–75, interpolated or extrapolated on basis of increase in assets from flow-of-funds figures (*RBIB*, various issues); 1976–77, extrapolated on basis of growth rate 1971–75.

TABLE 3-18. Growth Rates of Assets of Financial Institutions, 1951–1977 (Percent Per Year)

	1951–55	1956–60	1961–65	1966–70	1971–75	1976–77	1951–77 (current prices)	1951–77 (constant prices)
Reserve Bank	0.57	7.84	7.77	9.07	14.14	13.88	8.23	3.46
Commercial banks	4.64	11.71	9.63	13.73	19.84	28.08	12.93	8.16
Cooperative banks	9.93	25.42	17.80	15.32	13.74	11.66	15.98	11.21
Post Office Saving System	19.88	12.81	16.51	8.30	5.04	14.29	12.52	7.75
Development banks	28.81	43.82	10.92	14.24	18.68	24.64	22.88	18.11
Agriculture Refinance and Development Corp.	—	—	—	71.42	50.85	49.97	—	—
Finance and investment companies	.	.	6.81	5.49	-2.46	5.17	.	.
Unit Trust	—	—	—	29.77	12.66	23.57	—	—
Life insurance companies	5.87	10.18	11.98	12.28	13.26	13.70	10.92	6.15
Other insurance companies	9.98	11.92	11.69	14.14	13.91	14.43	12.48	7.71
Provident funds	17.57	17.19	16.08	15.03	16.72	17.36	16.56	11.79
All institutions, current prices	4.44	12.73	11.31	12.58	15.98	19.69	11.94	
All institutions, constant prices	6.51	9.55	4.51	6.79	5.34	14.60		7.17

SOURCE: Table 3.17.

TABLE 3-19. Distribution of Assets among Financial Institutions, 1950–1977a (Percent)

	1950	1955	1960	1965	1970	1975	1977
Reserve Bank	49.1	41.0	32.8	27.9	23.8	22.0	19.9
Commercial banks	29.7	30.0	28.6	26.5	27.9	32.9	37.6
Cooperative banks	5.3	6.9	11.7	15.5	17.5	15.9	13.8
Post Office Saving System	1.9	3.7	3.7	4.7	3.9	2.3	2.1
Development banks	0.3	0.7	3.1	3.1	3.3	3.7	4.0
Agriculture Refinance and Development Corporation	—	—	—	0.0	0.3	1.2	1.8
Financial and invest- ment companies	·	·	1.8	1.5	1.1	0.5	0.4
Unit Trust	—	—	—	0.2	0.4	0.3	0.4
Life insurance companies	8.5	9.1	8.1	8.4	8.3	7.3	6.6
Other insurance companies	0.9	0.9	0.8	0.9	0.9	0.8	0.8
Provident funds	4.2	7.6	9.2	11.3	12.6	13.0	12.5
All financial institutions	100.0	100.0	100.0	100.0	100.0	100.0	100.0

aDoes not include urban and rural moneylenders and a few small financial institutions.

SOURCE: Table 3-17.

declined from 80 percent in 1950 to 58 percent in 1977, having reached a nadir of 53 percent in 1969, which was due to the sharp fall of the share of the Reserve Bank from 50 to 20 percent. The share of the cooperative banks advanced sharply from not much more than 5 to 14 percent after a peak of 18 percent in 1969, and the share of insurance organizations rose from 12½ to 20 percent. These changes correspond to those commonly observed as a financial system develops. Although no comprehensive or continuous statistics are available on the resources of indigenous financial organizations, including rural moneylenders, there is no doubt that their assets increased much less than those of modern financial institutions, and they thus declined sharply in relative importance. Rough estimates put the average rate of increase of the indigenous financial institutions at less than 4 percent per year, so that their share in the assets of all financial institutions declined from nearly one-third in 1950 to less than 7 percent in 1975.[39,40]

(v) Reflecting their more rapid growth, the ratio of the assets of financial institutions to gross national product increased sharply from fully one-third in 1950 to more than one-half a decade later and continued to advance rapidly to more than two-thirds in 1975 and jumped to more than four-fifths in 1977, which is a rarely equaled rise in this ratio. The Reserve Bank was the only institution whose ratio failed to increase. Increases were largest, in comparison to the 1950 ratio, for development and cooperative banks and provident funds. However, even the ratios for commercial banks, the postal saving system, and life insurance companies increased by 90 to 210 percent.

(vi) The rapid expansion of the absolute and relative volume of financial institutions' assets was accompanied by far-reaching institutional changes. All of these changes increased public ownership and control of financial institutions, which was in line with the declared policy

39. Cf. table 3-56.

40. Comprehensive information on the assets of nidhis and chit funds, two types of small, indigenous financial institutions, mainly in southern India, is not available. At the end of the 1960s about 12,000 chit funds with capital of R. 80 mill., or 0.04 percent of the assets of all financial institutions, were registered in Kerala and Tamil Nadu, the two states that should have housed most of them (Nayar, pp. 165–66).

TABLE 3-20. Ratio of Assets of Financial Institutions to Gross National Product,
1950–1977 (Percent)[a]

	1950	1955	1960	1965	1970	1975	1977
Reserve Bank	16.2	15.4	16.3	14.2	13.5	14.6	16.0
Commercial banks	9.7	11.3	14.2	13.5	15.8	21.8	30.2
Cooperative banks	1.7	2.6	5.8	7.9	9.9	10.6	11.1
Post Office Saving System	0.7	1.4	1.8	2.4	2.2	1.6	1.7
Development banks	0.1	0.3	1.6	1.6	1.9	2.5	3.2
Agriculture Refinance and Development Corporation	—	—	—	0.0	0.2	0.8	1.5
Financial and investment companies	·	·	0.9	0.8	0.6	0.3	0.3
Unit Trust	—	—	—	0.1	0.2	0.2	0.3
Life insurance companies	2.8	3.4	4.0	4.3	4.7	4.9	5.3
Other insurance companies	0.2	0.3	0.4	0.4	0.5	0.6	0.6
Provident funds	1.4	2.9	4.6	5.8	7.2	8.7	10.0
All financial institutions	32.7	37.7	49.7	51.0	56.8	66.4	80.3

[a]Does not include urban and rural moneylenders and a few small financial institutions.

SOURCES: Tables 3-3 and 3-17.

of the Indian government to develop the country as a centrally planned socialist economy, although one in which much of the means of production would remain in private hands, particularly in agriculture. Thus the shares of the Reserve Bank were acquired by the government immediately after independence; the largest commercial bank, the Imperial Bank of India, was taken over by the government and renamed the State Bank of India in 1955; all life insurance companies were nationalized and merged into the Life Insurance Corporation of India in 1956; most of the development banks, organized in the 1950s and 1960s, were publicly owned and managed; by far the largest diversified investment company, the Unit Trust of India, was set up in 1964 as a public enterprise; the fourteen largest Indian private commercial banks were nationalized in 1969; and all property insurance companies were taken over by the central government in 1971. The Post Office Saving System, of course, has been part of the central government since its organization in the late nineteenth century. The provident funds for government employees are by their nature in the public sector, and those for other employees are closely regulated by the government. Although government ownership of the upper tier of the cooperative banking system is only partial and the lower tier is member-owned, the supervisory powers of either the Reserve Bank or the state governments are so extensive that the system may also be regarded as largely under public control. At the present time, therefore, there are hardly any modern financial institutions left in private hands, essentially only several sizable foreign banks, whose operations are limited to a few port cities and are controlled in their expansion; a limited number of medium-sized and small Indian commercial banks, subject to extensive government controls; a few investment-holding companies; and one development bank, the Industrial Credit and Investment Corporation of India. For practical purposes, therefore, the entire superstructure of modern financial institutions may be regarded as being in the public sector. Actually, central government control is not yet firmly exercised throughout the system (in the nationalized commercial banks, for instance, most of the old managements are still in place), and coordination between the various groups of nationalized financial institutions is still incomplete. Nevertheless, the centralized public direction of virtually the entire system of modern financial institutions is now a possibility that can be turned into reality by the central government at any time without the need for further legislation.

TABLE 3-21. Main Assets and Liabilities of Reserve Bank of India, 1948–1977 (Percent)

	1948	1950	1955	1960	1965	1970	1975	1977
Foreign assets	63.5	52.1	45.4	10.7	6.0	11.5	16.2	30.8
Claims against								
Government	35.2	47.2	51.3	82.2	87.3	76.3	69.1	55.9
Banks	1.1	0.3	2.6	6.4	5.6	11.0	10.5	7.7
Other assets	0.2	0.4	0.8	0.7	1.2	1.2	4.3[b]	5.5[b]
Currency								
Outside banks	75.6	75.8	84.0	78.2	78.4	73.9	58.9	59.4
In banks	2.7	2.7	2.7	2.2	2.4	2.9	9.0	14.7
Deposits								
Bankers	4.0	3.3	3.4	4.6	3.4	3.5	·	
Public	1.7	0.8	0.5	0.8	0.6	1.1		
Government	13.8	11.0	4.1	3.4	1.6	5.1	0.6	0.5
Liabilities								
Foreign	0.8	2.1	—	1.1	3.8	0.1	6.7	0.9
Other	0.8	3.8	4.8	4.4	4.1	3.5	12.3[c]	11.4[c]
Capital accounts	0.6	0.6	0.6	5.2	5.8	9.8	12.4	13.1
Total assets and liabilities								
Percent	100.0	100.0	100.0	100.0	100.0	100.0	100.0	100.0
R. bill.	16.81	16.76	17.24	25.14	36.55	56.42	109.32	141.77
Growth[a]	—	-0.15	0.57	7.84	7.77	9.07	14.14	13.88

[a] Growth rate between benchmark dates.   [b] Claims against other financial institutions.   [c] Net of unclassified assets and liabilities.

SOURCES: IFS, 1972 Supplement, pp. 242–43; January 1979, pp. 180–81.

b. Reserve Bank of India[41]

During the post-independence period the Reserve Bank of India, which had been in the first decade of its existence a traditional shareholder-owned central bank with a rather limited range of activities and powers, developed into a government-owned institution with wide powers over a large part of the country's financial system. It extended its operations well beyond managing the supply of money and controlling international financial transactions, in particular by setting up a system of development banks and becoming deeply engaged in developing the country's predominantly agricultural cooperative banking system. In all of these functions the bank seems to have acted primarily as the executor of policies laid down by the central government, although it apparently retained a certain amount of independence of action, if only because its headquarters in Bombay is more than 700 miles from the seat of the government in New Delhi.[42]

The total assets of the Reserve Bank increased from 1951 through 1977 at an average rate of 8 percent, or just in line with national product. As a result, the ratio of the bank's assets to national product stayed within the narrow range of from 14 to 17 percent. Because all other major financial institutions expanded much more rapidly than national product grew, the share of the Reserve Bank in the assets of all financial institutions declined in every year from 1950 on with the result that in 1977 its share of 20 percent was three-fifths lower than it had been three decades earlier. In particular, whereas the Reserve Bank's assets had exceeded those of the commercial banks in 1950 by more than two-thirds, they amounted in 1977 to not much more than one-half of those of the commercial banks. The decline is sharper still if the cooperative banking system is included: 140 percent in 1950, less than 40 percent in 1977.

At independence nearly two-thirds of the assets of the Reserve Bank consisted of sterling claims accumulated during World War II. These were rapidly reduced as a result of the import requirements of the plans, and from the late 1950s they did not exceed one-eighth of total assets. They were essentially replaced by government securities, whose share in total assets increased from fully one-third to about three-fourths from the late 1950s to 1970 but were reduced to not much more than 55 percent in 1977 as a result of the heavy balance of payment surpluses of the mid-1970s. In connection with the bank's increasingly close relation to the rapidly growing cooperative banking system, the share of advances to the latter, which had been very small in the 1950s, rose to 8 percent of total assets in 1977. The share of business credit in the form of bills purchased remained small.

Because other banks' deposits with the Reserve Bank have not been used as a tool of monetary policy, they have remained small—on the order of 3 to 5 percent of total liabilities—and have failed to show a definite trend. Government deposits have fluctuated substantially, between 14 percent and almost zero with a sharp downward trend interrupted only in the late 1960s. Thus the bulk of liabilities, between 75 and 85 percent, has always consisted of currency in circulation, more than nine-tenths of which is attributed in the flow-of-funds statistics to the household sector.

From the late 1950s to the early 1970s advances to the government have constituted between three-fourths and seven-eighths of the bank's total assets, and currency held outside banks, mostly by households, has represented an approximately equal share of the bank's liabilities. The bank, regarded as a financial intermediary, has thus been mainly a conduit

41. There is a vast literature about the development and policies of the Reserve Bank, partly official, partly academic. The operations of the bank are described in the bank's *The Reserve Bank of India—Functions and Working*, 1970. The detailed semiofficial history of the bank (Simha, 1970) unfortunately covers only the first few years after independence. The figures used in the text are taken from the various issues of *RBIB* and the Bank's annual reports.

42. Statements of this character can be made with confidence only by a limited number of persons with extended personal experience in the bank or the Finance Department or as a result of an exhaustive study of the relevant documents, many of which are not accessible to outsiders. The author obviously does not meet either of these tests.

TABLE 3-22. Basic Statistics of Commercial Banks, 1951–1975

	1951	1956	1961	1966	1970	1975
Number of banks	566	423	292	100	86	80
Whereof scheduled banks	92	89	82	73	73	72
Number of offices	4151	4067	5012	6593	11184	20435
Whereof scheduled banks	2647	2966	4390	6380	11040	20290
Offices per scheduled bank	29	33	53	87	151	282
Population (thou.) per office	87	98	88	76	49	27
Deposits (R. mill.)						
Per scheduled bank	6.4	9.6	21.2	47.0	77.0	187.3
Per office	0.22	0.29	0.40	0.54	0.51	0.66
Expense/earnings ratio	0.71	0.79	0.77	0.87	0.89[c]	0.98
Establishment expenses/earnings ratio[a]	0.34	0.33	0.29	0.30	0.33[c]	0.34
Profits/earnings ratio[b]	0.29	0.21	0.23	0.13	0.11[c]	0.11
Employees (thou.)	·	79	115	170	249	455
Employees per office	·	19	23	26	22	25
Employees per R. mill. deposits	·	6.8	5.7	4.7	4.4	3.9

[a]Excludes interest cost.   [b]Before taxes.   [c]1968.

SOURCES OF BASIC DATA: 1951–70, *RBC*, pp. 42–43; 1975, Research Department of Reserve Bank of India.

between the household and the central government sectors, except in the first and last few years of the period.

c. The Commercial Banking System[43]

(i) INSTITUTIONAL CHANGES. As it had in the preceding century, the commercial banking system has continued to be the centerpiece of India's financial structure since independence, although it has changed substantially in size, scope, and character.

The banking system left behind by the British Raj had been characterized by relatively small size, not only in relation to the country's area and population but also to its national product; by being practically limited to cities and to short-term commercial credit operations; by having virtually no direct connection with the two-thirds of the population dependent on agriculture; by the coexistence of numerous small banks with a few large institutions, particularly the Imperial Bank, which by itself accounted for about one-fourth of the assets of the system; by the importance of foreign banks, which controlled about one-sixth of total assets and were even more important in metropolitan areas; and, last but not least, by the high degree of independence of the government and the central bank. All of these characteristics were to change, some radically, during the first three decades of independence.

The change was most obvious, and also most radical, in the matter of ownership and control of the banks. Before independence only a few banks in some princely states had been government-owned. The new central government, in line with its goal of a democratic socialist commonwealth, probably envisaged from its inception the ultimate nationalization of the banking system, although it took more than two decades to reach this objective. The first step was the nationalization in 1955 of the Imperial Bank, which with the addition of the government-owned banks of some of the princely states became the State Bank of India. The next important step, apart from increasing control by the Reserve Bank over many aspects of the banks' operations, was the Credit Authorization Scheme of November 1965, which subjected the extension of new credits in excess of R. 1 mill. to prior approval by the Reserve Bank, and thus provided to the

43. The most detailed and best documented description of commercial banking since independence will be found in *RBC* and the accompanying volumes of technical appendices and special studies.

TABLE 3-23. Average Size of Deposits and Credits per Bank Office, 1974–1975 (R. Mill.)

Location	Current deposit accounts (1)	Saving accounts (2)	Cash credit and overdraft accounts[a] (3)	Ratio[b] (4)
Metropolitan areas	4.43	4.08	20.25	2.38
Urban areas	1.49	2.19	5.21	1.42
Semi-urban areas	0.64	1.45	1.33	0.64
Rural areas	0.15	0.60	0.24	0.32
All areas	1.19	1.68	4.45	1.55

[a]Approved credit limits.   [b]Col. 3 divided by col. 1 plus col. 2.

SOURCE: *RBIB*, 1978, p. 19.

bank a veto power over credit expansion of substantial size in directions disapproved by the authorities. The next step, this time in the direction of forcing banks to allocate credits in line with the wishes of the government, particularly to priority sectors hitherto neglected in the government's opinion—agriculture, small industries, artisans, backward areas—occurred in 1968. One year later, in July 1969, after considerable difficulties in Parliament and with the courts, the final step was taken, the nationalization of the fourteen largest privately owned commercial banks, which together accounted for considerably more than one-half of the assets of all commercial banks.[44] As a result, the share of the about sixty remaining private commercial banks was reduced to as little as one-sixth of the assets of the system, more than half of which was accounted for by fifteen foreign banks limited to operating in a few metropolitan areas. The objective of this last step was, in the words of the Banking Commission's report, "to control the heights of the economy and meet progressively and serve better the needs of development of the economy in conformity with national policy and objectives."[45]

(ii) CONCENTRATION AND BRANCH EXPANSION. A second important change, combining the pressure of market forces with that of government policy, was the rapid process of concentration within the commercial banking system (table 3-22). Between 1951 and 1975 the number of scheduled commercial banks declined from 92 to 72, and the group of smaller (nonscheduled) banks, which had numbered nearly 500 in 1951, practically disappeared as the result of mergers with larger (scheduled) banks or of dissolutions, both induced by their inefficient small size and incompetent management, competitive pressures, and government encouragement. The number of offices of the scheduled banks increased from about 2,650 in 1951 to nearly 6,600 in 1966, about one-half of the increase resulting from mergers, the other half from the opening of new branches. At that time the total number of commercial bank offices was already 60 percent higher than it had been a decade earlier, but the population per office, 76,000 (United States, about 10,000), was only one-fourth below the level of 1951, and offices were practically limited to the larger and medium-sized cities. During the 1960s, the banks, under strong government pressure, began a rapid expansion of their branch systems, and this time located or had to locate a substantial proportion of the new branches in rural or other hitherto neglected areas, a movement that accelerated after the nationalization of the fourteen largest banks in 1969. This expansion put a heavy strain on the internal organization of the banks, particularly on the

44. As far as I have been able to see, the *RBC* fails, in more than 700 pages, to mention these difficulties, which nearly produced a constitutional crisis.

45. *RBC*, p. 375.

TABLE 3-24. Distribution of Deposits among Large Commercial Banks, 1951–1975
(Percent of All Scheduled Banks)

	1951	1960	1970	1975	Ratio 1975 / 1951
State Bank and subsidiaries	37.01	37.62	26.87	28.42	0.77
Central	15.52	10.82	8.84	7.88	0.51
Bank of India	6.97	5.88	8.18	6.61	0.95
Punjab National	6.50	7.65	7.23	6.51	1.00
Baroda	3.92	4.96	6.75	5.79	1.48
United Commercial	3.70	4.74	4.49	3.58	0.97
Canara	0.94	1.65	3.74	4.56	4.86
United	3.67	2.83	3.29	3.49	0.95
Dena	1.05	1.94	2.48	2.45	2.33
Union	0.75	1.55	2.84	3.47	4.63
Allahabad	3.52	2.81	2.24	1.88	0.53
Syndicate	0.45	1.05	2.70	3.34	7.42
Indian	2.23	2.19	1.59	2.38	1.07
Indian Overseas	1.19	1.57	1.69	2.69	2.26
Maharashtra	0.33	0.83	1.65	1.85	5.61
15 banks (percent)	87.75	88.08	84.58	84.90	0.97
All scheduled banks (R. bill.)	7.98	18.07	61.94	134.82	16.89

SOURCE OF BASIC DATA: Reserve Bank of India, *Statistical Tables Relating to Banks in India,* various issues.

relations between staff and management, the more so because government policy changed several times.[46] It also substantially reduced the banks' profits, as most new branches necessarily operated at a loss for a shorter or longer period. Statistically, however, the results were spectacular. The number of bank offices tripled since nationalization, reaching 27,000 in 1977,[47] nearly one-half of the new offices being located in formerly unbanked places.[48] More than two-fifths of the branches were in rural areas, compared to not much more than 3,000 rural branches, or less than one-fourth of the total, in 1969 before nationalization. Of the fully 11,000 rural branches, more than 2,000 belonged to the State Bank; 5,000 to the fourteen nationalized large banks; about 2,000 to other still private commercial banks; and about 1,000 each to other public sector banks and to a new type, regional rural banks, which were generally subsidiaries of large commercial banks.[49] The population per office had been reduced to about 20,000, less than one-third of the situation before nationalization. The zealots, however, were still not satisfied.[50]

The speed of this advance and of the change in the distribution of offices, deposits, and loans is indicated by the fact that at the end of 1976 the offices opened after mid-1970 accounted for two-thirds of all offices, fully one-fourth of all deposits, and fully one-fifth of all credits. Even more pronounced is the expansion into rural areas, the main objective of government policy. Thus, at the end of 1976 considerably more than one-third of all offices were in rural areas, the result of about one-half of all new offices being placed in these areas. Because most of these offices were very small—on the average only R. 1.4 mill. in deposits and R. 0.8 mill. in loans—rural offices accounted for less than one-tenth of all deposits and 6½ percent of all loans, but for about 5 percent of the increase in total deposits or loans since 1969, both ratios far below the share of the rural population in national income.

46. On some of these problems, cf. summary of (then unpublished) *Report of the Committee on the Functioning of Public Sector Banks, RCF,* 1977–78, 1:139–40.

47. Shetty, p. 1441.

48. *RBIB,* July 1976, Supplement, p. 45.

49. Commerce Research Bureau, *Monthly Review of the Indian Economy,* July 1978.

50. See, e.g., Shetty, pp. 1407–51.

TABLE 3-25. Distribution of Commercial Bank Offices by Size of Locality, End of 1975

	All areas		Metropolitan	Urban	Semi-urban	Rural
			Amounts Percent			
	R. bill. (1)	(2)	(3)	(4)	(5)	(6)
Offices; number						
All offices	23485	100.0	14.2	18.7	30.3	36.7
Old offices	8163	100.0	18.4	23.2	39.6	17.7
New offices	15322	100.0	12.0	16.4	24.7	46.9
Deposits; R. bill.						
All offices	176.1	100.0	43.9	24.8	22.3	8.9
Old offices	129.8	100.0	47.0	25.0	23.4	4.6
New offices	46.3	100.0	35.3	24.3	19.4	21.1
Credits; R. bill.						
All offices	135.5	100.0	59.0	20.7	13.8	6.5
Old offices	105.3	100.0	64.0	20.8	12.5	2.9
New offices	30.2	100.0	41.7	20.4	18.6	19.3

SOURCE OF BASIC DATA: Shetty, p. 1441.

In terms of assets and deposits, the system is still predominantly metropolitan. In 1973 the five largest cities (Ahmadabad, Bombay, Calcutta, Delhi, and Madras), which contain about 3 percent of the population, though they may account for one-tenth of national product, had about 15 percent of all offices of commercial banks, 44 percent of all deposits, and 60 percent of all credits, Bombay and Calcutta alone accounting for 30 percent of all bank deposits and 45 percent of all bank credit.[51] At the end of 1977 fourteen metropolitan and urban centers still accounted for about two-thirds of bank credits and one-half of deposits.

In contrast to the rapid concentration within the commercial banking system as a whole, the relative position of the largest banks taken together has not changed substantially. The share

TABLE 3-26. Concentration of Bank Deposits in Large Cities,
1962 and 1973 (Percent of National Total)

	1962		1973	
	Bank deposits		Population	(2):(3)
Bombay	20.3	17.4	1.04	16.7
Calcutta	13.2	9.6	0.55	17.5
Delhi	14.5	8.7	0.57	15.3
Madras	2.9	3.3	0.44	10.5
Ahmadabad	2.1	1.9	0.28	6.8
Bangalore	1.7	1.6	0.27	5.9
Hyderabad	1.1	1.4	0.28	5.0
Dhanbad	0.2	1.2	0.07	17.1
Poona	1.1	1.2	0.15	8.0
Kanpur	1.0	1.0	0.20	5.0
11 to 15 cities	3.8	3.5	0.42	8.3
16 to 20 cities	2.5	2.6	0.37	7.0
21 to 25 cities	2.3	2.2	0.49	4.5
1 to 25 cities	66.7	55.7	5.13	10.9

SOURCE OF BASIC DATA: Commerce Research Bureau, *Basic Statistics Relating to the Indian Economy*, 1975, table 11-6.

51. *RBC*, p. 51.

of the fifteen largest banks in total deposits of all scheduled banks declined from 88 percent in 1951 and 1960 to 84 percent in the seventies. Because the share of the State Bank declined from 37 to 28 percent, that of the other fourteen large banks, virtually identical with those nationalized in 1969, increased from 51 to 56 percent, with considerable differences among individual banks.

An interesting picture of the local concentration of bank deposits, which should be close to the distribution of total assets of financial institutions, is provided by table 3-26, showing the share in these deposits and in population of the twenty-five cities with the largest bank deposits. The share of the individual cities in total bank deposits provides an idea of their relative importance as financial centers, and the ratio of their shares in deposits and in population is an indicator of the degree of financial importance relative to the weight of city size as reflected in population. The figures show a high degree of concentration in these two dozen cities. Although they shelter only 5 percent of India's population, they hold more than one-half of all bank deposits. Their share in bank deposits is thus ten times higher than corresponds to their population. Among cities, the ratio has a tendency to increase with size, reaching more than 15 in the three most important financial centers—Bombay, Calcutta, and Delhi—which in the latter case is probably also influenced by Delhi's role as the nation's capital. Madras, the fourth and less important center, has a ratio identical with that of the average of the twenty-five cities. The table also shows, and that may be as important as the present extent of concentration, that concentration has considerably declined during the last decade, in part a result of the government's policy requiring the banks extend their branch networks into smaller cities and even villages. Between 1962 and 1973 the share of the twenty-five cities declined from 67 to 56 percent, that of the three financial centers falling even more steeply from 48 to 36 percent, particularly in Calcutta and Delhi. In contrast, the next twenty-five cities almost held their own, their share declining only from 20 to 19 percent.

One effect of the rapid expansion of the banking system beyond the urban areas, together with limitations imposed by the government, has been the declining importance of foreign banks and their branches. In 1976 the share of foreign banks had been reduced to not much more than 5 percent compared with about 10 percent as recently as 1970.[52]

(iii) ASSET EXPANSION. From 1949 through 1977 the assets of the commercial banking system expanded at an average annual rate of nearly 12 percent, well ahead of the growth of national product or the money supply, which grew at rates of slightly more than 8 and more than $7\frac{1}{2}$ percent, respectively. Growth accelerated sharply from 4.6 percent in 1951–55 to 11.7 percent in 1956–60, slowed down to 9.6 percent in 1961–65, took a second sharp upward turn to nearly 14 percent in 1966–70, and further increased to 20 percent in 1971–75 and to as much as 28 percent in 1976–77. These movements were similar in direction to those of national product except for the slowdown in 1961–65. However, as a result of the more rapid expansion of bank assets, their relation to national product increased from the level of about one-tenth in 1950 to around 15 percent in the early 1960s and in a sharp sprint starting in 1970 to more than one-fifth in 1975 and almost one-third at the end of 1977. There was, however, little correlation in annual rates of change of commercial banks' assets and of national product.

The average rate at which commercial banks' assets expanded was for most of the period slightly below that of all other financial institutions, although considerably higher than that of the Reserve Bank. As a result, the share of commercial banks in the assets of all financial institutions kept close to 30 percent until the early 1970s, but then increased sharply to nearly 40 percent in 1977.

(iv) DISTRIBUTION OF ASSETS.[53] The main change in the distribution of assets since independence has been the increase in the share of advances to corporations from about one-fifth of

52. *RBIB*, 1977, S 548.

53. The discussion of the distribution of assets is based on the detailed combined balance sheet of banks in *D-V* and *V-S*. The much more aggregative data in *IFS* which underlie table 3–27, yield somewhat different ratios.

TABLE 3-27. Structure of Assets of Banking System, 1950–1970 (Total Assets = 100)

	1950	1955	1960	1965	1970
			I. Reserve Bank of India		
Foreign assets	52.1	45.4	10.7	6.0	11.5
Claims on government	47.2	51.3	82.2	87.3	76.3
Claims on banks	0.3	2.6	6.4	5.6	11.0
Other assets	0.4	0.8	0.7	1.1	1.2
			II. Commercial banks		
Reserves	10.5	8.4	7.6	5.9	5.3
Claims on government	36.5	32.4	29.2	24.0	20.2
Claims on private sector	47.0	53.8	56.9	67.4	70.7
Other assets	6.1	5.5	6.3	2.8	3.7
			III. Cooperative banks		
Reserves	5.6	2.4	1.3	1.2	1.5
Claims on government	} 94.4	34.1	13.9	10.7	8.9
Claims on private sector	}	63.4	84.8	88.1	89.7
			IV. Development banks		
Reserves	.	.	.	3.7	3.6
Claims on government	.	.	.	4.0	1.5
Claims on private sector	.	.	.	75.9	81.5
Other assets	.	.	.	16.6	13.4
			V. All banks (I + II + III)		
Reserves	4.0	3.5	3.5	2.8	2.8
Claims on government	42.9	43.2	56.1	54.4	44.2
Claims on banks	0.2	1.5	3.3	2.7	4.8
Claims on private sector	18.1	23.3	28.4	35.3	40.8
Other assets	2.5	2.7	3.2	1.9	2.4
Foreign assets	32.4	25.8	5.5	2.9	5.0

SOURCES: *IFS*, Supplement 1972, pp. 242–43.

total assets in 1950 to about two-fifths two decades later, a movement that reflects to a large extent the massive demands for credit connected with the expansion of industry. As a result, the share of claims against the private sector increased from about one-half in the early 1950s to close to two-thirds from the mid-1960s on. This increase was offset in part by a reduction in the share of funds made available to the government in the form of holdings of government securities or of advances from more than one-third to about one-fourth.

The sectoral breakdown of advances shows a dramatic change from the preponderance of wholesale trade, chiefly in agricultural commodities, which accounted for nearly one-half of all advances at independence but to less than one-fifth in 1975, to the dominance of industry, whose share rose sharply from one-third in 1947 to about three-fifths from the mid-1960s to the mid-1970s. The increase in the share of agriculture, which was minimal before nationalization in 1969, rose to more than one-tenth in the mid-1970s as a result of government directives to the banks. In this relatively short period the Indian banking system thus changed from a pattern common in underdeveloped countries to one approximating that in developed countries, a change that was the combined result of developments in the real infrastructure, namely, the increasing share of industry in output and particularly in investment, the government policy of putting obstacles in the way of the banks' financing transactions that were not in accord with the plan, particularly inventory accumulation, and the awarding of priority status to sectors formerly neglected, primarily agriculture, handicrafts, and small business.

A rapid change in the distribution of bank credit occurred from mid-1969 to early 1978, with total credits increasing from R. 36 bill. to R. 160 bill., or at an average annual rate of nearly 19 percent (table 3-29). During this period of fewer than nine years, the share of the specifically designated priority sectors in total bank credit increased from 14 to 25 percent, and that of government food procurement, which may be put in the same category, from 6½ to more than 12 percent. As a result, the share of all other borrowers fell from 72 to 55 percent, increasing at a

TABLE 3-28. Distribution of Advances of Scheduled Commercial Banks, 1947–1975 (Percent)

	June 1947 (1)	March 1951 (2)	March 1956 (3)	April 1961 (4)	March 1966 (5)	June 1972[a] (6)	December 1975[a] (7)
Industry	32.3	33.5	36.3	50.7	62.2	57.6	62.2
Commerce[b]	48.2	53.1	36.5	28.6	21.2	17.4	18.2
Finance	.	.	9.3	5.2	4.1	.	.
Agriculture[c]	3.7	2.1	2.0	0.5	0.2	6.8	10.7
Personal	8.0	7.3	7.5	6.7	4.5 }		3.1
Other	7.8	4.0	8.4	8.3	7.8	18.2	5.9
Total, percent	100.0	100.0	100.0	100.0	100.0	100.0	100.0
Total, R. bill.	4.76	5.85	7.70	13.06	23.47	53.00	100.15

[a]Only partly comparable with cols. 1–6.   [b]Mostly wholesale trade.   [c]Direct loans only.

SOURCES OF BASIC DATA: Reserve Bank of India, *Statistical Tables Relating to Banks in India*, 1968, pp. 24–25; 1975, p. 28; *RBIB*, various issues, e.g., 1972, 1680; *RCF*, 1976–77, p. 97.

TABLE 3-29. Share of Priority Sectors in Bank Credit, 1969 and 1978

	Amounts (R. bill.)		Distribution (percent)		Annual rate of growth 1969–78 (percent)	
	June 1969	March 1978	June 1969	March 1978	Nominal	Real[a]
Priority sectors	5.05	40.84	14.0	25.4	27.0	18.1
Agriculture	1.88	15.91	5.2	9.9	27.6	18.7
Small-scale business	2.86	16.67	7.9	10.4	22.3	13.8
Other	0.31	8.26	0.9	5.1	45.5	35.3
Exports	2.58	11.72	7.2	7.3	18.9	10.6
Food procurement	2.33	19.85	6.5	12.3	27.7	18.8
Others	26.03	88.49	72.3	55.0	15.0	7.0
Large and medium industry	·	61.51	·	38.2	·	·
Wholesale nonfood trade	·	12.79	·	7.9	·	·
Unidentified	·	14.19	·	8.8	·	·
Total	35.99	160.00	100.0	100.0	19.3	11.0

[a]Using gross national product deflator.

SOURCE: Shetty, p. 1421.

rate of 15 percent a year compared with one of 27 percent for the priority sectors and of 28 percent for food procurement. Even in real terms, using the national product deflator, the growth rate of credits to priority sectors and food procurement was spectacular, 18 percent for the former and 19 percent for the latter.

Notwithstanding the recent emphasis on credits to small borrowers, credits (limits) of less than R. 10,000 accounted in 1974 for only 9 percent of the total amount of credits used although they represented more than 90 percent of the total number of accounts. At the other end of the scale, credits with limits of more than R. 10 mill., accounting for only 0.03 percent of the number of accounts, absorbed 29 percent of total credits used. Although the interest charged seems to have differed little among the main groups of borrowers, the banks' servicing costs were much higher for small industry and farmers, with about 3 percent of loan amount, and for trade and individual borrowers, with nearly 2 percent, than for large and medium-sized industrial borrowers, with only about 0.3 percent.[54] As a result, the expense/earnings ratio increased from 1961 to 1975 from less than 80 to almost 100 percent.

Reflecting the increasing importance of advances, the share of the securities portfolio declined from about two-fifths in 1950 to about one-fifth two decades later. Within the portfolio, government securities dominated, but the share of central government securities declined from more than four-fifths to less than three-fifths, whereas that of state government and trustee securities advanced from one-tenth to two-fifths. Corporate securities, with a share of about 3 percent, and foreign securities, which declined from 5 to 1 percent of the portfolio, played an entirely secondary role throughout the period.[55]

(v) THE STRUCTURE OF DEPOSITS. The structure of deposits since independence is characterized by a sharp decline in the share of demand deposits from two-thirds in 1947 to less than two-fifths three decades later. This shift reflects primarily the declining share of money in total financial assets and is partly attributable to the fact that current deposits paid only very low rates of or no interest[56] in the earlier part of the period, econometric studies having shown a substantial degree of interest-elasticity by depositors.[57]

54. *RBC*, p. 282.
55. D-V.
56. Around 1970, the average interest rate paid was 0.1 percent on current deposits, 3.2 percent on saving deposits, and 5.6 percent on fixed deposits (*RBC*, p. 282).

TABLE 3-30. Distribution of Outstanding Credit of Scheduled Commercial Banks by Size of Credit Limit, June 1974

Credit limit (R. thou.)	Number of accounts	Credit limits	Credits used	Percent credits used
10 or less	90.31	7.2	8.9	71.4
10–100	7.99	11.4	13.1	67.1
100–500	1.23	12.0	12.7	61.4
500–1000	0.19	6.1	6.6	62.8
1000–2500	0.14	9.5	10.3	63.3
2500–5000	0.06	8.6	9.1	61.1
5000–10,000	0.03	9.9	10.1	59.8
10,000–50,000	0.02	19.9	17.1	50.1
50,000–100,000	0.00	5.2	5.1	56.7
Above 100,000	0.00	10.3	6.7	37.7
Unclassified	0.03	—	0.3	—
Total, percent	100.00	100.0	100.0	57.6
Total, amounts	55.20 a	137.76 b	79.99b	—

aThousands of accounts.   bR. bill.

SOURCE OF BASIC DATA: Reserve Bank of India, *Banking Statistics, Basic Statistical Returns,* 1975, p. 12.

TABLE 3-31. Ownership of Deposits with Scheduled Commercial Banks, 1951–1972
(Percent of Total of Each Type of Deposit)

	December 1951	April 1956	April 1961	March 1966	March 1969	March 1972
I. Current (demand) deposits						
Nonfinancial businessa	40.2	39.0	40.1	39.9	44.1	37.9
Manufacturing	11.6	14.6	13.7	13.2	20.0	16.3
Trade	25.2	22.4	26.4	26.1	23.3	20.9
Finance	11.5	10.0	14.5	15.3	15.6	17.5
Individuals	29.4	26.6	23.8	20.6	19.4	22.1
Government	} 18.9	11.6	6.7	10.2	4.8	7.9
Others		12.8	14.8	14.0	16.1	14.6
II. Fixed (time) deposits						
Nonfinancial businessa	23.0	18.2	21.0	14.6	11.7	10.6
Manufacturing	·	3.5	10.1	5.9	6.8	6.8
Trade	·	14.7	8.5	6.2	4.3	3.4
Finance	5.1	4.0	7.6	6.0	4.4	5.0
Individuals	54.1	55.2	48.7	58.0	59.4	59.5
Government	} 17.8	13.8	10.7	9.0	8.0	9.8
Others		8.8	12.0	12.4	16.5	15.1
III. Total depositsb						
Nonfinancial businessa	28.9	25.2	24.5	18.4	17.1	14.4
Manufacturing	·	7.1	9.8	6.6	8.5	7.3
Trade	·	15.9	13.6	10.5	8.1	6.7
Finance	7.8	6.2	8.8	7.3	6.2	6.9
Individuals	47.3	48.5	47.8	56.2	57.8	58.0
Government	} 15.9	10.4	7.4	7.3	5.2	6.8
Others		9.7	11.5	10.8	13.7	13.8

aIncludes other nonfinancial business.   bIncludes saving deposits, almost all of which are held by individuals.

SOURCES: Reserve Bank of India, *Statistical Tables Relating to Banks in India,* 1969, pp. 25 ff.; 1973, pp. 25 ff.; *RBIB,* 1978, pp. 77–78.

The changing share of demand, fixed, and saving deposits is, of course, in part the result of changes in the share of the different economic sectors in aggregate commercial bank deposits since these sectors distribute their total deposits in quite different proportions among their three types. Individuals keep most of their deposits as saving and fixed deposits, whereas most of the deposits of nonfinancial businesses are in their current accounts. However, even within each major group of depositors the share of demand deposits has shown a pronounced downward trend, whereas that of fixed and saving deposits has increased substantially, attesting to the power of interest rate differentials. Thus the share of demand deposits in individuals' total bank deposits has fallen between 1950 and 1970 from nearly two-thirds to below one-half. The same trend is evident in the deposits of nonfinancial business. The share of demand deposits, predominant at the beginning of the period with nearly three-fourths of the total, had been reduced to not much more than one-half in 1970. Even among the relatively small deposits of government, the share of demand deposits declined from more than one-half in the mid-1950s, when first reported separately, to less than one-fourth in the late 1960s. Finally, the share of fixed deposits of financial institutions rose from about one-sixth in the early 1950s to more than one-third in the late 1960s.[58]

These changes also influence the sectoral distribution of bank deposits. Individuals have throughout the period held almost all saving deposits, whereas their share in time deposits has shown a slight upward trend, bringing it to three-fifths since the mid-1960s, and that in demand deposits has declined from nearly three-tenths to not much more than one-fifth. As a result, individuals' share in total bank deposits has risen considerably from slightly below one-half to nearly three-fifths. The share of nonfinancial business in total deposits has been cut in half. The decline was concentrated in trade, evidencing its declining role in the Indian economy, and was particularly pronounced in time deposits but hardly noticeable in demand deposits.

A possibly better idea of the penetration of the commercial banking system is provided by the level and trends of the number of accounts and their average size. From 1951 to 1969 the total number of deposit accounts increased from 3.2 million to 18.3 million, or at an average rate of nearly 11 percent per year, approximately nine-tenths of which belonged to individuals. Thus, at that time possibly as many as 1 in 6 households possessed a bank account, compared with about 1 in 30 in the early 1950s, although the proportion was considerably higher in cities, where most bank offices and accounts were concentrated, and much lower elsewhere. These, however, were overwhelmingly saving and fixed deposit accounts of moderate size, averaging in 1969 about R. 900 and R. 3,900, respectively. Personal demand deposit accounts were not much in excess of 2 million, permitting the inference that only 1 in about 50 households had a checking account with an average balance of about R. 2,600, although the proportion again was considerably higher in urban areas. These figures nevertheless indicate a sharp increase in the use of bank money by households, as the number of personal checking accounts had been only 225,000 in 1951, or 1 in about 300 households. Although statistics of the size distribution of personal accounts are lacking, the decline in the average size of accounts between 1951 and 1969 (for current accounts from about R. 5,500 to R. 2,600, for fixed accounts from R. 4,500 to R. 3,900, for savings accounts from R. 1,000 to R. 870), in the face of a substantial increase in average incomes, indicates a shift toward smaller accounts as a result of the penetration of the banking and checking habit into more and more and almost necessarily less wealthy strata of the population and areas of the country. This tendency was particularly pronounced in the 1950s, whereas during the 1960s the average balance increased, at least for current and saving accounts, although considerably less proportionately than the increase in personal income. However, the

57. The most recent and detailed of these studies are those by Khusro and Siddharta in the supplementary volume to *RBC*, 1972, and the article by Divatia and Venkatachalam in *RBIB*.

58. V-S, pp. 129 ff.

TABLE 3-32. Regional Distribution of Banking System, 1973–1974 (Percent)

State or territory	Commercial banks (June 1974)			Working capital: cooperative banking system (1973–74) (4)	Agricultural loans (June 1974)	
	Offices (1)	Deposits (2)	Credit (3)		Commercial banks[a] (5)	Cooperative banks[b] (6)
Andhra Pradesh	7.3	4.2	4.7	6.9	11.0	7.0
Assam	1.1	0.8	0.5	0.8	0.3	0.4
Bihar	4.0	4.7	2.2	2.7	3.4	3.4
Gujarat	8.5	7.6	6.3	13.9	8.2	13.4
Haryana	2.3	1.4	1.3	2.9	1.9	3.2
Himachal Pradesh	0.9	0.6	0.1	0.6	0.1	0.6
Jammu and Kashmir	1.0	0.7	0.3	0.4	0.1	0.3
Karnataka	9.6	4.9	5.9	7.5	8.3	7.1
Kerala	6.4	3.2	3.0	3.6	2.8	3.1
Madhya Pradesh	4.0	2.8	2.3	6.8	4.1	7.5
Maharashtra	11.9	22.2	26.5	19.5	17.6	18.1
Orissa	1.5	0.8	0.6	2.2	0.9	2.5
Punjab	5.2	4.7	2.8	6.1	6.3	6.4
Rajasthan	4.4	1.9	1.5	2.7	3.4	2.6
Tamil Nadu	10.6	7.1	10.2	10.2	11.2	9.8
Uttar Pradesh	9.9	8.9	5.8	9.3	15.2	12.8
West Bengal	5.9	12.8	14.5	3.1	3.9	1.5
Union Territories	4.3	10.4	11.5	0.6	1.3	0.2
Indian Union[c]						
Percent	100.0	100.0	100.0	100.0	100.0	100.0
R. bill.	168.16[d]	107.55	80.65	68.65	5.20	19.70

[a]Outstanding commercial bank loans (direct and indirect finance for agriculture) as of June 30, 1974.   [b]Total of cooperative bank short-, medium-, and long-term loans for agriculture outstanding as of June 30, 1974.   [c]Including small amounts for four territories.   [d]Number.

SOURCES: Cols. 1–3 and 5: Reserve Bank of India, *Banking Statistics, Basic Statistical Returns,* June 1974.   Cols. 4 and 6: Reserve Bank of India, *Statistical Statements Relating to the Cooperative Movement in India,* 1973–74, p. 1.

rapid increase in the number of accounts was sufficient to impart a substantial upward trend to the ratio of total personal bank deposits, although not of demand deposits, to personal income, raising it from 5 percent in 1951 to more than 10 percent in 1970 and to nearly 20 percent in 1977.

(vi) REGIONAL DISTRIBUTION. At first sight, comparing, for example, the share of the different states in bank offices, deposits, and credits with their shares in total population, urban population, or national income, the banking system seems to be rather unevenly spread over the country. Karnataka, for example, to use only states without a major financial center, with 5 percent of total population, and fully 4 percent of urban population and of national income had nearly 10 percent of all bank offices and 6 percent of all bank credit. On the other hand, Bihar with 10 percent of total population, 2 percent of urban population, and 7 percent of national income in 1974 had only 4 percent of all bank offices, less than 5 percent of bank deposits, and not much more than 2 percent of bank credit. It would require a detailed econometric analysis, using a number of relevant demographic and economic variables, to ascertain whether the apparent regional unevenness of the distribution of the commercial banking system can be attributed to economically relevant variables or to historical accidents or institutional peculiarities.

Another aspect of the geographic distribution of commercial bank activities, the differences in the structure of deposits and credits in localities of different size, is provided in table

TABLE 3-33. Structure of Bank Deposits and Credits by Size of Locality, 1974–1975

		Centers with population (thou.)					
	All India	Less than 10	10 to 50	50 to 100	100 to 500	500 to 1,000	1,000 and over
Deposits	100.0[a]	100.0	100.0	100.0	100.0	100.0	100.0
Current deposits	41.3	20.2	28.8	34.4	40.6	40.0	52.1
Government	1.5	0.9	1.9	1.7	2.0	1.8	1.2
Government-owned enterprises	6.3	2.8	2.9	4.7	6.5	6.8	8.5
Private joint stock companies	6.2	1.4	1.7	3.1	3.4	2.7	11.0
All others	27.4	15.1	22.4	25.1	28.8	28.6	31.1
Saving deposits	58.7	79.8	71.2	65.6	59.4	60.0	47.9
Cash credits and overdraft limits	100.0[b]	100.0	100.0	100.0	100.0	100.0	100.0
Government	4.0	1.2	5.5	3.2	11.4	2.9	1.7
Government-owned enterprises	20.5	26.2	6.2	7.8	21.1	10.8	23.8
Private joint stock companies	41.8	16.1	24.6	31.6	22.2	37.7	53.3
All other	33.6	56.5	63.6	57.5	45.2	48.5	21.2
Population (mill.)	100.0	79.0	8.6	2.7	5.1		4.6

[a]R.48.37 bill.   [b]R.56.50 bill.

SOURCE: *RBIB*, 1978, pp. 35–38; figures apparently cover only part of the country.

3-33. Among deposits, the share of demand deposits increased with size of locality, rising from one-fifth in places with fewer than 10,000 inhabitants to fully one-half in cities with more than 1 million inhabitants. This was due in about equal parts to the increasing share of demand deposits of enterprises and of individuals. Among cash credits, private joint stock companies increased their share in the total from one-sixth in places with fewer than 10,000 inhabitants to more than one-half in those with more than 1 million inhabitants. The share of credits to households and unclassified borrowers correspondingly fell from nearly three-fifths in places with fewer than 100,000 inhabitants to only one-fifth in cities with more than 1 million people. These differences, of course, reflect the fact that large enterprises, public as well as private, generally are located or have their headquarters in large cities, particularly financial centers. Statistics of this type have led to complaints that the banking system was draining rural areas and small cities of part of their savings and making them available to metropolitan centers. A recent study found that in two-fifths of 391 districts there was no migration of credit out of or into other districts; that migration to the extent of up to 10 percent occurred in one-half of the districts; that migration exceeded one-tenth in only 8 percent of the districts; and that migration was mostly within states, 92 percent of outstanding credits being utilized within the state.[59] There was, however, a considerable outflow of funds from the four largest centers (Bombay, Calcutta, Delhi, and Madras), which supplied one-sixth of total credit utilized in other localities.

d. The Cooperative Credit System

The rapid development of the cooperative banking system, which is predominantly rural, has been one of the main objectives of the government in the financial field. There were probably at least two main reasons for this policy: first, the supposedly democratic and noncapitalist character of the cooperative movement, and, second, its potential contribution to the increase of productivity in agriculture by making funds available on a larger scale and on terms much less onerous than those of the village moneylender. On paper the results have been outstanding (table 3-34).

The rather complex system operates essentially on three levels—state, central (district), and

59. Tyagarajan and Saoji, pp. 802 ff.

TABLE 3-34. Development of Cooperative Credit Societies, 1951–1975[a]

	1951	1956	1961	1966	1970	1975	Annual rate of growth 1952–75 (percent)
Number (thou.)	125	179	234	213	184	160	1.0
Membership (mill.)	7.78	12.34	24.14	35.61	43.02	61.39	9.0
Working capital (R. bill.)	2.03	3.51	10.88	23.16	42.55	87.67	17.0
Deposits (R. bill.)	0.99	1.52	2.96	6.05	9.54	24.83	14.4
Loans outstanding (R. bill.)	1.23	2.12	3.62	14.81	31.46	59.41	17.5
Working capital ⎫ percent	1.87	2.97	6.85	8.44	10.58	12.06	8.9
Deposits ⎬ of	0.91	1.29	1.86	2.21	2.37	3.42	5.7
Loans outstanding ⎭ GNP	1.13	1.79	2.28	5.40	7.83	8.17	8.4

[a]Includes land development banks.

SOURCE: Reserve Bank of India, *Statistical Statements Relating to the Cooperative Movement in India, (Credit Societies),* various issues, e.g., 1975–76, abstract table 1.

primary (village, or in the case of urban cooperative banks, city).[60] There is a further distinction between short- and long-term credit, the latter being handled by central or primary land development banks. In 1975 there were at the apex about two dozen state banks, sizable institutions with average working capital of nearly R. 500 mill.; nearly 350 central banks with average working capital of about R. 60 mill.; and at the base, 140,000 primary agricultural and 18,600 non-agricultural societies, whose smallness is reflected in the average size of their working capital of only about R. 140,000 and R. 550,000, respectively. The degree of penetration of the primary agricultural credit cooperatives is indicated by their number, one for every four villages, and the number of their members, in 1975 equal to more than one-third of that of rural households.

As a result of the three-tier system, which involves extensive loans, deposits, and capital participation among institutions on the different levels, the volume of loans to members equals about two-thirds of the combined working capital of all agricultural credit institutions, most of the rest consisting of lending and borrowing within the system. In 1967 individual members contributed about three-fifths of the capital and two-thirds of the deposits of the system, but these had to be supplemented by borrowings, primarily from the Reserve Bank and secondarily from commercial banks and governments, and by the sale of debentures, which together were equal to about two-thirds of members' contributions.

Although the resources of the system expanded rapidly over the past quarter century, involving an increase by more than one-fourth of the number of primary agricultural societies and a ninefold increase in membership, during the 1960s and 1970s a government-fostered concentration process reduced the number of primary agricultural societies by more than one-fourth, even though the number of members continued to increase by more than 100 percent. As a result, the average membership per society increased between 1951 and 1975 from 85 to 320, and average working capital rose from less than R. 5,000 to more than R. 140,000. That the government's attempt to create a system of less minuscule but sounder organizations is still far from achieved may be inferred from the fact that even in 1975 one-fifth, in primary agricultural societies even more than two-fifths, of all loans outstanding were overdue, a substantial proportion of which must be regarded as uncollectible. This state of affairs is hardly astonishing in view of the fact that only a minority of cooperatives is in a position to afford even a single full-time salaried employee, and most of them have to rely on part-time, partly unpaid, work by members not trained in credit operations.[61] Similarly, the government's hope of developing the coopera-

60. For an organizational chart of the system, cf. *RBC*, p. 54. For an institutional description, cf. Tyagi.
61. For a discussion of some of the problems faced by the primary agricultural cooperatives, cf. *RBC*, chaps. 8 and 9.

TABLE 3-35. Cooperative Credit System, 1975–1976

	State cooperative banks	Central cooperative banks	Industrial cooperative banks	Agricultural credit societies	Nonagricultural credit societies	Central land development banks	Primary land development banks	All credit societies
	I. Amounts (R. bill.)							
Number (thou.)	0.026	0.344	0.010	139.9	18.6	0.019	0.890	159.8
Membership (mill.)	0.036	0.800	0.049	44.7	12.6	3.3	4.6	66.0
Own funds	1.59	3.60	0.06	4.41	2.43	1.54	0.72	14.35
Deposits	7.24	9.85	0.16	1.13	6.23	0.17	0.05	24.83
Working capital	12.87	20.48	0.30	19.99	10.32	16.67	7.04	87.67
Loans and advances								
Short	6.96	10.76	0.12	10.14	3.71	—	—	31.69
Medium and long	1.98	3.52	0.05	2.87	2.84	10.69	5.77	27.72
Overdue loans	0.43	4.60	0.03	5.63	0.51	0.64	0.31	12.15
	II. Distribution (percent)							
Number	0.0	0.2	0.0	87.5	11.6	0.0	0.6	100.0
Membership	0.1	1.2	0.1	67.7	19.1	5.0	7.0	100.0
Own funds	11.1	25.1	0.4	30.7	16.9	10.7	5.0	100.0
Deposits	29.2	39.7	0.6	4.6	25.1	0.7	0.2	100.0
Working capital	14.7	23.4	0.3	22.8	11.8	19.0	8.0	100.0
Loans and advances								
Short	22.0	34.0	0.4	32.0	11.7	—	—	100.0
Medium and long	7.1	12.7	0.2	10.4	10.2	38.6	20.8	100.0
Overdue loans	3.5	37.9	0.2	46.3	4.2	5.3	2.6	100.0

SOURCE: Reserve Bank of India, Statistical Statements Relating to the Cooperative Movement in India, 1975–76.

tives into democratically operated organizations to primarily benefit the poorer members of the agricultural community does not yet seem to have been realized.[62]

The less numerous, individually larger but in terms of aggregate assets considerably less important urban credit cooperatives expanded at a somewhat slower pace. In 1975 working capital per cooperative with an average membership of nearly 700 amounted to R. 550,000, nearly four times the corresponding figure for rural cooperatives. Working capital per member, however, was small in both types, about R. 550 for rural and R. 820 for urban cooperatives.

Notwithstanding these difficulties, the size of the cooperative banking system increased rapidly, both absolutely and relatively, aided by generous credits from the Reserve Bank and by multifarious government assistance. From 1950 through 1975 the combined, that is, partly duplicated, working capital of the system grew at an average rate of more than 16 percent, far above the rate of 11 percent for all financial institutions. Loans to members, not subject to duplication, also rose at an average rate of nearly 17 percent. The growth rate was considerably higher for agricultural than for nonagricultural primary societies, which expanded at an average rate of 18 and 12 percent a year, respectively. Expansion was even more rapid, averaging more than 20 percent a year, for land development banks, which make medium- and long-term loans. As a result, the share of the cooperative banking system in the assets of all financial institutions increased from fully 5 percent in 1950 to 12 percent in 1960 and more slowly to 14 percent in 1977, after having reached nearly 18 percent in 1970, whereas its ratio to national product rose from 1.8 percent in 1950 to nearly 12 percent in 1977. Both sets of ratios would have to be reduced considerably if lending and borrowing within the system are eliminated.

One of the important characteristics of the cooperative banking system is its regional unevenness.[63] Compared with a country average of 35 percent in the late 1960s, the share of rural member households fluctuated from one in six in West Bengal to two in three in Punjab and in Himachal Pradesh, formerly part of Punjab. The differences are not clearly associated with the relative level of agricultural income but reflect to a large extent historical and institutional differences. In general, the system is better developed in the western part of India than in the eastern states. As a result, the two states of Maharashtra and Gujarat, which contained only one-seventh of the population, accounted for nearly one-third of total agricultural loans outstanding throughout the country.[64]

e. The Post Office Saving System

The postal saving system is the only modern Indian financial institution that has hardly changed since independence in objective or operations. It still serves as a depository for small savings by the poorer sections of the community and turns over all its deposits to the central government's Ministry of Finance. Growing rapidly at an average annual rate of 12½ percent from 1950 to 1977, in part reflecting the increasing monetization in rural areas, the system increased its share in the assets of all financial institutions from less than 2 percent in 1950 to a peak of nearly 5 percent in 1965. In the last dozen years, however, its share has fallen back to not much more than 2 percent, a level already reached in the early 1950s, which is typical in an inflationary period. The annual increase of only about R. 1 bill. in the last five years represents only about 0.2 percent of personal disposable income.

Although the number of depositors has risen nearly sevenfold between 1950 and 1972, or at an annual rate of 9 percent, the number of depositors at the later date was still not much above 4 percent of the population. The fact that the average depositor's balance changed little, remaining slightly below R. 500 throughout the period in the face of a nearly fivefold increase in personal income, suggests that the new depositors had on the average considerably smaller

---

62. For a critical evaluation of the situation in the late 1950s, when most of the cooperatives seem to have been dominated, and primarily used, by the wealthier peasants, cf. Thorner.

63. Reserve Bank of India, *Statistical Statements Relating to the Cooperative Movement in India* (*Credit Societies*), 1975–76, abstract table 2.

64. *RBC*, pp. 151, 178; Reserve Bank's *Report on Trend and Progress in Indian Banking.*

TABLE 3-36. Post Office Saving System, 1950–1972

	1950	1955	1960	1965[b]	1970	1972
1. Offices (thou.)	9.9	12.4	17.1	14.6	18.4	19.6
2. Population per office (thou.)	36.2	31.2	25.1	33.1	29.3	28.7
3. Depositors (mill.)	4.09	5.99	9.21	13.73	20.58	27.70
4. Depositors (percent of population)	1.14	1.55	2.15	2.84	3.82	4.92
5. Deposits (R. bill.)	1.85	2.93	4.31	6.44	9.74	11.19
6. Deposits per depositor (R.)	452	489	468	469	473	404
7. Deposits (percent of GNP)	1.79	2.63	2.80	2.51	2.33	2.10
8. Deposit turnover (percent)[a]	0.46	0.46	0.56	0.52	0.54	0.56

[a]Withdrawals during the year divided by the deposits at the beginning of the year.   [b]Apparently excluding post offices acting as agencies only.

SOURCE: Lines 1, 3, 5, and 8: *SAIU*, various issues, e.g., 1974, p. 309. Deposits are considerably larger through 1960 and slightly smaller from 1970 on than in table 3-17 where they are taken from *IFS*.

balances as the system came in contact with increasingly poorer segments of the population. The velocity of turnover of deposits increased slightly but remained close to an annual rate of one-half, and hence an average turnover period of two years.

f. Non-bank Depositories

A number of nonfinancial enterprises, particularly in a few large western cities,[65] continue to solicit deposits for periods of up to several years, offering interest rates considerably above those paid by commercial or cooperative banks,[66] an arrangement specific to India's financial structure. They were joined in the 1960s by the new hire-purchase companies and a few other finance companies.

In 1960, when statistics began to be collected, deposits of this type were slightly in excess of R. 1 bill. They increased rapidly, reaching about R. 6 bill. at the end of the 1960s, an average growth rate of more than 22 percent, well above that of personal income, the assets of all financial institutions, or the time deposits of commercial banks, their nearest competitors. As a result, their relation to such deposits doubled during the 1960s from about 10 to more than 20 percent. Thus deposits with non-banking depositories must play a substantial role as outlets for household liquid saving at least in a few urban areas. In the early 1970s, the number of depositors exceeded 1 million with average deposits of about R. 6,500, indicating that deposits came mainly from middle- and upper-income households. As a result of increasing government controls, motivated by the desire to protect depositors and to avoid the possibility of these deposits interfering with monetary policy and interest regulations and other factors, growth in the early 1970s has been small, deposits reaching R. 10 bill. in 1974.[67]

g. Development Banks[68]

Development banks, which are generally referred to in India as term lending institutions, were inaugurated immediately after independence by the government through the organization of

65. The most important group of such non-bank depositaries are the cotton mills in Bombay and Ahmadabad, which in 1965–66 accounted for nearly one-third of total deposits of this type (Saravane, 1972).

66. Cf. annual statistics in *RBIB*, e.g., 1972, p. 803; 1973, p. 371; 1975, p. 237; 1978, p. 48.

67. For a list of 392 companies advertising the rates offered for deposits, cf. Commerce Research Bureau, *Companies Inviting Deposits*. Rates for one-year deposits ranged from 9 to 15 percent, longer maturities up to five years bringing 2 to 3 percent more.

68. The history and operation of development banks have constituted favorite topics for Indian financial economists; cf., e.g., Maitin, Saksena, P. N. Singh, Seturaman, and *Report of the Study Group of Non-Banking Financial Intermediaries* by a subcommittee of the Banking Commission, 1971. On installment credit, cf. Doodha.

the Industrial Finance Corporation of India (IFCI). The system was enlarged during the 1950s by the creation of (now eighteen) State Finance Corporations and the Industrial Credit and Investment Corporation of India (ICICI) and completed in the mid-1960s by the Industrial Development Bank of India (IDBI). The function of all these institutions is to provide long-term credit, usually for ten to fifteen years, to industrial enterprises and to underwrite securities issued by them. With the exception of the ICICI, all development banks were organized and controlled by governments or by the Reserve Bank, which in the 1960s became the dominating factor in this field. By now the development banks may be regarded as part of the nationalized financial system.

The IFCI, owned originally in equal parts by the government (now by the IDBI) and by a group of private financial institutions, which now have all been nationalized, was to provide medium- and long-term loans to industrial enterprises in the government and cooperative sectors and thus to assist in the country's industrialization. The State Finance Corporations have similar functions with respect to local small and medium-sized enterprises. The state governments usually put up about one-half of the capital, the Reserve Bank one-fifth, and financial institutions and individual investors the rest. The IDBI was organized in 1964 as a fully owned subsidiary of the Reserve Bank, taking over the six-year-old Refinance Corporation for Industry with the specific purpose of assisting in the development of strategic sectors of industry in private or government ownership. The only privately owned development bank (ICICI) was set up in 1955 in part to associate foreign financial institutions with Indian industrial development, 30 percent of its original capital and three of its twelve directors being supplied by foreign firms.

By 1977 development banks had made available (net after repayments) nearly R. 22 bill., mostly in the form of long-term rupee loans. Foreign currency loans amounted in 1970 to only one-sixth and the acquisition of corporate securities, mostly shares, to one-tenth of total investments. Operations were on a very moderate scale until the 1960s, with net funds made available averaging less than R. 30 mill. per year for 1949 to 1956 and still less than R. 200 mill. for 1957–60. In the second half of the 1960s annual disbursements rose to an average of R. 1.3. bill., and it was estimated that more than one-fifth of total investment in the private sector of industry was financed through development banks. The volume of lending accelerated in the 1970s, the increase in net claims on the private sector rising to more than R. 4 bill. in 1977, equal to about one-tenth of the increase in claims on the private sector by commercial and cooperative banks and by life insurance companies. The share of development banks in medium- and long-term loans would, of course, be much higher.

For all development banks taken together, borrowing from the central government was the main single source of funds with about two-fifths of the total. Debentures, mostly held by financial institutions, supplied about one-sixth; borrowing abroad somewhat more than one-tenth; and capital and reserves, mostly furnished by governments or the Reserve Bank, about one-seventh, again testifying to the dominant role of public authorities in the system. Notwithstanding this potentially unifying factor, coordination of operations among the various development banks and with other financial institutions operating in the same field, particularly the Life Insurance Corporation and the Unit Trust of India, appears as yet to be lacking or imperfect.

h. Insurance Organizations

At independence the insurance sector was fairly small, accounting for about one-tenth of the assets of all financial institutions and representing fully 4 percent of national product, and was privately controlled to the extent of two-thirds of its assets. In the following thirty years, however, the sector grew rapidly, reaching in 1977, by then completely nationalized, one-fifth of the assets of all financial institutions and more than one-sixth of national product.

The sector at independence consisted primarily of a large number of generally small, privately owned and operated life and property insurance companies, a minority of them foreign, whereas provident (pension) funds, though still fairly small, operated mainly in the government

TABLE 3-37. Assets of Life Insurance Companies, 1950–1975ᵃ (Percent of Total Assets)

	1950	1955	1960	1965	1970	1975
Cash	4.2	3.7	2.7	1.0	1.0	1.0ᵈ
Foreign assets	1.4	1.3	2.4	1.5	1.4	1.4ᵈ
Government securitiesᵇ	44.5	47.2	62.0	62.8	60.6	61.2
Corporate securitiesᶜ	14.9	21.4	16.0ᵈ	20.3	23.0	23.1
Policy loans	4.2	3.7	7.1	6.8	7.4	7.1
Real estate	3.5	4.4	4.3	3.0	2.0	1.6
Other assets	27.3	18.3	5.5	4.6	4.6	4.6ᵈ
Total assets, percent	100.0	100.0	100.0	100.0	100.0	100.0
Total assets, R. bill.	2.88	3.88	6.22	10.95	19.54	36.20

ᵃFrom 1960 on the Life Insurance Corporation of India.   ᵇClaims on government and official entities.   ᶜClaims on private sector other than policy loans.   ᵈAssumed equal to shares in 1970.

SOURCES: *IFS,* 1972 Supplement, pp. 244–45; January 1979, p. 180.

sector. The life insurance companies were nationalized in 1956 and merged into the Life Insurance Corporation of India (LICI), which since then has monopolized the sector. Property insurance companies were taken over by the central government in 1972 but as yet operate as separate entities.

The assets of life insurance grew at an accelerating pace, the rate of expansion rising from 6 percent in the early 1950s to 14 percent in the mid-1970s. This, however, was only in step with the growth of the assets of all financial institutions for the period as a whole, so that the share of life insurance companies stayed between 8 and 9 percent in the 1950s and 1960s but fell below 7 percent at the end of the period, thus showing, as is to be expected, a decline in the most inflationary part of the period. The ratio of assets to national product, however, rose fairly steadily and substantially from nearly 3 percent in 1950 to 5½ percent in 1977.

The limited degree of penetration of life insurance is indicated by the fact that in 1950 the number of policies, 3.3 million, was equal to well under 1 percent of the population; that the face value of policies, R. 7.5 bill., was on the order of one-tenth of personal income; and that premium payments absorbed less than one-half of 1 percent of personal income. During the 1950s the number of policies increased by nearly 130 percent, sums insured almost trebled, and premium payments went up by more than 150 percent to about three-fourths of 1 percent of personal income. The trend continued throughout the 1960s with the result that by 1970 the number of policies had risen to nearly 15 million, their face value to R. 70 bill., and premium payments to R. 2.8 bill. Even at that level the penetration of life insurance was still rather shallow. Thus the number of policies was equal to only about 3 percent of the population, sums assured represented only about three months' personal income, and premium payments absorbed not much more than 1 percent of personal income.[69] Ownership of life insurance was apparently very concentrated. According to one sample, the 1 percent of policyholders in the highest income class, seven in eight of whom were insured, accounted for more than one-tenth of all premiums, and the next 3 percent accounted for fully another tenth.[70]

Government securities have always constituted the largest single investment for life insurance funds, but their share in total assets was increased from fully two-fifths in 1950 to more than three-fifths after nationalization. Holdings of private corporate securities were also substantially expanded, in absolute terms, but were kept at about one-fifth of total assets, mostly in the

69. Kulkarni (p. 151) and annual reports of the Life Insurance Corporation of India.
70. Seturaman, without indication of source and reference date.

form of shares.[71] The LICI's investment policy with respect to corporate securities appears to have been rather passive, the corporation essentially limiting itself to acquiring such securities as the result of its participation in underwritings or when offered them by stockbrokers, particularly in periods of market weakness. As a result, LICI in the early 1970s owned shares in about 850 companies, or about one-half of all listed companies.[72] A considerable part of the holdings was nevertheless concentrated in the securities of a small number of issuers. Thus in early 1957 slightly more than one-half of the holdings of ordinary shares consisted of shares of companies belonging to the twenty largest industrial groups, and LICI was one of the largest shareholders, if not the largest single shareholder, in a number of them.[73] Policy loans have absorbed only a small, though increasing, fraction of assets, about 7 percent since 1960 compared with only 4 percent in the 1950s.[74]

Property insurance companies were of considerably smaller importance as investors. Their total assets expanded from 1950 through 1977 at an average rate of 12½ percent, and their share in the assets of all financial institutions remained below 1 percent, although the ratio of their assets to national product rose from 0.2 to 0.6 percent. The security portfolios of property insurance companies have always consisted mainly of corporate stocks and debentures, their share in total assets rising from one-fifth in 1955 to two-fifths ten years later.

Provident funds have been one of the most rapidly growing financial institutions as a result of the rapid spread of pension plans among government and private employees, the latter being administered by the Employees Provident Fund. From 1950 through 1977 their growth averaged 16½ percent per year. As a result, the share of provident funds in the total assets of financial institutions increased from fully 4 to 12½ percent, and their relation to national product rose from 1½ to more than 10 percent. More relevantly, the ratio of the increase in provident funds assets to personal disposable income advanced from only 0.3 percent in 1949–51 to more than 2 percent in 1975–77. Provident funds have thus become an important vehicle of compulsory household saving. Because their investments are limited by statute to government or similar securities, beginning with 1960 about evenly divided among funds for government and private employees, these funds have constituted an important source for financing government deficits and capital expenditures.

i. Investment Companies[75]

Two types of investment companies operate in India, neither exactly similar to the diversified investment trusts or the so-called mutual funds common in North America, Western Europe, and other developed countries. The first of these, already in existence before independence, was generally associated with one of the industrial groups and usually concentrated its funds on the securities of companies in the group, and thus is closer to the investment-holding companies of developed countries. The second, the Unit Trust of India, organized by the central government in 1964, operates on the sources-of-funds side like a mutual fund but differs from a mutual fund in the character of its portfolio.

There existed in 1971–72 about 350 companies of the first type[76] with total assets of R. 1,540 mill., indicating the modest average assets of less than R. 5 mill. These companies are

71. Cf. Mohsin.

72. This information is based on a conversation with one of the chief officials of the Life Insurance Corporation of India.

73. Cf. *Report of the Indian Licensing Policy Inquiry Committee,* 1969, pp. 169 ff.

74. The Post Office Life Insurance Fund, not discussed specifically and not included in the statistics used in this chapter, remained fairly insignificant throughout the period, with assets increasing from only about R. 100 mill. at independence to R. 200 mill. in the mid-1960s, thus representing only about 5 and 2 percent, respectively, of those of life insurance companies or the Life Insurance Corporation of India (*SAIU*, 1967, pp. 202–03).

75. Very little is known descriptively or statistically about these companies.

76. *RBIB,* 1978, pp. 574–ff.; total assets are nearly one-half in excess of the figures shown in table 3-17, col. 7, which cover fewer companies.

obviously of declining importance in the financial structure, as their assets increased at an average rate of less than 4 percent between 1957 and 1977.

The Unit Trust of India was organized to provide private, small investors with an inexpensive liquid instrument to own corporate stocks indirectly. The shares are sold on the basis of the current value of the Trust's assets, partly through the Trust's own four offices by agents who receive a commission of 1 percent and partly through Post Offices, but about three-fifths of the total shares are sold through banks, which are compensated by one-fourth of 1 percent of sales. Although the growth rate of the Trust's assets was rapid in relative terms, more than 21 percent per year from 1965 to 1977, it has remained small in comparison to other financial institutions, accounting in 1977 for less than 0.4 percent of their total assets.[77]

The Trust holds a diversified portfolio of securities, about one-half of which consisted in the early 1970s of about 350 different issues of stock, but astonishingly, for an organization of this type that is, moreover, publicly owned, it does not publish portfolio lists. If evenly spread, holdings would amount to less than R. 2 mill. per issue. In fact, they seem to be rather concentrated on a small number of issues, as the Trust is reputed to own about one-tenth of the shares of some of the largest private Indian corporations, the statutory limit being 15 percent of the capital of any company. Although most of the Trust's holdings of ordinary shares are bought on stock exchanges through brokers, most of the holdings of preference shares and debentures have been acquired directly from the issuers in connection with the Trust's role as one of the most important underwriters. Trading activities are apparently quite small.

At its organization, the Trust sold slightly less than R. 200 mill. of shares to 134,000 investors, or an average per sale of only R. 1,400. Since then, net sales have averaged about R. 140 mill. per year. In mid-1972 cumulated net sales as well as assets were slightly in excess of R. 1 bill. (about R. 1.8 bill. in 1974), and the number of holders had risen to 435,000. The fact that the average holding of about R. 2,500 was equal to more than four years' average income per head indicates that investment trust shares are an upper-class investment. The Trust's holdings of ordinary shares constituted more than one-third of its total assets but represented only a few percent of the market value of all ordinary shares listed on Indian stock exchanges.

j. Indigenous Bankers

Although statistical evidence is lacking, there is little doubt that the importance of the two main branches of professional lenders outside modern financial institutions, the rural money-lenders, by far the more numerous branch about whom very little is known statistically,[78] and the predominantly urban indigenous bankers, declined considerably in comparison to commercial and cooperative banks, their main competitors. Loans by rural moneylenders, who account for the bulk of the funds of indigenous bankers, are estimated to have increased from R. 11 bill. in 1951, to R. 12 bill. in 1961 and to R. 14 bill. in 1971, the slow growth being partly the result of increases in the volume of agricultural loans of commercial and cooperative banks (table 3-52). They would then have declined precipitously from almost one-third of the assets of all financial institutions in 1951 to less than one-sixth in 1962 and to a mere 5 percent in 1971.

Urban bankers, of whom there are about a half dozen main groups, form cohesive communities that usually are united by common caste or geographic origin.[79] They operate primarily in the southern and western parts of the country in the form of sole proprietorships or partnerships of generally modest size. Now probably the most important of these groups, and the only ones

77. This and the following two paragraphs are based on the Unit Trust's annual reports and discussions with its management.

78. The first, and only statistically founded, information on indigenous bankers in the post-independence period has been provided by a report by a subcommittee of the Banking Commission (*Report of the Study Group on Indigenous Bankers*, 1971), which is summarized in *RBC*, chap. 18. Earlier information was brought together in Karkal, and some original information is provided in Krishnan.

79. For a detailed firsthand description of one group of indigenous bankers, cf. Timberg.

for which a few statistical data are available, are the Shikarpuri and Gujarati shroffs, whose business is centered in the Bombay and Ahmadabad regions. Around 1970 nearly 700 bankers belonged to these two groups, with total resources of more than R. 800 mill., provided to the extent of about two-fifths each by their own capital and by deposits from associates and the general public, whereas the rest, sharply fluctuating seasonally, came from borrowing from commercial banks. Their lending takes the form of discounting indigenous, predominantly ninety-day, bills of exchange (hundi) in standard denominations of R. 2,500 and R. 5,000, which are issued by local small and medium-sized business enterprises, mostly in trade, to provide working capital, and are acquired by the shroffs either directly or through brokers. Part of the hundis are rediscounted with commercial banks. The size of the standard hundi as well as the average resources of the shroffs of not much more than R. 1 mill. indicates the small scale of the business.[80] In 1972 the discount rate for hundis, controlled by the Reserve Bank, was 17 percent, whereas they could be rediscounted at commercial banks at about 11 percent. The higher rates are apparently compensated in the borrower's view by the greater ease, lesser formality, and greater speed of accommodation provided by the shroffs.

Although the amount of funds made available by the urban indigenous bankers to business is in the aggregate minimal in comparison with the amount provided by commercial and urban cooperative banks, around 1970 probably well below 5 percent and now considerably less, they are of importance in the geographically limited areas in which they operate and for their clientele of small traders and manufacturers. In Bombay, in particular, the funds provided by the shroffs seem to be on the order of 5 percent of all commercial bank credit and thus must constitute a considerably higher proportion of the borrowing of smaller traders and industrialists.[81]

k. Sources and Uses of Funds

An overview of the sources and uses of all financial institutions for the period 1951 to 1975 and five subperiods on the basis of the Reserve Bank's flow-of-funds accounts is presented in table 3-38 in the form of distribution of sources and uses and in table 3-39 in that of percentages of national product.

The ratio of total sources or uses to national product rose with two jumps, one between the first and second plan period and the other in the early 1970s, from 1.5 percent in 1951–55 to nearly 8 percent in 1972–75. The upward movement of the ratio reflects once more the increasing importance of financial institutions in the Indian economy. Currency and deposits constituted the most important source of funds, with between two-fifths and three-fifths of the total, followed by insurance funds, whose share declined from more than two-fifths to one-sixth. During the 1950s, sales of foreign securities by the Reserve Bank, which are shown in the tables as a negative use, also were an important source of funds. Disregarding this item, the share of claims on the government in total uses of funds declined from nearly three-fourths in the 1950s to fully one-third from the mid-1960s to the mid-1970s. In contrast, the share of loans and advances, mostly to the private corporate and unincorporated business sector (including agriculture), increased from two-fifths in the 1950s to nearly one-half from 1960 on. It is interesting to see that whereas the ownership and control of the system of financial institutions by the government increased throughout the period, the share of the system's resources made available to the government, although high, declined substantially.

Table 3-39 shows the same picture from a different perspective. Both sources and uses of funds increased sharply in proportion to national product, once more reflecting the growing

80. Some of the information was obtained in discussion with the then head of the Shikarpuri Shroffs Association. Cf. also Narang.

81. A few other indigenous types of lending organizations, such as chit funds and nidhis, which operate mainly on lottery principles and are concentrated in the south and west, are quantitatively of negligible importance except possibly in the provision of housing credit. (Cf. *RBC* and V. H. Joshi.)

TABLE 3-38. Distribution of Sources and Uses of Funds of All Financial Institutions, 1951–1975 (Percent of Total)[a]

	1951–55		1956–60		1961–65		1966–71		1972–75	
	Sources	Uses	Sources	Uses	Sources	Uses	Sources	Uses	Sources	Uses
Currency and deposits	40.9	8.3	60.7	1.3	58.0	-0.3	56.0	2.0	60.7	1.4
Government securities	—	58.2	—	77.0	—	43.4	—	33.7	—	35.3
Corporate securities	—	4.0	—	1.8	—	4.2	—	2.3	—	1.3
Bank securities	2.5	—	3.7	0.0	4.2	0.8	6.0	1.5	3.4	1.9
Other financial institutions' securities	2.3	0.9	1.2	0.3	1.5	1.0	1.9	0.5	2.6	0.8
Foreign securities	0.0	-16.6	—	-26.1	—	-0.6	—	4.3	—	5.6
Loans and advances	1.8	38.9	1.9	41.0	7.3	48.0	4.2	51.8	4.5	44.3
Small savings	0.0	2.9	0.0	2.4	—	2.7	—	3.1	—	4.1
Life funds	15.8	—	8.6	—	10.0	—	10.2	—	7.2	—
Provident funds	29.4	—	16.8	—	10.9	—	11.5	—	9.9	—
Foreign claims n.e.c.	0.2	3.2	-0.6	1.6	-0.1	0.5	0.0	-0.2	—	4.0
Other items	2.2	—	2.4	-0.4	1.7	0.1	4.7	1.0	5.1	1.0
Financial surplus (or deficit)	5.1	0.0	4.9	0.9	6.5	—	5.5	—	6.6	1.3
Total	100.0	100.0	100.0	100.0	100.0	100.0	100.0	100.0	100.0	100.0

[a]Does not include urban and rural moneylenders and a few small financial institutions.

SOURCES OF BASIC DATA: 1966–71: *RBIB*, March 1967, July 1969, August 1975; 1972–75: *RCF*, 1975–76, II:18; 1976–77, II:20; 1977–78, II:6.

TABLE 3-39. Relation of Sources and Uses of Funds of All Financial Institutions to Gross National Product, 1951–1975 (Percent)[a]

	1951–55		1956–60		1961–65		1966–71		1972–75	
	Sources	Uses	Sources	Uses	Sources	Uses	Sources	Uses	Sources	Uses
Currency and deposits	0.63	0.13	2.15	0.05	2.50	-0.01	2.91	0.10	4.66	0.11
Government securities	—	0.89	—	2.74	—	1.89	—	1.75	—	2.71
Corporate securities	—	0.06	—	0.07	—	0.18	—	0.12	—	0.10
Bank securities	0.04	—	0.13	0.00	0.18	0.04	0.31	0.08	0.26	0.15
Other financial institutions' securities	0.04	0.01	0.04	0.01	0.06	0.04	0.10	0.03	0.20	0.06
Foreign securities	—	-0.25	0.00	-0.93	—	-0.03	—	0.23	—	0.43
Loans and advances	0.03	0.60	0.07	1.45	0.31	2.07	0.22	2.69	0.35	3.40
Small savings	—	0.05	—	0.08	—	0.12	—	0.16	—	0.32
Life funds	0.24	—	0.31	—	0.43	—	0.53	—	0.55	—
Provident funds	0.45	—	0.59	—	0.47	—	0.60	—	0.76	—
Foreign claims n.e.c.	—	0.05	-0.02	0.06	—	0.02	0.00	-0.01	0.39	0.31
Other items	0.04	—	0.08	-0.01	0.08	—	0.24	0.05	0.51	0.10
Financial surplus (or deficit)	0.07	—	0.18	—	0.28	—	0.29	—		
Total	1.53	1.53	3.54	3.54	4.33	4.33	5.20	5.20	7.68	7.68

[a]Does not include urban and rural moneylenders and a few small financial institutions.

SOURCE OF BASIC DATA: As for table 3-38.

TABLE 3-40. New Issue Ratio of Financial Institutions, 1951–1977 (Percent of Gross National Product)[a]

	1951–55	1956–60	1961–65	1966–70	1971–75	1976–77	1951–77
Reserve Bank	0.09	1.21	1.15	1.17	1.81	2.00	1.48
Commercial banks	0.49	1.43	1.29	1.85	3.33	6.44	3.07
Cooperative banks	0.21	0.93	1.15	1.25	1.28	1.20	1.15
Post Office Saving System	0.18	0.20	0.33	0.18	0.09	0.22	0.17
Development banks	0.06	0.31	0.16	0.23	0.36	0.63	0.34
Agricultural Refinance and Development Corporation	—	—	0.01	0.04	0.17	0.44	0.15
Financial and investment companies	—	0.22	0.06	0.04	−0.01	0.01	0.03
Unit Trust	—	—	0.03	0.04	0.03	0.05	0.03
Life insurance companies	0.18	0.37	0.48	0.51	0.58	0.67	0.53
Other insurance companies	0.03	0.04	0.05	0.06	0.07	0.08	0.06
Provident funds	0.34	0.59	0.79	0.89	1.19	1.48	1.04
Total	1.58	5.29	5.48	6.25	8.90	13.24	8.07

[a]Does not include urban and rural moneylenders and a few small financial institutions.

SOURCES: Tables 3-3 and 3-17.

importance of financial transactions in the Indian economy. The increase was particularly pronounced, as are many other phenomena, between the first and second plan periods and again in the inflation of the mid-1970s.

1. The New Issue Ratio of Financial Institutions

For the entire period from 1951 through 1975, the ratio of the net new issues of all financial institutions, measured by the change in their liabilities, averaged fully 8 percent of gross national product, rising from less than 2 percent in 1951–55 to nearly 6 percent from the mid-1950s to the end of the 1960s, advancing further to nearly 9 percent in the first half of the 1970s, and jumping to more than 13 percent in 1976 and 1977. This upward trend reflects the increasing importance of financial institutions in the post-independence Indian economy, particularly the gap between the first and second plan periods. These figures do not include the issues of indigenous urban bankers and credit organizations or rural moneylenders. The former are known to be insignificant in the overall picture. Even the latter are unlikely to have exceeded 0.1 percent of national product, that is, less than 4 percent of the calculated value of the new issue ratio.[82]

The banking system accounted for nearly three-fourths of total net new issues, the commercial banks contributing nearly two-fifths, the Reserve Bank nearly one-fifth, and the cooperative banking system one-seventh. Most of the remaining one-fourth of issues is attributable to insurance organizations. The changes in the distribution of total net new issues among the different types of financial institutions confirm trends beginning in the mid-1950s that have

82. Both the level and the share of the money issue ratio are very slightly overstated, the former by about 0.04 percent of gross national product for the period as a whole, because money includes one-rupee notes and coins issued by the central government rather than by financial institutions.

TABLE 3-41. Components of New Issue Ratio of Financial Institutions, 1951–1975

	1951–55	1956–60	1961–65	1966–70	1971–75	1951–75
	I. Amounts (percent of gross national product)					
1. New issue ratio	1.58	5.29	5.48	6.25	8.90	6.82
2. Money	0.41	1.00	1.56	1.43	2.02	1.53
3. Nonmonetary household claims	0.80	1.58	1.75	2.55	3.53	2.63
4. Interfinancial claims	0.70		1.34		} 3.35	} 2.66
5. Residual	0.95		0.87			
	II. Distribution (percent)					
1. New issue ratio	100	100	100	100	100	100
2. Money	26	19	28	23	22	22
3. Nonmonetary household claims	51	30	32	41	40	39
4. Interfinancial claims	19		22		} 38	} 39
5. Residual	26		15			

SOURCES: Line 1: Table 3-40. Line 2: Table 3-7. Line 3: Table 3-51. Line 4: Derived from V–S, p. 116; the underlying figures are available only for decadal totals 1951–60 and 1961–70.

already been discussed, such as the decline of the share of the Reserve Bank and of the postal saving system.

It appears worthwhile to attempt to break down the aggregate new issue ratio into a few components, in order to understand the determinants of the level and movements of the ratio.[83] Four such determinants are being distinguished: the money issue ratio (μ); the ratio of non-monetary claims of the household sector (which includes agriculture and unincorporated business enterprises) against financial institutions (ϵ); the ratio of interfinancial, that is, duplicative, issues (λ); and a catchall residual (ω), which includes non-monetary claims of the corporate, government, and foreign sectors as well as capital accounts and which absorbs all other discrepancies, for example, those resulting from the fact that some of the figures used in the calculations refer to fiscal years and others are based on calendar years. Table 3-41 shows the results of this attempt.

For the quarter century from 1951 to 1975, the increase in money in circulation equaled 1.5 percent of gross national product, and thus accounted for fully one-fifth of the aggregate net new issue ratio of financial institutions before, and to more than one-fourth after, elimination of the duplication involved in the inclusion of interfinancial claims among total assets and hence their issues and the issue ratio. Non-monetary claims of the household sector, that is, mainly time and saving deposits and equity in insurance and pension contracts, were the largest component, contributing issues of nearly 2 percent of national product and accounting for nearly two-fifths of total issues including, and nearly one-half excluding, interfinancial issues. Interfinancial issues averaged fully 1 percent of national product, or about one-fifth of total issues, their share being particularly high in the cooperative banking system. The residual, consisting mainly of non-monetary deposits of the nonhousehold sectors and of financial institutions' capital, accounted for nearly 1 percent of national product and contributed about one-fifth of the total new issue ratio before, and one-fourth after, elimination of interfinancial issues.

The distribution among the four components of the new issue ratio of financial institutions showed considerable differences as between the five subperiods. The share of money moved between 19 and 28 percent without trend. That of non-monetary household claims kept slightly below one-third from 1956 to 1965 but rose to two-fifths in the following decade. The share of

83. Cf. Goldsmith, 1969, chap. 2.

interfinancial claims was approximately the same in the 1950s and 1960s, whereas that of the residual declined from one-fourth to one-seventh.

One of the components, household non-monetary claims against financial institutions (ϵ), can usefully be further decomposed into four factors, the ratio of personal disposable monetized income to gross national product (ρ), the aggregate personal saving ratio (σ); the share of non-monetary financial saving in total saving (χ); and the ratio of non-monetary claims against financial institutions to total non-monetary financial saving (ν). These ratios are derived as follows:

$$\epsilon = \frac{CFI\text{-}M}{GNP} \quad \rho = \frac{PDY}{GNP} \quad \sigma = \frac{PS}{PDY} \quad \chi = \frac{PFS\text{-}M}{PS} \quad \nu = \frac{CFI\text{-}M}{PFS\text{-}M}$$

where *CFI* equals household claims against financial institutions, *GNP* equals gross national product, *M* equals money, *PDY* equals personal monetized disposable income, *PFS* equals personal financial saving, and *PS* equals personal saving.

We then obtain the following expressions:

	ϵ		ρ		σ		χ		ν
1951–55	0.0080	=	0.714	$\times$	0.0656	$\times$	0.362	$\times$	0.473
1956–60	0.0158	=	0.717	$\times$	0.0844	$\times$	0.475	$\times$	0.551
1961–65	0.0175	=	0.702	$\times$	0.0882	$\times$	0.434	$\times$	0.654
1966–70	0.0255	=	0.705	$\times$	0.0895	$\times$	0.483	$\times$	0.836
1971–75	0.0353	=	0.689	$\times$	0.1341	$\times$	0.447	$\times$	0.859
1951–75	0.0263	=	0.700	$\times$	0.1058	$\times$	0.450	$\times$	0.789

It is thus seen that the rise of the ratio of household non-monetary claims against financial institutions to gross national product (ϵ) from 0.8 percent in the early 1950s to 3.5 percent two decades later occurred in two steps, one a doubling of the ratio between the first and second halves of the 1950s, once again reflecting the shift from the first to the second five-year plan, and the second, another doubling between the early 1960s and the early 1970s, the ratio rising, but slowly, between the late 1950s and the early 1960s. Of the four components, the ratio of personal disposable monetary income to gross national product (ρ) showed no significant change, given the margin of error in the underlying estimates. Of the three others, the share of non-monetary financial saving in total personal saving (χ) fluctuated irregularly around slightly less than one-half after a sharp upward movement between the first and second half of the 1950s, again, the first and second plan. The rise in the ratio of household non-monetary saving to national product (ϵ) between the first half of the 1950s and the first half of the 1970s thus is due primarily to, first, increases in the personal saving ratio between the first and the second half of the 1950s, reflecting the generally relative rapid expansion of the Indian economy under the impact of the second plan, and between the second half of the 1960s and the first half of the 1970s, during which all monetary magnitudes expanded rapidly, a movement that more than doubled the personal saving ratio from 6½ to 13½ percent within a quarter of a century. It is due, second, to a substantial and fairly steady change in the structure of the personal financial saving ratio, an increase of the rate of non-monetary claims against financial institutions to total non-monetary financial saving (ν), from less than one-half to nearly seven-eighths. This movement once again reflects the increasing institutionalization of the financial saving process and implies a corresponding decrease in the role of government and private nonfinancial issues in household saving. These two factors (δ and ν) thus account for practically all the increase in the ratio of household non-monetary claims against financial institutions (ϵ)after 1955, which the decomposition is intended to explain, at least at the formal level.

5. FINANCING THE MAIN SECTORS OF THE ECONOMY

a. The Government

Beginning with the second five-year plan, that is, since the mid-1950s, the deficit of the central government has been the crucial factor in the development of India's financial superstructure. This has quantitative and qualitative reasons: the very large size of the deficit, which amounted to more than 4 percent of national product for the period as a whole, and the fact that a large part of it had been financed by the banking system or by foreign borrowing, thus strongly influencing the country's monetary policy, the trend of prices, and the balance of payments.

The central government's deficit has not been caused by its inability to cover its current expenditures by current receipts, which were increased from 5 percent of national product in the early 1950s to more than 9 percent in the 1970s, a low ratio but not astonishing in view of the country's poverty. In fact, the current account showed a substantial and increasing surplus, that is, gross government saving (disregarding depreciation allowances on government assets) to the extent of more than 1½ percent of national product for the years 1951 through 1975. The deficits have rather been attributable to capital expenditures and to lending to central government enterprises, to states and local authorities, and to others, which absorbed in the 1950s and 1960s between one-third and one-half of the total expenditures of the central government. The cash deficit, from the financial point of view the most important magnitude, rose from less than 2 percent of national product during the first plan to about 5 percent during the much more ambitious second and third plans and then declined to less than 4 percent in 1966–75.

To meet these large deficits, the central government had recourse to five main sources of funds, two internal and three external. The internal sources were primarily financial institutions and secondarily the nonfinancial sectors of the economy; the external sources were loans, which were practically all on concessionary terms, and grants and in the first few years after independence foreign balances. For the period as a whole, domestic sources furnished about two-thirds and foreign sources one-third of total borrowing. Among domestic sources, financial institutions predominated to the extent of about four-fifths of the total, the Reserve Bank alone absorbing

TABLE 3-42. Central Government Finance, 1951–1975 (Percent of Gross National Product)

Period[a]	1951–55	1956–60	1961–65	1966–70	1971–75
1. Revenue	5.02	6.41	9.08	8.40	9.34
2. Expenditure[b]	5.37	8.66	10.90	9.86	11.18
3. Net lending	1.51	2.54	3.16	2.47	2.07
4. Surplus or deficit	−1.87	−4.75	−4.98	−3.93	−3.91
5. Net borrowing					
Total	1.39	4.67	4.63	3.86	3.38
Domestic	1.23	3.66	2.68	2.35	2.24
Foreign	0.16	1.02	1.95	1.52	1.14
6. Foreign aid	0.16	0.19	0.37	0.16	0.72
7. Increase in debt held by					
Reserve Bank	0.18	1.80	1.13	0.66	1.11
Other banks[c]	0.08	0.37	0.20	0.24	0.67

[a]Fiscal years beginning April 1 for lines 1–6; calendar year for line 7.   [b]Including capital expenditures but excluding net lending.   [c]Commercial and cooperative banks.

SOURCES: *IFS*, 1971 Supplement, pp. 118–19; November 1972, p. 180; January 1979, p. 18.

about one-third, the commercial banks about one-eighth, and the life insurance companies one-tenth of the total, whereas most of the remainder was supplied by small savings certificates and pension funds. The sale of marketable government securities to households and business enterprises played a minor role, which is not astonishing in view of the relatively low yields offered on such securities. The share of government securities held by households is estimated to have declined from 4 percent in 1950 to 2 percent in 1970 after having reached 9 percent in 1960, and the increase in the amounts held between 1950 and 1970 was negligible.[84]

As a result, practically the entire increase in the central government's domestic debt was placed with institutions that either were by statute obliged to keep their funds entirely in government securities (such as the Post Office Saving System and provident funds) or were, or came, under government control or could be strongly influenced by the Treasury or by the Reserve Bank (insurance companies, cooperative banks, and commercial banks, the latter particularly after nationalization).[85] The main exceptions were the various forms of small saving, where the amounts placed depended on the decisions of millions of households. This source, however, provided only R. 36 bill. from 1951 through 1975, compared to an increase in the central government's marketable securities of R. 120 bill. and an increase in its total domestic debt of about R. 200 bill. The government was thus to a considerable extent autonomous in its debt management, although the amount of its debt that it chose to, or had to, place with the banking system, and particularly the Reserve Bank, had considerable influence on the expansion in the volume of credit, the movements of the price level, the balance of payments, and the international value of the rupee.

The results of these developments are shown in table 3-43, which sets forth the distribution of the central government's debt at five benchmark dates. It is evident that the structure of the central government's debt has undergone two significant changes in the past three decades. The first, and crucial one, is the sharp increase in the share of debt raised outside India from 1 percent in 1950 to one-fourth of the total in 1975 after having exceeded one-third in 1970, the result of net foreign borrowing of R. 75 bill., or more than 1 percent of the period's national product. Within the domestic debt, the main change was the decline of the share of marketable securities other than Treasury bills from considerably more than one-half of the total in 1950 to not much more than one-third in 1975, the reduction being concentrated in holdings by nonfinancial sectors. Treasury bills, almost all of which are held by the Reserve Bank, increased their share in domestic debt from one-seventh in 1950 to one-fourth in 1975, and the share of small savings rose from one-eighth to more than one-sixth. These and other changes resulted in a steady and substantial decrease of the share of marketable domestic debt held outside financial institutions from nearly two-fifths of such securities in 1950 to less than 5 percent in the 1970s. To put it in terms of the share of absorption of marketable securities of the central government, practically all net new issues of such securities during the period were absorbed by financial institutions. In the 1960s, indeed, financial institutions absorbed more than the total of net new issues of marketable central government securities, other sectors being net sellers to the extent of one fourth of net new issues.

In addition to the central government, the state governments issued considerable amounts of securities, again not to cover current deficits but to finance capital expenditures, either directly or through public companies and boards. With nearly R. 13 bill. from 1951 through 1971, these issues were equal to about one-eighth of the central government's total domestic borrowing but to more than one-fifth of its net issues of domestic marketable securities. In comparison, the net issuance of securities by local authorities was negligible, being in the

84. V-S, p. 134.
85. The flow-of-funds statistics show the following proportions of total uses of funds of all financial institutions as attributable to government securities: 1951–55, 58 percent; 1956–60, 77 percent; 1961–65, 43 percent; 1966–71, 34 percent; and 1972–75, 35 percent (table 3-38).

TABLE 3-43. Central Government Debt, 1950–1978

| | 1950 | March 31 of the year following | | | 1978[a] |
		1960	1970	1975	
		I. Amounts (R. bill.)			
Domestic securities	17.97	33.63	66.1	139.0	196.1
Treasury bills	3.58	11.06	25.2	58.1	73.7
Other	14.39	22.57	41.4	80.9	122.4
Small savings	3.39	9.82	22.1	39.5	52.6
One-rupee notes and coin	2.66	3.32	3.8	·	·
State provident funds	0.95	2.89	8.4	15.0	21.1
Other unfunded debt	0.06	2.53	9.1	33.1	64.8
Total domestic debt	25.00	52.19	109.5	226.6	334.4
Debt raised outside India	0.32	7.61	54.9	74.9	98.1
Total debt	25.32	59.80	164.5	301.5	432.5
		II. Distribution (percent)			
Domestic securities	71.0	56.3	38.1	46.1	45.3
Treasury bills	14.1	18.5	14.4	19.2	17.0
Other	56.9	37.8	23.7	26.8	28.3
Small savings	13.2	16.4	12.6	13.1	12.2
One-rupee notes and coin	10.5	5.6	2.2	·	·
State provident funds	3.8	4.8	4.8	5.0	4.9
Other unfunded debt	0.2	4.2	5.2	11.0	15.0
Total domestic debt	98.7	87.3	62.9	75.2	77.3
Debt raised outside India	1.3	12.7	37.1	24.8	22.7
Total debt	100.0	100.0	100.0	100.0	100.0
		III. Relation to gross national product			
Internal debt	0.24	0.34	0.26	0.30	0.34
External debt	0.00	0.05	0.13	0.10	0.10
Total debt	0.24	0.39	0.39	0.40	0.44

[a]Budget.

SOURCES FOR I: D–V; *RCF*, 1974–75, I:171; *RBIB*, 1975, S 929; *RCF*, 1977–78, II:192.

neighborhood of only R. 0.7 bill. for the entire period from 1951 through 1971. Most of the securities issued by state governments were bought by financial institutions.

During most of the period government securities have constituted more than one-third of all financial assets of financial institutions, their share reaching a peak of nearly one-half in the early 1960s. If interfinancial lending and borrowing is eliminated, the share of government securities would have been even higher. The share would be further increased by another few percentage points if account is taken of the fact that the available detailed statistics omit part of the provident funds, which are by statute almost entirely invested in government securities and loans.

For the period as a whole the share of government securities in total net acquisition of financial assets by financial institutions averaged considerably more than two-fifths but fluctuated between not much more than one-fourth in 1966–68 and nearly three-fifths in 1956–60. Consideration of the adjustments discussed in the preceding paragraph makes it likely that for the period as a whole the government absorbed approximately one-half of the total consolidated uses of funds of financial institutions, considerably more in the 1950s and considerably less in the 1960s and early 1970s.

The level and the movements of the share of government securities and advances in total financial assets varied considerably among the main types of financial institutions. In the case of the Reserve Bank, it rose sharply from more than one-third in 1950 to four-fifths in the 1960s but declined to not much more than one-half in 1977 as the surplus in the balance of payments permitted the accumulation of substantial foreign reserves. Commercial banks continued to hold slightly less than one-third of their assets in government securities.[86] The reduction, on the other hand, was pronounced among cooperative banks, namely, from 11 percent in 1950 to only 3 percent in 1971. Insurance companies reduced the share of government securities slightly before nationalization but afterward kept them close to three-fifths. Provident funds, finally, always kept most of their assets in the form of securities of, or advances to, governments.

For the nonfinancial sectors of the Indian economy, government securities constituted only a minor and generally declining part of financial assets and an even smaller proportion of their total assets. Among private companies, however, the share of government securities increased slightly and irregularly from one-sixth to one-fifth of total financial assets between 1950 and 1965 but were almost entirely liquidated in the late 1960s. Households kept between 10 and 15 percent of their financial assets in government securities, predominantly in the form of small saving certificates rather than in marketable issues, the share of which declined from 2 percent in 1950 to not much more than one-half of 1 percent in 1970 after having reached 3½ percent in 1960.[87]

Government companies, mostly organized and owned by the central government, have come to play an increasingly important role in the Indian economy, in particular in the manufacturing sector, where they operate the large new plants constructed under the plans. Early in 1970 the investment in ninety-one enterprises of the central government exceeded R. 43 bill., including R. 14 bill. in steel, R. 10 bill. in engineering and shipbuilding, and R. 8 bill. in chemicals and oil.[88] The enterprises owned by the states are much more numerous but smaller.[89,90] The bulk of these companies' funds have been provided by the government—to the extent of more than 95 percent by the central government, partly as capital and partly as loans. Loans of commercial banks have furnished about one-tenth of total borrowings and less than 5 percent of total funds. Thus the use of financial institutions by government companies has been mainly indirect, that is, by receiving a considerable part of the funds that the central and state governments raised by placing their securities with, or borrowing from, financial institutions. The often financially precarious situation of these companies is indicated by the almost complete absence of retained profits.[91]

b. Nonfinancial Business

The nonfinancial business sector of the Indian economy consists of two very different components. The first component, the traditional sector, is comprised of most of agriculture and of trade and services as well as a shrinking part of manufacturing. Very little is known in quantitative terms about the financial activities of this sector, certainly not enough to sketch with confidence a picture of its development since independence or to analyze its present financial status, partly because in most aggregative statistics, particularly in the Reserve Bank's flow-of-funds accounts, this sector is included in the broadly defined household sector. The statistical data available on the financial activities of the most important component of this sector, agriculture, mostly derived from sample surveys, will be discussed in subsection d.

The second component, the modern business sector, may be equated, and with only a

---

86. These ratios are derived from the detailed balance sheets in D-V and V-S. The ratios that can be derived for the Reserve Bank and commercial banks from *IFS* are somewhat higher, possibly because "claims against government" are more broadly defined.

87. Derived from the basic tables in D-V and V-S.

88. Information on individual central and state government companies will be found in Commerce Research Bureau, *Yearbook of Public Sector,* 1971; the figures in the text are taken from p. 23.

89. For a list of state enterprises, including their assets, see ibid., pp. 44 ff.

90. The share of government companies in the total assets of all (private and government) companies has risen from almost zero in 1950 to 18 percent in 1960 and to fully one-third in 1975 (based on data in V-S, ibid., and table 3-45). The increase in the assets of government companies during the 1960s was nearly half as large as that of private companies.

91. Commerce Research Bureau, op. cit., various issues, e.g., 1971, p. 26.

TABLE 3-44. Share of Government Securities in Financial Assets by Sectors, 1950–1971
(Percent)[a]

	1950	1955	1960	1965	1971
Reserve Bank of India	36.2	41.9	74.5	79.8	77.5
Commercial banks	31.6	29.4	28.0	27.3	32.3
Cooperative banks	11.0	12.5	6.2	5.4	3.2
Term lending institutions	44.7	24.1	6.5	5.6	2.8
Insurance companies	61.5	52.8	56.5	54.2	57.7
Provident funds	100.0	99.6	99.5	99.4	87.7
All financial institutions	35.5	37.0	46.7	45.6	42.5
Private companies	16.7	13.4	11.7	19.4	0.6
Government companies	·	·	5.4	6.4	4.3
Noncredit cooperatives	0	0	8.8	8.8	4.3
Central government	31.3	67.9	55.9	56.2	50.8
State governments	59.6	37.9	43.0	23.1	12.3
Local governments	35.2	31.8	39.6	35.1	·
Households[b]	12.8	14.6	15.4	13.8	10.1
All nonfinancial sectors	19.1	25.5	28.0	27.9	21.3
All sectors	25.8	29.4	34.2	33.5	28.8

[a]Includes loans and advances to, and securities of, central, state, and local governments.   [b]Includes small savings.

SOURCES OF BASIC DATA: D–V and V–S.

reasonable degree of inaccuracy, with the universe of nonfinancial companies and consists in turn, of four main subsectors: public domestic nongovernment companies; private domestic nongovernment companies, usually of smaller size and closely held; foreign companies, including the Indian branches of foreign companies; and government companies. Among the public domestic nongovernment companies, the available statistics permit a further separation of a group of between 500 and 1,500 large and medium-sized companies, predominantly in manufacturing, about which extensive data are available for most of the post-independence period; statistics are limited for the remainder of medium-sized and small public companies, as they are for private companies, to relatively small samples and to the period since 1960s.

Of the 35,000 companies operating in India in 1973, four-fifths were private and one-fifth public. The relations, however, in terms of assets or capital were quite different. Public (that is, not closely held) companies had nearly two-fifths and private companies more than three-fifths of the paid-up capital of all companies, and the average paid-up capital of public companies was R. 30 mill., twenty-five times as large as that of private companies.[92] The relatively high share of private companies is due to the private company form of most government and foreign companies. Although numbering only a few hundred each, government and foreign companies accounted for nearly one-half and more than one-tenth, respectively, of the paid-up capital of all companies. Domestic nongovernment private companies alone are not likely to have had more than about one-tenth of the paid-up capital of all companies and an average capital of only about R. 200,000.[93] The main change that has occurred in these relationships since independence is the sharp increase in the share of government companies and a less pronounced rise in the share of foreign companies. This section will be limited, in general, to nongovernment public companies, because government companies were already briefly discussed in subsection a and because

92. *Statistics of India,* 1975, p. 74.
93. In 1958 about 95 percent of all private nongovernment companies had a paid-up capital of less than R. 50,000 and about 8 percent of the total paid-up capital of all public and private nongovernment companies (Nigam and Chaudhuri, p. 7).

TABLE 3-45. Balance Sheet Structure of Nonfinancial Companies, 1971–1975 (Percent of Total Assets)

	All non-government companies	Public companies					Private companies	
		404 large	1,246 medium	750 small	1,001 large and medium	1,125 small	Foreign companies	Government companies
	1971–72	1975–76	1975–76	1974–75	1975–76	1974–75	1973–74	1975–76
	(1)	(2)	(3)	(4)	(5)	(6)	(7)	(8)
Fixed assets	34.9	39.4	28.2	26.0	26.3	21.2	37.4	49.5
Inventories	31.6	33.2	42.2	28.0	35.0	32.9	34.6	29.2
Tangible assets	66.6	72.6	70.4	53.9	61.3	54.1	72.0	78.7
Loans and advances	8.7	20.1	23.7	37.9	30.3	38.2	21.1	17.0
Investments	2.7	2.1	1.8	1.8	3.2	1.8	1.0	0.2
Cash and bank	4.0 }	5.1	4.2	5.5	4.5	5.5	4.9	3.2
Other assets	18.1			0.8	0.7	0.8	1.1	0.9
Financial assets	33.4	27.8	29.7	46.1	38.7	45.9	28.1	21.3
Total assets	100.0	100.0	100.0	100.0	100.0	100.0	100.0	100.0
Paid-up capital	18.9	17.1	15.1	15.4	14.0	15.0	23.7	32.7
Reserves and surplus	18.8	19.7	14.6	6.9	13.0	0.5	21.1	-0.6
Net worth	37.7	36.8	29.7	22.3	27.0	15.5	44.8	32.1
Provisions		.	.	3.4	5.1	2.8	6.9	2.2
Bank borrowings	24.9 }	16.7	23.9	17.7	23.5	19.4	14.4	8.1
Other borrowings	37.4 }	17.8	8.3	13.6	12.1	19.6	13.9	32.0
Trade dues		22.1	33.1	42.8	32.2	42.7	20.0	25.6
Total liabilities	62.3	63.2[a]	70.3[b]	77.6	73.0	84.5	55.2	67.9
Total assets and liabilities (R. bill.)	136.03	83.03	31.76	1.05	12.25	1.80	24.72	112.45

[a]Includes 6.6 other liabilities.   [b]Includes 5.0 other liabilities.

SOURCES: Col. 1: V–S, pp. 129–30.   Cols. 2 and 3: RCF, 1977–78, II, p. 67.   Col. 4: RBIB, 1977, p. 436.   Col. 5: RBIB, 1978, p. 348.   Col. 6: RBIB, 1977, p. 782.   Col. 7: RBIB, 1975, p. 467.   Col. 8: RBIB, 1978, p. 123.

statistical information is fragmentary on domestic nongovernment private companies, which, in any event, account for only a relatively small part of the financial activities of the private corporate business sector.

A synoptic view of the financial situation of the main groups of companies in the mid-1970s is provided in table 3-45.[94] It should be remembered that the combined balance sheets on which the ratios are based are comprehensive for all foreign and all government companies and nearly so for large public domestic companies, but that the data for small domestic nongovernment public and private companies are based on a small sample.

Quantitatively, the picture is dominated by large and medium-sized public and private nongovernment companies with assets around 1975 of R. 83 bill., and R. 32 bill., respectively; by foreign companies with R. 25 bill.; and by government companies with R. 112 bill. In comparison with these four groups, the assets of small public and private companies, which are not known, undoubtedly play only a minor role. The assets of the eight groups, close to R. 300 bill. (R. 180 bill. excluding government companies), or two-fifths of national product (one-fourth excluding government companies), attest to the relatively rapid development of corporate enterprise in India, as does the increase of assets from about R. 13 bill. in 1950, or at a rate of more than 13 percent per year (fully 11 percent excluding government companies), when their assets were equal to one-eighth of national product.

From a financial point of view, the main interest attaches to methods of financing and to financial assets held.[95] Although the picture refers to one point of time, the distribution of assets and liabilities in the mid-1970s should be quite similar to the distribution of uses and sources of funds during the preceding quarter century.

In 1971 internal sources accounted for nearly two-fifths of the funds of all nongovernment corporations, including one-fifth of paid-up capital.[96] Among liabilities, two-fifths were provided by bank loans, about 5 percent each by debentures, term lending institutions, and foreign lenders, leaving about two-fifths to trade accounts payable. Institutional lenders together provided nearly one-half of liabilities. These relationships should not have changed much by the middle of the decade. Differences in these ratios in the mid-1970s among the six main groups of nongovernment companies for which information is available separately, as well as the differences between private and government companies, can be followed in table 3-45. The share of external funds was much larger in small companies, with nearly four-fifths of the total, than in large public, and particularly foreign, companies with less than two-thirds and not much more than one-half, respectively. Bank loans represented about one-third of all liabilities of medium-sized domestic nongovernment corporations but only about one-fourth in the other groups except for government corporations, whose share was only one-eighth.

Financial assets constituted about one-third of the total assets of all nongovernment corporations, two-fifths of which (or fully one-eighth of total assets) had the form of trade accounts receivable. Cash and investments, mostly in affiliated companies, together accounted for about one-fifth of financial assets or 7 percent of total assets. Financial assets were considerably larger in comparison to total assets for small public and private companies than for large and medium-sized domestic public nongovernment or foreign companies. The role of financial assets is, not astonishingly, considerably smaller for the large government companies concentrated in the heavy industries than for any of the groups of nongovernmental companies.[97]

---

94. Somewhat more detailed figures for a slightly larger group of nongovernment nonfinancial large and medium-sized public limited companies for the fiscal year 1971–72 have been published in *RBIB*, 1978, pp. 402–48.

95. Cf. K. G. K. S. Rao, pp. 138–84.

96. The share of external sources of funds differs somewhat from the reported share of borrowings and paid-up capital in total assets because reserves have probably been increased by some upward revaluations, but this may have been offset by the capitalization of part of earned reserves in the form of bonus shares.

97. Cf. Bhole, pp. 453–70, and Menon (pp. 149–72), concluding that "the liquidity position of the Indian corporate sector during the period from 1965/66 to 1974/75 was on the whole comfortable" (p. 157).

TABLE 3-46. Sources of Funds of Nongovernment Companies, 1951–1976 (Percent)

	1951–55 (1)	1956–60 (2)	1961–65 (3)	1966–71 (4)	1972–76 (5)
Paid-up capital	26.9	16.8	13.2	7.4	10.4
Reserves and surplus	22.5	36.7	30.6	6.5	22.4
Debentures	1.7	0.8	2.3	1.3	.
Borrowings	25.2	28.8	34.3	52.8	50.7
From commercial banks	11.8	17.8	22.4	28.9	40.0
From development banks	1.4	1.9	2.6	6.9	7.8
From government	1.0	1.2	1.3	0.7	5.8
From affiliated companies	1.0	0.6	0.8	−0.6	.
From rest of the world	1.2	2.1	2.1	0.6	−2.0
From others	8.8	5.1	5.2	16.3	−0.9
Other liabilities[a]	23.7	16.9	19.6	32.1	16.5
Total liabilities	50.6	46.5	56.3	86.1	67.2
Percent	100.0	100.0	100.0	100.0	100.0
R. bill.	14.5	22.7	33.1	31.0	160.0
Percent of GNP	2.8	3.5	3.3	1.5	4.9

[a]Mainly trade accounts payable.

SOURCES OF BASIC DATA: D–V and V–S, (derived from first difference in balance sheets), for cols. 1–4; flow-of-fund accounts (RCF, various issues) for col. 5.

A better view of the financing of nongovernment companies and the changes in it since independence can be obtained from table 3-46, which shows considerable change in the ratio of total financing to national product as well as in the structure of financing. Although total financing amounted to about 3 percent of national product from 1951 to 1965, the share of nongovernment companies was cut in half in the late 1960s but increased sharply to 5 percent in the inflationary 1970s. In the first period, sales of capital stock and retained earnings provided one-half of total funds, but their share declined to one-third in the 1970s after having almost disappeared in the second half of the 1960s. Among external sources, bank borrowings increased from one-eighth to one-half, an important change in view of the nationalization of most commercial banks in 1969 and the consequent increased indirect influence of the government over private companies' financing and other policies. Direct borrowing from the government also increased, although it remained small even in the 1970s.[98]

On the basis of data for 1973–74, the financial characteristics of public nongovernment corporations show some associations with size. Whereas the ratios of gross profits to sales and assets rise with size, the ratio of net profits to net worth declines, reaching its highest level for companies with the relatively low paid-up capital of R. 2½ bill. to R. 5 bill. The retention ratio falls fairly steeply with size, declining from about four-fifths for companies with a capital below R. 5 mill. to less than one-half for the largest companies. Bank borrowings are considerably less important as a source of external funds for large corporations than for small or medium-sized firms. The cash ratio shows no clear association with size.

The open capital market has been only a secondary source of funds for corporate business or, more correctly, for nongovernment public limited companies, as the issues of private limited companies are not publicly offered. From 1951 through 1976, total public issues amounted to nearly R. 18 bill. This compares with an increase of about R. 13 bill. from 1951 through 1971 in

98. An econometric study of 1,540 firms in six industries for the 1950s and 1960s found that "the main source of financing growth in Indian industries is long-term borrowing against mortgage of fixed assets" and that "the retentions are generally found to be insignificant" (Pandey, p. 379), contrary to table 3–47.

TABLE 3-47. Financial Characteristics of 1,650 Public Nongovernment Companies of Different Size, 1973–1974

	Paid-up capital (R. mill.)							
	0.5 to 1.0	1.0 to 2.5	2.5 to 5.0	5.0 to 10.0	10.0 to 20.0	20.0 to 50.0	50.0 and over	All sizes
Gross profits as percent of								
Sales	7.30	7.21	9.02	9.12	10.07	12.01	11.65	10.47
Assets	9.90	10.18	11.60	10.05	11.34	11.84	10.74	11.04
Net profits (percent of net worth)	14.48	17.01	19.93	14.36	11.40	10.45	8.77	10.24
Dividends (percent of net worth)	3.13	3.35	4.15	4.05	4.71	4.85	4.62	4.54
Relation to total assets of								
Net worth	0.330	0.264	0.279	0.302	0.327	0.395	0.437	0.367
Borrowings	0.366	0.285	0.295	0.285	0.343	0.392	0.462	0.377
Net fixed assets	0.366	0.285	0.295	0.285	0.343	0.392	0.462	0.377
Inventories	0.307	0.384	0.412	0.423	0.366	0.313	0.302	0.346
Cash	0.046	0.046	0.036	0.055	0.035	0.053	0.050	0.059
Bank borrowings: external sources of funds	0.341	0.360	0.374	0.343	0.395	0.279	0.222	0.307
Saving ratio[a]	0.784	0.803	0.792	0.719	0.587	0.536	0.473	0.557
Gross sales (R. bill.)	0.95	6.37	10.73	14.53	14.42	21.44	26.30	94.73
Number of companies	160	415	408	298	172	140	57	1650

[a]Retained profits : profits after tax.

SOURCE OF BASIC DATA: *RBIB*, September 1975.

paid-up capital and debentures outstanding of all nongovernment companies.[99] This figure excludes foreign companies' increase in paid-up capital of about R. 5 bill., because these companies do not use the Indian market. It appears, therefore, that about two-thirds of all new stock issues result in public offerings. The new issue ratio for corporate stock, based on changes in paid-up capital, is low, approximately 0.3 percent of national product for the entire period, rising from below 0.2 percent of national product in the early 1950s to nearly 0.4 percent in the early 1960s, only to decline to below 0.2 percent in the 1970s. Thus the market for corporate issues seems not to have developed since independence, and, in addition, to have lost considerably in importance.

The low and relatively declining volume of private capital issues reflects the shrinking importance of the private corporate sector in the Indian economy as well as the absence until late 1950s of a developed investment banking machinery.[100] Nearly nine-tenths of new corporate capital issues underwritten in the 1955–63 period by commercial and development banks, the Life Insurance Corporation of India, and the Unit Trust, practically all now government-owned, were sold to a large extent by the underwriters to financial institutions rather than to the general public. This gives the central government another means of influence over nominally independent corporations.

The cost of flotation of new stock issues appears to be modest, averaging from 1958 to 1970 about 5 percent, of which a little more than one-fourth constituted underwriting commissions.[101]

One of the characteristics of the modern corporate sector in India, the institution of managing agencies, came to an end in the late 1960s, partly because it became redundant as the financial superstructure grew and became better able to take care of the needs of corporate borrowers, and partly as a result of the opposition of the government, which frowned on the institution because of its alleged monopolistic and concentrating tendencies, and also because most of the agencies were of foreign, primarily British, origin and some remained under foreign control after independence.[102]

In the middle 1950s, when the situation had but little changed since independence, the nearly 4,000 managing agencies managed more than 5,000 public and private limited companies. Nearly 9 out of 10 agencies managed a single company and thus constituted just one more layer above the officers and directors. The 17 largest agencies together, however, managed about 360 companies, or an average of 21 companies. How prevailing the institution was is indicated by the fact that 1 in 6 of all companies operating in India with nearly one-half of their total paid-up capital were agency-managed and that the companies managed by the 17 largest agencies accounted for about one-eighth of the paid-up capital of all companies. In some industries, primarily cotton and jute textiles, iron and steel, cement, coal, and electricity, the managing agency system was entirely predominant, applying to more than four-fifths of the paid-up capital of all companies in the industry.[103]

From the mid-1950s on the scope of the managing agency system declined, partly under government pressure of various sorts. By 1968, the number of managed companies had been reduced to fewer than 700, only one-seventh of that of 1954, although their paid-up capital was slightly higher at nearly R. 6 bill. This, however, represented only about 30 percent of the capital

99. V-S, pp. 1929–30.

100. For an institutional description, cf. Bhatia. For an evaluation of investment banking and underwriting, more positive than that in the text, cf. L. C. Gupta.

101. Bhatia, p. 73.

102. Managing agencies have been another favorite subject of governmental investigation and academic study in India. The most extensive recent publications are Nigam and the *Report of the Indian Licensing Policy Inquiry Committee* of the Ministry of Industrial Development, 1969. Others are, without attempt at exhaustiveness, Basu, 1958; Kidron, and Kothari.

103. Nigam and Chaudhuri, pp. 55–56.

TABLE 3-48. Capital Issues of Nonfinancial Nongovernment Companies, 1951–1977
(Percent of Gross National Product)

	1951–55 (1)	1956–60 (2)	1961–65 (3)	1966–70 (4)	1971–75 (5)	1976–77 (6)
Ordinary shares[a]	0.10	0.20	0.26	0.17	0.14	0.08
Preferred shares	0.02	0.05	0.03	0.03	0.01	0.00
Debentures	0.05	0.03	0.07	0.07	0.04	0.00
Total, percent	0.17	0.28	0.36	0.27	0.20	0.08
Total, R. bill.	0.85	1.85	3.65	4.47	5.74	1.38

[a]Excludes bonus issues.

SOURCES OF BASIC DATA: **Cols. 1–3:** Kulkarni, p. 143.   **Cols. 4 and 5:** *RCF,* various issues, e.g., 1977–78, I:204.

of all nongovernment companies and one-sixth of that of all companies, a sharp reduction from the level of nearly one-half in the mid-fifties when government companies were as yet of small importance.[104] The end of the system came in 1970 when the contractual relations between the agencies and the companies they managed were dissolved by statute.

In contrast to the decline of the managing agency device of industrial concentration, the formation of exclusively Indian groups of corporation, which are similar to American conglomerates, has greatly increased since independence. This development is of importance for financial structure, because an increasing proportion of corporate financing has been concentrated in a small number of economic units. In 1972 the twenty largest industrial groups had assets of more than R. 30 bill., equal to about one-fourth of the assets of all domestic nongovernment companies. The two largest groups—Tata and Birla—each accounted for one-fifth of the assets, as well as the sales and profits, of all twenty groups, and no other group accounted for more than 6 percent of the total.[105]

Individual Indian shareholders hold only about one-half of the total capital of the approximately 30,000 public and private nongovernment companies, and their holdings appear to have declined from nearly three-fifths of the total in the 1950s to somewhat below one-half in the late 1960s.[106] If government companies are included, the share of individuals' holdings is, however, only on the order of one-fourth.

The main change in the distribution of ownership of nongovernment companies shown in table 3-49, is the rise in the share of holdings by financial institutions, primarily development banks and the Life Insurance Corporation, from less than 7 percent in the 1950s to 17 percent in 1971. Intercompany holdings, mainly within groups, have fluctuated around one-fifth of total capital, declining to one-eighth in 1971. Foreign holdings, which are concentrated in a relatively small number of large private limited companies, have throughout the period also accounted for about one-fifth of the stock of nongovernment companies.

Although direct ownership by the government in nongovernment companies has remained small, it had risen to 8 percent in the early 1970s. Inclusion of government companies, however, increases the share of the government in the paid-up capital of all limited companies to about one-half. The government, moreover, has indirect control over the holdings of financial institutions, now practically all nationalized, in nongovernment companies, a circumstance that brings its direct and indirect ownership to about one-sixth in the early 1970s.

104. *Company News and Notes,* January 1, 1969.
105. Commerce Research Bureau, *Monthly Review of the Indian Economy,* April 1978, p. 41.
106. A proportion of individuals' holdings of about one-half has also been shown in a few sample inquiries, as reported by S. C. Gupta, pp. 151 ff., and Hazari, 1965, pp. 259 ff.

TABLE 3-49. Distribution of Holdings of Stock of Nongovernment Companies, 1950–1971
(Percent)

	1950	1955	1960	1965	1971
Commercial banks	1.4	0.8	0.6	0.8	0.8
Cooperative banks	—	—	0.0	0.0	0.6
Term lending institutions	—	0.1	4.0	6.5	7.3
Insurance organizations	5.3	5.2	6.6	9.7	8.4
Companies	17.6	22.2	21.5	16.9	11.9
Government	0.1	0.1	1.0	2.4	7.7
Households	57.1	59.3	45.4	42.8	44.5
Rest of world	18.5	12.3	20.9	20.9	18.8
Total, percent	100.0	100.0	100.0	100.0	100.0
Total, par value, R. bill.	4.73	8.63	12.45	17.66	27.74

SOURCES OF BASIC DATA: D–V (1950 tentatively corrected for a misprint) and V–S.

The government's share is even higher for large public limited companies because the holdings of financial institutions are concentrated in companies of this type. Thus the direct and indirect holdings of the government should be on the order of one-third for all public companies together. Because of the concentration of the stockholdings of the nationalized financial institutions, and probably also the direct shareholdings of the government, in the larger public domestic companies, the direct and indirect share of the government in these is considerably higher. It is evident, therefore, that by now the government controls directly or indirectly the largest single block of stock in many, if not in most, large public companies and in quite a number of them actually has majority control. The government, for instance, is supposed to control 45 percent of the shares of the largest nominally private corporation, the Tata Iron and Steel Company.[107] Although in practice the government's control has hitherto only been potential, it obviously can be exercised whenever the government chooses and must already now enable the government to influence the policies of a large proportion of the large companies that nominally are still in the private sector. A large part of the modern business sector, other than the foreign-owned private companies, which still account for about one-fifth of all nongovernment companies, has thus been, in effect, nationalized without need for specific legislation.

The role of the government within corporate business, although considerably understated because of the government's indirect holdings, is shown in table 3-50, which classifies the 100 largest nonfinancial companies according to their ownership. It shows that one-third of the 100 largest companies were government-owned, including 7 of the 10 largest. One-fifth of the largest 100 corporations, and nearly one-third of the nongovernment corporations among them, were foreign-owned. Of the remaining 47 corporations, many or most are in fact government controlled through direct or indirect stock ownership.

Little is known about the distribution of ownership of that part of the capital of nongovernment domestic companies that is owned by Indian individuals, which amounted in the early 1970s to approximately R. 16 bill. in par value and more than R. 20 bill. in market value.[108]

The total number of shareholders has been estimated at about 450,000 in 1954–55 and at about 625,000 (for ordinary shares only) in 1961.[109] The number of shareholders is not likely to be much in excess of 1 million at the present time, indicating that fewer than 1 in 100 families

107. For slightly different distributions for 63 companies, cf. L. C. Gupta, pp. 145–47; for 228 companies, Hazari, *Economic and Political Weekly*, November and December 1960; and for 70 companies, *RBIB*, 1959.

108. The figures in the text are obtained by assuming a proportion of individual ownership of fully two-fifths; a par value of nongovernment company stock of R. 22 bill. in 1970 (*Statistics of India, 1972–73*, p. 69); and an average ratio in March 1976 of market to par value of 1.5 (*RBIB*, 1977, p. 405).

109. L. C. Gupta, (1965–66): 251, 253; estimate for 1954–55 is by Nigam.

TABLE 3-50. Ownership of 100 Largest Nonfinancial
Companies, Mid-1970s

Rank	Government	Indian private	Foreign
1–10	7	2	1
11–20	4	3	3
21–30	6	3	1
31–40	2	5	3
41–50	4	4	2
51–60	0	8	2
61–70	1	5	4
71–80	4	5	1
81–90	2	5	3
91–100	2	7	1
1–100	32	47	21

SOURCE OF BASIC DATA: Commerce Research Bureau, *Basic Statistics of the Indian Economy*, 1975, table 9-18.

owns any stock. In 1957–58 about 12 percent of all income-tax assessees, who in India constitute only a small fraction of the population, owned stock, the proportion rising to nearly 60 percent for assessees with declared incomes of more than R. 100,000.[110] The value of the average individual shareholder's portfolio would then be on the order of R. 15,000, producing an average dividend income of only about R. 1,000.

Not much is known about the size distribution of individuals' shareholdings. In 1965, a sample covering 1.065 million holdings in about one-half of all listed companies showed that the 92 percent of all holdings with par value of less than R. 5,000 accounted for slightly less than half the value of all holdings, whereas the relatively few holdings of more than R. 50,000 each represented nearly one-fifth of the value of all holdings.[111]

The number of shareholdings in listed companies in the early 1970s has been put at 2.75 million, an average of less than 3,000 per listed company, of which 0.82 million were in 100 large companies and 0.08 million in the company with the largest number of shareholders (Tata Iron and Steel).[112] Because the average number of shareholders is much lower for unlisted public companies and still lower for private companies, the number of shareholdings in all public and private limited companies is not likely to be much in excess of 3 million. This would indicate that on the average a shareholder's portfolio contains about three issues[113] and that the average shareholding has a modest value of about R. 5,000.[114, 115, 116]

110. L. C. Gupta, op. cit., p. 251.

111. *RBIB*, February 1968.

112. Estimates of Bombay Stock Exchange.

113. Although this figure is reasonable in international comparison, it cannot be reconciled with the results of a sample survey that indicated the unlikely median number of shareholdings per shareholder of 15, rising from 8 for shareholders with a portfolio worth less than R. 6,000 to 26 for portfolios worth more than R. 50,000 and implying average values per shareholding on the order of only R. 1,000 (National Council of Applied Economic Research, 1966, III).

114. On the Indian stock market, cf., e.g., K. L. Gupta, 1971.

115. For an attempt at an econometric explanation of stock price movement cf. Sarkar, pp. 151 ff., who finds a positive relation to the profit rate of corporations and a negative relation to government security yields.

116. The most intensive study of the financial aspects of private limited companies will be found in the "Structure of Private Limited Companies in Maharashtra in 1963–64," *Economic and Political Weekly*, July 3, 10, and 17, 1971. The nearly 3,200 companies with a paid-up capital of R. 1.1 bill. covered in the study represented about one-sixth of the number and one-tenth of the capital of all private nongovernment limited companies in India. It was found that about 70 percent of the capital was owned by individual Indians, 13 percent each by Indian and by foreign companies, and 4 percent by foreign individuals. Ownership by financial institutions was negligible. The average company had nine shareholders. In 70 percent of the companies, ownership was limited to one to three families, and in only 3 percent of the companies were more than fifteen families involved.

TABLE 3-51. Components of Household Financial Saving, 1951–1975 (Percent)

	Distribution					Relation to personal disposable income				
	1951–55	1956–60	1961–65	1966–70	1971–75	1951–55	1956–60	1961–65	1966–70	1971–75
Total gross financial saving	100.0	100.0	100.0	100.0	100.0	2.92	5.26	6.35	5.97	8.51
Currency	14.9	20.5	20.6	17.3	12.5	0.43	1.07	1.30	1.03	1.06
Bank deposits	14.8	22.3	31.1	36.2	47.9	0.43	1.17	1.97	2.16	4.07
Loans to companies	.	3.8	5.4	5.3	2.8	.	0.19	0.34	0.31	0.24
Corporate securities	13.5	11.9	5.3	1.3	0.7	0.39	0.62	0.33	0.08	0.06
Securities of financial institutions	.	0.7	0.1	0.2	0.0	.	0.03	—	0.01	0.00
Trade credit, net	.	.	0.4	0.7	} 4.5	} 0.23	0.04	0.02	} 0.04	0.39
Debtors	7.0	.	.	0.8			.	0.05	0.05	
Life insurance	11.9	7.7	10.1	12.4	9.8	0.34	0.40	0.63	0.74	0.83
Provident funds	16.2	15.7	17.6	21.3	20.3	0.47	0.82	1.11	1.27	1.72
Claims on government	21.5	17.5	9.1	5.3	1.3	0.63	0.92	0.58	0.22	0.11
Unit Trust	—	—	0.4	1.0	0.4	—	—	0.02	0.06	0.03
Total liabilities	25.3	23.8	25.9	35.5	23.7	0.74	1.22	1.64	2.07	2.02
Bank advances	14.2	15.7	14.9	28.2	18.0	0.41	0.82	0.94	1.66	1.54
Loans from life insurance	1.9	0.3	1.3	2.2	1.8	0.05	0.01	0.08	0.12	0.15
Loans from government	9.5	4.7	6.4	4.2	1.8	0.27	0.24	0.40	0.24	0.15
Loans from noncredit cooperatives	.	0.6	1.0	0.6	0.7	.	0.03	0.06	0.03	0.06
Creditors	.	2.3	2.3	0.4	1.5	.	0.12	0.14	0.02	0.12
Net saving, percent	74.7	76.2	74.1	64.5	76.3	2.18	4.04	4.70	3.90	6.49
Net saving, R. bill.	8.5	18.8	32.8	45.6	130.7	—	—	—	—	—

SOURCES OF BASIC DATA: RCF, various issues; NAS, 1970/71–1975/76, pp. 106–07.

c. Households

Flow-of-funds and other financial statistics define the household sector very broadly, so that it includes three large groups of units: consumer households, that is, the households of wage and salary earners and persons living on pensions or on rent, interest, or dividend income; unincorporated nonagricultural business units; and cultivators, who operate or lease land, for whom a separation of household and business-type financial activities is conceptually difficult and statistically virtually impossible. For analysis, these groups should be reviewed separately, because the nature of their financial assets and liabilities and their financial transactions are likely to differ greatly; but, unfortunately, the only figures available, apart from those for the entire household sector, are limited data for agriculture, which will be reviewed in the following section.

The household sector as a whole has been the main net supplier of funds in the economy, as the sector's borrowing from financial institutions and the government has for the entire period from 1951 to 1975 offset only fully one-fourth of the sector's total gross financial saving. Consideration of debt to urban and rural moneylenders and other unorganized sources of funds (for which only very rough estimates are available, as they are not included in the flow-of-funds statistics), indicating an increase in indebtedness on the order of R. 20 bill. (table 3-51), would increase this proportion but slightly. However, inclusion of these borrowings would not reduce net financial saving of the household sector because the lenders also belong to the broadly defined household sector. Given the still very low level of consumer and housing credit,[117] one may assume that most of the reported borrowing of the household sector from financial institutions and governments consisted of business-type loans to unincorporated nonagricultural enterprises and to agriculture. Such loans, supplied primarily by commercial and cooperative banks, increased steadily, but with substantial annual fluctuations, from only 0.7 percent of personal monetized disposable income in the first half of the 1950s to close to 2 percent in the first half of the 1970s. Government loans, primarily to agriculture, accounted for about one-fourth of total household borrowing. Policy loans remained small, at less than 10 percent of total reported borrowing of households.

Total gross financial saving increased sharply between 1953 and 1954[118] and continued to grow, although slowly and irregularly, throughout the rest of the 1950s and the 1960s, accelerating its rise during the inflationary mid-1970s. Its ratio to personal disposable monetized income advance from just below 3 percent in 1951–55 to an average of about 6 percent in 1956–70, but increased in the first half of the 1970s to 8½ percent and reached 11½ percent in 1976 and 1977. The net saving ratio rose meanwhile from not much more than 2 to 9½ percent of personal disposable income. This may be regarded as remarkable in a country with as low a real income per head as India in which most of household saving remained within the discretion of the population.

Among types of gross financial household saving, currency, with between one-eighth and one-fifth of the total, and money, including demand deposits that rose from one-fifth in the 1950s to one-third in the 1960s, played important roles. The high, though declining, ratios of currency to deposits and the persistently high ratios to total gross financial saving and to disposable income of more than 1 percent for the period as a whole are characteristic of a low-

117. Institutional housing finance is still in its infancy. In 1976 outstandings were estimated at about R. 6 bill., up from not much more than R. 2 bill. in 1970, or at only about 1 percent of the value of dwellings and the underlying land. Even if it related to only the value of urban dwellings and including the loans made by government and public employers to their employees, the ratio would still be very low, probably well below 5 percent of the value of dwellings. About one-half of the total is supplied by the Life Insurance Corporation of India directly or through housing cooperatives, and there are no private organizations specializing in financing housing construction (Cf. Chitre, pp. 140 ff.)

118. The reasons for this sudden increase of gross financial saving from 1.4 percent of personal disposable monetized income in 1953 (and an average of less than 1 percent in 1950–53) to 4.6 percent in 1954, never to fall thereafter below 4 percent, are not clear. In particular, personal disposable income was somewhat lower in 1954 than in 1953.

income, predominantly rural country. The bulk of all household financial saving had the form of deposits mainly time and saving deposits, with financial institutions. The share of these deposits in total financial saving increased from only one-seventh in 1951–55 to two-fifths in 1971–75. As a result, their ratio to disposable personal income rose sharply from less than ½ percent to 4 percent. Saving through insurance organizations contributed with little change fully one-fourth of total gross financial saving, rising from 0.8 to 2.6 percent of personal disposable income. Both saving through life insurance and through provident funds, the latter the only important type of compulsory household saving, increased more rapidly than personal income, although only roughly in step with total gross financial saving. The category of claims against the government, which includes government securities, special types of small saving certificates, and deposits with the postal saving system, hardly grew at all in absolute amount until the 1970s. As a result, both its share in total gross financial saving and its relation to personal income declined sharply between 1951–55 and 1970–75, the first from more than one-fifth to virtually zero, the latter from about 0.6 to 0.1 of personal disposable income. Indeed, in the case of ordinary government securities not only relative but absolute holdings also declined. Saving through the acquisition of corporate securities declined even in absolute amount, and their share in total financial saving fell from 14 percent in 1951–55 to 5 percent in 1961–65 and almost disappeared since the late 1960s, their ratio to personal income falling from a high of 0.6 percent in the second half of the 1960s to below 0.1 percent. The predominance of indirect household saving through financial institutions thus became further accentuated, exceeding nine-tenths toward the end of the period.

Little is known about the distribution of income of financial assets among the non-agricultural population.[119] There is no agreement about the exact shape of the income distribution or on the question of whether income distribution has substantially changed since independence, and if so in what direction and to what extent. It is certain, however, that the distribution is very unequal. Thus, it has been estimated that in 1971–72 more than one-third of the urban population had monthly expenditures of less than R. 18 (at that time $2.40 at the rate of exchange, although more than three times as much in purchasing power), whereas the expenditures of the top tenth of the urban population exceeded R. 60 per month.[120]

Numerous attempts have been made to explain the saving behavior of Indian households, using either time series for aggregate household sector saving or cross-section data derived from relatively small samples of households.[121] These analyses are only of little use in understanding the participation of households in the financial process because they try to explain aggregate household saving, often without distinguishing between urban and rural households, rather than household financial saving, that is, their acquisition of financial assets and their borrowing. One of the few studies devoted to financial saving, based on time series for the period 1950 to 1966,

119. An idea of the material available and its analysis is provided by fourteen articles and nine abstracts on various aspects of income distribution in India in *Indian Economic Journal* 25, no. 2 (1977).

120. R. K. Choudhury, *Indian Economic Journal* 25, no. 2 (1977):38, using data of Madagli.

121. Among the numerous analyses of saving in post-independence India, most of which are based on data of the 1950s or early 1960s, the following may be mentioned, again without any attempt at comprehensive coverage: V. V. Bhatt, "Savings and Capital Formation in India," *Economic Development and Cultural Change* 7, no. 3 (April 1959); I. Friend, "The Propensities to Save in India," in *Problems of Economic Development,* 1966; K. L. Gupta, "Personal Saving in Developing Nations—Further Evidence," *Economic Record* 46 (1970), "On Some Determinants of Rural and Urban Household Saving Behaviour," *Economic Record* 46 (1970), and "Household Savings in Financial Assets—A Case Study of India," *Indian Economic Journal,* 1970; V. H. Joshi, "Saving Behaviour in India," *Indian Economic Journal* 17 (1969–70); D. R. Khatkhate and K. L. Deshpande, "Estimates of Saving and Investment in the Indian Economy: 1950–51 to 1962–63," in P. C. Malhotra and A. C. Minocha, eds., *Studies in Capital Formation, Savings, and Investment in a Developing Economy,* 1971; A. C. Minocha, "Estimates of Saving and Captial Formation in India—A Review of Existing Estimates and Methodology," in Malhotra and Minocha, eds., *Studies in Capital Formation;* National Council of Applied Economic Research, *Urban Income and Saving,* 1962, and *Saving in India—A Monograph,* 1965; P. G. K. Panikar, *Rural Savings in India,* 1970; K. N. Raj, "The Marginal Rate of Saving in the Indian Economy," *Oxford Economic Papers* 14 (1961); *Reserve Bank of India Bulletin,* March 1960, August 1961, March 1965.

TABLE 3-52. Agricultural Debt by Type of Lender, 1951, 1961, and 1971 (Percent)

Outstandings, June 30	1951 (1)	1961 (2)	1971 (3)
Government	3.7	6.6	6.7
Cooperative banks	} 3.5	10.4	20.1
Commercial banks		0.3	2.2[a]
Moneylenders, agricultural	25.2	47.0	23.1
Moneylenders, professional	46.4	13.8	13.8
Trade and commission agents	5.1	7.5	8.7
Landlords	3.5	1.1	8.6
Relatives and friends	11.5	5.8	13.8
Others	1.1	7.5	3.0
Total, percent	100.0	100.0	100.0
Total, R. bill.	15.5	19.6	37.5

[a]The absolute amount of R. 0.8 bill. is well below the amount of loans to agriculture shown in commercial banking statistics, which is somewhat above R.2 bill., either because of underreporting in sample survey or because of more comprehensive definition of agriculture in banking statistics.

SOURCES: **Col. 1:** Reserve Bank of India, *All-India Rural Credit Survey*, 1954, vol. 1, pt. 2, p. 3. **Cols. 2 and 3:** Reserve Bank of India, *Indebtedness of Rural Households and Availability of Institutional Finance*, p. 36, 40.

found as the main determinants of saving (all items expressed in constant prices) a three-year average of income per head, the ratio of agricultural to nonagricultural prices, and changes in the price level and interest rates.[122] Of these four determinants, saving was positively related to the level of income and interest rates and negatively to inflation and the relative prices of agricultural commodities. The analysis was limited to total net financial saving without distinguishing the acquisition of financial assets from the incurrence of indebtedness and without separating the different types of financial assets or liabilities. For aggregate financial saving, a high marginal rate was found, the value usually exceeding 20 percent, but the specific ratio depended on the form of the estimating equation used. An intensive and up-to-date econometric analysis of financial saving of Indian households distinguishing different types of households, in particular separating rural from urban households and wage-earner from small entrepreneurial households, and separating the main forms of financial assets and debts is apparently still to be done.

d. Rural India

Although agriculture has continued to employ more than two-thirds of the labor force and to contribute two-fifths of its national product, the importance of agricultural finance, and particularly of its noninstitutional part, has declined substantially, a result primarily of the rapid expansion of nonagricultural credit. Thus, the volume of agricultural credit has fallen from nearly twice total domestic institutional credit in 1951 to about two-thirds in 1961 and less than one-third in 1971.

According to the estimates of the official sample agricultural debt surveys conducted in the early 1950s, 1960s, and 1970s,[123] total agricultural debt increased from less than R. 16 bill. in 1951 to R. 20 bill. in 1961 and to R. 38 bill. in 1971, or at an annual average rate of 4½ percent, rising from fully 2 percent in the first decade to nearly 7 percent in the second. It thus fell from less than one-third of agricultural product in 1951 to one-fourth in 1961 and to less than one-fifth

122. K. L. Gupta, 1970.
123. The results of the 1951 Survey have been published in three volumes (*All-India Rural Credit Survey*, 1956 and 1957). For a summary of the results of the 1962 Survey, cf. *RBIB*, September 1965. For the 1971 Survey, cf. Reserve Bank of India, *All-India Debt and Investment Survey 1971–72*, p. 197, and *Indebtedness of Rural Households and Availability of Institutional Finance*.

in 1971. Practically all the increase in debt was attributable to cultivators, the debt of agricultural laborers and rural artisans remaining in the neighborhood of R. 2 bill. and falling from about 15 to only 6 percent of total agricultural debt. Although burdensome for many borrowers, for the entire country the ratio of debt to total farm households' assets was astonishingly low, less than 5 percent in 1971.

The outstanding characteristic of agricultural finance and debt is the small, though now rapidly increasing, share accounted for by financial institutions. In 1951 the cooperative and commercial banking system held less than 4 percent of the total agricultural debt, most of which was being supplied by cooperatives. A decade later these two types of institutions held more than one-tenth of the total debt, thus having supplied about one-third of the increase in the debt between 1951 and 1961. Both cooperative and commercial banks, particularly the latter, rapidly expanded their credit to agriculture during the 1960s with the result that together they accounted for more than one-fifth of total debt outstanding in 1971 and for more than one-third of the increase in debt between 1961 and 1971. The government, which administers numerous schemes of credit to agriculture, often at concessionary interest rates, increased its share from 4 percent in 1951 to nearly 7 percent in 1961 and 1971. This still left nearly nine-tenths of the total agricultural debt in 1951, about five-sixths in 1961, and about 30 percent in 1971 to be supplied by professional rural moneylenders,[124] on the one hand, and by landlords, suppliers, relatives, friends, and other unorganized lenders, on the other. Although the share of moneylenders declined between 1951 and 1961 from 72 to 61 percent and fell to 37 percent in 1971, that of unorganized lenders rose from about one-fifth in 1951 and 1961 to one-third in 1971.[125]

The present status of agricultural debt is not entirely clear. As part of the reform legislation of 1975, an indeterminate moratorium was proclaimed for agricultural debt, both the capital and interest payments, not owed to financial institutions. This should have affected a total of nearly R. 30 bill. of debt. It remains to be seen how completely the debtors will take advantage of this moratorium, given the unfavorable effect repudiation would have on their future chances of borrowing from the same sources.[126]

A basic problem of Indian agricultural finance is the high ratio of total debt contracted for nonproductive purposes. The 1961 survey found that less than one-fourth of total agricultural debt had been raised to pay for capital expenditures in farm business, and even the inclusion of current farm business expenditures would raise the share to less than one-third. Household expenditures, on the other hand, were given as the use of slightly more than half of total debt outstanding, the ratio being close to two-thirds for noncultivators, and another 5 percent for repayment of debt. In line with this character of the bulk of agricultural debt is its short maturity, less than one-sixth having a maturity of more than five years and nearly two-fifths being due within one year, and the fact that more than 70 percent was made on personal security and less than 20 percent on mortgages. The high proportion of unproductive debt is particularly serious in view of the high interest rates reported, which may well understate the true burden—a median of more than 9 percent, an average of nearly 11 percent, and a share of nearly one-third of loans with an interest rate in excess of 12½ percent.

As with many other characteristics of Indian agriculture, regional differences in indebtedness are substantial (table 3-53). Thus in 1971 the average debt per household ranged, disregarding small territories from R. 160 in Orissa to R. 1,040 in Punjab, compared with a country

124. An idea of the penetration of unorganized lenders is given by a survey of 276 villages in West Bengal, Bihar, and the eastern part of the Uttar Pradesh, according to which nearly one-half of the villages in 1975–76 had their moneylenders and more than four-fifths had money-lending farmers (Bardhan and Rudra, p. 371.)

125. The sharp increase in the share of institutional lenders is limited to cultivators, who account for most of the debt. Among noncultivators, the share of institutional lenders remained close to one-tenth.

126. Cf. the statement by A. K. Ganguli, (p. 41) that the drying up of the traditional sources of rural credit in "the wake of the declaration of a moratorium on rural debts has created a vacuum."

TABLE 3-53. Regional Differences in Agricultural Debt, June 1971

State	Proportion of households reporting debt (1)	Average debt Reporting households (2)	Average debt All households (3)	Total debt (4)	Share of Organized lenders (5)	Share of Loans for farm business (6)	Assets per household (7)	Debt/asset ratio (8)
Andhra Pradesh	115	114	131	11.4	47	98	71	183
Assam	61	60	36	0.9	118	83	69	53
Bihar	93	64	59	6.6	37	45	113	52
Gujarat	115	165	191	9.4	161	122	114	168
Haryana	85	221	189	2.6	90	118	240	79
Himachal Pradesh	91	130	118	0.7	82	57	200	59
Jammu and Kashmir	115	63	73	0.5	70	27	135	54
Karnataka	119	126	150	8.1	102	105	89	169
Kerala	83	90	75	2.5	150	58	103	73
Madya Pradesh	97	83	81	6.2	108	110	93	87
Maharashtra	109	111	121	9.5	231	162	103	118
Manipur	38	50	19	0.0	49	19	65	30
Meghalaya	14	17	2	0.0	26	94	53	4
Orissa	71	47	33	1.6	103	58	53	63
Punjab	132	162	213	4.3	123	105	281	76
Rajasthan	135	136	183	7.5	32	59	113	163
Tamil Nadu	120	120	145	12.1	76	122	60	240
Tripura	95	51	49	0.1	45	55	57	86
Uttar Pradesh	90	78	71	12.6	80	83	120	59
West Bengal	84	46	39	3.0	105	85	65	60
All India, percent	100	100	100	100	100	100	100	100
All India, amounts	41	1179	487	37.5	29	45	11310	4.31
Unit	percent	R.	R.	R. bill.	percent	percent	R.	percent

SOURCES: **Cols. 1–6:** Reserve Bank of India, *Statistical Tables Relating to Cash Dues Outstanding Against Rural Households as on 30th of June, 1971*: **Cols. 7 and 8:** Reserve Bank of India, unpublished tables.

average of R. 490; and the debt-asset ratio extended from 2.4 percent in Assam and Bihar to 10.3 percent in Tamil Nadu, compared with a country average of 4.3 percent. With the exception of the proportion of households in debt, the range between the extreme state values is well in excess of the country average, thus indicating wide regional dispersion. An even wider dispersion is shown in the amount of agricultural loans of commercial and cooperative banks per rural inhabitant, which ranges from R. 6 in West Bengal to R. 107 in Gujarat.[127]

Much less is known with any degree of confidence about the size and structure of agricultural saving, particularly the acquisition of financial assets.[128] On the basis of the evidence, mostly derived from sample surveys, it has been concluded that "only an insignificant proportion of savings of rural families is held in the form of financial assets."[129] The absolute level of the available estimates varies so much that little confidence can be put in any of them. All, however, indicate that agricultural, or even all rural, households account for only a small proportion, well below their share in population or income, of total financial saving or of all financial assets outstanding in the country or held by all households. One rough estimate puts the volume of financial saving of the rural population at fully one-fourth of that of all Indian households in the early 1960s as well as in 1970–71. About one-half of total financial saving of rural households is estimated to have been, averaging figures for 1960–61 and 1971–72, in the form of contributions to life insurance companies and provident funds, about one-fourth in currency, very little in deposits with financial institutions, about one-seventh in small saving certificates of the government, and about one-tenth in the shares of cooperatives. These ratios are fairly similar to those for urban households.[130] Another comparison for the early 1960s indicates larger differences, which may have been attenuated since then.[131] In particular, it shows a much higher share of notes and coins in rural household saving, which is probably the result of the extraordinarily low level of average total financial saving per household in the rural sector, the lack of familiarity with financial instruments by most of the rural population, and the absence until the late 1960s of branches of financial institutions in almost all villages. These factors may also explain the considerably higher share of "small savings" (special government small denomination certificates of deposit and postal saving deposits) among the rural population, about one-fifth of total financial saving compared with about one-tenth for the nonrural population. These differences are offset by the much lower shares of saving through insurance, securities, and particularly through bank deposits in total financial saving of the rural population. Thus the share of bank deposits of only one-eighth of saving for rural households compares with one three times as large for urban households, a difference that should to a good extent have been attributable to the scarcity of branches of commercial banks in rural areas as late as the early 1960s.

Considerably more reliable, detailed, and recent information is available on the holdings of a few important types of financial assets from the large-scale decadal agricultural financial sample surveys. Some results, summarized in table 3-54,[132] indicate for all 78 million agricultural households in mid-1971 total holdings of deposits of R. 8.3 bill., of shares in cooperatives of R. 1.6 bill. and of receivables (partly debt of other rural households) of R. 3.8 bill., a total of R. 13.6 bill. (not including, of course, currency and hoards of precious metals, which are

127. *RBC,* pp. 151, 178.

128. Cf. Divatia, 1977, pp. 1–57.

129. Panikar, p. 164.

130. Sarkar and Murthy, 1977, p. 174.

131. For rural households this comparison is based on National Council of Applied Economic Research, *Rural Household Saving Survey,* 1962, Summary Statement, p. 7, and for all households, on D-V, 1961–65 average.

132. For some analysis of the data, cf. Divatia and Shaw, pp. 84–135, and Reserve Bank, *Indebtedness of Rural Households.*

TABLE 3-54. Financial Assets and Liabilities of Rural Households, Mid–1971[a,b]
(R per household, except cols. 1 and 8)

Assets per household (R. thou.)	Percent of households	Financial assets				Liabilities[c]	Net financial assets	Share of financial assets (percent)[d]
		Deposits	Coop shares	Receivables[c]	Total			
Below 0.5	11.4	3	0	1	4	76	−72	1.7
0.5–1.0	8.4	10	1	3	14	129	−115	1.9
1.0–2.5	15.5	38	3	6	47	217	−170	2.8
2.5–5.0	16.1	60	6	12	78	298	−220	2.1
5.0–10.0	18.3	69	11	18	98	412	−314	1.4
10.0–15.0	9.7	92	21	36	149	572	−423	1.2
15.0–20.0	5.7	98	26	65	189	677	−488	1.1
20.0–30.0	6.2	189	43	85	317	973	−656	1.3
30.0–50.0	4.8	245	75	149	469	1329	−860	1.2
50.0–100.0	2.9	499	141	255	895	1969	−1074	1.3
Above 100.0	1.0	2464	266	1438	4168	3865	+303	2.6
All households	100.0							
percent		106	20	48	174	491	−317	1.5
R. bill.[e]		8.26	1.56	3.75	13.56	38.25	−24.69	—

[a]Notes, coins, and precious metals not included.   [b]R. per household except cols. 1 and 8.   [c]Cash, receivables and liabilities only.   [d]Percent of total assets.   [e]Based on 77.9 million households.

SOURCE OF BASIC DATA: Reserve Bank of India. All-India Debt and Investment Survey 1971–72, Statistical Tables, 2:18.

many times larger than the three reported assets,[133] and holdings of other unreported financial assets, which are probably very small). To put these figures in perspective, it is well to realize, first, their absolute and relative smallness, R. 174 per household ($23 at the exchange rate); 1.5 percent of total assets of rural households; and not much more than one-third of their debt. The penetration, or lack of it, of financial assets holdings in rural India is indicated by the fact that only 1 in 7 farm households held any deposits, 1 in 15 owned shares in cooperatives, and 1 in 30 had any other claims. The proportion holding some currency would, of course, be near to unity, and that of owning some gold or silver fairly high.

The sample surveys also permit a rough estimate of the financial saving rate of the agricultural population for the two decades between 1951 and 1971, if it is assumed that asset holdings in 1951 must have been very small compared with those of 1975, given the rapid rise in personal disposable agricultural income over the period from about R. 35 bill. to R. 140 bill. On that assumption, saving through the three types of financial assets covered by the sample surveys in the two decades ending in 1971 would have been slightly below one-half of 1 percent of agricultural personal disposable income, of which about three-fifths had the form of deposits, three-tenths that of other claims, and one-tenth that of shares in cooperatives. This compares with a rate of saving through the three financial instruments by all households of fully 2 percent. The difference for all financial saving would probably be larger, as agricultural households probably hold fewer government and private securities and have less equity in life insurance and provident funds. On the other hand, agricultural households are likely to hold relatively more currency. Finally, the precious metal hoards of the agricultural population probably are considerably larger than those of town dwellers.

There are, of course, substantial differences in these relationships among poorer and wealthier rural households (table 3-54). Thus total reported financial assets of the richest 1 percent of rural households represent about one-fourth of the financial assets of all households, whereas the bottom 25 percent account for only 5 percent of the total; put otherwise, the average financial assets of the top 1 percent was more than 100 times that of the bottom half. The ratio of financial to total assets of households, on the other hand, varied only between 1.1 and 2.8 percent, and there was no simple relationship between the level of the ratio and household total wealth. In fact, the ratio was highest for the poorest and richest households and lowest in the middle-wealth ranges. The probable reason for the relatively high ratios among the lower-wealth classes is the inclusion of most of the landless farm laborers whose total assets are minuscule for that very reason.

Regional differences were also great.[134] Average financial assets per household varied, again omitting small territories, from R. 55 in Orissa to R. 460 in Punjab, compared with R. 174 for the entire country. Differences in the distribution of total financial assets among the three components were also large. The ratio of financial to total assets, however, again fluctuated only within a relatively narrow range from 0.8 to 3.2 percent, and there was no clear relation between the ratio and a state's position in the average wealth hierarchy.

e. New Issues of Nonfinancial Sectors

Because the characteristics and the trends of the different types of financial instruments issued by nonfinancial sectors have been discussed previously, this section is limited to a brief overview of

133. In a sample inquiry in three districts in western India, gold and jewelry accounted for between 1½ and 5 percent of total assets of rural households and were much larger than their financial assets, which were put at 0.2 to 2.0 percent of total assets (Rangarajan). If these ratios could be applied to the R. 885 bill. of assets of all 78 million rural households (derived from the 1971 survey), gold and jewelry hoards would amount to between R. 13 bill. and R. 44 bill. They would then be equal to between 3 and 10 percent of national product, between nearly 1 and nearly 3 percent of total national wealth, and between 1¼ and 4 percent of reproducible tangible assets.

134. They can be followed in the two Reserve Bank publications dealing with the 1971 survey that are cited in footnote 123.

TABLE 3-55. Sectoral New Issue Ratios, 1951–1975[a]

	Ratios (percent of GNP)			Distribution (percent)		
	1951–60 (1)	1961–70 (2)	1971–75 (3)	1951–60 (4)	1961–70 (5)	1971–75 (6)
			I. By sector			
Banking	2.37	4.14	5.31	20	21	32
Other financial institutions	0.79	1.40	1.84	7	7	11
All financial institutions	3.16	5.54	7.15	27	28	43
Private corporations	2.41	2.39	1.53	21	12	10
Government	6.19	10.18	6.15	53	51	36
Households	0.77	1.50	1.42	7	8	8
Nonfinancial sectors	9.37	14.07	9.10	81	71	54
All domestic sectors	12.54	19.61	16.26	107	98	97
Rest of the world	−0.80	0.29	0.44	−7	2	3
Total	11.74	19.90	16.70	100	100	100
			II. By instrument			
Currency	0.69	0.87	0.61	6	4	4
Deposits	0.96	2.12	4.06	8	11	24
Loans	4.84	9.45	4.38	41	48	27
Government securities	2.79	2.88	3.18	24	14	19
Private securities	0.32	1.14	0.79	3	6	5
Insurance funds[b]	0.86	1.40	1.75	7	7	10
Other	1.29	2.04	1.91	11	10	11
Total	11.74	19.90	16.70	100	100	100

[a]Uses of funds divided by period's gross national product. Does not include noninstitutional agricultural debt issues, which amounted to about 0.17 percent of national product in 1952–61, 0.41 percent in 1962–71, and 0.33 percent in 1972–75.   [b]Includes social security funds.

SOURCES OF BASIC DATA: Flow-of-funds accounts, *RBIB*, various issues, for cols. 1, 2, 4, and 5; *RCF*, various issues, for cols. 3 and 6.

the new issue ratios, that is, the change in amounts outstanding divided by gross national product, for the main nonfinancial sectors and the main types of their financial instruments.

The new issue ratio for all domestic nonfinancial sectors together increased from 9½ percent in the 1950s to 14 percent in the 1960s and decreased to 9 percent in the first half of the 1970s, declining from three-fourths to not much more than one-half of the issues of all domestic sectors. This indicates an increase in the role of financial institutions in the financing process. Among nonfinancial sectors, the government predominated to the extent of about two-thirds of the total. The share of private corporations fell from one-fourth to below one-fifth, whereas that of households doubled from 8 to 16 percent.

The annual new issue ratio of the nonfinancial sectors has shown, after a sharp step up in 1955, only moderate fluctuations within a slight upward trend, ranging from 1955 to 1975 between 7.7 and 11.1 percent. Both trends and annual fluctuations differ considerably, however, among the main types of issues, and for most of them, small savings being the exception, the year-to-year fluctuations are much more pronounced than in the aggregate issue ratio for all nonfinancial sectors. This indicates a substantial degree of substitution among these different types of issues. The domestic issues of the government, mostly sold to financial institutions, averaged 6 percent of national product in the 1950s and 1970s and exceeded 10 percent in the 1960s, but kept close to two-thirds of the issues of all nonfinancial sectors throughout the period. The issue ratio of private corporations, most of the issues being absorbed by financial institutions, moved rather erratically around a slight downward trend from nearly 2½ percent in the 1950s and 1960s to 1½ percent in 1971–75. The borrowings of households, again mostly from domestic financial institutions because the figures do not include agricultural borrowings from moneylenders, show an irregular upward trend from 0.8 percent in 1955–57 to 1.4 percent in 1971–75. Among both total and domestic issues of the nonfinancial sectors, short-term fluctuations have apparently been determined mostly by the extent to which the government has borrowed from either domestic financial institutions or abroad, its issues absorbing in most years between one-half and three-fourths of total domestic nonfinancial issues.

6. THE NATIONAL BALANCE SHEET OF INDIA, 1950–1975

Although the estimates of tangible and financial assets in 1950, 1960, and 1970 (table 3.56) are rough, they should nevertheless be sufficiently accurate to support a number of conclusions about the structure of India's national balance sheet and the changes in it since independence.[135]

The summary that follows is based essentially on six tables. Table 3-56 shows the absolute and relative amounts of the main components of the unsectored national balance sheets for 1950, 1960, 1970, and 1975. These figures are put in perspective by relating them in table 3-57 to national product and by indicating their rates of growth between benchmark dates. Table 3-58 rearranges some of the data in the form of a from-whom-to-whom matrix for 1970. Similar matrices, omitted because of space limitations, have been drawn up for 1950 and 1960 and will be used in the discussion. Finally, table 3-59 summarizes some of the results in the form of a number of national balance sheet ratios.

(a) The value of national assets rose by more than 80 percent, or 6¼ percent per year, in the 1950s, and its growth accelerated to 180 percent, or 11 percent per year, in the 1960s. Preliminary estimates indicate that the rise further increased to 105 percent or over 15 percent per year, during the first half of the 1970s. Much of this increase was due since the 1960s to an increase in the price level of tangible assets.

(b) Up to 1970, the value of financial assets increased more rapidly than that of tangible assets. As a result, the financial interrelations ratio (financial assets divided by tangible assets) advanced from fully one-fourth in 1950 to two-fifths in 1960 and to 45 percent in 1970, indicating a substantial increase in the importance of the country's financial superstructure and raising the level of the ratio to that observed in semideveloped countries. In the early 1970s the rise in the price levels of tangible assets was so sharp that the financial interrelation ratio fell back to not much more than two-fifths, notwithstanding an increase by more than 90 percent in the value of financial assets.

(c) Within tangible assets, the value of reproducible assets (excluding gold and silver) has grown more rapidly than that of land.[136] The indicated changes in the relation is so great—from equality in 1950 to a predominance on the order of three to one in 1975—that there can be no

135. An earlier attempt at constructing a national balance sheet for India was made by M. S. Joshi, showing national and four sectoral balance sheets for 1950 and 1961. Joshi's aggregate figures are fairly close to those used here, although there are substantial differences in some components, partly because Joshi uses a somewhat broader concept of financial assets. More recently a national balance sheet for 1965 was published by Kumar, Sarkar, and Narain (p. 143). Their estimates seem to be compatible with those in table 3-56 for 1960 and 1970.

136. The level of the value of land is somewhat understated for all dates because the estimates make no allowance for land owned by business and government (*RBIB*, 1972, p. 1720). It is difficult to see how this land could have been worth less than 5 percent of the value of land included in the estimates. This omission leads to an overstatement of the financial interrelations ratio by about 0.01. A second, probably smaller, overstatement results from the omission of part of reproducible tangible assets, namely, assets of local authorities and nonprofit organizations (*RBIB*, 1972, p. 1722). These understatements of national assets may be offset, and probably are more than offset, by the understatement of financial assets resulting from the narrow definition used by D-V and V-S. The omission of gold and silver finally may lead to an under- or overstatement of the financial interrelations ratio, depending on whether these hoards are regarded as financial or tangible assets. It thus is not possible to be definite about whether a ratio calculated on a more complete and comprehensive basis would be higher than the figures of table 3-62, although this seems likely; and if so, by how much, although it is felt that the difference would be relatively small.

doubt about the direction and the approximate order of magnitude of the changes, even allowing for the roughness of the estimates of both the numerator and the denominator.

(d) The extremely large rise in the value of reproducible tangible assets (excluding gold and silver)—a fourteenfold increase within a quarter of a century—which after elimination of price level changes implies an increase of about 340 percent, or about 6 percent per year in real terms, is evidence of a rapid acceleration of the country's infrastructure and modern sector.

(e) This characteristic is emphasized by the fact that within reproducible tangible assets the stock of dwellings increased much more slowly than that of the other, mostly industrial, reproducible assets, namely, in constant prices, by 5 percent per year between 1950 and 1975, compared with an increase of 6½ percent per year for other reproducible assets.

(f) Within the nondwelling capital stock, increases were particularly pronounced in the 1950s and 1960s in electricity with, in real terms, nearly 12 percent per year; public administration with nearly 10 percent; finance with 8½ percent; communication with nearly 8 percent; and registered manufacturing with fully 7 percent. Expansion, on the other hand, was slow in agriculture with less than 2½ percent and in trade with one-half of 1 percent.[137]

(g) Capital imports have significantly contributed to the growth of the capital stock. The net foreign balance, substantially positive in 1950 as a result of the large balance of payments surpluses of World War II, had by 1975 become negative to the extent of nearly R. 90 bill., or 4 percent of the total stock of nondwelling reproducible assets.

(h) Claims are the predominant form of financial assets. The share of equity securities declined from 9 to 5 percent notwithstanding a large increase in the stock of government companies. The amounts held by households have declined even more sharply.

(i) Among claims, structural changes have been pronounced. The share of currency and deposits, mainly held by the household sector, has declined from more than one-fourth in 1950 to below one-fifth in 1975, most of the decline attributable to the sharp fall in the share of currency from 16 to 5 percent, a sign of financial maturation. Insurance funds, wholly held for individuals, doubled their share from 4 to 8 percent. On the other hand, the share of loans and advances, absorbed mainly by the business and government sectors has risen sharply from one-twelfth to nearly one-third indicating a rapid expansion of the use of credit within the Indian economy. The share of government securities, which is held mainly by financial institutions, remained close to one-seventh. Private corporate securities have declined from 11 to 7 percent of all financial assets. Agricultural noninstitutional debt has fallen precipitously from 15 to 3 percent of all claims. More of these changes occurred during the 1960s than in the following fifteen years.

(j) Financial interrelations matrix for 1970 is presented in table 3-58 by expressing each cell as a percentage of the sum of all cells, which equals total outstandings of financial instruments, rather than in absolute figures in order to facilitate intertemporal and international comparisons. It is then seen that the largest cells refer to intergovernmental loans and borrowings with 18 percent of the total, evidence of the government's extensive activities as a financial intermediary; to household claims against the banking system with nearly 13 percent; to the government's borrowing from domestic banks with 8½ percent. Fairly substantial, with 4 to 6 percent each, are interbank loans; household borrowing from banks; household claims against the government and against non-bank financial institutions; and corporate and government loans to others.[138]

137. Choudhury, 1977, p. 155.137. Choudhury, 1977, p. 155.

138. If account were taken of agricultural borrowing from unorganized lenders, the share of intrasectoral credit would increase by less than 4 percent of total financial assets. The share would be further increased if accounts receivable and payable among unincorporated business, now omitted, were added; and if accounts receivable and payable of nongovernment companies were shown separately instead of being netted, as they now appear to be. The share of all intrasectoral

TABLE 3-56. National Balance Sheet 1950–1975

	Amounts (R. bill.)				Distribution (percent)			
	1950 (1)	1960 (2)	1970 (3)	1975 (4)	1950 (5)	1960 (6)	1970 (7)	1975 (8)
I. Tangible assets	392	676	1865	3910	69.0	65.1	63.7	65.0
1. Land	188	215	615	980	33.1	20.7	21.0	16.3
2. Reproducible assets	204	461	1250	2930	35.9	44.4	42.7	48.7
a. Dwellings	44	131	230	500	7.7	12.5	7.9	8.3
b. Other structures ⎱ c. Equipment ⎰	85	208	740	1900	15.0	20.0	25.3	31.6
d. Inventories	32	50	140	250	5.6	4.8	4.8	4.2
e. Livestock	28	26	50	80	4.9	2.5	1.7	1.3
f. Consumer durables	15	46	90	200	2.6	4.4	3.1	3.3
II. Gold and silver	50	65	150	350	8.8	6.3	5.1	5.8
III. Financial assets	126	297	914	1758	22.2	28.6	31.2	29.2
1. Claims against financial institutions[a]	34	77	237	497	6.0	7.4	8.1	8.3
a. Banks	28	56	164	352	4.9	5.4	5.6	5.8
b. Insurance and pension organizations	5	14	52	105	0.9	1.3	1.8	1.7
c. Other	1	7	21	40	0.2	0.7	0.7	0.7
2. Loans by financial institutions	7	25	107	240	1.2	2.4	3.7	4.0

3. Loans by government	3	34	135	300	0.5	3.3	4.6	5.0
4. Agricultural debt[b]	14	16	27	35	2.5	1.5	0.9	0.6
5. Domestic government securities	18	56	129	225	3.2	5.4	4.4	3.7
6. Corporate securities	11	22	62	91	1.9	2.1	2.1	1.5
7. Trade credit	30	45	125	220	5.3	4.3	4.3	3.7
8. Other	9	22	92	150	1.6	2.1	3.1	2.5
IV. National assets	578	1038	2929	6018	100.0	100.0	100.0	100.0
V. Net foreign assets	10	−18	−83	−89	1.8	−1.7	−2.8	−1.5

[a]Includes equity.   [b]1951, 1961, and 1971: noninstitutional debt.

SOURCES: Line I-1: 1950–70, *V.S.*, p. 117. The estimate for 1950 is close to that of the Reserve Bank (*RBIB*, 1963, pp. 10) and that for 1960 is almost the same as that of Gothoskar and Shankar (op. cit., Oct. 1972). These estimates omit land in the government and private corporate sectors, which may be equal to about 5 percent of that of the household sector. Estimate of 1970 extrapolated on basis of movements in agricultural prices and in cultivated areas. Lines I-2a, 2e: 1950–60, Choudhury, 1976, Appendix I, adding in 1950 estimate for consumer durables; 1970, 1975, extrapolated from 1965 estimate (loc. cit.) on basis of net capital formation and change in prices (United Nations, *Yearbook of National Accounts Statistics*, 1979). Line I-2b: 1950–75, residual. Line I-2d: 1950–75, based on Kumar's estimate (''National Balance Sheet for India,'' 1976–77, p. 143) of R. 84 bill. for 1965, equal to about one-third of national product. Line I-2f: 1950, 1960, Choudhury (1976), Appendix I; 1970, 1975, rough estimates, for 1970 based on Choudhury, loc. cit., for 1965. Line II: 1950–75, obtained by multiplying Bombay prices of gold and silver, relative to 1956 (*RBIB*, various issues, e.g., 1976, S 48, and *SAIU*, 1962, pp. 352–53 and 456), with estimated quantities. These have been taken for 1946, 1950, and 1957 from Prakash, pp. 273, 275, and 291–92, and have been estimated to increase from 1960 on by 2 million ounces per year for gold (semiofficial unpublished estimate) and to remain unchanged for silver. Line III-1: 1950–75, table 3-17. Lines III-2, 3, 5, 6, 8: 1950–70, V−S, table 1; 1975, derived by cumulative use of funds from flow-of-funds estimates (*RCF*, 1974–75, II.18: 1975–76, II.19; 1976–77, p. 21; 1977–78, p. 117) except for line III-8, which is a rough estimate. Line III-4: 1950–71, table 3-52; figures refer to 1951, 1961, and 1971, respectively; 1975, assumed to have increased at same rate as between 1961 and 1971. No allowance has therefore been made for the extension or remission of agricultural debt to noninstitutional lenders, which was legitimated in 1975. Line III-7: 1950–75, estimated at about 90 percent of inventories (line I-2c).

TABLE 3-57. Relation to Gross National Product and Rate of Growth of National Balance Sheet Components, 1950–1975

	Ratio to gross national product				Rate of growth (percent)			
	1950 (1)	1960 (2)	1970 (3)	1975 (4)	1951–60 (5)	1961–70 (6)	1971–75 (7)	1951–75 (8)
I. Tangible assets	3.79	4.29	4.47	5.23	5.6	10.7	16.0	9.6
1. Land	1.82	1.39	1.47	1.31	1.4	11.1	9.8	6.8
2. Reproducible assets	1.97	2.99	3.00	3.92	8.5	10.5	18.6	11.2
a. Dwellings	0.43	0.85	0.55	0.67	11.5	5.8	16.8	10.2
b. Other	1.55	2.14	2.44	3.25	7.5	11.9	17.9	11.5
II. Gold and silver	0.48	0.42	0.36	0.47	2.7	8.7	18.5	8.1
III. Financial assets	1.22	1.92	2.19	2.35	9.0	11.9	14.0	11.1
1. Claim against financial institutions	0.33	0.50	0.57	0.66	8.5	11.9	16.0	11.3
a. Banks	0.27	0.36	0.39	0.47	7.2	11.3	16.5	10.7
b. Insurance organizations	0.05	0.09	0.12	0.14	10.8	14.0	15.1	13.0
c. Other	0.01	0.05	0.05	0.05	21.5	11.6	13.8	15.7
2. Financial institutions } Loans	0.07	0.16	0.26	0.32	13.6	15.6	17.5	15.2
3. Government	0.03	0.22	0.32	0.40	27.5	14.8	17.3	20.2
4. Agricultural debt	0.14	0.10	0.06	0.05	1.3	5.4	5.3	3.7
5. Domestic government securities	0.17	0.36	0.31	0.30	12.0	8.7	11.8	10.6
6. Corporate securities	0.11	0.14	0.15	0.12	7.2	10.9	8.0	8.8
7. Trade credit	0.29	0.29	0.30	0.29	4.1	10.8	12.0	8.3
8. Other	0.09	0.14	0.22	0.20	9.3	15.4	10.3	11.9
IV. Net foreign assets	0.10	-0.12	-0.20	-0.12	—	.	.	.
V. National assets (I + II + III)	5.59	6.73	7.02	8.04	6.0	10.9	15.5	9.8
VI. National wealth (I + II − IV)	4.37	4.69	4.63	5.58	4.8	10.3	16.6	9.3

SOURCE: Table 3-56.

TABLE 3-58. Financial Interrelations Matrix, 1970 (Percent of Total Financial Assets)

Borrowing sector	Banking	Other financial institu- tions	Private corporate business	Govern- ment	House- holds	Rest of the world	Total
		Lending sector					
Banking	4.84	0.70	0.65	1.20	12.53	0.19	20.11
Other financial institutions	0.27	0.32	—	0.48	4.87	0.10	6.04
Private corporate business	3.30	1.33	0.62	0.89	2.21	2.23	10.58
Government	8.55	3.62	0.04	17.93	4.99	10.35	45.48
Households	4.50	0.38	0.16	1.32	—ᵃ	—	6.36
Other domestic	0.68	0.24	4.06	4.57	—	—	9.55
Rest of the world	0.63	0.04	0.01	1.20	—	—	1.88
Total	22.77	6.63	5.54	27.59	24.60	12.87	100.00

ᵃNoninstitutional agricultural debt (3.50 percent) not included in total.

SOURCE OF BASIC DATA: V–S, p. 116.

(k) The patterns of the matrices for 1950 and 1960 are fairly similar to that of 1970. The degree of similarity can be expressed as the absolute sum of the differences between the ratio of the values of individual cells in the two years being compared to the sum of all cells. It is then seen that the difference between the 1950 and 1960 matrices is considerably larger than that between the 1960 and 1970 matrices (.57 against .27). This indicates larger changes in the pattern of financial interrelations in the 1950s than in the 1960s, a conclusion that is corroborated by the evidence presented throughout this chapter. The difference between the 1970 and 1950 matrices is only slightly smaller than the sum of the differences between the 1960–50 and 1970–60 matrices (.72 against .81), suggesting that only a small part of the changes in the pattern between 1950 and 1960 was reversed in the following decade.

(l) Table 3-59, finally, brings together a few important ratios that can be derived from the national balance sheet. The capital-output ratio showed only small movements from 1950 to 1970, around a level of about 4¼, movements that may not be significant given the roughness of the estimates, but rose to nearly 5 in 1975. The share of land in all tangible assets declined substantially, though irregularly, from nearly one-half to fully one-fourth, as one would expect in the early stages of financial development. The financial interrelations ratio (financial assets : tangible assets), possibly the most important of the ratios, almost doubled between 1950 and 1960 but fell back sharply to below the 1960 level in the first half of the 1970s. The net increase from less than one-fourth to fully one-third is the clearest indication of the rapid increase of the relative importance of the financial superstructure in the Indian economy since independence. It remains to be seen whether the reverse movement in the early 1970s will turn out to be significant. The financial intermediation ratio (share of financial institutions in all financial assets) declined slightly in the 1950s, an unexpected movement in a developing country,[139] which is explained by the large-scale activity of the central government as a financial intermediary,[140] but increased sharply in the 1970s. The same fact is reflected in the increase of the share

credits more broadly defined might then be well above one-third of all financial assets. From the point of view of the analysis of the country's financial superstructure, the broader concept of financial assets is preferable as there is no reason to eliminate intrasectoral credits.

139. Goldsmith, June 1971.

140. Because of the relatively slow expansion of borrowing from unorganized lenders, and presumably also of trade credit, the decline would be smaller if a broader concept of financial instruments was used.

TABLE 3-59. National Balance Sheet Ratios, 1950–1975

Numerator	Denominator	1950	1960	1970	1975
National assets	Gross national product	5.49	6.73	7.02	8.04
National wealth		4.37	4.69	4.63	5.57
Tangible assets A		4.27	4.80	4.83	5.69
Tangible assets B		3.79	4.38	4.47	5.23
Financial assets A		1.70	2.35	2.55	2.82
Financial assets B		1.22	1.93	2.19	2.35
Financial assets A	Tangible assets A	0.45	0.54	0.57	0.52
Financial assets B	Tangible assets B	0.29	0.40	0.45	0.41
Assets of financial institutions	All financial assets	0.19	0.21	0.22	0.24
		0.27	0.26	0.26	0.28
Assets of banks	Assets of financial institutions	0.82	0.73	0.69	0.71
Land	Tangible assets A	0.43	0.29	0.31	0.23
	Tangible assets B	0.48	0.32	0.33	0.25
Net foreign balance	Tangible assets A	0.02	−0.02	−0.04	−0.02
	Tangible assets B	0.03	−0.03	−0.04	−0.02
	Tangible assets C	0.06	−0.05	−0.08	−0.07

NOTE: A includes and B excludes gold and silver; C includes reproducible assets other than dwellings and gold and silver.

of the government's debt to all financial instruments outstanding from one-third to considerably more than two-fifths. It also explains, although only in part, the decline in the share of money and even of currency plus all deposits in total financial instruments outstanding.

(m) The formula used in chapters 1 and 2 to break down the financial interrelations ratio into its main components[141] can also be applied to the ratio of 0.39 for 1975 derived from the national balance sheet. In this case, however, the formula

$$[\tau\alpha\beta^{-1}\,(\delta + \phi)\,(1 + \nu)] + F_{1950}/W_{1975}]$$

yields a calculated value ($0.60 \times 13.2 \times 0.22 \times 0.19 + 0.03$) of 0.36—$\nu$ is difficult to ascertain but small enough to be disregarded—somewhat below the observed ratio of 0.41.

141. Cf. Goldsmith, 1969, chap. 2.

List of Publications Cited

Anstey, V. *The Economic Development of India*. New York: Longmans, Green, 1929.

Arora, H. C., and Iyengar, K. R. R. "Long-term Growth of National Income in India, 1901–1956." In V. K. R. V. Rao et al., eds., *Papers on National Income and Allied Topics*, vol. 1. New York: Asia Publishing House, 1960.

Atkinson, F. J. "Silver Prices in India." *Journal of the Royal Statistical Society* 60 (1897).

_____. "A Statistical Review of the Income and Wealth of British India." *Journal of the Royal Statistical Society* 65 (1902).

Bagchi, A. K. *Private Investment in India 1900–1939*. Cambridge: Cambridge University Press, 1972.

Balwant Singh, S. *An Inquiry into Mortgages of Agricultural Land, in the Kot Kapura Utar Assessment Circle of the Ferozepore District in the Punjab*. Lahore: Civil and Military Gazette Press, 1925.

Banerjee, A. K., ed. *India's Balance of Payments, 1948–49 to 1961–62*. Bombay: Reserve Bank of India, 1963.

Barbour, D. *The Theory of Bimetallism and the Effects of the Partial Demonstration of Silver on England and India*. London: Cassell, 1885.

Bardhan, P., and Rudra, A. "Interlinkage of Land, Labor and Credit Relations." *Economic and Political Weekly*, annual number, 1978.

Baster, A. S. J. *The Imperial Banks*. London: P. S. King & Son, 1929.

Basu, S. K. *Industrial Finance in India*. Calcutta: University of Calcutta, 1950.

_____. *The Managing Agency System in Prospect and Retrospect*. Calcutta: World Press Private, 1958.

Bauer, P. T. *Indian Economic Policy and Development*. London: Ruskin House, G. Allen Unwin, 1961.

Bell, H. *Railway Policy in India*. London: Percival, 1894.

Benjamin, N. "Some Aspects of Agricultural Indebtedness in British India (1850–1900)." *Indian Journal of Economics* 51 (1971).

Bhagwati, J. N., and Srinivasan, T. N. *Foreign Trade Regimes and Economic Development: India*. New York: National Bureau of Economic Research, 1975.

Bhagwati, J. H., and Desai, P. *India: Planning for Industrialization*. New York: Oxford University Press, 1970.

Bhargava, B. K. *Indigenous Banking in Ancient and Medieval India*. Bombay: D. B. Taraporevala Sons, 1934.

Bhatia, B. *New Issue Market in India*. Bombay: Vora, 1976.

Bhatt, V. V. "Savings and Capital Formation in India." *Economic Development and Cultural Change* 7, no. 3 (April 1959).

_____. *Structure of Financial Institutions*. Bombay: Vora, 1972.

Bhole, L. M. "An Empirical Study of Liquidity Preference of the Corporate Sector in India." *Indian Journal of Economics* 59 (1978).

Blyn, G. *Agricultural Trends in India, 1891–1947*. Philadelphia: University of Pennsylvania, 1966.

Bose, A. "Foreign Capital." In V. B. Singh, ed., *Economic History of India: 1857–1956*. New York: Allied Publishers, 1965.

Brunyate, J. B. *An Account of the Presidency Banks*. Calcutta: Superintendent of Government Printing, 1900.

Buchanan, D. H. *The Development of Capitalistic Enterprise in India*. New York: Macmillan, 1934.

Calvert, H. *The Wealth and Welfare of the Punjab*. Lahore: Civil and Military Gazette Press, 1922.

Cameron, R., ed. *Banking in the Early Stages of Industrialization*. New York: Oxford University Press, 1967.

Chandavarkar, A. G. "The Nature and Effects of Gold Hoarding in Underdeveloped Economies." In P. C. Malhotra and A. C. Minocha, eds., *Studies in Capital Formation, Savings, and Investment in a Developing Economy*. Bombay: Semaiya Publications, 1971.

Chaudhuri, B. B. "Rural Credit Relations in Bengal, 1859–1885." *Indian Economic and Social History Review* 6 (1969).

Chaudhuri, R. K., ed. *Trends of Socio-Economic Change in India 1871–1961*. Simla: Indian Institute of Advanced Study, 1969.

Chitre, K. "Financing of House Construction in India." *Reserve Bank of India Bulletin* 30, no. 2 (February 1976).

Choksey, R. D. *Economic Life in the Bombay Deccan 1881–1939*. Bombay: Asia Publishing House, 1955.

Choudhury, U. D. R. "Income Distribution and Economic Development in India Since 1950–51." *Indian Economic Journal* 25 (October–December 1977).

______. "Industrial Breakdown of Capital Stock in India." *Indian Journal of Income and Wealth* 2 (1977).

Cirvante, V. R. *The Indian Capital Market*. Bombay: University Publications, Economics Series, no. 6, 1956.

Clarke, G. R. *The Post Office of India and Its Story*. London: John Lane, 1921.

Coale, A. J., and Hoover, E. M. *Population Growth and Economic Development in Low Income Countries: A Case Study of India's Prospects*. Princeton, N.J.: Princeton University Press, 1958.

Commerce Research Bureau. *Commerce Yearbook of Public Sector*. Bombay.

______. *Basic Statistics Relating to the Indian Economy*. Bombay, 1975.

______. *Companies Inviting Deposits*. Bombay, 1975.

______. *Monthly Review of the Indian Economy*. Bombay.

Cooke, C. N. *Banking in India*. 1863.

Coyayee, J. E. *The Indian Currency System*. Madras: University of Madras, 1930.

Darling, N. *The Punjab Peasant in Prosperity and Debt*. 1925.

Datta, K. L. *Report on the Enquiry into the Rise of Prices in India*. Calcutta: Superintendent of Government Printing, 1914.

Davis, K. *Population of India and Pakistan*. Princeton, N.J.: Princeton University Press, 1951.

Desai, T. B. *Economic History of India under the British, 1757–1947*. Bombay: Vora, 1968.

Digby, W. *"Prosperous" British India: A Revelation from Official Records*. London: T. F. Unwin, 1901.

Divatia, V. V. "Inequalities in Asset Distribution of Rural Households." In Reserve Bank of India, *Reserve Bank Staff Occasional Papers*, no. 1. Bombay, 1976.

_____. "Patterns of Assets of Rural Households." In Reserve Bank of India, *Reserve Bank Staff Occasional Papers,* no. 2. Bombay, 1977.

_____, and Shaw, C. H. "Financial Assets of Rural Households at the End of June 1971." In Reserve Bank of India, *Reserve Bank Staff Occasional Papers,* no. 1. Bombay, 1976.

_____, and Venkatachalam, T. R. "Household Demand for Money in India: Some Evidence from Time Series." *Reserve Bank of India Bulletin* 26, no. 6 (June 1972).

Doodha, K. D. *India: Installment Credit, Extent, Stability and Growth.* Bombay: University of Bombay, 1965.

Doraiswami, S. V. *Indian Finance, Currency and Banking.* Madras: S. V. Doraiswami, 1915.

Dubey, D. L. *The Indian Public Debt.* Bombay: D. B. Taraporevala Sons, 1930.

Dubey, V. "Railways." In V. B. Singh, ed., *The Economic History of India, 1857–1956.* New York: Allied Publishers, 1965.

Eastern Economist. Records and Statistics, quarterly.

Friend, I. "The Propensities to Save in India." In *Problems of Economic Development.* 1966.

Frykenberg, R. E., ed. *Land Control and Social Structure in Indian History.* Madison: University of Wisconsin Press, 1969.

Gadgil, D. R. *The Industrial Evolution of India in Recent Times, 1860 to 1939.* 5th ed. Bombay: Oxford University Press, 1971.

Ganguli, A. K. "Rural Banking—A Point of View." *Margin* 9, no. 2 (1976–77).

Ganguli, B. N. "Rammohun Roy on India's Contemporary Economic Problems." In S. L. N. Simha, ed., *Economic and Social Development.* Bombay: Vora, 1972.

Ghose, B. C. *A Study of the Indian Money Market.* London: Oxford University Press, 1943.

Gokale Institute of Politics and Economics. *Notes on the Rise of the Business Communities in India.* New York: International Secretariat, Institute of Pacific Relations, 1951.

Goldsmith, R. W. *Financial Structure and Development.* New Haven, Conn.: Yale University Press, 1969.

_____. "Prolegomènes à l'analyse comparative des structures financières." *Revue d'économie politique* 80 (1970).

_____. "The Development of Financial Institutions during the Postwar Period." *Banca Nazionale del Lavoro Quarterly Review,* no. 97 (June 1971).

Gothoskar, S. P., and Shanker, K. "Estimates of Tangible Wealth in India." *Reserve Bank of India Bulletin* 26, no. 10 (October 1972).

Green, T. *The World of Gold.* New York: Walker, 1968.

Gubbay, M. M. S. *Indigenous Indian Banking.* Bombay: D. B. Taraporevala Sons, 1928.

Gulati, I. S., and George, K. K. "Centre-State Financial Flows in 1969/70." *Economic and Political Weekly* 13 (1978).

Gupta, K. L. "Household Savings in Financial Assets—A Case Study of India." *Indian Economic Journal* (1970).

_____. "Personal Saving in Developing Nations—Further Evidence." *Economic Record* 46 (1970).

_____. "On Some Determinants of Rural and Urban Household Saving Behaviour." *Economic Record* 46 (1970).

_____. *Stock Exchange and Securities.* Bombay, 1971.

Gupta, L. C. "The Ownership of Industrial Securities in India." *Indian Economic Journal* 13 (1965–66).

_____. *The Changing Structure of Industrial Finance in India: The Impact of Institutional Finance.* Oxford: Clarendon Press, 1969.

Gupta, S. C. "Land Market in the North Western Provinces (Uttar Pradesh) in the First Half of the Nineteenth Century." *Indian Economic Review,* vol. 4

Gupta, U. L. *Working of Stock Exchanges in India.* New Delhi: Thomson Press, 1972.

Gurtoo, D. N. *India's Balance of Payments, 1920–1960.* Delhi: S. Chand, 1961.

Habib, I. M. "Banking in Mughal India." In T. Raychaudhuri, ed., *Contributions to Indian Economic History,* vol. 1. Calcutta: K. L. Mukhopadhyay, 1960.

Hanson, A. H. *The Process of Planning.* London: Oxford University Press, 1966.

Hazari, R. K. "Pattern of Inter-sectorial Shareholding in 418 Companies." In V. K. R. V. Rao et al., eds., *Papers on National Income and Allied Topics,* vol. 3. Bombay: Asia Publishing House, 1965.

_____. *The Structure of the Corporate Private Sector: A Study of Concentration, Ownership, and Control.* Bombay: Asia Publishing House, 1966.

Heston, A. In *Cambridge Economic History of India.* Cambridge: Cambridge University Press, 1979.

Hirsch, F. *Money International.* Garden City, N.Y.: Doubleday, 1967.

Howard, H. F. *India and the Gold Standard.* Calcutta: Thacker, Spink, 1911.

India Currency and Banking Enquiry Committee. *Report.* 1930.

India, Department of Commercial Intelligence and Statistics, *Statistical Abstract for India.* New Delhi, annually.

India (Republic), Banking Commission. *Report of the Banking Commission.* New Delhi: Manager of Publications, 1972.

_____. *Report of the Study Group on Indigenous Bankers.* 1972.

_____. *Report of the Study Group of Non-banking Financial Intermediaries.* 1972.

India (Republic), Central Statistical Organization. *National Income Statistics: Estimates of Gross Domestic Capital Formation in India 1948/49–1960/61.* New Delhi: Department of Statistics, Cabinet Secretariat, 1961.

_____. *Estimates of National Income, 1948/49 to 1962/63.* New Delhi: Central Statistical Organization, 1964.

_____. *National Accounts Statistics 1960/61–1973/74,* 1976.

_____. *Statistical Abstract of the Indian Union.* New Delhi: Manager of Publications, annually.

India (Republic), Department of Economic Affairs. *Pocket Book of Economic Information.* New Delhi: Ministry of Finance, Department of Economic Affairs, annually.

India (Republic), Department of Labour and Employment. *Pocket Book of Labour Statistics.* New Delhi, annually.

India (Republic), Industrial Licensing Policy Inquiry Committee. *Report.* New Delhi:, 1969.

India (Republic), Planning Commission, Statistics and Surveys Division. *Basic Statistics Relating to the Indian Economy.* New Delhi: 1975.

Indian Central Banking Committee. *The Indian Central Banking Inquiry Committee.* Calcutta: Government of India Central Publication Branch, 1931.

Indian Economic Conference (Bombay). *The Monetary Policy of the Reserve Bank of India.* Bombay: Popular Prakashan, 1964.

Indian Insurance Yearbook. New Delhi: Manager of Publications.

Indian Merchants Chamber, Economic Research and Training Foundation. *National Income of India, Growth and Distribution, 1950–51 to 1960–61.* Bombay, 1963.

Islam, N. *Foreign Capital and Economic Development.* Rutland, Vt.: Tuttle, 1960.

Iyer, K. V. *Indian Railways.* London: Humphrey Milford, 1929.

Jain, L. C. *Indigenous Banking in India.* London: Macmillan, 1929.

Jathar, G. B., and Beri, S. G. *Indian Economics.* 7th ed. Madras: Oxford University Press, 1942.

Jefferies and Co., Inc. *Investment Seminar.* Tokyo, 1970.

Jenks, L. *The Migration of British Capital to 1875.* New York: Knopf, 1927.

Jevons, H. S. *Money, Banking and Exchange in India.* Simla: Government Central Press, 1922.

Johar, R. S. "Determinants of Business Investment in India." *Indian Journal of Economics* 56 (1978).

Joshi, M. S. *The National Balance Sheet of India.* Bombay: University of Bombay, 1966.

Joshi, V. H. "Saving Behaviour in India." *Indian Economic Journal* 17 (1969–70).

Kapoor, J. L., and Khera, R. N. "Estimate of Wealth in the Public Sector." *Journal of Income and Wealth* 2 (1977).

Karkal, G. *Unorganized Money Markets in India*. Bombay: Salvani Publishing House, 1967.

Keynes, J. M. *Indian Currency and Finance*. Vol. 1. London: Macmillan, 1913.

Khatkhate, D. R., and Deshpande, K. L. "Estimate of Saving and Investment in the Indian Economy: 1950–51 to 1962–63." In P. C. Malhotra and A. C. Minocha, eds., *Studies in Capital Formation, Savings, and Investment in a Developing Economy*. Bombay: Semaiya Publications, 1971.

Khusro, A. M., and Siddharta, N. S. "An Econometric Model of the Banking System." *Technical Studies Prepared for the Banking Commission*. Bombay: Reserve Bank of India, 1972.

Kidron, M. *Foreign Investments in India*. London: Oxford University Press, 1965.

Kothari, M. L. *Industrial Combinations*. Allahabad: Chaitanya Publishing House, 1967.

Krishnan, V. *Indigenous Banking in South India*. Bombay: Bombay State Cooperative Union, 1959.

Krishnaswami, A. "Capital Development in India." Ph. D. dissertation, University of London, 1941.

Kulkarni, V. G. *Statistical Outline of Indian Economy*. Bombay: Vora, 1968.

Kumar, D. *Western India in the Nineteenth Century*. Toronto: University of Toronto Press, 1968.

Kumar, J.; Sarkar, A. K.; and Navani, P. "National Balance Sheet for India—An Exercise." *Indian Journal of Income and Wealth* 2 (1977).

Lakdawala, D. T., and Mody, R. J. *Financial Assets and Instruments for Mobilization of Saving*. Ahmadabad: Sardar Patel Institute of Economic and Social Research, 1975.

Lal, R. N. *Capital Formation and Its Financing in India*. Bombay: Allied Publishers, 1977.

Lall, V. D. "Structure of Private Limited Companies in Maharashtra." *Economic and Political Weekly* 6 (July 1971).

Lamb, H. "The State and Economic Development in India." In S. Kuznets et al., eds., *Economic Growth: Brazil, India and Japan*. Durham, N.C.: Duke University Press, 1955.

Laumas, P. S. "Monetization, Economic Development and the Demand for Money." *Review of Economics and Statistics* 60, no. 4 (November 1978).

Lokanathan, P. S. *Industrial Organization in India*. London: Allen & Unwin, 1935.

Macpherson, W. J. "Investment in Indian Railways, 1845–1875." *Economic History Review* 8, no. 2 (1955–56).

————. "Economic Development of India under the British Crown 1858–1947." In A. J. Youngson, ed., *Economic Development in the Long Run*. London: Allen & Unwin, 1972.

Madagli, S. "Trends in Monetization in the Indian Economy (1961–62 to 1974–75)." In Reserve Bank of India, *Reserve Bank Staff Occasional Papers,* 1 Bombay, 1976.

Maddison, A. *Class Structure and Economic Growth: India and Pakistan since the Moghuls*. London: Allen & Unwin, 1971.

Maitin, T. P. *Institutional Finance in India*. Agra: Sahitya Bhawan, 1971.

Malenbaum, W. *Modern India's Economy*. Columbus, Ohio: Merrill, 1971.

Malhotra, D. K. *History and Problems of Indian Currency 1835–1959*. New Delhi: Minerva, 1960.

Malhotra, P. C., and Minocha, A. C., eds. *Studies in Capital Formation, Savings, and Investment in a Developing Economy*. Bombay: Semaiya Publications, 1971.

Manchester Man, A. *A Guide to Indian Investments*. London, 1861.

Mann, H. H. et al. *Land and Labour in a Deccan Village*. London: Milford, 1917.

Marx, K. *Articles on India*. Bombay: Peoples' Publishing House, 1951.

Mehta, M. M. *Structure of Indian Industries*. Bombay: Popular Book Depot, 1955.

Mehta, R. C. *Capital Market in India for Planned Growth*. Gwalior: Kitak Ghar, 1965.

Menon, K. A. "Liquidity in India's Corporate Sector." In Reserve Bank of India, *Reserve Bank Staff Occasional Papers*, no. 2. Bombay, 1977.

Minocha, A. C. "Estimates of Saving and Capital Formation in India—A Review of Existing Estimates and Methodology." In P. C. Malhotra and A. C. Minocha, eds., *Studies in Capital Formation, Savings, and Investment in a Developing Economy*. Bombay: Semaiya Publications, 1971.

Mohsin, M. *Investments of Life Insurance Corporation Funds*. Aligarh: Aligarh Muslim University, 1966.

Moreland, W. H. *India at the Death of Akbar*. London: Macmillan, 1920.

Morris, M. D., et al. *Indian Economy in the Nineteenth Century: A Symposium*. Delhi: Indian Economic and Social History Association, 1969.

Mukerji, K. "Land Prices in Punjab." In M. K. Chaudhuri, ed., *Trends of Socio-Economic Change in India 1871–1961*. Simla: Indian Institute of Advanced Study, 1969.

Mukherjee, M. *National Income of India, Trends and Structure*. Calcutta: Statistical Publishing Society, 1969.

———. "Sources of Growth of the Indian Economy." *Sankhya*, B. 35 (1973).

Mukherjee, R., ed. *Economic Problems of Modern India*. 2nd ed. London: Macmillan, 1939.

Mukherji, K. "Levels of Living of Industrial Workers." in V. B. Singh, ed., *Economic History of India: 1857–1965*. New York: Allied Publishers, 1965.

Muranjan, S. K. *Modern Banking in India*. Bombay: New Book, 1940.

Myers, C. A. *Labor Problems in the Industrialization of India*. Cambridge: Harvard University Press, 1958.

Myrdal, G. *Asian Drama: An Inquiry into the Poverty of Nations*. New York: Pantheon, 1968.

Nanavati, M. B., and Anjaria, J. J. *The Indian Rural Problem*. 6th ed. Bombay: Indian Society of Agricultural Economics, 1965.

Naoroji, D. *Poverty and Un-British Rule in India*. 1873.

Narang, H. "The Development of the Hundi Business by the Shikarpuri Shroffs." In Shikarpuri Shroffs Association, *Silver Jubilee Souvenir*, 1969.

Natarajan, B. *An Essay on National Income and Expenditure in India*. Madras: Economic Advisor to the Government of Madras, 1949.

National Council of Applied Economic Research. *Saving in India—A Monograph*. New Delhi, 1961.

———. *Rural Household Saving Survey*. New Delhi, 1962.

———. *Urban Income and Saving*. New Delhi, 1962.

———. *Capital Market in a Planned Economy*. New Delhi, 1966.

Nayer, C. P. S. *Chit Finance: An Exploratory Study of the Working of Chit Funds*. Bombay: Vora, 1973.

Nicholson, F. A. *Report regarding the Possibility of Introducing Land and Agricultural Banks into the Madras Presidency*. Madras: Superintendent of Government Press, 1895.

Nigam, R. K. *Managing Agencies in India: Basic Facts—First Round*. New Delhi: Ministry of Commerce and Industry, 1958.

———, and Chaudhuri, N. C. *The Corporate Sector in India*. New Delhi: Research and Statistics Division, Department of Commercial Law Administration, Ministry of Commerce and Industry, 1961.

Paish, G. "Great Britain's Capital Investments in Individual Colonial and Foreign Countries." *Journal of the Royal Statistical Society*, 1910–11.

Pandey, D. P. "Financial Policy of Growth: A Study of the Corporate Private Sector of the Indian Economy." *Artha Vijñana* 19 (1977).

Pandit, Y. S. *Indian Balance of Indebtedness, 1891–1913*. London: Allen & Unwin, 1937.

Pani, P. K. *A Macroeconomic Model of the Indian Economy*. 1977.

Panikar, P. G. K. *Rural Savings in India.* Bombay: Semaiya Publications, 1970.

Pendharkar, V. G., and Narasimham, M. "Recent Evolution of Monetary Policy in India." *Reserve Bank of India Bulletin* 20, no. 4 (April 1966).

Prakash, V. "An Estimate of Stock of Precious Metals in India." In V. K. R. V. Rao et al., eds., *Papers on National Income and Allied Topics,* vol. 1. New York: Asia Publishing House, 1960.

Prasad, A. *Indian Railways.* Bombay: Asia Publishing House, 1960.

Raj, K. N. "The Marginal Rate of Saving in the Indian Economy." *Oxford Economic Papers* 14 (1962).

Ramana, D. V. "Determinants of Money Supply in India, 1914–1950." *Indian Economic Review* 3 (1957).

Ramanadham, V. V. *Indian Railway Finance.* Delhi: Atma Ram and Sons, 1956.

————. *The Finances of Public Enterprises.* Bombay: Asia Publishing House, 1963.

Rangarajan, C. "Innovations in Banking: The Indian Experience." Indian Institute of Management, Mimeographed. 1978.

Rao, K. G. K. S. "Shifts in the Pattern of Financing Capital Formation in the Private Corporate Sector." In Reserve Bank of India, *Reserve Bank Staff Occasional Papers,* no. 2 Bombay, 1977.

Rao, R. B. *Present Day Banking in India.* 4th ed. Calcutta: University of Calcutta, 1938.

Ray, P. *India's Foreign Trade since 1870.* London: Routledge, 1934.

Ray, R. M. *Life Insurance in India.* 1941.

Raychaudhuri, T., ed. *Contributions to Indian Economic History,* vol. 1. Calcutta: K. L. Mukhopadhyay, 1960.

Reddaway, W. B. *The Development of the Indian Economy.* Homewood, Ill.: 1962.

Report of the Indian Central Banking Enquiry Commission, 1931.

Reserve Bank of India. *All-India Rural Credit Survey; Report of the Committee of Direction.* Bombay, 1954.

————. *Banking and Monetary Statistics of India.* Bombay, 1954.

————. *India's Balance of Payments, 1948–49 to 1961–62.* Bombay, 1963.

————. *Banking and Monetary Statistics of India, Supplements 1 and 2.* Bombay, 1964.

————. *Financial Statistics of Joint Stock Companies in India,* 1950–51 to 1962–63 and 1960–61 to 1970–1971. Bombay, 1967.

————. *The Reserve Bank of India—Function and Working,* 2nd ed. Bombay, 1970.

————. *Technical Studies Prepared for the Banking Commission.* Bombay, 1972.

————. *All-India Debt and Investment Survey 1971–72, Statistical Tables.* Bombay, 1973.

————. "Financial Assets of Rural Households (as at the End of June 1971)." In Reserve Bank of India, *Reserve Bank Staff Occasional Papers,* no. 1. Bombay, 1976.

————. *Statistical Tables relating to Cash Dues Outstanding against Rural Households as on 30th of June, 1971.* Bombay, 1976.

————. *Indebtedness of Rural Households and Availability of Institutional Finance.* Bombay, 1977.

————. *Banking Statistics, Basic Statistical Returns.* Bombay, annually.

————. *Report on Currency and Finance.* Bombay, annually.

————. *Statistical Statements relating to the Cooperative Movement in India.* Bombay, annually.

————. *Statistical Tables relating to Banks in India.* Bombay, annually.

————. *Reserve Bank of India Bulletin.* Bombay, monthly.

————. *Reserve Bank Staff Occasional Papers.* Bombay.

Roy, B. "Estimation of Capital Formation in India." Ph.D. dissertation, University of Calcutta, 1975.

Roy, R. *Questions and Answers on the Revenue System of India.* 1831.

Roy, S. C. *Agricultural Indebtedness in India and Its Remedies.* Calcutta: University of Calcutta, 1915.

Rungta, R. S. *The Rise of Business Corporations in India—1851–1900.* London: Cambridge University Press, 1970.

Rutnagur, S. M. *Bombay Industries: The Cotton Mills.* Bombay: Indian Textile Journal, 1927.

Saini, J. N. *Indian Railways: One Hundred Years, 1853 to 1953.* New Delhi: Ministry of Railways, 1953.

Saini, K. G. "Some Measures of the Economic Growth of India: 1860–1913." Ph.D. dissertation, Columbia University, 1968.

————. "The Growth of the Indian Economy, 1860–1960." *Review of Income and Wealth* 15 (1969).

Saksena, R. M. *Development Banking in India.* Bombay: Vora, 1970.

Samant, D. R., and Mulky, M. A. *Organization and Finance of Industries in India.* Bombay: Longmans, Green, 1937.

Sandara Rama Sastry, N. *A Statistical Study of India's Industrial Development.* Bombay: Thacker, 1943.

Sanyal, N. *Development of Indian Railways.* Calcutta: University of Calcutta, 1930.

Saravane, M. *The Demand for Money in India.* Delhi: Vikas, 1971.

————. *Deposits with Non-bank Companies and Monetary Policy.* Delhi: Vikas, 1972.

Sarkar, A. K., and Murthy, G. S. "Estimates of Household Savings in India by Rural and Urban Areas." *Journal of Income and Wealth* 2 (1977).

————. "Household Saving in India: Indicator Approach." *Journal of Income and Wealth* 1 (1977).

Sarkar, D. "Factors Affecting Industrial Security Prices in India, 1950–66." *Margin* 3, no. 3 (1970–71).

Sarma, I. R. K. "Growth of Income and Changes in Inequalities." *Margin* 9 (1976).

Sastry, N. S. R. *A Statistical Study of India's Industrial Development,* 1947.

Savkar, D. S. *Joint Stock Banking in India.* Bombay: Popular Book Depot, 1938.

Sen, S. K. *Studies in Economic Policy and Development in India (1849–1926).* Calcutta: Progressive Publishers, 1966.

Sethuraman, T. V. *Institutional Financing of Economic Development in India.* Delhi: Vikas, 1970.

Shah, K. T., and Kambata, K. J. *Wealth and Taxable Capacity of India.* Bombay: D. B. Taraporevala Sons, 1924.

Sharma, K. S. *The Institutional Structure of the Capital Market in India.* New Delhi: Writers and Publishers, 1969.

Sheldon, C. D. *The Rise of the Merchant Class in Tokugawa Japan.* Locust Valley, N.Y.: Augustin, 1958.

Shergill, H. "The Moneyness of Savings Deposits." *Indian Journal of Economics* 59 (1978).

Shetty, S. L. "Performance of Commercial Banks since Nationalization: Promise and Reality." *Economic and Political Weekly,* annual number, 1978.

Shirras, G. F. *Indian Finance and Banking.* London: Macmillan, 1920.

Shrivastava, N. N. *Evolution of the Techniques of Monetary Management in India.* Bombay: Semaiya Publications, 1972.

Shukla, T. *Capital Formation in Indian Agriculture.* Bombay: Vora, 1965.

Simha, S. L. N. *History of the Reserve Bank of India, 1935–51.* Bombay: Reserve Bank of India, 1970.

————, ed. *Inflation in India.* Bombay: Vora, 1974.

Singh, H. "Structural Changes in the Size Distribution of Holdings—A Macro View." *Indian Journal of Agricultural Economics* 31 (1976).

Singh, P. N. *Role of Development Banks in a Planned Economy.* Delhi: Vikas, 1974.

Singh, S. B., and Calvert, H. *An Inquiry into Mortgages of Agricultural Land . . . in the Punjab,* 1925.

Singh, V. B., ed. *Economic History of India: 1857–1956.* New York: Allied Publishers, 1965.

Sinha, H. *Early European Banking in India.* London: Macmillan, 1927.

Sinha, J. N. "Demographic Trends." In V. B. Singh, ed., *Economic History of India: 1857–1956.* New York: Allied Publishers, 1965.

Sivasubramonian, S. "National Income of India, 1900–01 to 1946–47." Ph.D. dissertation, University of Delhi, 1965.

Soni, H. R. *Indian Industry and Its Problems.* London: Longmans, Green, 1932.

Soyeda, J. "Banking and Money in Japan." *History of Banking in All Leading Nations, Journal of Commerce.* New York, 1896.

Spaulding, R. M., Jr. *Imperial Japan's Higher Civil Service Examinations.* Princeton, N.J.: Princeton University Press, 1967.

Spear, T. G. P. *The Oxford History of Modern India, 1740–1947.* Oxford: Clarendon Press, 1958.

Srinivasan, E. S. *Financial Structure and Economic Development (with Special Reference to India: 1951–1966).* 1977.

Statistical Abstract for British India. New Delhi: Indian Department of Commercial Intelligence and Statistics, annually.

Streeten, P., and Lipton, M., eds. *The Crisis in Indian Planning.* London: Oxford University Press, 1968.

Tata Services Limited, Department of Economics and Statistics. *Statistical Outline of India.* Bombay, annually.

Thakurdas, P. *A Plan of Economic Development for India.* Harmondsworth: Penquin Books, 1944.

Thavaraj, K. "Capital Formation in the Public Sector in India: A Historical Study, 1898–1938." In V. K. R. V. Rao, et al., eds., *Papers on National Income and Allied Topics,* vol. 1. New York: Asia Publishing House, 1960.

Thomas, P. J. *The Problem of Rural Indebtedness.* Madras: Diocesan Press, 1934.

———. "Rural Indebtedness." In R. Mukherjee, ed., *Economic Problems of Modern India.* 2nd ed. London: Macmillan, 1939.

———. *Report on the Regulation of the Stock Market in India.* New Delhi: Indian Ministry of Finance, 1948.

Thorburn, S. S. *Musalmans and Moneylenders in the Punjab.* Edinburgh: Blackwood, 1886.

Thorner, D. *Agricultural Cooperatives in India.* New York: Asia Publishing House, 1964.

Thorner, D., and Thorner, A. "The Working Force of India, 1857–1946." Mimeographed. Bombay, 1960.

——— *Land and Labour in India.* Bombay: Asia Publishing House, 1962.

Thorp, W. L. *Business Annals.* New York: National Bureau of Economic Research, 1926.

Timberg, T. A. *The Marwaris.* New Delhi: Vikas, 1978.

Tiwari, R. D. *Railways in Modern India.* Bombay: New Book, 1941.

———. *Indian Agriculture.* Bombay: New Book, 1943.

Tripathi, A. *Trade and Finance in the Bengal Presidency, 1793–1833.* Bombay: Orient Longmans, 1956.

Tyagarajan, M., and Saoji, S. H. "Migration of Credit: An Aspect of Banking in Metropolitan Centers." *Reserve Bank of India Bulletin* 31 (1977).

Tyagi, R. B. *Recent Trends in the Cooperative Movement in India.* Bombay: Asia Publishing House, 1969.

Vakil, C. N. *Financial Developments in Modern India, 1860–1924.* Bombay: D. B. Taraporevala Sons, 1925.

———, and Muranjan, S. K. *Currency and Prices in India*. Bombay: D. B. Taraporevala Sons, 1927.

Vasudevan, A. "Demand for Money in India: A Survey of Literature." In Reserve Bank of India, *Reserve Bank Staff Occasional Papers,* no. 2, Bombay, 1977.

Venkatachalam, T. R., and Sarma, Y. S. R. "Structure and Trends in the National Balance Sheet of India." *Indian Journal of Income and Wealth* 2 (1977).

Wacha, D. E. *A Financial Chapter in the History of Bombay City*. Bombay: Cambridge, 1910.

———. *Indian Railway Finance*. 1912.

———. *Premchund Roychund: His Early Life and Career*. Bombay: Times Press, 1913.

Wadia, P. A., and Joshi, G. N. *Money and the Money Market in India*. London: Macmillan, 1926.

Wilson, J. G. S. "The Business of Banking in India." In R. Sayers, ed., *Banking in the British Commonwealth*. Oxford: Clarendon Press, 1952.

Wingate, G. *A Few Words on Our Financial Relations with India*. London, 1859.

Index